Will Hutton is chief executive of the Work Foundation and a columnist for the *Observer*, where he was editor, then editor-in-chief for four years. He began his career in journalism as economics correspondent for the BBC's *Newsnight* and for the *Guardian*.

Will Hutton is the author of *The Revolution That Never Was*, the bestselling *The State We're In*, *The State to Come* and *The World We're In*.

Praise for *The Writing on the Wall*

'There is much to be learned by reading *The Writing on the Wall*. Hutton is right to rub the noses of starry-eyed Western governments and investors in the formidable difficulties China faces'
Guardian

'Compelling'
Observer

'The case he lays out is stark and well argued . . . this book makes uncomfortable reading in Beijing – and for the rest of us whose fate is now bound up with the gamble that they can pull it off'
New Statesman

'A big, booming book bristling with combination punches'
Independent

'It is high time for a fresh look at China, and this intellectually searching, politically challenging book by one of Britain's most incisive economic journalists sparkles with new ideas'
John Gittings, *South China Morning Post*

'A lively and informative read . . . engaging, like a robust conversation with a super-enthusiast'
Irish Independent

'Hutton is surgical in his arguments'
Magill

'Hutton certainly knows his economics and any reader can profit from what he has to say'
Jagdish Bhagwati,

THE WRITING
ON THE WALL

China and the West in the
21st Century

WILL HUTTON

ABACUS

First published in Great Britain in 2007 by Little, Brown
This paperback edition published in 2008 by Abacus

Copyright © Will Hutton 2007

A CIP catalogue record for this book
is available from the British Library.

ISBN 978-0-349-11882-6

Papers used by Abacus are natural, recyclable products made from
wood grown in sustainable forests and certified in accordance
with the rules of the Forest Stewardship Council.

Typeset in Caslon by M Rules
Printed and bound in Great Britain by Clays Ltd, St Ives plc
Paper supplied by Hellefoss AS, Norway

Abacus
An imprint of
Little, Brown Book Group
100 Victoria Embankment
London EC4Y 0DY

An Hachette Livre UK Company

www.littlebrown.co.uk

To Jane, Alice, Andrew and Sarah.
And to my mother and father.

He would have liked this book.
I surprise myself at how often I think of him.
He would have liked that too.

CONTENTS

PREFACE

China is a continent-wide country whose land area is eerily close in terms of square miles to that of the United States. Look at a map and imagine that China's western border was bounded by sea and the analogy becomes even more eerie. For the Rockies read the Himalayas. For the heavily industrialised north-east of the United States, read the heavily industrialised north-east of China, including Manchuria. For Washington's location read Beijing. For Florida read Guangdong province in the south-east. The Yangtze may flow west–east while the Mississippi flows north–south, but each is an enormous river that bisects its country. And for Shanghai read New York.

Similarities stop there. China boasts a civilisation at least three thousand years old. It is home to 1.3 billion people. It is authoritarian and formally communist. And, since 1978, it has burst back on to the world scene in a manner paralleled in scale and speed in world history only by the rise of the United States between the Civil War and the First World War in 1914. The open question is whether the twenty-first century is going to be the Chinese century in the way the twentieth century was American and the nineteenth century British. Is the baton of global leadership going to pass from Anglo-Saxon hands, which held so many values in common, to Chinese hands? If so, the implications could not be more profound. The world would have to accommodate a wholly different civilisation and values; the character of global institutions, our culture and the primacy of the English language would be challenged. If China remained communist there would be substantial implications for the organisation of Western economies and societies. The answer to this question is one of the most important of our age.

The central argument in this book is that if the next century is going to be Chinese, it will be only because China embraces the economic and political pluralism of the West in general, and our Enlightenment institutions in particular modified, of course, for the Chinese experience. I use the Enlightenment as shorthand to capture the full panoply of institutions, processes and ways of thinking that were launched by the European Enlightenment and embodied in its quintessential expression, the constitution and public processes of the United States. The rule of law, the independence of the judiciary, the freedom of the press, the scientific and research processes in independent universities, or the very idea of representative, accountable, checked and balanced government – all these flowed from the great intellectual, philosophical and political wellspring that we call the Enlightenment. Above all, it endowed Western societies with the idea of the public realm and an approach to living whose spirit the great Enlightenment philosopher Immanuel Kant summed up simply: to 'dare to know'.

What I try to show is that these are not 'Western' but indispensable components of any well-functioning economy and society. Their lack in China is increasingly showing through in a myriad of dysfunctions and internal contradictions that will have to be confronted. The current Chinese economic model is unsustainable, which will have important implications for the capacity of the Communist Party to run China as a single-party authoritarian state.

That is why the simple extrapolations of China's continued growth at current levels for the next forty or fifty years are misleading. And why it is wrong for so many Western politicians, business leaders and opinion formers to use China as an ominous threat before which the West must change or else wilt. This idea is normally code for the proposition that ordinary Americans and Europeans should accept stagnating living standards, diminished welfare states and fend for themselves, acquiring the educational and skill levels – more and more at their own expense – necessary to compete with China's advancing hordes. Those in the higher echelons of society, meanwhile, can continue to enjoy the trappings of growing inequality.

China is not such a threat. Rather, it is a sophisticated civilisation beset by profound and deepening problems that is making a difficult transition from a primitive and poor peasant society to modernity. It requires our understanding and engagement – not our enmity and suspicion, which could culminate in self-defeatingly creating the very crisis we fear. China's vulnerability is not widely understood; Europe and the United States should stay open to China in both our trade and in the realm of ideas.

Above all we should be confident. The Enlightenment values and institutions that propelled the West past China in the nineteenth century remain no less important sources of competitive advantage and social well-being today. They lie at the heart of the emerging 'knowledge economy'. The problem is that they are being neglected and, in consequence, are fading. In the United States public institutions, representative government, the media, secondary education, corporations, investment institutions and, especially, general supports for developing the individual capabilities of its citizens are simply not working as well as they should. Britain is in a very similar position. In particular, we have an underdeveloped concept of the public realm that consistently makes the expression of public purpose – vital in a market economy and society – uncertain and weak. And both countries have actively undermined the system of international law and multilateral governance in their pre-emptive war of choice in Iraq. If we want to persuade China and the world of the virtues of pluralism, Enlightenment values and democracy, the United States and

Britain have to practise what they preach at home and abroad. At present they do not.

This, then, is the heart of this book's case. After an introductory overview chapter the next five chapters explore how China has developed up to today, the structure of its economy and the increasing unmanageability of the contradictions upon which it rests. Chapters 7 and 8 investigate the advantages of economic and political pluralism more fully in theory, and trace how they are emerging in other parts of Asia. Chapter 9 sets out the areas of political and economic tension between the United States and China, and Chapters 10 and 11 use the same framework and criteria through which I look at China to assess the United States. In the Conclusion I briefly examine the knowledge economy, assess the British position and set out a prospectus for potential change in our international priorities, processes and institutions. The numbers have all been updated for the paperback edition

The relationship between the United States and China, and that between China and the rest of Asia are delicately poised. There are myriad problems – most tellingly, the environment and global warming, which now threaten so many ecosystems that in the view of the bulk of the scientific community we are fast approaching a tipping point where humanity as a species is in danger. All require an international response and appreciation of our shared fate. China and the United States are an indispensable part of the response. My ambition for this book is that it will help tilt the balance towards international collaboration, contribute to a reappraisal of the so-called China threat and a recognition of the situation as an opportunity and, above all, reaffirm Enlightenment values and the importance of economic and pluralism. All this is already too long for the Preface. Read on – and I hope you enjoy.

1

The Last Great Powers

It is a truth universally acknowledged that a great power will never voluntarily surrender pride of place to a challenger. The United States is the pre-eminent great power. China is now its potential challenger. The great questions of our time are, first, whether China can translate that potential into reality without democracy and without genuine capitalism. And, second, whether the United States will be wise enough to keep its markets and the wider world system open as this Chinese drama plays out, and by so doing accelerate the fundamental reform that must come to China. Our prosperity and even global peace depend on the answers.

For the Americans and Chinese are different from the rest of us. Every state in the world may harbour ambitions to have the autonomy of the archetypal nineteenth-century nation-state, but most must come to terms with the constraints of their relative small size compared with the scale of global markets. Only China and the United States, with their continental economies, vast populations and huge military machines, can genuinely think in old nation-state terms. They calculate their spheres of military, diplomatic and economic influence. They are prepared to use military power to secure national ends. Each believes its civilisation and culture have a special destiny. They are intensely nationalistic. They are, in short, the last genuine great powers. The world's future hangs on whether they can resist the temptations of rivalry and find a constructive accommodation that allows them to do business.

This comes at a critical and delicate juncture. For sixty years the United States has overcome its protectionist tradition – no other country in the nineteenth century and the early twentieth century had tariffs on industrial imports for so high for so long – to lead the development of an open global economy. Flows of trade, investment and technology have reached an unsurpassed intensity. Growth and living standards have risen remarkably. True, there are disturbing and dangerous new inequalities between countries whose capacity to take advantage of these opportunities varies hugely. But the overall balance sheet is positive. The United States itself is up to $1 trillion richer as a result of globalisation.[1] The Asian miracle, including the rise of China, would have been impossible without it.

But within the United States anxiety has grown about the stagnating incomes and increased insecurity of much of its middle class. Because these have come at the same time as globalisation, they are too often said to have been caused by it. In fact, the principal causes lie within the United States (see Chapter 11), including the onward march of new technologies, changing tastes of consumers, an epidemic of mergers, take-overs and acquisitions and the increasing unwillingness of American businesses and policy makers alike to accept a duty of care to the American workforce.

Even before 9/11, doubts were voiced in the United States about whether the network of multilateral treaties and institutions that had developed under American leadership since the end of the Second World War was still working. Was it right for the proud United States to be constrained in a fabric of international law with foreigners of doubtful reliability, whether over trade or weapons systems? Since 9/11 the historical American tendency towards unilateralism and suspicion of foreigners has become rampant. The expensive, deadly and poorly executed involvement in Iraq is reinforcing the distrust of foreign entanglements, and the threat from Islamic fundamentalist terrorism has spurred calls for clamping down zealously on immigration and sealing the United States' borders.

The globalising economy is blamed by critics for the outsourcing of jobs, squeezing American wages and for unfair competition from foreign goods. It has allowed the United States to be challenged by China, plainly exploiting the order America has built, to force the country into the largest bilateral trade deficit with any single country in its history – a stunning $233 billion in 2006 and projected to approach $300 billion in 2007.

As a result, popular support for the idea that the United States should take the lead in further integrating the world economy is eroding. The congressional majority in favour of international treaties and free trade, always hard to put together, is challenged. The hysterical campaign in 2006 against plans to have Dubai Ports World manage six United States ports when it took over the British company P&O is symptomatic of a new attitude. Every Democrat candidate for the presidential nomination has declared a readiness to get tougher on China. The United States, however, is not alone. Around the world, almost no country or trading bloc now looks at the global economy as something that needs to be built and sustained for collective benefit. Rather, it is considered a juggernaut only admissible in so far as one can exploit it to one's own advantage. The World Trade talks aimed at extending trade liberalisation were suspended in July 2006, with none of the key actors prepared to initiate concessions for the sake of a settlement for the global good. They remain suspended.

The global economy is not an unstoppable force. What has been made by political choices can be unmade by political choices. If everyone bends, disobeys and ignores the rules, soon

there are no rules. The architecture that sustains the world's growing interdependence is under great strain. It needs to be
re-crafted and reinvigorated, but this requires preconditions that
are lacking: intellectual conviction and a high degree of trust and
common values between the great powers. The current climate,
and accompanying impasse over constructive collaboration over
everything from trade to finance, is extremely dangerous.

Which is why China's rise is so significant. China's economy in
2007 is more than nine times larger than it was in 1978, and is the
fourth largest in the world, after the United States, Japan and
Germany. If current trends continue it is set to become the second
largest within a decade.[2] The only comparable rise of an economy
as a proportion of world GDP in such a short time is that of the
United States at the end of the nineteenth century.[3] Between
1981 and 2001, 400 million Chinese people had been brought out of
poverty. Between 1978 and 2003, the average per capita income
rose by a multiple of six. The proportion of the population living in
towns and cities has doubled to nearly two-fifths. Up to 150 million
workers have moved to China's booming cities – the biggest
migration in history.[4] It is a head-spinning achievement.

China is the new factor in global politics and economics. No
global architecture can be constructed without it. By the end of
2007 it will have more than $1.5 trillion of foreign-exchange
reserves. The United States could not be running an annual
current-account deficit of $800 billion without consistent selling
pressure on the dollar if Chinese purchases of United States
Treasury bills and bonds were not so high. China is the world's
second largest importer of oil. Before 2010 it will be the world's
largest exporter of goods.[5] It is comfortably the world's second-
largest military power: the Pentagon believes that China's defence
expenditure is up to three times more than the $30 billion offi-
cially declared. The Pentagon's four-yearly defence review stated
that the scale of China's military build-up has already put 'regional
military balances at risk' and that China is the power most likely to

'field disruptive military technologies that could over time offset traditional US military advantages'.[6] In January 2007 China used one of its missiles to shoot down one of its weather satellites: a reminder that the Pentagon's view of its military muscle (this was to show China had the capability to destroy the United States' satellite capacity) is more than justified. If you are prepared to compare China's output not on the basis of current market foreign-exchange rates but on estimates of the real purchasing power of what China produces, then it is already the second-largest economy in the world. On this basis China could overtake the United States within twenty years.[7] The problem is that this new great power is communist, and its rise to power has been masterminded by the Communist Party.

The party may have made major ideological changes; it praises only 70 per cent of Mao's record, for example, condemning the disastrous Cultural Revolution and the Great Leap Forward in which more than thirty million Chinese died. It now aims to build a 'socialist market' economy rather than the planned communist economy. It has permitted the dismantlement of twenty-six thousand communes in rural China. Hundreds of millions of peasants are again farming plots on long leases held by their ancestors. China wants its state-owned enterprises to compete as autonomous companies largely free to set prices as they choose in an open economy. China's communists have declared that the class war is over. They now claim to represent not just the worker and peasant masses but entrepreneurs and business leaders, whom it welcomes into its ranks. The party refers to this meta-morphosis as the 'three represents' – meaning that the party today represents, in the ideological categories in which it thinks, 'advanced productive forces', 'the overwhelming majority' of the Chinese and 'the orientation . . . of China's advanced culture'.[8] Party representatives abroad say that the country wants to rise peacefully, not to play power politics or to aim for any kind of hegemony. China has joined the World Trade Organization and is a judicious member of the United Nations Security Council, using its veto only five times, for matters of immediate concern.

Yet it remains formally a communist power adhering to the doctrines of Marxism, Leninism and Mao. It is a one-party state with no regular competitive elections, no independent rule of law, no freedom of speech, no right of association and no entrenched basic human rights. Although it condemns 30 per cent of Mao's legacy, it praises 70 per cent. Difficult as this may be for many foreigners and even some Chinese to accept, a majority of China's 1.3 billion people and its communist rulers regard the Communist Revolution of 1949 as a significant, important and legitimate event analogous to the American and French revolutions. Today's China could not have happened without the revolution. Mao's mass murders are condemned, as the French might condemn Robespierre and the Terror, but Mao is seen as part of a process that also included some good, notably a dramatic increase in literacy and the shattering of the imperial Confucian system which had held China back for 150 years. Deng Xiaoping, China's great pro-market reformer, did not build contemporary China out of nothing; he built on foundations left by Mao and always aimed to preserve the primacy of the Communist Party.

That foundation is now a profound problem for China, the United States, Britain and the rest of the world. It makes China a difficult partner internationally because there is an objective clash of interests over the importance of democracy, the rule of law and human rights and how they should be represented in the world's architecture. Meanwhile, at home, China's communists, notwithstanding their success to date, are confronting limits regarding how far they can develop a pluralist market economy without pluralist political institutions. The evidence is all around: in a disastrous environmental performance, in an emergent inflation, in a gathering crisis over the quality of Chinese goods – reflected in a string of recalls of toys and contaminated foods – and in a dangerous inequality. The party leadership has not yet embraced the 'soft' institutional infrastructure that accompanies successful capitalism: impartial courts, clear property rights, proper commercial processes for bank lending, independent auditors, accountability to a free press, independent trade unions, effective corporate governance, transparent anti-monopoly rules, free intellectual inquiry and even a properly functioning welfare system. The party is also facing a growing issue of legitimacy. If it no longer rules as the democratic dictatorship of peasants and workers because the class war is over, why does it not hold itself accountable to the people in competitive elections? Answers are not easy for it to find.

China is confronting an ideological crisis. With the collapse of the Soviet Union, communism in China cannot now justify itself as part of an international movement whose success is historically and scientifically preordained. Instead, it has to justify itself through its domestic accomplishments as well as its historic role in enabling China to regain the pride and international respect that had been lost ever since the Opium War of 1839–42. Successful economic development has thus been one strand of policy to legitimise the party; the other has been nationalism.

This latter sentiment has deep roots. Confucian emperors portrayed China as the centre of the universe and foreigners as barbarians. As a result, China's reversals during the nineteenth century were felt particularly keenly; by the 1870s there was already a patriotic 'self-strengthening' movement, aiming to copy foreign methods to recover China's power, and the mood intensified after defeat by Japan in 1895. After the First World War, when German concessions in China were handed over to the Japanese as part of the Treaty of Versailles with no regard for China's views, this was felt to symbolise all that was wrong. The spontaneous demonstrations that erupted on 4 May 1919 developed into a loose nationalist political movement that was one of the antecedents of the Communist Party's own official foundation in 1921. Thus today's introduction of 'patriotic' education to inculcate pride in China and in the party's achievements builds on long-standing instincts. China has to be permanently on guard against its enemies, who have not changed their spots. 'The Chinese people must never again be humiliated by foreign aggressors,' runs the official interpretation of history.[9] China must avoid disunity at home and be protected abroad by a vigilant communist government.

The weakness of communist ideology, assuaged only partially by this nationalism, is matched by a growing awareness that the logic of reform is rapidly confronting China with a choice. The current halfway house of trying to retain political control of what is in truth only half a market economy is unsustainable. Is China to accept that economic pluralism, along with an institutional infrastructure to confer political pluralism, is the only way a market economy can flourish? After all, in March 2007 China's premier Wen Jiabao declared that China's economy was 'unstable, unbalanced, uncoordinated and unsustainable'. Or can it hold the line and manage today's ambiguities and economic contradictions?

The economy provides an unwelcome answer for the conservative wing of the Communist Party, whose instinct is to retreat and retrench. So far, China has few great companies capable of competing internationally, and almost no global brands. Its private sector consists of a plethora of small transient companies typically dependent on political patronage. China's state-owned, state-directed or state-influenced corporations may have the freedom to set prices and wages, but only within limits laid down by the party. Their productivity is disastrous.

The system that has brought China this far is Leninist corporatism, rather than anything approaching a proper market economy, let alone a socialist market economy. It is Leninist in the primacy it affords the Communist Party, and corporatist rather than capitalist because it does not foster capitalist economic pluralism. It is neither a communist nor a capitalist economy. The central argument of this book is that, for all China's success to date, ultimately the system that the communists have created is structurally unstable, as they themselves acknowledge. The next phase of China's economic and political development must solve the ambiguity but permit more economic pluralism. That will set in train a process that must challenge the pre-eminence of the Communist Party.

The face-off

China does not face this conundrum in a vacuum. Its sheer scale forces it into structural tension with the United States. There are three primary flashpoints between the two countries: oil, trade and currency. Looming over all of them is Taiwan and the possibility that one day China will test the commitment of the United States to defend Taiwan against a Chinese invasion.

The peak of world oil production is clearly imminent. According to some estimates it is already on us; if it is not, very few expect the peak much after 2020. So it is hardly a surprise that the last two great powers eye each other's intentions concerning oil with suspicion.[10] A network of Chinese-financed pipelines that will take oil away from the United States and towards its challenger is appearing or planned in Canada, Venezuela, Sudan and Iran. Four-fifths of China's oil is transported through the Strait of Malacca between Malaysia and Indonesia. At one end of the Strait is an American fleet at the Changi Naval Base in Singapore. At the other end, the United States' Indian Ocean fleet operates from Diego Garcia. From Beijing's perspective, the United States has its fingers on China's windpipe; President Hu Jintao makes frequent reference to the 'Malacca problem'. China wants more oil brought in by pipeline across Asia and by tanker across the Pacific. It wants a deep-sea fleet to protect its interests. Richard Nixon's former Secretary of State, Henry Kissinger, has warned of a potential great-power conflict over oil: this is it.[11] China's 'ring of pearls' strategy, developing close relationships with Pakistan, Cambodia,

Thailand and Myanmar (Burma), is intended to give it access to ports for its naval and merchant vessels if ever hostilities broke out with the United States.

However, the most pressing issue is over trade and currency. It may be true that up to 70 per cent of Wal-Mart's sales are produced in China, to the advantage of the American consumer. Cumulatively American consumers are $100 billion better off, as one authoritative economist estimates, because China's cheap exports have lowered consumer prices in the United States.[12] Britain, with its more open economy, has enjoyed an even larger benefit. China's role in financing the United States' trade deficit is critical, as I have already noted. After 9/11, however, these advantages may not outweigh, in the American public's mind, the perceived damage from free trade with China. The United States did not become a genuinely open economy until the 1940s, when it became clear that the country's industry had no serious rivals abroad and that there was a strategic interest in accepting imports from Japan as well as the rest of capitalist Asia and Europe. By encouraging trade, the argument went, the United States would advance the cause of capitalism against communism.

In the mid-1980s there was a ferocious backlash against Japanese imports, and we are now seeing a backlash against China. There is no obvious strategic interest in boosting communist China's economic base; indeed, the American public may be unsure that it wants its trade deficit financed by the People's Bank of China or wants to depend on China at all. The spate of product recalls and challenges of Chinese-made goods over safety has hardly helped matters, prompting one Democrat candidate for the presidential nomination, Governor Bill Richardson, to propose an 'import' Czar to monitor the quality of, in particular, Chinese imports. The forces that want the United States to pull up the economic drawbridge are becoming ever more powerful, drawing on the nation's historical ambiguity about its relationship with the rest of the world and its belief in its own special destiny. Rationality is made immeasurably more difficult by George W. Bush's warnings that the United States is now in a long war against terrorism.

Non-Americans have difficulty coming to terms with the virulence and contradictory complexity of American nationalism. The United States regards itself as the exceptional country, a view it arrives at through the (partly justified) belief that it is still a new civilisation whose constitution and values insulate it from making the same mistakes as Old Europe commingled with a (less justified) belief that it is especially blessed by Providence. It is an exceptionalism that can sometimes inspire generosity and enlightened leadership, and can sometimes excuse the pursuit of narrow self-interest even when that proves self-defeating in its own terms. Global warming is one example. Although the United States accounts for about 25 per cent of the world's carbon-dioxide emissions, George W. Bush could unblinkingly oppose the Kyoto Protocol in March 2001 because 'it exempts 80 per cent of the world, including major population centres such as China and India, from compliance, and would cause serious harm to the US economy'.[13] Thus the United States abdicated its leadership role, pursued its own interests and stood aside from serious concerns that affect global humanity. The stance was and is profoundly troubling to a significant part of the American public and to the United States' allies. Yet Bush suffered little. He was putting America first.

Public opinion and political leadership in the United States are divided, between this amalgam of an 'America first' tendency and protectionism justified by a belief in an American exceptionalism granted by God and Providence, and an opposing internationalist tendency that favours free trade and a multilateral foreign policy. Under President Bush, the 'America first' strain, which was already gaining ground before 9/11, has become fiercely predominant. The reaction to 9/11 recalls the analysis by the American political historian Richard Hofstadter, who identified what he called a 'paranoid style' in American politics. There have been periods in American history when conspiracy theories about alien influences, ranging from suspicion of international bankers during the Greenback and Populist era at the end of the nineteenth century to McCarthy's witch-hunts in the early 1950s, have given a paranoid, even xenophobic style to American politics. China is provoking such paranoia as well as the 'America first' tradition. The resulting spectacle is not edifying.

The anti-China sentiment that has surfaced in the past two or three years is obvious. Some of the twenty bills introduced in this period aimed at retaliation against China or its imports would have disastrous consequences if passed. Two have crystallised. One, now passed by the Senate Finance Committee by a 20–1 majority and backed by leading candidates for the Democrat presidential nomination Hillary Clinton and Barack Obama, mandates the United States government to impose punitive duties on the imports from any country whose currency is 'fundamentally misaligned'. The other would set conditions for China's investigation by (or even expulsion from) the World Trade Organisation because of alleged currency manipulation. Either bill would have economic impact analogous to a unilateral missile attack. Flows of Chinese finance to support the dollar and United States asset prices would collapse; there would be a sell-off in world stock markets. Britain and Europe would find themselves on the front line as China redirected its exports away from the United States to the European Union. The fissures between a protectionist Southern Europe, already evident in its calls for protection against Chinese shoe and textile imports, and a Northern Europe more convinced of the merits of free trade would become explosive. The tensions could even call into question the ability of the European Union to maintain its single market, and thus its cohesion. For its part, the Chinese economy would rapidly slow down, with incalculable implications for the country's political stability.

The scope for miscalculation by either the United States or China is huge. These are two nationalist titans, and the Chinese have very limited room to manoeuvre when responding to the United States' demands, which are presented with mounting intensity. In the first place a sudden revaluation of the renminbi would have a very depressive effect on the incomes of the 900 million Chinese living in peasant households, because it would lower China's food prices, keyed as they are to world price levels. It would damage savings, arrest export growth, slow down the economy and raise the spectre of a banking crisis. Second, to call for China' s immediate compliance with Western and best Asian standards of corporate governance, transparency and accountability is to force systemic change on China. Such change is inevitable, but these reforms must be handled with great sensitivity. Change can and will come; and external pressure should be applied, but not to the point that the fallout causes at least as much pain for the West as it does for China.

Seen from Beijing, the call to revalue the renminbi or transform the Chinese economic system is a de facto act of aggression that will destabilise the government. Seen from Washington, the refusal to become a good international economic citizen is wilful neglect of what former Deputy Secretary of State Robert Zoellick regards as China's duties as a responsible stakeholder in running the world system. It is an eyeball-to-eyeball confrontation, a great-power game to see who blinks first. The strength of sentiment on both sides should not be underestimated. Only fifteen members of Congress voted in 2005 to allow one of China's national oil companies – CNOOC – to take over the United States company Unocal, arguing that concerns about the endangering of national security were specious, as they largely were; 398 voted against the takeover. In China, suspicion of American intentions runs no less high: in the summer of 2007 senior Chinese officials talked openly about the possibility of using China's financial muscle as a counter-threat to American threats.

Never far beneath the surface of conflict is Taiwan, Japan's former colony, which was commandeered in 1949 by the Nationalist armies, who claimed to have taken the genuine republic of China with them. Now a functioning democracy, China wants it to rejoin the motherland like Hong Kong and Macau; this would remove the last stain of a century of humiliation and, far more important, eliminate an ideological rival. What stands between China and its goal is the United States' fleet. China continues a military build-up that the Pentagon and senior military analysts agree is congruent only with a projected invasion of Taiwan. The United States maintains substantial military strength in the region, and promises to stand by its understandings with Taiwan in the event of a Chinese attack. The question is whether China will ever choose to test the American commitment.

Underneath the tension lies a greater truth. The two sides are co-dependent and essentially benefit from their relationship. The internal difficulties on either side are home-grown, a much harder political analysis for either to accept, rather than the fault of the other. The United States needs to remind itself that as an $11-trillion economy it is still four times larger than that of China, and many times richer in terms of per capita income. It still produces more than one-fifth of the world's output. Thirteen of the world's top twenty brands, and fifty-three of the top hundred, are American.[14] The United States leads the world in innovation and patents. Its military power is overwhelming: its annual military R & D spending alone is $50 billion, dwarfing that of China; it can deploy an army of five hundred thousand, as it showed in the Gulf in 1990.[15] The United States' soft power is also overwhelming. This is the country with the Enlightenment inheritance of free speech, free association, rule of law, free thought and pluralist checks and balances, even if today these look somewhat tattered and even fly-blown. Some self-confidence and generosity of spirit are in order. China has people, exports, foreign-exchange reserves and enormous potential; it is the only country capable of challenging the United States. But the United States remains in the driver's seat in determining how the challenge will play out and what the final settlement might be.

Indeed, the more China grows, the more likely it is to develop its middle class and an appetite for institutional changes that will make it a more comfortable partner. Alistair Iain Johnston, a China-watcher at Harvard, notes that according to opinion polls China's middle class is already more internationalist than its poor.[16] On the other hand, the party is keenly aware that it must bind China's burgeoning middle class to the Communist Party in a strategy of co-option in which entrepreneurs and businessmen become privileged insiders. The tension between wanting change and benefiting from the status quo is palpable: the Party debates anxiously whether reform has gone too far and what it must do to retain control.

The American interest is to make it impossible for China to turn back rather than to strengthen Beijing's conservatives by behaving as they always worried; the British interest is to make sure the Americans see it that way – and that they act appropriately. It is not just an economic issue that the bigger and more open China is, the better the prospects for American and Western companies to sell in its market. It is that a plural democratic China is more likely to be the stakeholder in the international system that we need it to be. For its part, China has an interest in carrying on with reform and peaceful progress to resolve its acute economic dilemmas, and accepting the logic of where that takes it. These may be objective interests. History, however, is littered with examples of where the temptation not to follow objective interests leads.

Globalisation: a short history

With China's rise, globalisation has entered a new phase. Companies, especially from Hong Kong and Taiwan, have flocked to China, attracted by unlimited supplies of low-wage workers. On average, wages are a tenth of those of in Europe and the United States; for unskilled workers they can be as little as a thirtieth.[17] On top a first-world infrastructure of ultra-modern ports and roads, along with cheap container ship transport and low factory building costs, are together up to 70 per cent cheaper.[18] Through the Internet, telephones and ever cheaper air travel, companies have the capacity to keep in close touch with operations on the ground. The question whether to produce domestically or outsource production to China has loomed larger in multinationals' strategic planning. Outsourcing precludes the rise of a Chinese competitor (by capturing the same cost structure) and offers an advantage over a company's existing rivals. These are powerful countervailing arguments: there are costs to doing business in China, from intellectual property theft to sheer distance from Western markets, that offset low manufacturing costs – which in any case are increasingly low as a proportion of the final sales price, as I explore in Chapter 11 and the Conclusion.

On the other hand, the Chinese market itself is an opportunity for Western producers. Indeed, China is still largely a final-assembly exporter, with most of its plants producing exports owned and managed by foreigners, and so is still heavily dependent on the necessary imports to be assembled for export. The number of jobs directly lost to China so far through offshoring is paltry, while there are direct gains through producing for its markets, and indirectly through the higher real wages and consumption in the West through having access to cheaper Chinese goods. Overall job gains will almost certainly affect losses, but in both the United States and Britain politicians, unionists and businesspeople are already predicting darkly that 'China is coming', as if the only trajectory is more and more global economic integration which necessarily brings job losses. Neither the job losses, nor even globalisation itself, is inevitable.

If over the course of five hundred years there has been more and more interpenetration of national economies the process has not been linear. Periods of opening have been followed by partial or complete closure as societies have sought relief from competition, immigration and social and cultural change. In periods of economic and social openness, nothing seems more inexorably natural than interdependence. The journalist and Labour parliamentarian Norman Angell, who won the Nobel Peace Prize in 1933, made a famous prediction of peace four years before the First World War. In *The Great Illusion*, a book that was translated into eighteen languages, he argued that war would be self-defeating because countries were now so economically and financially interdependent. By contrast, in times of closure and depression, like the mid-1930s, nothing seems more obvious than loyalty to the national unit and the fragility of globalisation. The British economist John Maynard Keynes, once a strong advocate of free trade, found himself praising a world of little trade, homespun production and national rather than international systems of finance.[19] He could no more imagine today's globalisation than Angell could imagine war. Both were wrong, as we may be.

The lesson is that globalisation is and always has been vulnerable to setbacks. The historian Harold James describes Europe's first embrace of globalisation, arguing that the Reformation, the consequent religious wars and the creation of nation-states in the seventeenth century were in part a reaction to the disruptive, inflationary impact of Latin American gold and silver, and of the profits from the Asian trade on the settled societies of late-medieval Europe. In 1524 Martin Luther railed against the effect of Indian silks on the culture and attitudes of solid, God-fearing Germans.[20] Although the trade in such luxury goods might have been small relative to European output, its economic and cultural impact was much greater. Venice, then Portugal, then the Netherlands and France were all beneficiaries of long-distance trade. British economic and political history is inexplicable without it. The institutions needed to foster such trade, then interacted with the institutional creativity of the Enlightenment to give Europe a decisive advantage over China, which until then had been ahead, both scientifically and technologically. The result was the Industrial Revolution.

In the 1820s a second phase of globalisation began, based on the European factory system. This was an era of exchange of cheap manufactured goods produced within national economies for increasingly mass markets. Trade grew at between 3 and 4 per cent annually for nearly a century until 1914 – a sustained upward growth that was unprecedented. The architecture and rules of the game were created by the hegemonic power Britain, which insisted on free trade throughout its formal and informal empire, and instituted this with most of Europe through bilateral trade treaties. Sterling and the gold standard held sway. During this period China's backwardness and insularity became painfully evident. Not only did it not see any need to catch up, it lacked the institutional wherewithal to do so had it wanted. Only towards the end of the nineteenth century did it begin to recognise the need for change, but by then the unequal die had been cast.

For all the growth in trade, the years just before 1914 brought increasing strains. The gold standard operated by imposing periods of austerity and growth on economies as gold stocks mounted or shrank. Unemployment jumped violently: there were massive movements of people between countries and continents. Between 1871 and 1915, thirty-six million people left Europe for the Americas, Africa and Australasia.[21] Europe and North America both witnessed powerful reactions against social distress, and Europe saw the birth of socialist parties and, eventually, communism. Between 1914 and 1950 the global system simply broke down. There was neither the international architecture nor the internal domestic social consensus on which the pre-war system had depended, and the world retreated from globalisation.

Britain was too weak and the United States too reluctant and inward-looking to enforce the rules of the game and sustain a common economic, trading and financial architecture. No other candidate country was powerful enough to do so in their stead. In Europe tariffs on manufactures had been rising ominously towards 20 per cent before the First World War, except in Britain (which espoused free trade). In the United States tariffs were over 40 per cent. After 1918 tariffs rose again everywhere as countries tried to protect themselves from unemployment, economic slowdown and social protest.[22] The growth of trade shrank to the lowest level ever recorded,[23] either before or since. Countries retreated into their national economic citadels; exchange and capital controls were imposed. It was an era of depression, war and a clash between communism and fascism – which in China manifested itself as the Communist Revolution.

Then, starting in 1950, a third phase of openness began. The leading developed countries were determined to establish a global financial and trade architecture, and at home a commitment to social welfare and full employment helped to construct a more stable social order that could alleviate the pain of adjusting to international competition. The United States instituted and maintained trade openness with the dollar as the world's reserve currency and medium of exchange. Tariffs on manufactured imports fell to an average of less than 4 per cent. Trade ballooned, achieving an astonishing 8 per cent growth rate in the golden years from 1950 to 1973 and subsequently an impressive 5 per cent.[24] Multinational companies, with Americans in the vanguard, began multi-sourcing their production and distribution within a small but growing pool of developed countries; foreign direct investment exploded.

Since the mid-1990s this type of globalisation has become even more vigorous and ambitious. In a sense it is 'true' globalisation. Multinationals have outsourced more production in selected low-wage developing countries, thereby producing a surge of exports based on a dramatic cheapening of the price of manufactured goods. There has been a phenomenal build-up of assets held overseas, together with international capital movements amounting to $250 trillion a year – five times world output. Two trends have come together. The first is the arrival of new information and communication technologies that have prompted a tipping point in the intensity, sophistication, cheapness and scope of exchange of goods, services, money and ideas. The second is that these cross-border technologies have emerged just as border obstacles themselves have come down. Low average tariffs are now extending into the less developed countries as exchange controls melt away.

Crucially, huge countries that were formerly closed have entered the world system. China has redefined communism to indulge markets and trade; India has decided that openness is a better development strategy than protection; the former Soviet Union has repudiated communism and its former satellites in Eastern Europe have joined the European Union. There is a new sense of security among multinationals in the north and the south alike that they could and should take advantage of low wages, low transport and communication costs and low tariffs. Manufacture has become increasingly commoditised, with most economic value being generated from research, financing, marketing, branding and distribution, which takes place at home. Production can be more foot-loose, dictated by cost. A successful commercial strategy now necessitates developing global capacities, a global reputation and global brands.

This last phase of true globalisation is one in which China, by virtue of its size and its readiness to be open, has taken a principal role in intensifying and structuring new interdependencies. During the Cultural Revolution and the Vietnam War, a growing number of the Chinese communist elite, including Deng Xiaoping, observed how China's Asian neighbours were profiting from globalisation. Deng saw that by following the route of the Asian tigers China might develop successfully in a way in which Mao had failed, and that paradoxically this was the sole means of sustaining communism. He has been proved right.

The danger is that the increasing presence of China, along with India, Brazil and Russia, will destabilise the global system. We could see a rerun of the period leading up to 1914, with internal social strains and a fragmentation of the global architecture.

Germany's rise in Europe and the rise of the United States in the world economy between 1870 and 1914 led to tension in Europe and the North Atlantic that in turn led to war and depression. The world system led by Britain was not sustainable; there was no intellectual or political imperative for countries to stay open and keep the peace, given the internal tension that was mounting as a result of rapid industrialisation and urbanisation. German protectionism was at odds with the prevailing British norms, and as Germany grew ever larger it could not but destabilise the balance of power and interests on which the world system then depended. The result was war.

The question for the world is if today's conditions are analogous. Suppose that today's China is yesterday's Wilhelmian Germany, on a collision course with Asia's top regional power, Japan, as Germany was with France. Then does the superpower United States, any more than Britain in 1914, have the economic power, or the political and intellectual conviction, to sustain the present order? Can countries continue to maintain openness and internal social stability? Globalisation may, historically, advance or retreat. The possibility of another retreat, unless the United States, Europe, Japan and China are mindful of the dangers, is all too obvious.

The China effect

The growth of exports from China, always impressive, has recently become startling. For more than fifteen years exports have grown by over 20 per cent a year, with the rate of growth accelerating since China joined the World Trade Organization in 2001. Over the past twenty-five years Chinese exports and imports have each grown from 1 per cent of the world's total to more than 6 per cent. Not only has China grown very rapidly, it has been exceptionally open to the world. In 1980 the share of trade (exports plus imports) in China's GDP was 15 per cent; in 2005 it exceeded

70 per cent. The United States is the only continental economy ever to have matched China's impact on the world economy,[25] as noted earlier, and even it was not as open to trade as China.

The flood of manufactured exports at what Western consumers regard as unnaturally low prices has been largely directed at the United States, which takes around 40 per cent of the total. I have already mentioned the benefit to American consumers, but Britain, Europe and Japan have also profited. Another way of looking at this trend is to see how China has lowered the global inflation rate. Dresdner Kleinwort Wasserstein, a major German investment bank, calculates that American inflation over the past few years is one percentage point lower as a result of the competition from China. The United States Federal Reserve agrees that China has driven inflation down, although more recently rising prices in China and the slight upward movement of the renminbi has reduced the effect.[26]

The resulting cheap money contributed to a housing boom in both Britain and the United States. The Federal Reserve and the Bank of England have been able to keep interest rates much lower than could have been expected, given the growth of credit, because the world prices of manufactured goods have been falling and the growth of wages has been so low. In Britain, the United States, Canada and Australia, home owners have benefited as the price of housing has soared in response to low interest rates. The deregulated financial systems in these countries are particularly aggressive in marketing money – and home owners are borrowing it widely. Consumers have borrowed against the increase in equity in their homes and spent the cash, reducing savings in both the United States and Britain to ever lower levels. The continual rise in consumption has spawned shopping malls, restaurants and whole new industries that rely on buoyant personal spending; all this in turn has generated new jobs; and the new jobs have made people confident that they can borrow more. The process has kept the economic wheel spinning.

Nor is that all. The mushrooming United States trade deficit has happened at the same time as dollars have poured out of the country to be invested in factories all over Asia and financial assets everywhere while the government has been paying for Iraq and Afghanistan on top of its already vast and growing network of United States military bases and fleets.[27] The United States' current account has soared to 6.5 per cent of GDP – almost double the previous record. In more normal times you might expect even more weakness in the dollar than it has shown, and more upward movement in American interest rates as a result. One estimate is that American long-term interests have been 1 to 1.5 per cent lower than they otherwise would have been.

But no: another aspect of the 'China effect' is that China's anxiety to promote its exports means it maintains its exchange rate artificially low, building up the massive surplus of foreign-exchange reserves it holds in dollars. Indeed, it is so concerned to maintain the renminbi at a stable rate against the dollar, to promote exports abroad and social stability at home, that it will offer trillions of renminbi to stop the exchange rate rising. This has been doubly important since the People's Bank of China, under intense pressure from the United States, adjusted the currency upwards by 2 per cent in July 2005 (after holding the same rate for more than a decade). The People's Bank has countenanced further rises in its new phase of managed floating – whetting the appetite of international financiers for the Chinese currency because now they might make a profit as it rises. Meanwhile China's purchases of bonds and bills mean that the price of American bonds has risen and their yields have fallen, despite the mountainous domestic and overseas debts of the United States (the country's international debts now approach an astonishing $3 trillion). The low yields on bonds reinforce the trend for money to stay cheap, helping to keep the boom going. The counterpart, of course, is the $1 trillion of China's foreign-exchange reserves.

It is fashionable to blame China for downward wage pressures in the United States. Median wages in the United States have grown only slowly for a generation; and the argument is that with 760 million potential new Chinese workers joining the global labour market, the impact on American and European jobs and wages will become even stronger.[28] In 2003 China also produced seven hundred thousand science graduates, compared with sixty thousand in the United States. It is easy to make the situation seem very alarming. However, despite the sense of panic, the statistics so far indicate only a tiny effect (see Chapter 11). The more reliable impact may have been to make workforces more fearful and accommodating, anticipating the arrival of China's hordes; also, examples of successful outsourcing are being exaggerated to terrify workers into accepting lower wages. The rhetorical deployment of China to subdue wage inflation is at this stage more important than any direct effect.

Still, China is having direct and indirect effects on our lives. The prices we pay for goods, housing and oil are being radically shaped by the big new kid on the economic block. The soaring price of petrol as oil prices approach $80 a barrel, signalling a new period of high or very high oil prices, is inexplicable without the rise in demand from China, now the world's second-largest oil importer. And over the past two years Chinese buying has driven world commodity prices to record highs. To the extent China's exports have helped keep inflation down, cheap credit has inflated property prices.

China has given new force to the arguments environmentalists have been putting forward for decades. Debates over how soon oil production will peak[29] have become more urgent, as has the imminent exhaustion of copper and zinc reserves, predicted by industry analysts within fourteen and eleven years respectively.[30] If China continues growing at the same rate, it will start to press against the limits of some world resources within the next decade. Moreover, its growth is having an impact on the Chinese environment. China is extraordinarily wasteful of energy: to generate every dollar of GDP, China uses three times more energy than the global average, four times more than the United States and eight times more than Japan.[31] In 2006 China's carbon dioxide emissions exceeded those of the United States, according to the Dutch Environmental Assessment Agency; by 2008, says the International Energy Agency, it will be the largest emitter of all greenhouse gases. Worryingly, the growth is explosive and apparently unstoppable. China is becoming globally toxic, even as it protests that on a per capita basis its emissions are a quarter of those of the United States. The sense of grievance at being in the dock for causing global warming is thus partially understandable; the fact remains that while China's plans call for emissions to be frozen by 2010, compared to 2005, on these trends they will have doubled! Pollution is endemic: four hundred thousand Chinese die prematurely every year from air pollution. And in addition, all China is chronically short of water.

China is also beginning to flex its muscle as an Asian power. Americans, and Europeans in the peaceful tranquillity of the European Union, have little idea of how edgy and raw relationships are between China and the surrounding states, or how nationalistic and warlike the rhetoric and – sometimes – actions can become. China readily entered the Korean War in 1950; fought India in a bloody border war in 1962; invaded Vietnam in 1979, with a loss of fifty thousand men; and has had skirmishes with the Russians. Borders are contested; ownership of islands in the East and South China Seas is not accepted; and old wounds from the Second World War and even earlier are unhealed. Asia knows that China wants Taiwan back. The region frequently sounds and feels more like pre-1914 Europe than part of twenty-first-century globalisation.

For example, in February 2005 Japan formally took possession of the Senkaku Islands, whose control is the key to claiming sovereignty over vast offshore oil and gas reserves. In April 2005 China sent an official warning to Tokyo to withdraw or 'take full responsibility' for any consequences. It was the kind of ultimatum a great power might have issued during the nineteenth century. Japan's defence ministry drew up contingency plans to deploy fifty-five thousand troops if China invaded the islands. In September 2005 five Chinese naval ships, including a guided-missile destroyer, were found near the Chunxiao gas field in the East China Sea. Eventually both sides drew back; but this kind of brinkmanship over a territorial dispute is now almost unknown in the rest of the developed world. The *People's Daily* has declared that the competition for oil resources in the East China Sea is just 'the prelude of the game between China and Japan over international energy'.[32]

China feels ideologically isolated, encircled by enemies and rivals. There are also challenges at home, even if they are currently submerged. In 1989 China was rocked to its foundations by a coalition of workers, students and intellectuals like the one that brought down communism in Eastern Europe and Russia. The same causes for complaint exist today, arguably with even more force and a repeat of Tiananmen today might succeed. It is an ever-present fear of China's communist leadership, even if in the West the memories fade. To understand today's China, we must first understand Tiananmen and its legacy.

The internal bargain

Tiananmen was China's own attempted perestroika and velvet revolution rolled into one. Not only did the protests convulse Beijing for six weeks in 1989; there were demonstrations in 181 cities, including all of the provincial capitals, the major cities and special economic zones.[33] Nearly every city with a university experienced some kind of public march.[34] Official records indicate that students from 319 Chinese universities were represented in Tiananmen Square.[35] The party itself was divided over how to respond, as was the army; 150 officers openly declared that they would not fire on demonstrators after martial law was declared, and at least a third of the Central Committee wanted to reach a compromise with the protestors.

At the beginning of the 1980s, China of the Deng-inspired opening was much more intellectually free and easy than it is today. Political and economic reform were more obviously proceeding hand in hand. But there were problems. In 1986–7 inflation had been rising sharply and the growth in general living standards had halted, in stark contrast to the extravagant lifestyles of party officials. Corruption was rampant.

In the spring of 1989 a group of students at Beijing University, impressed by the events unfolding in Eastern Europe and by Gorbachev's reforms in the Soviet Union, began to wonder if they dared engage in public street protests. The movement was an uneasy, incoherent coalition.[36] It included party members from the reformist wing who wanted the pace of reform to be matched by a commitment to social justice; it also included those who wanted to accelerate privatisation and market liberalisation as well as those who wanted Western-style democracy and were agitating for a thoroughgoing regime change. The only common ground was a fierce hatred of corruption. This was not enough in the first phase of protests to let the protesters find an effective common line in their negotiations with the compromisers among the party leadership. From that breach disaster would follow.

An initial daring march by a motley group of students on the morning of 27 April 1989, with banners proclaiming '*vive la liberté*', was not opposed by police gunfire; it spontaneously swelled into a street march of more than half a million people that lasted all day. For the next six weeks more than one million people manned barricades and blockades, effectively occupying central Beijing. They made their headquarters Tiananmen Square, the vast square outside the Forbidden City that is the totemic public heart of China. Alongside a makeshift statue of the goddess of democracy, the newly formed Beijing Workers' Autonomous Federation set up a tent and began to recruit and mobilise workers, copying Solidarity in Poland.

Deng and the party elders – the so-called eight 'immortals', veterans of the Revolution – were furious. They were unafraid to shed blood if necessary to repress what they deemed a counter-revolutionary rebellion. However, the party's general secretary, Zhao Ziyang – the reformer whom Deng had elevated first to the presidency in 1980 and then to the general secretaryship of the party in 1987 – was opposed. He wanted compromise, proposing a partial meeting of demands for reform rather than systemic change, and the avoidance at all costs of bloodshed.[37] He had publicly insisted in early May that the 'just demands of the students be met' and encouraged extensive news coverage of the events to bolster his position, which he allowed to be understood as a challenge to Deng.[38] As a result the protests grew.

Alarmed at the scale of the demonstrations, the elders finally acted. Zhao lost the argument, his job and his official reputation; he remained under house arrest until his death in 2005. Martial law was imposed on 19 May and a fortnight later the tanks rolled into Tiananmen Square. However, Deng had to leave Beijing to ensure that army groups 28 and 29, personally loyal to him, would provide the core of the force rather than the uncertain army groups based around the capital. It was a bloody and murderous engagement. The General Office of the State Council reported to the Committee of Elders afterwards that five thousand soldiers and police officers, and two thousand civilians, were wounded in the action. Of the 443 dead, 223 were soldiers and police officers, thirty-six university students and the rest were ordinary Chinese citizens.[39] At least as many were arrested and disappeared into the Chinese prison system. In sharp contrast to what was to happen in the Soviet Union, the party had reasserted its authority, but at a terrible long-term cost. The image of the anonymous student single-handedly stopping a tank is one of the most arresting of the twentieth century.

The scale of the international response shook the leaders, although privately they congratulated themselves on having shown their willingness to act, irrespective of the views of foreigners. Negotiations over membership in the General Agreement on Tariffs and Trade (GATT, a forerunner of the World Trade Organization) that had begun two years earlier were immediately suspended; a European arms embargo was imposed, joining the American embargo, which has continued to today. The pace of inward investment from foreign companies levelled off, and investors were persuaded to return only by being given generous tax concessions that continue to distort and weaken the government's fiscal position.

Equally serious was the crisis of legitimacy at home. The citizens that the party had killed were not just any citizens. Young students have for millennia held a special place in Chinese life as the generation studying to promote China's greater good, and Beijing University is the country's elite institution. The rhetoric applied to defend the suppression – that the whole event was a 'counter-revolutionary riot' – was so obviously false and self-serving that the official language of communism lost any vestigial respect. To call for an official reassessment of Tiananmen has become the most potent and politically challenging declaration in China.

The Communist Party leadership and its seventy million members know that they might not survive another Tiananmen. There would be no Committee of Elders with revolutionary credentials who could command the loyalty of the military or the personal loyalty of some army groups. The divisions that incapacitated the protesters of 1989 would be unlikely to be repeated; there would be more willingness to campaign for system-wide change as the only way to stem corruption and establish the rule of law. Also, repression imposed as in 1989 would today incur even more international odium and, given China's integration into the world economy, the reaction would make China more vulnerable. The argument for democracy is more strongly entrenched internationally, despite its association with Bush's foreign policy. More states have converted to democracy since 1989, and resisting it seems retrograde.

There is no possibility of an ideological renewal, a 'back to basics' reassertion of core communist values such as a modified Cultural Revolution. When Mao tried that in the mid-1960s, communism was still a live ideology at home and abroad – and even then it failed. The party has now acknowledged that the class war is over, but it finds itself in a catch-22. It resists elections because they would expose it to political competition, but without elections there are no channels except protest through which to express dissent and anger. China's communists confront the same conundrum as the old Confucian emperors. Legitimacy depends completely on continued economic success and urgent appeals to nationalism.

Yet the gap between the booming cities and the depressed rural areas grows ever wider. There is a stark contrast between Shanghai, where adjusted per capita income exceeds $15,000 and provides almost first-world living standards, and poverty-stricken Guizhou province in the rural west, with a per capita income of $1247.[40] Roughly half of China's people, mainly in the rural west, live on comparably low incomes. Income gradually rises towards the coast, but even within the rich coastal cities and provinces there is phenomenal inequality between the migrant workers and the richer middle classes. Eight of China's thirty-one provinces, comprising 40 per cent of its population, have provided almost three-quarters of China's growth since 2000. The UN World Development Report ranks China, with its formal communist commitment to equality, as more unequal than both the United States and Britain.[41]

Regarding employment, the best estimate is that to stave off a potential avalanche of dissent and protest, China has to create some twenty-four million new jobs a year for migrants leaving the countryside, for students leaving schools and colleges and for people left newly unemployed by the rationalising of state-owned enterprises.[42] Yet employment is growing by only slightly more than 1 per cent a year. Open and disguised unemployment, according to some estimates, is as high as 170 million, or 23 per cent of the labour force.[43] Another problem is corruption. A leading Chinese economist and intellectual, Hu Angang, who has an edgy relationship with the Chinese leadership because of his outspokenness, calculates that in the late 1990s corruption resulted in an economic loss to China of between 13.3 and16.9 per cent of GDP.[44]

The number of public protests demanding social justice – especially protests against unfair compensation for compulsory land purchases – has increased significantly. According to official Chinese sources, the numbers involved in public protests increased from 740,000 in 1994 to 3.7 million in 2004. Strikes have risen as well: from 1909 in 1994 to 22,600 in 2003, with the number of people involved jumping from 77,704 to approximately 800,000. Even the larger numbers are, of course, a small proportion of the total population but, given the bravery it takes to dissent in an authoritarian state, the fact that some four million protesters and one million strikers have run the risk is testimony to the growing strength of feeling. Importantly, numbers are no longer disseminated publicly. The Ministry of Labour and Security has warned that the growing income gap is likely to make the system unstable by 2010 if no effective solutions are found.[45]

The debates within the party about whether to maintain the pace and structure of reform have become increasingly acute. The left has become more vocally critical; the 2007 law to enshrine private property rights has been significantly watered down, allowing for the renewal of leases in towns but reasserting that rural land is collectively owned. Critics claimed any more would undermine Chinese socialism: it was 'surnamed capitalist, not surnamed socialist'.[46] Communist Party committees are to be established in private enterprises as in state-owned enterprises. President Hu Jintao, also general secretary of the party, has cracked down on the

Internet and the media. He praises the communist parties of Cuba and North Korea and eulogises Mao, using Maoist rhetoric about the danger of bourgeois liberalism in internal party speeches. He has appealed to Chinese journalists to write in the spirit of 'Marxist journalism' in the run-up to the Olympics in 2008. The returning economic liberals educated at American and British universities are regarded with growing suspicion. Liu Guoguang, one-time reformer and member of the party's Standing Committee, now says that introducing Western reforms into China was a mistake; Liu Guoguang societies are growing dramatically without party opposition. The party's priority is now 'harmonious development', lowering inequality, giving rights to migrant workers, sustaining rural incomes and trying to limit rural protests. Its mounting worry is that if ever the growth machine slows down, it will be in mortal trouble. It is right.

The reckoning

For fifteen years China's economic growth has approached an average of nearly 10 per cent a year. Its planners have pencilled in a more modest growth rate of 7.5 per cent for the eleventh five-year plan or 'guidelines', which extends to 2010; but the reality is that the average growth rate the Chinese have become accustomed to must be maintained. China needs to maintain the highest growth rate possible more or less indefinitely if it is to prop up the Communist Party.

This is not possible with the current economic structure. The model that has taken China thus far will have to be transformed, because it cannot withstand the strain of a near tripling of the economy's current size over the next fifteen years. If the current structure of growth continues, by 2020 Chinese exports would constitute nearly $5 trillion, or some 100 per cent of its then GDP – and approaching half the likely merchandise exports of the world at that time. Since China's export growth has mainly been driven by non-Chinese companies, to reach this total we have to suppose that there are sufficient non-Chinese companies with the capacity to transfer production on such a scale to China, and that Western markets have the capacity to absorb such enormous flows of imports. Already 80 per cent of American toy imports come from China. So far, some four hundred of the Fortune 500 in the United States and a comparable proportion of European and Japanese producers have invested in China. In other words, most of those who could move production to China have done so already.[47] Growth projections that extrapolate current trends have to suppose that over the next fifteen years Western multinationals in China are going to be able to continue increasing Chinese production and exports at six or seven times the rate of growth of their domestic markets.

This is both a mathematical and an economic impossibility. The law of large numbers is going to start kicking in. To maintain its growth record, China will have to start exporting under its own steam, with its own companies, its own technology, its own new product lines and its own brands. But to achieve that in the time-frame is equally impossible. At the time of writing, there are no Chinese brands in the world's top hundred; and so far only two Chinese companies – Huawei and Lenovo – both very small, can be called genuine multinationals. In short, some time in the next decade export growth from China is necessarily going to subside to more normal levels.

Thus China must be pulled along more by domestic consumption; it must allow investment in its infrastructure to decline relatively, develop indigenous Chinese enterprise and begin to revolutionise its approach to the use of resources. These are iron laws of economics and, increasingly, of nature. But here is the rub. Chinese enterprise under the current rules has so far shown itself incapable of meeting such challenges. It has developed neither a viable concept of the company nor the institutional network to support a company. The vast majority of its state-owned enterprises still have political rather than business priorities and its plethora of quasi-governmental, local government and cooperative organisations do not have the balance sheets, the culture or the organisational capacity to produce at such a scale without escalating subsidy. Meanwhile its small companies tend to be built around families and kinship relationships (*guanxi*) or to depend so much on links with corrupt officials that they cannot build themselves up to be high-volume producers. Many are extraordinarily short-lived. One sign of weakness is that since the mid-1990s each additional increment of capital investment has been producing declining returns.[48] The incentives in the system are soft options, quick returns and corrupt profits. The party interest trumps building a business.

In comparison with where China started nearly thirty years ago, reform has been extraordinary. It has introduced the 'hard' processes of a market economy – free movement of prices, wages and rents – permitted limited ownership of private property and recognised the fundamental role of profit. It has opened to overseas investors. State capacity has been built up, and China now possesses the machinery of modern government. It has lowered tariffs and become a genuinely more open economy adhering to the rules of the World Trade Organization.

But what has been achieved has been comparatively easy compared with what now lies ahead. The party has to recognise that an essential adjunct of capitalism is a morality as vigorous in its own terms as that associated with communism, and certainly more effective. Building a great company is not just a matter of assembling workers, capital and land and selling the resulting product for profit in a market. Long-term success involves the construction of a common culture and shared purpose that in turn depend upon the establishment of an overriding business aim and organisational reason for existence that binds the company together and relates it to its market and customers. In this respect successful capitalism has a moral dimension.

China has almost no enterprises, no critical mass of executives and no business tradition that understands this moral facet of capitalism. The 'soft' institutions of capitalism and a live public realm are as integral to growth and sustainability as the hard processes of private companies and markets. If China wants to triple the size of its economy over the next generation it has no option but to develop these soft institutions. One storm warning that the current economic model is reaching the end of its usefulness is the accelerating increase in inflation – a consequence of the interaction of rapid economic growth with the astonishing build-up of cash and liquidity in the Chinese financial system, itself closely linked to the growth of foreign-exchange reserves. China's foreign-exchange reserves are growing at an annualised rate in excess of $500 billion a year – up $266 billion in the first six months of 2007 – and not even the efforts of the People's Bank of China can stop liquidity growth equivalent to around a quarter of GDP every year from leaking into the financial system. The rise in the Chinese stock market, the property booms in the major cities, wasteful investment and yet more non-performing loans are already testimony to the results. The impact of inflation – the precursor to Tiananmen and even the backdrop to the defeat of Chiang Kai-Chek's nationalist armies – is justly feared by the party. Already the authorities are allowing the renminbi to move up sooner than they planned and allowing individuals to buy securities offshore in 2008 in an attempt to curb the growth of foreign-exchange reserves. But the better solution would be to have an economic system less reliant on exports, investment and a rigged exchange rate, and with more inherent capacity to boost domestic consumption and generate innovation itself. That requires reform.

The reforms so far proposed in the plan and under consideration – such as selling minority shareholdings in the banks to foreigners and trying to professionalise the hopelessly compromised judiciary – are all steps in the right direction and were unthinkable just twenty years ago. But they are piecemeal and reactive. The pace of institutional change must accelerate, and a genuine Chinese enterprise culture must develop; otherwise some shock will force a sharp deceleration in the growth rate. That shock could be a prolonged water shortage, a further increase in the price of oil, a destabilising rise in inflation or unilateral tariff increases by the United States against Chinese exports. A relapse into repression at home and nationalism abroad would be likely to follow.

What the West must do

Because China must change, it will. The question is what constitutional and political spasms it may experience and what their internal and global impact might be. Given the inevitability of the outcome, it would be rational to get there peacefully, with as few hiccups and alarums as possible. If China needs to invent a soft institutional infrastructure, then equally the West will have to breathe new life into its own and the Enlightenment tradition that gave it birth. The global institutional architecture – from the International Monetary Fund to the World Trade Organization – must be reformed around the same reassertion of principles. Whether climate change or the approaching energy crisis as oil production peaks, the world faces a choice of responding collaboratively through revived or new institutions – or relapsing into competitive nationalisms.

The changes are far-reaching for both parties. Eventually, the communist leadership will have to accept that China must become a pluralist representative democracy; similarly, the West will have to accept a major reorganisation of its own economic and social structures to accommodate China and the implications of the international division of labour. The United States and Europe are going to rely increasingly on China and the rest of Asia for commodity manufactures and commodity services, and on the rest of the world for food and raw materials.

What this means for the West is an intensification of recent trends – a future built not just on science and technology but on knowledge in its widest sense, everything from the creative and cultural industries to financial services and revolutions in energy provision and use. So it should be. The West took a lead over China with a combination of scientific, technological and institutional prowess; now it has to reassert these skills in order to maintain its place in the global economic order.

However, Western economies will not be able to keep their side of the new global bargain if their own soft institutions are not appropriate. In this respect there is nearly as much cause for concern as with China's institutions. The West in general, and the United States in particular, is failing. American economic dynamism has always been characterised by a tension between its soft institutional infrastructure and the hard processes of its tough market-oriented capitalism – but now its soft infrastructure is weakening. If China needs a free press; corporate accountability; a duty to care for its workforce; intelligent, responsive government; proper concern for equality; and an impartial judicial system, then so does the United States. But the United States' Enlightenment legacy is fraying. The American political system is increasingly compromised by inequality, overt political fixes and the erosion of the concept of the public interest. It is becoming less responsive to public needs. Its media fails more and more in the duty to speak truth to power. American companies and financiers, scrambling for self-enrichment, increasingly deny they have a duty to care for their workforces. America's social bargain, which promotes social mobility and education in exchange for the acceptance of inequality, has been allowed to decay. And the lack of respect for international law in the response to Islamic terror has been appalling.

Britain's record is not dissimilar. The understanding of the contribution of our Enlightenment legacy to the operation of a market economy is hardly notable. We may have a stronger welfare system than the United States, but the pulse of public purpose beats ever weaker; our media uncertainly prosecutes its obligation to hold power to account in an era of celebrity, and our grip on what the rule of law means grows more insecure. Too many company leaderships see their role as boosting their own pay and share price rather than building great companies. Internationally, we have chosen to make common cause with an American government that undermines international law.

This makes achieving the Western side of a new bargain much harder. Maybe the world will have to go through spasms or set-backs first. We of course hope not. But to understand how the West might respond, we first have to understand more about China, why it has developed as it has and its capacity to complete the reform it has started. To do that we have to start with an assessment of how China, its government and its culture first began, which takes us to 1030 BC.

2

Pride and Fall

Understanding China has always been a struggle for the West. Nineteenth-century Western critics of China's endemic backwardness and its peasant poverty were counterbalanced by admirers of its civilisation, the quality of its Confucian government and its astounding advances in science and technology long before Europe achieved them. Now comes a new riddle to superimpose on the old debate. The current Western consensus is that political liberty and capitalist success go hand in hand, but here is a communist authoritarian government presiding over an economic success story. Moreover, the Chinese Communist Party was largely shaped by a murderous ideological zealot, Mao Zedong. What happened to put a China long outrun by the West back into the race?

China's rise, stagnation, fall and subsequent rise, along with its potential sustainability, constitute a puzzle that is becoming one of the most important to solve. It is made more difficult still by a long tradition of Western theorists only too willing to see their own prejudices confirmed by what they imagine to be the

Chinese experience. Thus Marx, in the nineteenth century, had to dismiss China as the creature of backward orientalism in order for his theory to hold. 'A rotting semi-civilisation, vegetating in the teeth of time' defined the first, most primitive Asian mode of production, he argued, which had not even reached the ancient, let alone the feudal, level of development that were the basis for European capitalist dynamism and the creation of an industrial proletariat.[1] This framework could hardly explain how China's iron production exceeded Europe's as late as 1750, or how China's agricultural yields had exploded from the eighth to the thirteenth century, when European peasant agriculture languished. It also neglected the problematic truth that Chinese feudalism had mainly disappeared by the third century BC.

The German sociologist Max Weber criticised the Chinese for their 'incomparable dishonesty', 'absolute docility' and 'distrust for one another' which, together with their lack of the Protestant incentive of a virtuous afterlife earned by saving and hard work, condemned China to economic backwardness.[2] Again it was hardly useful in explaining how China had got so far ahead of Europe only to fall back. Weber needed to explain how the Chinese had become more docile, dishonest and distrustful over the nineteenth century. He could not.

More recently, American economists, historians and sociologists have had a similar proclivity to look at China through the ideological prism of conservatism, usually some combination of American exceptionalism and an insistence that because markets and property rights are the route to economic success lack of success means necessarily that they did not or could not have existed. The Nobel laureate Douglass North, for example, has stressed the weakness of the system of Chinese property rights, permanently at the discretion of the emperor, as the chief cause of China's backwardness.[3] But as early as the third century BC, China had entrenched diffused private property rights which in many ways were better developed and more sophisticated than either

Europe's or America's. Today, for example, an embedded culture of private property and a sense of legal entitlement are provoking protests against the Communist Party when proper compensation is not offered for the compulsory acquisition of peasants' land. North is a pioneer in stressing the importance of institutions to development, but he overemphasises China's lack of property rights and thus oversimplifies the deficiencies of its institutional structure.

On the other hand, there is a Western tradition that is too much in awe of what it sees in China. Marco Polo, the Venetian explorer, arrived there in the thirteenth century and marvelled at the skills involved in silk and ceramics manufacture, and at the sophistication of the government. It did not occur to him that no Chinese explorer had reciprocated his initiative by similarly spending decades in Venice, whose leadership of medieval Europe was no less intriguing. Five hundred years later Voltaire celebrated the disinterested intelligence of the secular Confucian government and its success in creating such an advanced civilisation just as, unbeknown to him, China's Confucian system was being overtaken by a dynamic Europe.

More recently there is the British economic historian Joseph Needham, whose twenty-eight-volume masterwork *Science and Civilisation* details how the Chinese were ahead of Europe in almost every invention: the compass, the clock, gunpowder and the printing press. Needham argued that only China's commitment to harmony and cooperation, which he contrasted with Europe's addiction to bloody conquest and capitalist acquisition, had prevented China from reproducing Europe's economic success.[4] This thesis ignores the fact that China doubled its land area by conquest under the Qing in the eighteenth century, one of the greatest imperial land-grabs in history,[5] and Needham fails to explain its sudden conversion to capitalist-style growth today. China remains an elusive intellectual quarry.

Yet it does seem clear that as late as the 1800s China constituted

33 per cent of the world's GDP, according to the economic historian Angus Maddison,[6] before plunging to around 5 per cent in 1950. China had created a political and social system that successfully governed a land area equivalent to Europe or the United States, offering a continent-wide order in which the peasant, the key actor in pre-industrial China and Europe, was genuinely more prosperous and peaceful, aided by a scientific and technological advance that was ahead of Europe's. By the standards of pre-industrial humanity, China had provided the good life to one-fifth of the world's population for the best part of two thousand years. But throughout the nineteenth century it became more and more dysfunctional and by the early twentieth century the Chinese system was obviously the principal obstacle to economic and political modernisation. To understand today's China we need to understand how and why imperial China succeeded and failed, and how it illuminates economic development in the past and present.

The Chinese achievement

Imperial China, with antecedents stretching back to the Zhou dynasty 1030 years before the birth of Christ, lasted from 221 BC, with the first emperor of all China, Qin Shihuang, until the collapse of the Qing dynasty in 1912 – one of the world's most extraordinary achievements. Geography, nature and relative ethnic homogeneity all made the establishment of a common governmental system across a continent immeasurably easier. Nature had been kind: the soil was fertile, rainfall was plentiful, much of the country enjoys a temperate or subtropical climate, rivers are extensive and crop yields are good. Farming came naturally.

The purpose and basis of the Chinese imperial system was cultivation of the land, raised to the standing of what the historian

Kent Deng describes as a 'cult of agriculture'.[7] As early as 2800 BC the worship of the land god Shennong was well established, as was the idea of *xiangtu*, that establishing a home required the possession of cultivatable land. In contrast to the Western antecedents of the word 'society', the ancient Chinese word *sheji* has its roots in the veneration of agriculture. '*She*' means land or earth god, while '*ji*' refers to millet. Society is based on the land and what the land produces. But the Latin word *societas* indicates human relationships; the Western notion of society has to do with citizenship, situated in aggregations of people in cities rather than the isolated countryside. Even as late as the 1780s only 6 per cent of China's then 290 million people lived in cities.[8]

The genius and durability of the imperial system lay in the triangular relationship between the land-owning, small-scale farming family; the imperial order that protected it, drawing income from rural prosperity; and the Confucian mandarinate who attempted to govern fairly and objectively to boost agricultural production. The English economic and social historian Richard Tawney observed that 'the typical figure in Chinese country life is not hired labour, but the landholding peasant'.[9] Thomas Rawski comments, 'for at least the last millennium, Chinese agriculture has been dominated by a large number of free, small-scale farmers, working under a system of private land-ownership'.

By the eighteenth century as much as 92 per cent of registered land was privately owned. Among the property-owners, smallholders were the majority, with an average farm size of 1.7 acres.[10] European-style feudalism, in terms of land ownership, existed in China, but it was always on the defensive and finally disappeared on any large scale during the Qin dynasty (221–207 BC). European feudalism would last until the fourteenth century, but the Chinese had left this system more than a thousand years earlier.

The task of successive emperors was to support the fecundity of the venerated land, the incomes of those who owned and cultivated it and to ensure that the population at large did not starve.

And this they did with imagination and energy. By the 1500s China had an unparalleled transport infrastructure of twenty-eight national highways and fifty-three provincial main roads intersecting with a dense system of canals and navigable rivers, the cumulative result of two thousand years of investment.[11] Private land ownership had been enshrined by Shang Yang (390–338 BC), an adviser to the Qin state, who created a land registry to establish property titles over two thousand years before the Declaration of Independence. It proved a master stroke, motivating peasants to boost production and so equipping the Qin with plentiful food and well-fed armies, thus laying the basis of their later dynastic success.

More than four hundred years before the birth of Christ Li Kui initiated what was to develop into a national system of granaries that stored more than a six-month supply of grain, with minimum prices to guarantee farm incomes and a capacity to buy surpluses for future famine years – a combination of the European Union's Common Agricultural Policy and the United States' farm support system. Low-interest loans were available to farmers. In irrigation, famine relief, improving seed types and farming techniques the Chinese were ahead of Europe by hundreds of years. Needham shows that by the end of the twelfth century the Chinese had invented the compass and sternpost rudder, and by the end of the fourteenth century gunpowder and the mechanical clock, inventions that Europe copied. Taxes were kept low, never more than 10 per cent of GDP,[12] largely because there was so little war. Chinese emperors can be seen as archetypal political pragmatists, combining a Conservative approach to taxes with a Labour approach to public improvement.

For a long time it worked. What Shang Yang had proposed in recognising title to property was no more than following what happened on the ground. Peasant families cultivated the land of the forebears they worshipped, so developing a virtually unchallengeable sense of entitlement. Their right to farm originated in the legitimacy of their ancestors' first claim and the continuation of the farming tradition. They did not have the feudal European notion that the monarch was charged by God to hold land, thus justifying his absolute rights over it. In China, imperial authority might be associated with heavenly purpose, but that conferred no rights over land. Rights came from one's ancestors.

Patterns of land ownership became increasingly sophisticated.[13] Renting, for example, had been supplemented in the early Song period (around 1000 AD) by a system of leasing which went beyond granting rights for topsoil cultivation to separate leases for the exploitation of minerals or for access to water, each right creating its own lively market. Not only could a sublease be bought and sold, but so could any mortgage attached to it. Thus the world's first secondary mortgage market emerged more than a thousand years ago: infinitely better developed than any comparable financial instrument in Europe.

The system was certainly effective. Although China has less cultivable land than Europe, and a denser population, agricultural productivity was significantly higher. Historical data on nutrition and daily caloric intake are notoriously difficult to assemble, but Kenneth Pomeranz, a professor of history at the University of California Irvine whose path-breaking book *The Great Divergence* made him the co-winner of the World History Association Book Prize in 2001, estimates that the average Chinese, at least until the 1800s, was as least as well fed as his or her European counterpart. We also know that from the Tang period to the Ming period, between 618 and 1644, total grain output averaged about fifteen million tons a year, almost twice as much as was needed for subsistence consumption. Not only did the Chinese have a well-established system of property rights and a market in those rights, they also produced a great deal more food per hectare. Seven per cent of the world's cultivable land fed between one-fifth and a quarter of the world's population.

Confucianism in theory and practice

All this required predictability and order, provided by the third leg of the Chinese system, the mandarin official class of Confucian scholars who administered China. The starting point of Confucianism is that the heavenly purpose (*tian*), independent of any particular monarch, is to ensure the well-being of the people (*minben*). The task of the Confucian scholar or official is to interpret in government the day-to-day means of achieving the Confucian goal of perfect harmony (*dao*) and hold the emperor accountable for his decisions. Nothing can be more sacred than the promotion of human well-being: those who are entrusted with governing have to be moral and seek to construct harmony, cooperation and order all around them. There developed an elaborate etiquette of interpersonal behaviour and conduct that was meant to signify adherence to this commitment.

Crucial to the integrity of the governmental and administrative machine was the willingness of the emperor to accept, and Confucian officials to offer, criticism of his decisions. This was the system of remonstration and admonition (*jianzheng*). It was taken very seriously and sometimes demanded extreme bravery from the officials concerned. Le Yun of the Northern and Southern dynasties and Hai Rui of the Ming dynasty both brought their coffins to court, recognising that their challenge might end in their death.[14] In a system in which executive, legislature and judiciary were rolled into one, *jianzheng* was a crucial counterbalance.

Another was the *huibi* system, or law of avoidance. Officials were assigned to provinces and cities other than their own in order to minimise the temptation to favour friends and family; also, it was forbidden for an official to buy land in his home town. Moreover, there was a systematic rotation: officials were regularly moved on so that they would not be incorporated into local merchant and landlord networks and would not govern in a partisan or unfair way. The design of the system thus reinforced the overriding obligation of the Confucian official to behave with integrity and to administer and adjudicate objectively and impartially, both upwards and downwards. Among the Confucian virtues, the supreme virtue was *li*: the cultivated, intense self-discipline with which the aspirant scholar or official went about his daily business. But *li* was not meant to be achieved by too great a demonstration of hard work; it was meant to be effortless, the consequence of having reached inner peace through inner discipline. The long nails, knotted hair and elaborate gown of the Confucian gentleman, at once teacher and exemplar of his creed, signalled that he was above manual labour. What counted was the propriety of his conduct and the scrupulousness of his judgements, in which he had considerable discretion. The essence of Confucian government was that it was executed by men embodying moral purpose rather than a system of impartial rules.

Confucius died in 479 BC, after some years of wandering throughout China trying unsuccessfully to persuade its vying rulers and warlords to adopt the principles set out in his *Analects*. His disciple Mencius, who refined the Confucian system, had only marginally better luck 150 years later. It was not until 136 BC that Confucianism became the official state ideology, offering emperors a source of legitimacy and a code of good government. The emperor could thus acquire an official and administrative class whose secular religion was to further the interests of millions of family smallholders justly and fairly in a spirit of community, harmony and public-mindedness. The result was to boost their agricultural production, secure their land and protect them from bullying neighbours, criminals and arbitrary rule. As the farmer families prospered, so would the empire.

Confucianism was unable to modernise China in the nineteenth century – a condemnation made by every shade of opinion from the Communist Party to Western intellectuals, and it clung to its apparently other-worldly goals of harmony and virtue. All this has coloured our understanding of its achievements. But in practice the economic importance of trade and industry was recognised, even if land ownership and becoming part of the rural gentry offered superior social status. Aspiring Confucian scholars chose to write essays on economic development;[15] in office they built roads and canals and worked closely with merchants in developing business. The Confucian tradition was much more focused on development than its caricature would suggest.

The efforts made to legitimise the Confucian bureaucracy were intense and impressive. Competitive written examinations were the key to entry. These were first established in the second century BC, and they were open to all, even the lowliest peasant. In Europe the first comparable written examinations began in 1702; in the United States they began in 1883 and were opposed for some years as a Chinese import and therefore un-American.[16] By the time of the Northern Song dynasty (960–1127 AD) the system had become as fair as possible. Examination papers were kept secret, locked in safe rooms; essays were read by at least two independent examiners only after they had been transcribed into identical calligraphy to avoid bias; examinees were body-searched to avoid cheating; and the emperor himself read the best papers. The penalties for abuse were severe and included death. In 1657 seven imperial examiners found guilty of irregularities were beheaded immediately, their private property was confiscated and 109 of their close relatives were exiled. So that the bureaucracy would not become self-perpetuating, quotas were established to limit the entry of sons of serving officials.

The process achieved its objectives. As far as can be established, the Chinese mandarinate drew its members from across Chinese society. One study found that 83 per cent of those who came out on top in the intensely competitive exams, so-called champions, were from lower-class families, with the rest from the upper class, almost exactly mirroring China's social structure.[17] A study of successful applicants between 1015 and 1874 AD found that one village, Liukeng, a tiny backwater in the relatively underdeveloped Jiangxi province, supplied nearly three hundred officials, of whom some became ministers and one became prime minister.[18] Far from being a closed caste, China's Confucian bureaucracy was organised as the world's first genuine meritocracy. It offered social mobility and legitimacy, and it kept officials close to the interests of the people – proof positive of the governmental concept of the 'people as foundation'. The Confucian official has sometimes been described as the embodiment of the impractical and the other-worldly, who achieved his status by committing the Confucian classical texts to memory and writing stylised 'eight-legged' essays; the truth is more complex. The structure worked so well for so long because of these officials' dedication to the national cause, the public interest and the well-being of the people. This vision of how a mandarinate should work was later deployed by both nationalist and communist leaders, even while they criticised it for being anti-modern.

The system was an interdependent whole. The emperor relied on his prime minister, imperial secretariat and liaison office, which in turn linked up to the provincial bureaucracies and magistracies that administered justice, collected taxes and developed the economy. The family property holders looked to the imperial government to maintain their rights, secure their incomes and keep order. There were built-in checks and balances. Young officials were the emperor's watchdogs, keeping an eye on the integrity of the older officials, who in turn ran the system of remonstrance that kept an eye on the imperial bureaucracy, along with the censorate that inspected it.[19] Administration was relatively decentralised. Successive emperors understood their own place in the scheme of things: Emperor Taizong (627–649 AD) even wrote a book titled *The Norm for Monarchs* (*Difan*), which systematically instructed his descendants in how to behave and govern the country by Confucian standards, and warned them that if they did not they risked revolt and being deservedly deposed.[20]

The trouble was that despite all these efforts, and even the inevitable autonomy in the provinces of so large a continent, formal power lay at the centre and Confucian internal checks and balances were an inadequate counterbalance to arbitrary and, sometimes, just plain bad government. Ominously for today's Communist Party, whose centralised rule by enlightened officials governing for the general good has obvious resonances with China's imperial past, the system was seriously weakened by its lack of institutions and processes that could have held power to account and represented interests and grievances. China's peasants responded in the only way they could; they engaged in periodic violent and sustained protests, so that China has a history of bottom-up rebellion unsurpassed anywhere else in the world.

Revolt came to be understood as a justified, almost legitimate, expression of dissent and anger. It was a kind of institutional cleansing, holding the imperial system to account but stopping short of revolution. The ruler might change, but not the system. The rebellions could be awesome, involving millions of peasants and lasting for decades; two lasted more than forty years each, with enormous costs in deaths and loss of output. At least five Chinese imperial dynasties (Qin, Han, Sui, Yuan and Ming) succumbed to these monumental protests. There were many more provincial and regional rebellions. The structural difficulty was that, despite good intentions and moral rhetoric, the network of landlords, officials and Confucian scholars tended to harden into what became known as the gentry; pitiless and hard-headed in looking after its own interests by tax-farming and imposing the highest possible rents. Meanwhile the imperial government was too distant to respond: heaven is high and the emperor is far away (*tian gao, huangdi yuan*) in the words of an old Chinese aphorism. The salaries of Confucian mandarins were linked to middle-income peasants and as officials were promoted their salaries fell, the assumption being that the more senior they became, the more they should demonstrate their morality. They could keep pace with the incomes of the rich landlords and merchants only by tax-farming and accepting bribes.

By the end of the nineteenth century the system was not only challenged by the incursion of foreigners with obviously superior technology and superior financial, communication and weapons systems, but was beginning to fail on its own terms. As the historian John Fairbank notes, during the Qing dynasty the actual income of a Confucian governor-general was as much as 140 times his nominal salary, the difference having been earned by corruption.[21] One-third of China's peasant households were now tenants, the majority renting from a network of landlords who included slightly richer peasants and absentee merchants in far-off cities. It is estimated that in the last years of the Qing dynasty (the late nineteenth century) as much as 25 per cent of cultivable land was owned by absentee landlords. As in earlier times, resentment directed against the officials and landlords was building up to rebellion, just as Confucius, Mencius and the emperor Taizong had warned. Fatally, it also included disaffected gentry who acted as leaders of peasant rebels. What was different when the Qing fell was that there was no dynasty-in-waiting; the imperial system was understood by the governing elite and the governed alike to have reached its end. Rebellion would not just be an institutional cleansing as before; it would be the signal for wholesale change that would culminate in the Communist Revolution of 1949.

Why did Europe overtake China?

Yet the mystery remains. China had markets, technology, sophisticated agriculture and private property rights. The ingredients that had produced economic success in Europe all existed in China. Anything up to two-fifths of China's agricultural output was traded in any one year; at least as much as in Europe. As we now know, its fleets and seafaring skills were comparable to Europe's; no fewer than seven Ming fleets ranged far across the Indian and Pacific oceans in the early fifteenth century. China could and should have had self-generated industrialisation. Yet Europe, not China, was to industrialise and expand overseas. Why?

The answer is that Europe succeeded in creating a network of independent, empowering, non-state but nonetheless public institutions that acted as mediators and arbitrators of relationships between the state and the individual. The public institutions might range from scientific associations to the concept of the company, from an independent judiciary to an independent press, but all reinforced a plurality of interests whose experimentation, cross-learning, openness and competition gave rise to cultural and economic dynamism. They allowed space for a process of rational argument: valuing and protecting the process of justification (a concept to be explored more fully in Chapters 7 and 8), marshalling evidence to support or dispute a case or point of view. Ultimately such values and cultural momentum would make the case for representative government accountable to the people indisputable, so that state and government became a discrete part of the same public sphere rather than opposed to it.

The crystallisation of these forces in the European Enlightenment is thus the phenomenon that enabled Europe to overtake China with implications that continue today. Rival claims and disputes were settled on their merit in sometimes intoxicatingly fresh and addictive open argument. New institutions developed, in a process and spirit that were independent of top-down fiat, whether by monarch, pope or Confucian official obeying some ancient textual formula. This was the bursting into life of the eighteenth-century coffee houses, the first newspapers and the associations for the advancement of science described by Jürgen Habermas.[22] Their counterpart was the urgent discussion of government in New England town squares in the years before the American Revolution. If the competition between warring

European states set in motion the construction of this public space and the accompanying institutions and culture, then the European Enlightenment completed it, so beginning the Western democratic tradition.

In parallel it ignited the revolution in industrial production techniques that during the nineteenth century would enable European economic hegemony in general, and British dominance in particular. Immanuel Kant summed up the spirit of the philosophical Enlightenment as 'dare to know'. The economic historian Joel Mokyr of Northwestern University argues that this spirit was transplanted to the economic sphere in a parallel 'industrial Enlightenment'.[23] Innovation did not stop with individual inventions, as it did in China; what distinguished the Industrial Revolution was that each invention and scientific advance led to more, in a continual process, creating waves of technical innovation that characterised the nineteenth century and were at the heart of the European miracle.[24] Whereas the Chinese would use mathematics and astronomy, for example, to reconceive how historical ceremonial bronze bells or ancient carriages might be built under the patronage of the emperor, Europeans would use the same techniques to develop means to sail the oceans or cast ever-stronger cannons. To dare to know gave an impetus to move restlessly forward. China could not offer the space for those who dared to know to do anything but work within the constraints of what was already around them.

China and Europe both had markets, private property and profit-hungry entrepreneurs, both possessed science and technology. Europe's system became successful capitalism with its propensity for growth, technological advance and creative destruction because of Enlightenment institutions and Enlightenment attitudes. And the Enlightenment itself, by objecting to the irrationality of barriers to trade – monopolies, local tolls, special exemptions and licences and discretionary taxes – made the intellectual case for the development of first national and then international markets. It is no accident that Adam Smith, father of free-market economics, was the quintessential expression of the Scottish Enlightenment.

The invention of the public realm

The creation of this 'public' tradition was not a seamless process of advance, but the jerky and unintended result of an interaction of a series of forces. One of the most powerful was the European proclivity for war, creating a monarchical need for taxes, which in turn created the first faltering public institutions. Europeans were not necessarily more warlike than the Chinese, as Needham suggests; rather, the geography of Europe divided them into a kaleidoscope of kingdoms, duchies and baronies with different languages, mores and loyalties, all vying for expansion.[25] For ninety-five years in the sixteenth century and ninety-four years in the seventeenth, one major European state or another was at war.[26] China certainly had spasms of warfare, dynastic change and peasant revolt, but in between there were long periods of relative peace unknown in Europe.

The unintended consequences of preparing for and waging war were far-reaching. To pay for wars, taxes had to be levied and loans raised, serviced and repaid; and, bit by bit, this created a new ongoing, iterative relationship between governors and governed; taxpayers wanted something in return. Nor was it just a matter of more pressure to raise money because there was more war. The European aristocracy and merchant classes alike were harder to take over and repress because they had distinct power bases, initially from the structure of feudalism and then, between 1500 and 1800, increasingly from the profits of long-distance oceanic trade. In Britain in particular, early feudalism, followed by the profits from international trade, created power centres that monarchs found hard to coerce. Similar effects were occurring in western France and the Netherlands. It was more rational and cheaper to gain the support of these interest groups by making political concessions to them; this was in contrast to China, where the repression was less costly.[27]

Edward I recognised this political reality by calling representatives of the English shires and towns to attend London's parliament and give him exceptional 'grants of supply'. The representatives seized this opportunity to present lists of wrongs that should be righted as a quid pro quo. Similar political institutions appeared all over Europe, such as the French *Parlement* and the Spanish *Cortes*. If taxation was to rise without civil resistance, then the monarch had to create political space to build consent; and if he didn't, then he risked a political crisis.

As warfare became more intense and expensive, the demand for taxation grew inexorably, and with it the political risk of mishandling the civil reaction. In England, Charles I could not subjugate Scotland without taxes that forced the recall of Parliament after eleven years' suspension; this led to the English Civil War and to a monarchy bounded by a representative constitution. Louis XVI could not pay for a French victory over England in the American Revolution without recalling the *Parlement*, so leading to the French Revolution. Both kings paid for their political miscalculation with their heads; both opened the way not merely for more representative government, but for the creation of a public realm.

War also spurred the creation of financial institutions and power centres beyond the state that required superintendance by independent public institutions. The great medieval Italian banking families grew fat by financing war; the same demand would spur banking families to become the first commercial banks. These could then experiment with lending to the private sector. Economic expansion could be financed from bank loans or – as in the case of England's South Sea Company – from issuing shares on nascent stock markets.

As the financial system developed it drove the creation of public banks of superintendence as well as independent courts alike. The Bank of England was established in 1694 and the Swedish Riksbank in 1688 to superintend the new markets in government bonds and to maintain the integrity of the consequent financial system in the wider public interest. Also, loans required collateral and impartial courts through which to enforce loan contracts if they were not repaid. Europe's emerging representative institutions always insisted not only that merchants, producers and financiers should have a voice in shaping commercial and contract law, but also that the law should be predictably and impartially administered.

One of the first acts of the Dutch, newly independent from Spain in the late sixteenth century, was to insist that law in the Netherlands was jointly made by king and parliament, and that Dutch courts would be independent of the monarchy. The restoration of Charles II in England, and the later accession of William, the Dutch king, to the English throne in the Glorious Revolution of 1688–9, established a similar system in England. English and Dutch commerce required a predictable, independent, impartial legal system adjudicating law that was neither arbitrary nor biased against merchants' interests. The early fight for democracy in both countries was as much a fight for disinterested justice and enforceable contracts as for representative government.

War in China was too infrequent to have the same political and institutional consequences; long periods of peace had the effect of reinforcing the basic political apparatus and its accompanying philosophy, which became more and more difficult to budge.[28] For example, the unwillingness of the Confucian system to pay for more naval expeditions by the eunuch Admiral Zheng He in the early fifteenth century has been taken as proof of its backwardness. But a system consecrated to rural self-improvement and stability did not need to spend a fortune on overseas exploration with uncertain returns: it needed to prioritise financing the internal system of canals and irrigation. The choice was rational. The system was set up to venerate agriculture and family ancestors; as long as it delivered, it was doing its job. And with a powerful emperor behind the 4400-mile Great Wall, symbol both of its unity and its intent to promote its own objectives undisturbed by others, the priority was to do just that. Its success was enlisting the vast peasantry with a vested interest in the continuance of the system, so braking the processes that might force institutional change. The peasants became guarantors of the status quo.

The state was firmly in charge, so that even while Chinese merchants and bankers enjoyed European-style property rights, these never led to the creation of autonomous European-style public companies, or to the development of public institutions that were not state institutions, or to a space between individual and state. In Europe, monarchs enfeebled by war had to accept terms imposed on them by banks for loans and the bills of exchange that the banks developed independently. In China merchants and bankers used bills of exchange created by the imperial government. This is a crucial distinction. Peace locked the Chinese system into stasis, so there was no impetus for institutional development or creativity.

It was further hardened by China's turning away from foreign trade, as part of the same logic. By the late fifteenth century overseas trade was restricted, as the peasants wanted, to favour trade on the inland waterway system, not only cutting China off from an important source of profit, but also cutting it off from another stimulus to the development of public institutions.

It all connects

Capitalist development can never be conceptualised as a wholly internal, national achievement of one country or culture without relation to the wider world economy and the opportunities of that economy. This is the insight of the French historian Fernand Braudel into growth in Western Europe.[29] In his view, Europe's growth from 1550 on cannot be explained without reference to its place in the world economic system. The list is long. Spain's discovery of gold and silver in Peru; the Netherlands' domination of the spice trade in the sixteenth and seventeenth centuries; the Venetians' capture of the Middle East and the silk road trade; and then the English and the slave trade, and their later access to raw materials and food from North America. This European story is about groups of merchants profiting hugely through their relationship to the far-flung world economy, enforcing their position violently with their superior military technology, forming at first the nucleus of cities and city-states, and later of nations. They then reinvested in the profitable trade to make more profit still, and their growing imports of key resources removed the constraints on growth.

All this also prompted institutional innovations. The commercial needs of long-distance traders stimulated industrial investment, and their complex linkages demanded the development of new forms of organisation, notably the company and the commercial bank as successors to the medieval guilds and fairs. John Maynard Keynes suggested that Francis Drake's *Golden Hind*, completing the circumnavigation of the globe in 1580 with a cargo of gold stolen from the Spanish and worth more than $100 billion in today's prices, effectively paid off all of England's international debt and provided the risk capital for the City of London's first trading and banking institutions, and thus the economic foundation of the British Empire.[30] But London was only following a trail blazed by Genoa, Venice, Cadiz and Amsterdam.

The profitability of the long-distance trade was important in itself, creating a source of surpluses outside the city or emerging state system that could be reinvested. But commercial trade relations also begat production: merchants wanted to fill their outgoing vessels with goods, offer them for exchange and bring back the exchanged goods as cargoes of imports. European vessels would make outward-bound voyages with their cargoes of textiles, linen, dyes, mirrors, glass, engines and clocks; they would return with sugar, tea, spices, cotton, hides, timber and silk – and, as the trade grew, grain and meat in large volumes. Trade created opportunities for industrial specialisation, but it also allowed the trading countries to escape national resource, food and raw material constraints.

The most obvious case of this process at work is Britain – the first industrial nation. In order to industrialise, Britain had to transfer its workforce from agriculture to factories while maintaining the supply of food. It could square part of this circle with increased agricultural productivity, but it also needed to import food and fuel from overseas, crucially North America and, later, Australasia. Although it was blessed with fast-running rivers in the Pennines that provided water power, and then easy access to coal, it also needed wood to burn for charcoal, wood to construct ships and wood with which to build houses and farms. The timber, sugar and grain trade were indispensable ingredients of industrialisation.

But what is also evident is that trade, finance and industry had to be given organisational shape – another key and frequently undervalued part of the development equation. Long-distance trade in sixteenth- and seventeenth-century Europe was hazardous. Vessels might not survive the vicissitudes of the voyage, whether from piracy, the weather or bad seamanship. The outgoing cargoes and the costs of the voyage had to be financed. The prices of the traded commodities fluctuated alarmingly. It also took a long time; the thirty-thousand-mile round trip from the Netherlands to the Dutch East Indies and back occupied eighteen months. First in the Netherlands and later in England, Dutch and English merchants developed the idea of the company as a formal partnership of merchants who would obtain a licence to trade from the sovereign, share the risk in financing the trade and build the organisation over time to create an ongoing infrastructure to support the trade. This meant everything from the stocks of key supplies along the trading route allowing boats to replenish their needs, to armies of clerks who kept an inventory of what was bought and sold.

The formation in London in 1600 of the East India Company, and that of a Dutch forerunner on which it was modelled, are thus watershed moments in the development of European capitalism. Although in one sense the early company was still part of the family and guild relationships that characterised economic organisation in both medieval Europe and China, with members' or partners' trust based on personal acquaintance, the company nonetheless crossed a vitally important line. It moved from a paradigm of personalised relationships to the paradigm of an organisation with a personality and life of its own. It was the company that organised the voyage, assumed the risks and paid the bills; it was the company that owned and developed the infrastructure and, because it expected to be long-lived, could be more long-sighted.[31] The company was to grow into the organisational invention without which European and Western capitalism would have been impossible.

It was the apogee of a rapidly developing soft Enlightenment infrastructure. The story of England between 1600 and 1750 is the gradual putting in place of the world's first viable soft-capitalist infrastructure – the development of the idea of the company; the establishment of a system of law that could be reliably and impartially adjudicated by an independent judicial system; and the emergence of a financial system that allowed external finance to be raised through both creditworthy, trusted banks and the stock market.

The profits of long-distance trade, vital imports of raw materials and a coherent soft infrastructure with trustworthy public institutions were essential preconditions for Britain's Industrial Revolution. But they were not sufficient. The application of technology and new techniques of production were also necessary, not as one-offs that might stop or even be reversed as they were in

China, but rather as the ceaselessly restless driver of industrialisation, embedded in the very heart of the production process.[32] In
effect this was the nineteenth-century knowledge economy, the
production of knowledge, its translation into practical application
and then subsequent use.

The first European university had been established in Bologna in
1080 and by 1500 Europe boasted no fewer than seventy centres of
largely secular learning; they transmuted into independent engines
of knowledge production. The spirit of science existed not apart
from the production system but as its handmaiden: for Joel Mokyr,
the interpenetration of Europe's *savants* (thinkers) and *fabricants*
(manufacturers) was essential to the chemistry of its development.[33]

Advances in European technology were not just national: they
drew upon pools of inventiveness that were global. For example,
the history of mathematics, science and technology is bound up
with advances in Muslim thinking. The results were disseminated
around the continent. In this respect the printing press was as
important as the university; as early as 1500 Europe possessed 220
presses that had already printed eight million books.[34] This,
together with Europe's complex dynastic rivalries and wars, meant
that European monarchs, whether Habsburgs or Bourbons, could
not establish hegemony as China's emperors had done. A competitive political pluralism held sway, which was central not merely to
Europe's political but economic momentum. If a technology or
scientific advance worked in country A, then countries B, C and D
quickly had to adopt it or else find themselves at an industrial and
military disadvantage – and the printing presses spewed forth the
books and manuals containing the informational gold that could
transform industrial and military capacity. Countries who refused
to move with the times would find themselves marginalised.
Spain's economic decline in the eighteenth century was an awesome warning of the consequences of not accommodating new
technologies. The leadership role passed first to France and then
Britain, with other European countries quickly adopting the factory

system, the water-driven looms and first steam- and latterly coal-driven engines. Europe's pluralism was an essential driver of change: the practitioners of science might find themselves exiled from Catholic Europe, but in Protestant England, the Netherlands or Germany they could follow where inquiry led – with the results being eminently reproducible.

These four key elements – the pluralism developed by near-continual war and state competition; profitable long-distance trade and the companies it created; a robust soft institutional infrastructure and the universalisation of technology – kindled Europe's miracle and allowed it to overtake China despite what the two continents held in common and China's early leadership. Uniting, underpinning and embodying all four elements was the Enlightenment and the public institutions it underwrote. For what the growth produced was its own culture of modernity, a willingness to accept that economic and social systems would not remain static but constantly evolve. Other propositions also had to be accepted: that the gods of one's ancestors could not provide a compass with which to navigate this ever-changing present; that societies had to find collective responses to change or experience serious dislocation; and that technology and science would relentlessly force the continual ageing and obsolescence of what seems indisputably contemporary today and would deliver predictable gains in productivity which are not only the roots of wealth and riches, but of military superiority. China, ahead of Europe for millennia, would find by the early nineteenth century that its divinely inspired order was no match for Europe's. The legacy of the resulting turmoil is with us yet.

The century of humiliation

At the beginning of the nineteenth century a structural problem was emerging in Europe's relationship with China. Europe's demand for Chinese tea, silk, porcelain, furniture and decorative goods was large and growing – but China had little demand for the products that Europe's nascent factories and mills were producing.[35] The Celestial Kingdom demanded payment in silver and gold, which caused an escalating balance of payments problem – a flashpoint for Britain, overwhelmingly its largest trading partner. Britain could not expect to underpin the global position of the pound and its ascendant military, trading and industrial position after beating France in the Napoleonic wars if its still-inadequate reserves of gold and silver were to be transferred to the Chinese.

For most of the eighteenth century the British had preferred to offer another substance in exchange for Chinese goods: opium. A trade that had begun with no more than a few hundred chests in the 1730s had grown to more than thirty thousand chests by 1835 and was a growing source of friction with the Qing dynasty. Within China, opium addiction was reaching dangerous levels. Also, there was an increasing shortage of silver to back China's growing economy, lifting the price of silver in relation to other goods – and as taxes were paid in silver, so raising the real tax burden, with potentially fatal consequences for the regime. In 1838 came the fateful decision; the import of opium was banned.

The British reaction was forceful, made yet more effective by the deployment of a steam-driven battleship, the *Nemesis*, that could operate in as little as five feet of water – decisive in the shallow bays and key river estuaries where the war was waged and in emphasising China's technological backwardness. The British could win any battle as they chose. The peace treaty of Nanjing in 1842 reflected the scale of China's reverse and became the most telling symbol of the empire's humiliation. The Celestial Kingdom that claimed to rule 'all that was below heaven' and held foreigners in contempt had to concede that the destructive trade in opium had to continue, that it pay every pound of Britain's war costs and more, that it cede Hong Kong to Britain, and that it allow British merchants freely to operate in its five leading ports. The emperor also had to deal directly with emissaries from the British state and accept Chinese being taught to foreigners, and that any concession made to any other Western power would immediately extend to Britain.

The Treaty of Nanjing was the beginning of a series of defeats at the hands of every foreign power China fought. No fewer than twenty-six treaties[36] followed, in effect opening up the entire Chinese coast and navigable river system to foreigners on their own terms, which might include their own system of education, communication, armed forces, steamship lines, courts, factories, free access and trading rights. By the 1890s the indebted, militarily weak Qing dynasty was on the point of collapse, prompting a kind of feeding frenzy by the Western powers. By 1900 Russia had secured a large part of Manchuria, Japan had colonised Taiwan after its victory in the 1894–5 war, Britain added Kowloon to Hong Kong, France expanded its Indo-Chinese empire northwards and Germany entered the frame by seizing the Shandong port city of Qingdao and the mineral rights of the surrounding province. China was being carved up, it was said, like a melon. The Western powers did not need to colonise China; the treaties secured them all they wanted without having to go to the expense.

If this was not enough, the dynasty suffered a series of violent internal revolts from parts of the empire emboldened by Qing weakness. These revolts not merely challenged the Qing right to rule, but for the first time in Chinese history contested the values and legitimacy of the combination of Celestialism and Confucianism that underpinned the empire. The Muslim revolts in the west demanded independence from infidel rule; the Nian revolt in north-central China was fuelled by the incapacity of the imperial system to deliver plentiful supplies of food, its side of the old bargain; and, most durable of all, the Taiping rebellion that lasted from 1850 to 1864 embraced Christianity and sought to organise land ownership on egalitarian principles. All despised the Qing for their decadence and the subjugation of the Chinese by foreigners: the Boxer uprising between 1898 and 1901 was explicitly anti-Western, killing two hundred Westerners and wanting to restore China's glory by reinvigorating the integrity of the Chinese imperial system. It was subjugated by a largely foreign army, whose eight constituents afterwards insisted that they could maintain their armed forces for protection – another humiliation for China.

In fact, the capacity of the Qing to suffer so many simultaneous blows and yet survive for so long was tribute to the continuing resilience and resourcefulness of the Confucian system, despite China's economic backwardness, and the loyalty of so many senior officials and generals to the imperial idea. The domestic rebellions were, after all, subdued. But so many defeats at the hands of foreigners could hardly fail to prompt the most profound soul-searching. China could not match the industrial and technological pre-eminence of the West or even Japan. The whole edifice of Confucian thought seemed inward-looking and anti-modern, locking China into economic and social backwardness with concomitant poverty, misery and lack of self-respect summed up by widespread opium addiction. In the final dog days of the Qing dynasty the regime conceded that China needed more representative government, more systematic modern education, a thorough overhaul of its military machine, a fairer distribution of land and a commitment to industrialisation symbolised by the creation of a national rail network.

However, the collapse of its legitimacy and the accompanying mushrooming of alternative prospectuses to modernise China had gone too far. For example, the newly created provincial parliamentary assemblies became not a constructive force for change, as the Qing hoped, but crucibles for the expression of dissent. When an army mutiny that began in the autumn of 1911 culminated in its forty-four senior commanders insisting that China become a republic, the five-year-old Emperor Puyi and the Qing court, their power base gone, had no choice but to abdicate. China was left with a constitutional and governmental vacuum. The Celestial Kingdom had not just fallen to earth; it had shattered, and its prestige evaporated.

3

Mao's Bequest

China's urgent requirement in 1912 was to build a state that worked. The country needed to be held together, justice and order offered and China prevented from being the victim of more defeats by foreigners. The founder and first leader of the Guomindang (or Nationalists, as I shall call this party from now on), Sun Yat-sen, put it more ambitiously: China simultaneously had to build a state, democratise, create order, reconcile competing interests, take on foreigners and modernise economically. He even argued for applying the untried precepts of socialism to drive development because corrupt Chinese capitalism and its *guanxi* insider networks were evidently not powerful enough. It was a call that his party never followed up.

The challenge was huge. With the implosion of the imperial centre in the Forbidden City had gone the linchpin of the Confucian mandarinate that had held China together. In the country the landlords, unchecked, tightened their grip on the land. No longer were they part of a civilisation that purported to generate harmony and benevolence. Into the political vacuum of the 1910s and 1920s stepped a network of provincial barons or warlords who sustained themselves with personal armies, paid for by tribute and any profitable trade, including opium dealing, and who enlisted the old imperial official gentry to serve them, thus tightening their own grip on the peasants. Every aspect of the economy – agriculture, industry, finance – was behind that of the West and desperately primitive. Public education and health care were rudimentary. Poverty was widespread and life expectancy was low, less than forty years. Corruption was endemic. Opium addiction grew exponentially; in the 1930s, according to one estimate, 20 per cent of Chinese agricultural land was devoted to opium production.[1] Secret societies flourished.

Above all, China was violent. In the absence of imperial or democratic legitimacy many warlords held power through force of arms and fear. Zhang Zongchang in Shandong was an extreme example, delighting not merely in murder but in splitting human heads open 'like melons' and hanging them on telegraph poles as a warning to those minded to challenge his authority.[2] Others did not go quite so far, but human life was cheap. Lu Xun, China's most influential twentieth-century author, wrote after a student massacre by warlords in Beijing in 1926, that 'a few lives count for nothing in China'.[3] And militaristic Japan was not to be forgotten; its colonies in Korea and Taiwan could be readily used as launch pads for bringing a Japanese colonial empire to China.

Sun Yat-sen, in the years before the collapse of the Qing, had argued for a post-imperial Chinese state to be modelled on a Western-style division of powers between executive, legislative and judiciary branches with an independent non-Confucian civil service dedicated to economic improvement. But none of the preconditions existed. Without them, Nationalist China would struggle to create any kind of legitimate government to counteract the inexorable drift to warlordism, disorder and hyperinflation against an international background of beleaguered capitalism, weakening liberal democracy and the invasion of Japan.

Even had political conditions been more favourable, the Nationalists still lacked a prospectus for the economy. The alpha and omega of China's economic problem was its poverty-stricken, unproductive, backward peasant rural economy. The causes – landlordism, inability to raise credit, lack of mechanisation and the tiny size of most plots – had to be tackled, and an agricultural surplus generated. But even if that problem could be solved, there was no national banking system capable of mobilising the resulting savings into investment. The Chinese banking system was more of a money transmission system than an investment system as there had been no demand for anything else. Companies were family concerns or insider *guanxi* networks; the idea of a corporate organisation based on rules and capable of marshalling production resources in volume barely existed beyond Shanghai. Typically, Chinese enterprise hardly reached out beyond the town or province in which it was located. Nor was there any state capacity to step in to do what the banking and investment systems could not. To those Chinese who were burning to create constitutional order and economic prosperity, restore their self-respect and catch up with the West, the scale of what had to be done on so many fronts must have seemed daunting, if not impossible.

Sun Yat-sen, for all his vision of how China should develop, never succeeded in reunifying China's provinces and died, unfulfilled, of cancer in 1925. Chiang Kai-shek, who succeeded him, managed in 1927 to construct a semi-unified Chinese Republic through force of arms, clever politics and bringing key warlords into his coalition. The rest of the task was beyond him. He now had to build state capacity and modernise the economy, but with the additional deadly complication of unsuccessfully trying to beat back the Japanese invasion that had begun in 1931 and which, by 1937–8, had captured Shanghai, Nanjing and Canton. By 1941 Japan had conquered the northern, central and southern coastal regions of the country, leaving only the remote, mountainous west to the Nationalists and communists. China also had to defeat the communists in what, after 1945, became a fully fledged civil war.

This was not necessarily an impossible task. Chinese peasants might hate their landlords, but they hated even more losing their property rights and their links with their ancestors; this was why classic Marxist analysis (and the Communist Party's advisers from the Soviet Union) initially regarded them as too reactionary to be the class base for a transformational communist revolution, and early efforts at radicalising them within orthodox communist guidelines failed. There was a window of ten or fifteen years from 1927 in which the Nationalists could have won both the ideological and the military argument with the communists if they had been more skilful and capable of building mass support. As it was, the Communist Party's forces and organisation were very nearly exterminated by the Nationalists after the Long March in 1935 to the rural redoubt of Yan'an in the provincial west of China and the sustained attack on their organisation in the cities; less than 10 per cent of those who began the march ended it.[4] As for Japan, after Pearl Harbor and the United States joined the war it was inevitable that Japan would lose. Even after their exile in Sichuan it was possible that the Nationalists could emerge as the country's prime organising force.

The insurmountable difficulty was that the prerequisite for such success were a viable state, an enduring political coalition to sustain it and a workable programme of economic development. The Nationalists could achieve none of those targets. To build an effective state they needed a national bureaucracy; and to begin developing the economy they had to confront some of the interests in their own coalition – warlords, landlords and the Confucian gentry. As Jonathan Fenby says in his biography, Chiang Kai-shek never had the political strength, the ideological programme or the practical policies that might have begun to approach what was needed.[5]

Chiang could not, as the communists proposed, attack landlords and the gentry to raise agricultural productivity by means of land reform, because they constituted the officer class in his army and raised what revenue he could muster in the country. Nor did he have the resources or the political plausibility to tackle systematic corruption, tax-farming and the maladministration of justice by his officials. He and the Nationalists might want them to display the Confucian virtues of order, harmony and self-discipline, but he could offer no compelling moral or pragmatic reason for them to abandon their habits.

Chiang Kai-shek found himself experimenting with a soft version of fascism – again, international influences had an impact on national politics when he began the 'new life' movement in 1934 to 'remoralise' and regenerate China. It certainly showed his recognition of the need for a better political philosophy, but it also showed the Nationalists' own ideological and moral weaknesses. The movement was soon discredited. It issued a stream of petty regulations aimed at improving individual morality – specifying, for example, that the hem of a skirt should fall four inches below the knee – but did nothing against the secret societies, opium dens and gangsters on which the regime depended.[6]

The lack of effective reform revealed itself in the performance of the economy and public finance. There had been a significant increase in industrial production during the 1930s, with considerable investment in textile and chemical manufacturing from foreign investment – and some of the coastal cities, especially Shanghai, experienced rapid economic growth. But the Chinese had no industrial infrastructure that would enable them to match the Japanese military machine. And the administration was too weak to ensure that the few taxes collected would actually find their way to the republican government in its capital, Nanjing. Every year from 1929 until 1937, before the Japanese overran China, the Nationalist government ran a deficit that rose from 12 per cent of its total spending in 1933 to 25 per cent in 1937 – an unsustainable amount. Between 1937 and 1943, during the war against Japan, the deficits soared out of control and the Nationalists resorted to printing money. Inflation reached 300 per cent in the early 1940s and the yuan's international value collapsed.[7]

Meanwhile the communists managed to turn a humiliating debacle, the Long March, into a propaganda success – a sign that after many false starts since their foundation in Shanghai in 1921 they were beginning to learn how to make a revolution in Chinese conditions, and how to become genuinely popular. Whatever happened after 1949, the Chinese Communist Revolution resulted from a popular mass movement. The Soviet Union under Stalin was savagely cruel, and we know now that communism necessarily leads to authoritarianism. Nevertheless, throughout the Japanese war Mao's base camp in Yan'an was the focal point for a wide range of intellectuals, students, workers and businessmen who were fleeing the Japanese and who saw communism as the most effective way of modernising China and winning the war.

The appeal of communism

The communists had more appeal than may seem obvious today. Capitalism was in disarray and, according to its critics, the prolonged global depression of the inter-war years proved that it was inherently flawed. The dominant intellectual theory in the West was that states had to organise economic development. Roosevelt's New Deal in the United States, Stalin in the Soviet Union and Hitler in Germany were all obvious examples. Obviously, if China wanted to industrialise it would have to be state-led and would have to reform rural land tenure. But this implied constructing a state and political coalition that could confront the landlords and the gentry. The Nationalists could not do this, because they relied on the landlords and the gentry; but it was the communists' avowed programme. Moreover, the communists' idea was in the long Chinese tradition of changing a regime by mobil-ising a peasant revolt.

Communism in China had another, more subtle advantage. It could be understood as a modern transmutation of Confucianism, retaining the commitment to service, social harmony and integrity but dropping some of the obviously unnecessary and dysfunc-tional elements.[8] Communism, like Confucianism, promised fairness, incorruptibility and responsiveness to the preferences and wants of the people. Unlike Confucianism, it celebrated sci-ence rather than superstition, progress rather than tradition, economic development and, importantly for many, equality between men and women. Communism lived, and lives, uneasily with Confucianism, sometimes condemning it, sometimes using it as a source of legitimacy. But in the early days it was a valuable support. For example, Liu Shaoqi, one of the five-strong leader-ship group with Mao in the early 1940s, drew a parallel in his book *How to Be a Good Communist* between the Confucian scholar and the aspiring communist: each raised his integrity through con-stant self-discipline and self-criticism. Confucius, wrote Liu, did not see himself as a born sage. He had gone through a 'process of steeling and self-cultivation' to reach an understanding of what was right, and so must the good communist.[9] The thousands of refugees rallying to Mao's banner recognised the continuity between the revolution and Chinese culture, and were reassured. Communism, in short, seemed to combine the best of the past and the best of the future.

Communism also offered a face-saving explanation of China's humiliation – and a solution. China had been a victim of Western imperialism, and its quasi-colonial status had resulted from a global quest for markets, cheap labour and raw materials. As John Fairbank, Edwin Reischauer and Albert M. Craig put it, commu-nism 'provided a self-consistent, universalistic and scientific view of the world's history which enabled one to reject the imperialist West in the name of Western "scientific thought" and explain

China's humiliating backwardness as due to her bondage to "capitalist imperialism"'.[10] A communist revolution in China, along with domestic modernisation, would be part of an international defence against exploitation. This alignment between communism and Chinese nationalism still exists today.

So far, so good. But throughout the 1920s and 1930s the problem was how to get the communists' story to correspond to actual conditions in China, and not frighten the people with too much talk about revolution and the abolition of private property. According to Marx, a communist revolution was meant to arise spontaneously from an oppressed working class whose existence and consciousness of its exploitation had been created by bourgeois industrial capitalism. But China had neither industrial capitalism nor an industrial working class outside Shanghai, Wuhan and Canton. If there was to be revolution it could come only from the peasants, being organised and led by the Communist Party – a dauntingly difficult logistical and ideological task. Few would have bet on the communists even as late as 1935.

Understanding how the communists succeeded is fundamental to understanding today's party, and the debt it knows it owes to Mao, notwithstanding his later failures and his cruelty. There were three important changes to Marx's template. The first change was to follow Lenin and argue that the party would need to be the vanguard of the revolution, which in a peasant society could not be a spontaneous class revolt. Marxism became Marxism–Leninism. The second change was a departure from orthodoxy. Because peasants were culturally hostile to the maxims of socialisation and collectivisation, their radicalisation would require much more work in the villages by party cadres. The cadres would have to persuade the peasants of the merits of communist ideas; help them articulate grievances; take political action; and then, by helping them achieve their new goals, get them to 'own' the revolution. Lenin could use the party in Russia to impose change from above, but Mao developed the concept of the 'mass line'. 'All correct leadership is necessarily from the masses to the masses,' Mao wrote. 'This means: take the idea of the masses (scattered and unsystematic ideas) and concentrate them (through study turn them into concentrated and systematic ideas), then go to the masses and propagate and explain these ideas until the masses embrace them as their own.'[11]

The mass line, as it was developed in Yan'an, had immediate implications from which the third change – another key difference between Chinese and Soviet communism – emerged. Instead of confiscating land into collectivised soviets (the Chinese communists had tried to do this in the late 1920s and early 1930s, but the peasants had resisted), the new approach was more reformist. Land would be redistributed from rich peasants to poor, but property rights would be respected. Taxes would be lowered, as would usurious interest rates. Above all, Mao said, individual party members working in villages had to be extremely responsive to local political conditions instead of behaving as if they were writing an 'eight-legged' essay – the classic essay for Confucian examinations. In other words, the party should not rigidly impose communist doctrine where it might not work. Only one-third of the candidates in village, town and provincial government elections should be communists; another third should be other leftists; a last third would be more genuine progressives. The aim should be inclusion, decentralisation and the redressing of real grievances. Party cadres had to be responsive, flexible and unbureaucratic while still developing a communist position. This tough mandate required much education and 'rectification'.

If the old imperial system had still existed, Mao might have been the leader of a peasant rebellion, but the challenge was now bigger than cleansing the old order. It was to build a new system from the foundations up. Communism provided the ideology, the political script and guidelines about what to do in power – all validated by being scientific, modern, Western and part of a global movement. Mao's political talent was to see all this, translate it into a Chinese idiom and make it work in practice. For many Chinese, communism became the only viable choice.

The sudden capitulation of the Japanese in 1945 was followed by a full-scale civil war. The Nationalist army was larger but, despite extensive American support, was exhausted by eight years of war against the Japanese. Also, the Nationalists had no political strategy for winning popular support; the state was weak; China's financial position was precarious; inflation steadily escalated, eventually to more than 6000 per cent in 1948. Mao, who was now the party's undisputed leader – he had been the chairman of the Military Council since 1937 and chairman of the Central Committee and Politburo since 1943 – rolled out the Yan'an strategy. By developing popular support in areas under their control, the communists could concentrate all their forces – armed by the Soviet Union – at the front line. The Nationalists had to dissipate their disintegrating forces in quelling village and urban unrest, which was mounting under the strain of hyperinflation. Despite their superior numbers, the Nationalists could not marshal equivalent forces at the front.

Their collapse came sooner than either side had anticipated. The communists controlled the rich province of Manchuria in north-eastern China, which gave them a base for taking control of northern China, and the Nationalist armies fell back. On 1 October 1949, Mao Zedong declared the establishment of the People's Republic of China in Tiananmen Square. Chiang Kai-shek and his armies fled to the island of Taiwan, which they called the Republic of China, claiming sovereignty over the mainland. The communists insisted that Taiwan should be returned to the motherland, but with the United States protecting Taiwan, the People's Republic has never attempted an invasion. Nearly sixty years later Taiwan retains all its capacity to inflame mutual enmity.

The Chinese Communist Party had made a seismic coup. It had led a popular communist revolution in the world's most populous country. It faced the monumental work of reconstructing a devastated economy and building state structures – two tasks at which the Nationalists had failed. But the ups and downs that were to follow would be led by a Communist Party profoundly different from others, notably its counterpart in the Soviet Union. It would be a vanguard Leninist party characterised by the pragmatism, reformism, democracy and decentralisation of Mao's mass line. Pragmatic reformism would ultimately be its salvation. The question is whether it will ever rediscover its commitment to democracy.

Challenging a 2000-year-old stasis

The overriding economic challenge for the new communist government in 1949 was to repair the devastation of war and to invest in industrialisation, infrastructure, education, health care and agriculture. Even if China had been an open economy in the early 1950s, it would have had very little capacity to finance investment from borrowing external savings by the international capital markets or institutions like the early World Bank. The funds were not available, and today's sophisticated capital markets did not exist. Investment therefore would have to be financed from an increase in domestic saving, and the only route to that destination was from agriculture, which then represented more than 85 per cent of the Chinese economy. To produce a surplus, peasants could live on less, work more or become more productive, or some combination of all three. That, in turn, would involve land reform and the reorganisation of agricultural production.

The state would have to lead the process; it could not be left to market forces. This was the iron truth that would have faced any government, whatever its ideology. Even the Nationalists began a land reform programme in Taiwan to create larger plots and achieve greater productivity – goals that had eluded them in China. The communists would quintuple the 1600 medium and large state-owned enterprises they inherited from the Nationalists. They would use the state to create a national education system capable of lowering the male illiteracy rate (70 per cent) and the female illiteracy rate (which, in rural areas, was an incredible 99 per cent).[12] The state would also develop a health infrastructure to raise life expectancy (now around fifty years). And the state would need to be reorganised so that it could credibly borrow savings rather than print banknotes, if hyperinflation was to be reduced.

Communist leaders knew that this was only a beginning. The goal was radical egalitarianism and elimination of the economic base of class relations. The means would be collective enterprise and the mobilisation of investment through planning. The end would be the gradual establishment of the communist utopia. In towns this would mean the abolition of private capitalist enterprise; in the country it meant abolishing landlordism and even, more controversially, abolishing the property title peasants held for their land. An agricultural surplus would be created to finance the first five-year plan that would deliver economic modernisation. Mao, who in Yan'an and before had dissected the Chinese class system in elaborate detail as a guide to communist strategy to win the war in the country, now undertook the same analysis at the national level. Everybody in China was given a class position on which his or her fate would be determined. Radical egalitarianism had begun.

The land reform of 1950, in which more than two-fifths of China's land was redistributed in a series of nationwide village meetings from those higher up in the hierarchy to those lower down, was based on this carefully calibrated class position. It was the precursor of first cooperativisation and then communisation. Hence the nationalisation of private enterprise in the towns and the major initiatives to improve the condition of women in the name of equality. Women, like men, were given the right to petition for divorce; girls were to be educated alongside boys in the new national education system. Mao declared that 'women hold up half of the sky'. Even though China was to plunge into the Korean War, supporting communist North Korea against an American-led Western coalition in the south and incurring a terrible loss of life, the early, genuine popularity of the revolution was undimmed. Chinese history validated both land redistribution and fighting foreign encirclement; supporting the communists in North Korea was necessary, both ideologically and for security.

In the first five-year plan, between 1952 and 1957, China was to experience rapid economic growth – an average of 9.2 per cent. Industrial production more than doubled, with spectacular gains in industries as disparate as bicycles and steel. Advised by technocrats from the Soviet Union, the Chinese maintained the pace of investment throughout the entire five-year period, creating the necessary savings by forcing the newly established cooperatives to sell one-fourth of their grain production to the state at low prices. The build-up of communism in rural China was gradual but relentless; small-scale work teams gave way to larger 'lower-stage' agricultural cooperatives, which gave way in turn to 'higher-stage' cooperatives. The majority of peasants volunteered to participate, accepting that the more they organised themselves collectively, the more their economic position would be improved. By allowing peasants to withdraw income (the amount was based on a combination of the land they had contributed and the work they had put in), by abolishing rent, by supplying cheap credit through new credit cooperatives and by organising the process through village leaders, the communists commanded consent. In the early years they offered a genuine improvement in peasants' incomes, if not in productivity.

At the same time as an agricultural surplus was being forcibly confiscated, industrial investment was being forcibly initiated.

Inflation was brought under control when savers responded to a call to display patriotism and buy government bonds. The communist revolution seemed to be bearing fruit. But already there were problems and tensions. Mao believed that political will, exercising itself through the permanent dialectic of political conflict, would drive progress; he believed in political institutions only in so far as they permitted the exercise of that will, and he saw politics as a succession of conflicts each transmuting itself into the next and so propelling progressive change.[13] Thus the cooperatives established during the first five-year plan were political stepping stones on the way to true communism; by building on this political achievement China would increase both agricultural production and industrial investment.

Mao's colleagues were less certain. Grain production had stabilised at around 167 million tonnes; the breakthrough to modern agriculture was not happening, and so the prospect of raising the surplus to fund the next five-year plan was fading.[14] There was a limit to how much cooperatives could raise productivity without fertilisers, new types of seed and mechanisation. Also, as the government began to base members' incomes solely on their work and not on the historic contribution of land to the cooperative, peasants began to supplement their meagre income by working their ancestors' individual plots more intensively and selling the extra produce on the market. The class of rich and semi-rich peasants the revolution was meant to abolish was being recreated, while production from the unmechanised, low-technology cooperatives stagnated. Mao wanted to solve the problem politically, by full-scale communisation, while other Politburo leaders – notably Liu Shaoqi – felt that the political justification was inadequate. There had to be a parallel economic effort to raise agricultural production, and that meant more mechanisation and accepting the role of incentives and markets. Liu now began to be associated with an argument which Mao would consider counter-revolutionary and which led to Liu's eventual death under house arrest during the Cultural Revolution.

Another problem had to do with the class of what we would today classify as knowledge workers – scientists, technologists, writers, researchers and teachers. Sustained economic success would obviously depend on their brains, commitment and ingenuity; and they would also form the cornerstone of a new communist civil society. The party could attempt to browbeat them into loyalty to the revolution through ideological training, as it had tried initially, but this was unsatisfactory. Mao wanted to create a genuine communist civil society, in which intellectuals would freely exchange views, perhaps critical, but always within a communist paradigm. This would reinforce communism and the revolution socially and intellectually. By early 1957 Mao was so confident that the achievements of the revolution were obvious, compared with the past, that he deemed 'a hundred flowers' should be allowed to bloom and a communist civil society should begin. For five weeks in May and June, intellectuals were allowed to debate freely what had been and should be happening. But, as with Tiananmen thirty-two years later, there was a crescendo of complaint: party officials were criticised for corruption, communist democracy was ridiculed as a sham and the low standard of living was described as intolerable. Mao responded with a crackdown; thirty thousand intellectuals were arrested as counter-revolutionary 'rightists' and imprisoned, exiled or sent to labour camps. Mao complained that his trust had been abused. Debate still rages as to whether his intent had ever been genuine, or was merely a ruse to ensnare his critics. His subsequent actions suggest the latter interpretation.

Either way, it was a turning point. There was stagnation of agricultural output in the countryside, a crisis of legitimacy among the intelligentsia and a re-emergence of the rich peasant class that the party was pledged to abolish. On the other hand, the first five-year plan had matched or exceeded the expectations for industrialisation. The Politburo – including, as he would later acknowledge, Deng Xiaoping – came around to Mao's view that the only response was to intensify the political fight. Peasants tempted away from cooperatives and sceptical intellectuals needed to be shown emphatically that more communism was the answer to the Chinese predicament. The party must intensify the egalitarian moralisation of the Chinese through communist principles, raise the peasantry to new heights of revolutionary fervour that would permit greater collective efforts, eliminate any signs of a new rich peasant class and build on cooperatives as the principal economic institution, expecting them to supply their members' needs. The sums in the second five-year plan could add up if the locus of industrialisation was moved to newly established decentralised communes. These communes would have the incentive of lifting agricultural production to fund the investment in order to meet the raised targets for industrial output – a variant of the 'mass line' that had won the revolution. The communes, for Mao at least, were also vehicles for constructing the communist civil society that had just been aborted. The inexorable economic and political logic of the situation, and of communist thinking, led to the Great Leap Forward. There seemed to be no other option.

For the next eighteen years Mao never abandoned his conviction that radical egalitarianism would achieve the goals of modernising China, eradicating for ever the legacy of the Confucian gentry and unleashing the potential of individual peasants, to whom he was romantically, if remotely, attached. If this egalitarianism required violence and death, so be it. The more the programme failed, the more he blamed weak implementation and the opposition of his colleagues, rather than seeing anything wrong with the theory. In any case, he was more and more isolated from reality. The twenty-six thousand communes set up for the Great Leap Forward that were meant simultaneously, through revolutionary will, to raise farm productivity dramatically and develop light industries. Self-sufficient collectives could not deliver all this. They lacked manpower, incentives, equipment and skills – but Mao, seeing from his special train fields that were artificially adorned with food crops, would learn only belatedly of the scale of the disaster. The backstreet foundry, in which pots, pans and farm implements were melted into unusable steel to meet the production targets, was symptomatic of the whole debacle. As for food, after the communes had given their dwindling stocks of grain to the government (which in turn used it to service the debt to the Soviet Union) they did not have enough to live on. Famine, starvation and death stalked the land; the combination of communisation and the mass line had backfired spectacularly. Estimates of the deaths range up to thirty-seven million.[15]

Between 1961 and 1965 there was a brief return to more pragmatic policies. This was when Deng, believing that he was being only as pragmatic as Mao urged, declared that 'it doesn't matter if a cat is black or white as long as it catches mice' – a position that was to condemn him, during the Cultural Revolution, to loss of office and exile for being the second 'capitalist roader' after Liu. Mao was never reconciled to the peasants selling surplus produce in the country markets, to their urban counterparts engaging in small business in towns or to anyone's deviation from the plan. Deviation constituted a reproach to Mao's belief in communism as a source of cultural and psychic fulfilment, and as the road to prosperity and a new society.

The mass violence of the Red Guards during the Cultural Revolution lasted for less than two years from 1966, but the flat-earth political commitment to equality and class warfare continued until Mao's death in 1976, although it was mainly focused on the towns. Private business was still outlawed. But, as times became calmer, the investment engine kept propelling state-owned enterprise forward; production quickly recovered, although with declining productivity. All the vocational training schools were closed until 1978 because they were said to foster bourgeois skills, and the curriculum in general schools in the education system was reorganised to focus on ideological and political education.[16] Teacher training was abandoned until 1971; no new undergraduates were admitted to universities until 1972, and no postgraduates until 1978.

Around Mao there could be no public complaint, even though the scale of the economic costs were obvious to all. In 1970 Mao's designated successor, Lin Biao, learned that he was to be passed over and, rather than accept this verdict, he planned an assassination. The details have never been released, but allegedly he was found out and died in an aircraft crash in Mongolia as he attempted to flee to Russia without sufficient fuel or crew. Mao had now beaten all his political opponents and China was set on a course of self-sufficient communes, industrialisation in heavy industry by state-owned enterprise and aggressive egalitarianism.

There were two saving graces in an otherwise dismal economic situation. First, peasant savings had been channelled into investment in infrastructure, education and industry on a grand scale. Industrial output had climbed more than thirteen times and by 1978 constituted 46.8 per cent of national income, compared with 12.6 per cent in 1949.[17] The size of the rail network had more than doubled. The proportion of irrigated land rose from 20 per cent in 1952 to 50 per cent in 1978.[18] Moreover, male literacy had now climbed to 81 per cent and female literacy to 45 per cent as a result of a generation of educational investment, despite the Cultural Revolution.[19]

Second, Mao's commitment to decentralisation was real. Central direction, he recognised, was nonsensical in a country as large as China. In 1970 China's provinces were asked to manage most state-owned enterprises with the central government running only 8 per cent of industrial output. By 1975 provincial and local governments were responsible for about 60 per cent of all state investment and for the greater part of the plan; only the production of key commodities like coal, timber and cement was organised from the centre.[20] State-owned industries might have their inputs, outputs and prices set by the plan, but a report by the World Bank argues that thirty thousand medium-sized and 150,000 small industrial organisations were largely free of the plan.[21] A new rudimentary form of light industry was emerging in the rural areas; it would take off during the reform period and was unintentionally a great boon.

However, China's advance overall was pretty much disastrous. Per capita income in 1978 was only $210. The growth rate between 1957 and 1978 was only 4.3 per cent, though the generation of reformers who succeeded Mao doubled that rate, another indication of the waste that took place during the Mao years. Eighty per cent of industrial output was in the state sector. More than 70 per cent of the labour force worked on the land in conditions of severe poverty. External trade and access to foreign technology were effectively non-existent; the economy was sealed off from foreigners. Also, the institutions of civil society had been snuffed out and only the artificial, greatly disliked commune system had taken their place. As Mao lay dying and the leaders of the Communist Party jockeyed for position, they all knew that, one way or another, policy had to change.

Coming to terms with Mao

On 5 August 1966, the fifty-year-old headmistress of a leading girls' school in Beijing had become the first victim of the Cultural Revolution. The excoriation of teachers for 'rightism', for organising bourgeois exams, for being sympathetic to capitalism and the cultural icons of reactionary imperial China, had been going on for some months, but in early August its intensity mounted. In a spasm of collective violence the headmistress's pupils, now self-styled 'Red Guards' indoctrinated into believing they were fulfilling Mao's higher purpose, poured boiling water over her.

She died from the battering she received from belt buckles and sticks studded with nails. The student leader was honoured less than two weeks later at a review of hundreds of thousands of Red Guards at Tiananmen Gate; she put an arm-band on Chairman Mao, who told her to rename herself 'Be Violent'.[22]

Similar abuses would kill up to half a million others during the Cultural Revolution. Mao had become convinced that every vestige of China's imperial past and the Confucian gentry class that had suffocated China had to be violently and irrevocably smashed. Only thus could the revolution escape its tendency to relapse into the temptations of capitalism, the antithesis of communism, stalling the economic and social egalitarianism that he genuinely believed was the route to individual prosperity and personal well-being. Thus the state consciously, and with no judicial process, systematically encouraged the mass killing of its citizens.

This was only forty years ago – a tremendous event in the history of China and still within living memory. The Communist Party, in whose name the killing was done, is still in power. South Africa formed a Truth and Reconciliation Commission after the end of apartheid, but in China there has been no honest and sustained attempt to come to terms with the crimes that were committed. Many critics of modern China say that no good can ever come from evil; but the advances in general well-being – from the reduction in poverty to the transformation in the position of women – suggest otherwise. The reforms that began in 1978 built on Mao's legacy. What sense are we to make of the extraordinary cruelty of his regime? Can there be any gains from such evil? Can China ever become a normal state when the enormity of what was done is not recognised, and when no safeguards have been created so that it might never happen again?

Jung Chang and her husband Jon Halliday argue in their best-selling biography *Mao: The Unknown Story* that the Cultural Revolution was further evidence of Mao's deranged, amoral lust for power and thus a condemnation of communism, which allowed it to happen. It took Chang – who also wrote the compelling *Wild Swans*, a story of today's China through the eyes of three generations of women – and Halliday ten years of research to produce a comprehensive indictment. They estimate that seventy million people died as a direct or indirect result of Mao's policies. The Great Leap Forward and the disastrous conditions of workers cynically sacrificed in building dams, railways and irrigation systems under lethal conditions are evidence of an indifference to human life.

That indifference sprang from a callous, self-absorbed, immoral human being who treated his wives and children contemptuously, did not even walk the Long March (he was carried in a bamboo litter), owned more than fifty personal estates and thought nothing of having fresh fish from Wuhan carried more than six hundred miles to please his palate. He, and the system which bred him and which still does not acknowledge or offer redress for what was done, are beyond the pale.

Nobody wants to be an apologist for Mao. Even the Communist Party, five years after his death, as I reported in Chapter 1, delivered the famous verdict that he was only 70 per cent right. The Cultural Revolution and the Great Leap Forward have had the paradoxical result of delegitimising Maoist communism, and thus were self-defeating even in Mao's terms. But the wider question with which we all have to wrestle is, what part of Mao's thought system delivered the good – if any – alongside the acknowledged evil, whatever the relative percentage may be? Or does the scale of the inhumanity and injustice of the Mao era put it beyond the traditional boundaries within which ethical questions are normally discussed?

In the first place, we must recognise, if not accept, the context. Mao was the leader of a revolutionary Communist Party that believed in egalitarianism, collective will and an ongoing political struggle against reaction as the means to solve China's profound problems. Its civilisation had collapsed; it had been despoiled by invasion and civil war; it was economically backward. There was a craving for a complete and decisive rupture with all that had produced this.

China is a proud culture. To plumb such depths was humiliating personally as well as nationally. In the nineteenth century foreigners had treated the Chinese as little more than animals – a reversal of what the Chinese believed the relationship should be. When Mao said that the Great Leap Forward would lead to China's overtaking Britain within fifteen years, he was not articulating his own deluded personal ambitions, he was speaking for a collective desire to restore China and the Chinese to the proper scheme of things.

For the majority of Chinese the revolution of 1949 ranks alongside the world's other great revolutions. The communist revolutionaries were like the French revolutionaries, who violently ended monarchy and aristocratic government and inaugurated much-needed modernity. A survey published in Beijing in August 1995 by the Beijing magazine *Chinese Youth* named Mao Zedong, Sun Yat-sen and Deng Xiaoping as China's three greatest figures.[23] There is respect for Mao's commitment to radical egalitarianism and an understanding, if not an endorsement, of why he did what he did. Hu Jintao's invocations of Mao today are not empty or ritualistic; they are his way of expressing unease about the values of the market, in contrast to Mao's collectivism.

Maurice Meisner argues that empathy is needed. Communism sought an unalterable break with the past to deliver a future in which everyone could achieve personal fulfilment, genuine equality, cultural depth and economic prosperity.[24] 'Deprived of its ability to inspire hope for the future, the revolution congeals into an image of "madness" which seemingly transforms it from a problem in history to an aberration outside history,' Meisner writes. 'And socialism, its ideological motive force, is similarly transformed into a pathological ideological escape from present reality.' Unless that is understood, many of Mao's actions seem inexplicable. For the first decade after 1949 most Chinese were behind Mao; what followed in the late 1950s and 1960s is seen not only as a crime against humanity but also as a process through which China reached its present position and its present possibilities. Some elements of the dream of 1949 have been delivered while others have been shown to be impossible and irretrievably compromised. More – even, ultimately, political liberty, the rule of law and freedom of expression – is expected in the future, although such things are uncertain and will have to be fought for.

This raises the question whether any violent means is justified for a morally 'good' end, or whether there is a dividing line if the morally good result was unintended. President Truman, authorising the use of the atom bomb against Japan in 1945, argued that the violent means justified the ultimate end of bringing the war to an earlier end and saving American lives. That has not ended the anguished debate about whether it was right to use such a weapon on civilians, which continues today. In an influential essay of 1918, on what it means to be a political leader, German sociologist Max Weber observed that political leadership necessarily places politicians in a moral universe where they make decisions about how to achieve ultimate ends – equality or justice, or winning a war – the ramifications of which may involve moral 'ills' for which the leaders cannot be held to account in the same way.[25] The 'ethic of ultimate ends', Weber argues, cannot be reconciled with the 'ethic of responsibility' whereby politicians are deemed to know in advance whether the consequences of their actions will actually be worth whatever progress is secured in the pursuit of an ultimate end. The political leader is in uncharted territory, as he has been throughout history; his vocation damns him to have an ultimate end and he has perforce to strive to achieve it. Truman's action is still intensely criticised, even though it led to the ultimate end he wanted.

Communist egalitarianism – the justification that Mao would offer for his action – is a far more debatable ultimate end; we do not share it, so for us, any associated 'ills' have no moral justification. Mao would counter that our view does not matter; his beliefs were sincerely held and thus he belongs to the same moral universe as Truman, even if we do not share his beliefs and values.

But there is an important difference. The American system both before and after the decision to use the atom bomb has held Truman to account for what he did despite the good of the ultimate end – as he knew it would. This meant that the threshold for justification had to be high. It will be if a similar decision is ever made again, and so the threshold will act as an important constraint. Weber would have approved. However, no such process has taken place in China.[26] Mao was in his own thought bubble while violently rooting out an 'infestation' of cultural reaction, as he would put it, that stood in the way of his egalitarian utopia. The authoritarian system permitted only Mao to judge the case and set the threshold for justification of murder; the decision, the results and the immediate and continuing lack of redress are all wrong. Even Meisner's plea for empathy towards revolutionaries cannot escape these truths. The moral superiority of liberal democracy is that it has a process to hold politicians to account even when they plead that their end justified the means – and it gives civil society some chance of linking, even if imperfectly, the moral universes of ends and responsibility.

This does not mean that good can never come from bad, or that communism had zero utility. If good can never come from bad, then it becomes impossible in any circumstance for a political leader to make a decision like Truman's. Weber's point is that we may not like it, but politicians occupy a universe in which such decisions have to be made. Truman's critics must accept that the war probably ended earlier than it otherwise would have, even if they think the price was too high. Similarly, we know the negative side of the communist balance sheet: murder, injustice and economic waste. But even the Mao years cannot be wholly written off. It is true that they constituted a period of economic futility and famine, with a tiny Maoist court within the inner government compound of Zhongnanhai in their own secret Forbidden City obsessively playing paranoid, murderous and vengeful political games.

There is also a plus side. There was a vast build-up of industrial production, extension of the rail network and agricultural irrigation and a dramatic lowering of innumeracy and illiteracy. Life expectancy rose and the circumstances of women, as argued earlier, were transformed. Moreover, Mao's commitment to political decentralisation was genuine; as a result, state planning and collectivisation of agriculture could be reversed more quickly in China than in the Soviet Union when the opportunity for reform came.

There is also a remarkable lack of self-knowledge, and even of history, among some Western critics who seem unaware how Western economies developed from predominantly agrarian communities into capitalist market societies. Too many commentators ignore the degree to which states have had to lead the creation of market economies, and the extraordinary social dislocation and pain involved in moving from a predominantly rural economy to an industrialised one. In his *Social Origins of Dictatorship and Democracy*, Barrington Moore observes that slavery was the core of the United States' agricultural system in the south before 1865, and that the American Civil War should be seen in part as the dislocation of moving to the wage system on which the industrialised north depended. Indeed, no country has succeeded in industrialising without some pain.[27] Karl Polanyi in *The Great Transformation* shows how the nineteenth-century laissez-faire system in Britain – with workers paid in money (rather than as in feudal times food and housing), free trade, enclosed privately owned land and the gold standard – was created deliberately and painfully by the British state.[28] The fact that the Chinese state has had to build its halfway house between capitalism and the market, and that there have been severe costs in moving hundreds of millions of people from a system of low-productivity agriculture built up over two thousand years to higher-productivity industry, should not be seen as aberrant. It is in fact typical.

Today's China could not have started from nothing in 1978. It built on foundations laid by Mao, not least of which was the experience of the Great Leap Forward and the Cultural Revolution as an approach not to adopt again. The unifying thread was the vanguard role of the Communist Party. Lenin expected it to build communism; instead it has led it towards capitalism – or, as Jiang Zemin would have it, the 'socialist market economy'. The success has been so stunning that just as critics of China's political system have abstracted it from context, history and the issues of political morality that exist elsewhere, so there is much praise of China's economic system and policy which is similarly abstracted from history and reality.

Andrew Neil, former editor of the *Sunday Times*, cites today's China as evidence of the enduring validity of Hayekian truths about the superiority of markets and economic and political freedom.[29] Sir Digby Jones, former director-general of the Confederation of British Industry (CBI), warns the British that an avalanche of Chinese free-enterprise entrepreneurialism awaits them. As we will see, Neil and Jones both wildly misinterpret what is happening in China. Its economic model is a conflation of markets and political authoritarianism that cannot be sustained. Reform will require genuine economic pluralism. The problem is that China's worrying failure to come terms with Mao points to a wider political incapacity to create independent, pluralist institutions vital for economic development. The party's ducking of the moral consequences of mass murder because it might threaten the legitimacy of the Communist Party will, if not addressed, fatally damage this next economic transition. Just as we need to be hard-headed about the beneficial outcomes of the Mao years if we are to understand today's China, so we need to be equally hard-headed about how the inability to challenge Mao's actions, tradition and legacy undermines the future. Jung Chang and Jon Halliday are right to insist that before China can move on it must come to terms with the enormity of Mao's crimes; on the other hand neither their comprehensive indictment, in my view, any more than the praise of an Andrew Neil of the subsequent reform programme help us navigate the complexities sure-footedly. But then neither do the ideological simplicities and avoidance of the truth by the Communist Party itself. China, past and present, evokes strong emotions. That increases the importance of seeing through them to the truth.

4

The Odd Couple: Communism and Capitalism

Deng Xiaoping was the inspirational architect of contemporary China, and is thus among the pole figures of the twentieth century. He was a canny survivor of the Mao years, but in 1976, when he was a seventy-two-year-old bureaucrat, there was little to suggest the depth of his radicalism. He was known as an economic pragmatist, certainly, but scarcely anyone could have guessed the extent of his ambition for change or his willingness to take risks to advance the cause of reform. He was, after all, an original communist from the 1920s, and had earned his revolutionary credentials as a high-ranking army commander, first in the war against the Japanese and then in the civil war against the Nationalists, when he performed with distinction.

After 1949 he effectively ran one of the six regional bureaux – the south-west China bureau – established to entrench the revolution. He was brought to Beijing in 1952, and by 1956 his combination of organisational skills and political suppleness led to his appointment as general secretary of the party. Between then and 1967 he cast himself as an inscrutable technocrat, effective administrator and communist loyalist. None of this protected him during the Cultural Revolution. He worked on the floor of a tractor factory under house arrest and was badly scarred by the experience. His eldest son, taken for questioning to expose his father's 'rightist' tendencies, had instead thrown himself out of the window and was left partially paralysed for life. That incident profoundly coloured Deng's view of Maoism. Deng re-emerged in politics in Beijing in 1973, when Mao recalled him to take eventual charge of the army. He was the only high-ranking communist Mao could turn to with the standing to stabilise the army, a clear signal of Mao's waning ability to find radical recruits who could sustain the Cultural Revolution.

Mao's allegation was right. Deng was inclined to be a 'capitalist roader', and he represented a growing tendency within the upper echelons of the Communist Party. The Great Leap Forward and the Cultural Revolution had convinced Deng that Mao's approach to economic development was all wrong. He would say in 1988 that if there was consensus on reform and China's opening up, 'This should be attributed to the ten-year Cultural Revolution, the lessons from this disaster are too profound.' He also said, 'The Cultural Revolution has become our wealth' – without it there would have been no new policies.[1]

After Mao's death, reform had to be fought for. Mao had designated Hua Guofeng as his successor. Within a month of Mao's death Hua arrested the Gang of Four, Mao's leftist clique who had led the Cultural Revolution, accusing them of planning further destabilisation. Despite this, Hua could not be the champion of reform. As Mao's designated successor his own legitimacy depended on that of Mao, so he could not repudiate him and had to hold the line. The Chinese, he said, should 'obey whatever Mao had said and ensure the continuation of whatever he had decided' – a policy that the group around Deng derided as the 'whatever approach'. With a feeble base, doubtful legitimacy and a policy that attracted few adherents Hua was in trouble from the beginning.

In any case, Deng was a formidable opponent. As a veteran of the revolution he had considerable legitimacy; as a former army commander, regional bureau chief and general secretary of the party he had an unequalled network to access and mobilise; and he had the better argument. China did not want more of the same. It did not want to follow Mao 'whatever'. It ached for genuine economic progress, especially because by 1978 its neighbours – Japan, Hong Kong, Taiwan and Singapore – had established an enviable pattern of economic growth.

Deng had seen peasants and state enterprises respond to incentives in the pragmatic reconstruction after the Great Leap Forward. His initial objective was clear, even if the means were not. He intended the Communist Party to retain its iron political control of China, which he signalled with his closure of the 'Democracy Wall' in 1978 and imprisonment of human rights activist Wei Jingsheng when critics began to advocate democratisation of China. But in the economy he wanted to get the party out of the day-to-day management of communes, state-owned enterprises, education and agriculture, instead allowing managers to take responsibility, respond to incentives and raise growth and productivity. There should be no fear of recreating a capitalist class. Rather, the party had to 'make practice the sole criterion of truth'[2] and recognise there is no communist virtue in poverty; on the contrary, it is glorious to be rich.

Economic development had to be at the heart of the Communist Party's intent, Deng would say in 1992, or else the party was lost; 'it was the only hard truth'.[3] Ideological egalitarianism, whether in the school system or the organisation of agriculture, had obstructed development. It would have to go.

During 1978 Hua Guofeng was outmanoeuvred intellectually and politically, and in December 1978, at the famous Third

Plenum of the Eleventh Party Congress, the party committed itself to modernisation, broad-based economic development and the rule of law – rather than the class struggle, further peasant collectivisation and heavy industrialisation to which Hua had pledged himself. It was an historic and decisive moment. Deng moved fast, and within months his people, many, like him, restored from exile, were in key positions in the Politburo and the state. The Dengists – the 'practice' party[4] – had the political momentum, and the conservatives were on the defensive. Reform could and would begin.

What followed was an extraordinary and triumphant vindication of Deng's approach, 'crossing the river groping for stepping stones', as Deng put it. China has made up its own rules and processes at each stage of reform, oscillating between *fang* (opening up) and *shou* (tightening) as it has moved forward, responding to ebbs and flows of confidence and balance between reformers and conservatives.[5] There has been no top-down 'big bang' initiation of privatisation, price liberalisation and democratisation as in Eastern Europe.[6] Rather, it has been some of the bottom-up movements – such as the dismantling of the commune system – that most clearly resembled a 'big bang'.

The centrepiece of economic development has been the ability to maintain investment at a stunning 35–40 per cent of GDP for twenty-five years (an unparalleled rate, higher than that of Korea or Japan). This was possible because of continued high savings and the single-minded capacity of the state-owned banking system, protected by capital and foreign-exchange controls, to channel the savings to state-owned enterprises and infrastructure. This has entailed serious costs: waste, low productivity, bad loans and white-elephant infrastructure projects. Also, the banking system has neglected rural China; this neglect has been scandalous and a source of dangerously rural poverty (which I discuss in more detail in Chapter 5). But the fact remains. The World Bank estimates that from 1978 to 1998 two-thirds of the 9.4 per cent annual growth rate in China's GDP resulted simply from having more machines and infrastructure every year. The proportion of growth attributable to this source rose from 63 per cent in the first decade of reform to 67 per cent in the second decade.[7] Even today the boom in foreign direct investment has been a relative sideshow; it amounted to $60 billion in 2004, but represented just 10 per cent of China's total investment.

In much of the Chinese reform programme there has been a significant element of luck, which has then been cleverly exploited. One example is the continuation of high personal and enterprise savings available for investment, averaging 37 per cent of national output between 1978 and 1995; this could not have been anticipated in 1978. Another example is globalisation, which has lead to greater foreign direct investment over the 1990s and 2000s. This too could not have been anticipated. The main cause – again, unexpected – of high and rising personal savings has been the one-child policy introduced in 1980 to slow down China's population growth and relieve pressure on the land. Urban and rural people have built up their savings because they can rely on no more than one child to look after them in old age, and because of the roll-back in the system of social support – the 'iron rice bowl' – provided by state-owned enterprises under growing financial pressure.

Also, according to Shahid Yusuf of the World Bank, after many decades of austerity the Chinese are keenly aware that belt-tightening could quickly return, so they have held back from increasing their spending in line with their higher incomes. In fact, the risk of unemployment has been rising. The demographics begin to look less favourable from now on as the population ages and people draw on their savings. China is probably at the peak of its saving capacity now, but saving, nevertheless, has been indispensable to its development story.[8]

The regime's pragmatism and gradualism have resulted from a

lack of political consensus at the top about what to do, how radically to do it and in what sequence – together with uncertainty about how specific initiatives would work in practice. There has been as much responding to events, and capitalising on lucky breaks, as directing them. Almost all the developments in rural China have emerged from the bottom, with the state essentially letting the bottom do what it will as long as it does not obstruct the prime objective: reorganising and supporting state-owned enterprise, investing in infrastructure and phasing out planning with as few losers as possible. The insistence that the sole test is 'practice' disguises an unwillingness to create new constitutional and institutional forms. Focus on 'practice' has involved offering incentives, increasing production and creating transitional institutions while crucially leaving the legal, social and political structures that buttress communism pretty much undisturbed.

When the West sees sound money, balanced budgets, market incentives and encouragement of small firms, it thinks it is seeing elements of Western-style capitalism and an embrace of free-market fundamentalism. What it is in fact seeing is the Chinese 'flexing' their system in ways that do not upset its essential components. Balanced budgets and incentives make macro sense and do not disturb the wider system: indeed, budget discipline is a prerequisite for capping inflation, the social implications of which the party fears. The real preoccupation of the Chinese is shown in their unwillingness to privatise, to sell majority control of state-owned enterprises to private investors on the stock market, to reduce the party's influence on the banking system, to allow independent trade unions, to develop an impartial judicial system or to relax capital controls. In these terms some of the Western debate over the virtues of gradualism is beside the point.

China's approach has certainly meant that the mistakes made in Eastern Europe and Russia have not been repeated. For example, in Russia premature privatisation led to a pillaging of state assets before regulations, legal and property rights could be put into place; this has not occurred in China. But it was not economic far-sightedness that allowed the Chinese to avoid this mistake. Their eclectic policy has been driven by an overriding political reality: the vanguardist Communist Party must stay firmly in control, keeping hold of the key power levers while managing the reform process so as to minimise the number of powerful losers. This is not free-market capitalism but Leninist corporatism.

More communist institutions in China have adapted to this policy and proved their economic utility than any Western observers would have guessed. Columbia University's Jeffrey Sachs and Wing Thye Woo of the University of California Davis have argued[9] that China was fortunate to start with so much of its labour force in agriculture and with a relatively underdeveloped industrial sector; there were fewer people to feel the pain of restructuring and China could begin afresh. China was also lucky to have Hong Kong and Taiwan on its doorstep to provide an example of what the Chinese economy could do and to provide an inside track of family and friendship connections within daily commuting distance, showing others how profitable investment in China could be.

Even Sachs and Woo concede that the Maoist legacy of decentralisation helped. The Chinese plan governed only 1200 commodities; the Russian plan, by contrast, governed twenty-five million – so again the Chinese had less to unscramble.[10] This was not so much a result of China's needing less planning because it was a more backward economy, as Sachs and Woo argue. Rather, it resulted from Mao's view that the self-sufficient decentralised unit was the strategic driver in revolutionary success, whether a guerrilla group or a state-owned enterprise. Such units could decide for themselves, in the light of local conditions, how best to further communist objectives. As I remarked in Chapter 3, China's decentralised organisation reflected Mao's belief. When Deng, in the initial reform period, gave more autonomy to the provinces over how they spent and raised money and how they could respond to the demolition of the communes, he was operating within precedents and structures established by Mao.

And if the international environment was more benign, Deng had acted to make it so by seeking peace with the United States. On 1 January 1979 the United States and China announced the opening of full diplomatic relations. Washington severed its formal ties with Taiwan and China agreed to step back from anything but a titular claim to Taiwan, and to accept the United States' rules for the international game in trade, finance and investment. Although it did not seem so at the time, and is not understood even today in these terms, this represented a de facto victory for the United States in the Vietnam War – in effect, a surrogate war against China. By delaying communist government in Vietnam, with its Chinese backing, until 1975 the United States had bought a crucial decade for the Asian economy to begin its growth – led by exports – and to show, indisputably, that capitalist development was more successful than communist. The normalisation of relations included China's buying three American Boeings, allowing Coca-Cola to open a bottling plant in Shanghai and setting up four 'special economic zones' later in 1980 to attract foreign investment. China had admitted ideological defeat; from now on it intended to develop a market economy, though that economy would have strongly Chinese characteristics. This was a remarkable unsung success for American policy.

The accommodation was part of Deng's greater plan. He was not content to increase agricultural production and accelerate industrialisation by offering incentives to Chinese peasants and managers. He also wanted to reproduce in China the kind of success that Hong Kong, Singapore and, gallingly, Taiwan had achieved, building up exports through inward foreign investment and gaining access to foreign technology. Of the four new special economic zones established in 1980, tellingly one was in Shenzhen, just across the border from Hong Kong, another near Macao and two across the straits from Taiwan. They were to be tax-free, bounded zones where foreign multinationals (especially Chinese from Hong Kong and Taiwan) could build up export capacity on their own terms. Normalisation of relations with the United States gave the Taiwanese and Hong Kong Chinese, the most likely initial investors in China, the green light. Foreign direct investment began to move back into China for the first time since the early 1930s.

Phase one: 'responsibility'

China in 1978 was directly or indirectly run by the state, with party cadres involved in the day-to-day management of every nook and cranny of the country. Apart from 150,000 individual proprietorships representing 1 per cent of GDP, the rest was wholly state-owned and state-run. The first step was to take the Communist Party out of management and turn the responsibility over to the managers in industry; teachers in education and so on. Deng focused on the industrial sector. In 1980 he proposed a 'factory manager responsibility system' that would 'take the Party Committee out of day-to-day affairs and allow it to concentrate on party and ideological work and organisational supervision.'[11] Organisations, instead of being subject to detailed planning, would contract with state purchasers regarding how much they would produce and would be given more autonomy to decide how to produce it. In 1984 the 'Ten Regulations' allowed organisations to sell any surpluses they produced over and above the targets set by the plan, at prices that could be set 20 per cent above or below the planned price. To weaken the hold of the party, enterprise managers could make mid-management appointments. By the late 1980s almost all state-owned enterprises were entering long-term planning contracts, negotiating prices, promoting on merit and retaining an increasing share of their profits for reinvestment. Also, managers were able to qualify for bonuses.[12] This was a small revolution of sorts but, as we shall see, it did little to improve the dismal productivity of state-owned enterprise.

Still, it did begin a phased freeing-up of prices. China did not go for a one-off bonfire of price controls; the economic reaction could not be predicted, and if inflation resulted, the social consequences would be dire. The combination of a responsibility system on the land and the Ten Regulations meant that by 1985 the prices of 40 per cent of farm products, 34 per cent of consumer goods sold in shops and even 13 per cent of factory products at the gate were free of government regulation.

Deng now wanted to go further. The scope for arbitrage between planned and market prices was sometimes huge, making the whole transition unstable and opening up the possibility of massive fraud. He wanted to move fast to remove the temptation, and introduced a sudden relaxation of prices in 1988. Inflation rose sharply, arousing memories of the hyperinflation of 1949 and a run on the banks. Price reform was dropped almost immediately, but even so there was a rise to double-digit inflation. This was one of the grievances that provoked Tiananmen the following year, the event above any other that showed the Politburo it was presiding over a powder keg.

However, by the early 1990s Deng felt politically secure enough to do what he had wanted to do three years earlier: complete the liberalisation of prices. By 1995, 78 per cent of farm prices, 89 per cent of consumer goods in shops and a whopping 79 per cent of factory-gate prices had been decontrolled.[13] Today virtually all prices have been liberalised, except those for some key utility and energy prices. China's degree of price freedom matches that of most industrialised countries that, like the Chinese, regulate key prices.

China's phased decontrol thus involved a dual system of pricing: one within the plan and one progressively set by the market. It has been widely praised as a striking example of successful pragmatism. However, the Chinese had no choice. If the Communist Party was to stay in power, it dared not risk a social revolt. As Qian

Yingyi of Stanford University argues, it allowed reform to be phased in so that there were few losers, thus preventing a wider economic and political crisis.[14] Nobody went bust, because inefficient firms could obtain supplies at the planned prices, but at the same time there was plenty of opportunity for efficient firms to expand production to profit from the new opportunities to sell on the freer market. In coal and steel, for example, the planned targets were met at the planned prices, but there was also a booming market in coal and steel produced outside the plan, with prices set by supply and demand. However, the longer the dual system lasted, the more corruption took hold: local officials lined their pockets by procuring production under planned prices and selling the products at higher market prices. The People's Liberation Army, with its own network of factories producing a range of goods, some of which could easily be supplied to civilian buyers, was also able to profit illicitly from the reform process. Gradualism was the right policy for reform, but it did not come without costs.

Deng was directing the process in industry, but in rural China the communes themselves seized the initiative, taking the opportunity that the 'responsibility system' gave them. Even before the Third Plenum in 1978, a group of communes in Fenyang county of Anhui province had persuaded the provincial government to accept that individual peasant households – rather than the commune – would contract to deliver quotas of grain and that the province would thus get more grain.[15] This would set off a revolution from below; a Chinese-style big bang. The Fenyang arrangement swept through rural China like a social hurricane. Peasants simply closed down the commune system and insisted on farming individual plots, almost always the plots of their ancestors. By 1983, 98 per cent of peasant households were individually contracting with their counties or provinces to produce food, sweeping away the detested Maoist communes.

Deng called this the 'household responsibility system' and nearly 300 million households were operating in this way just four years after the process began. What made the transition happen so quickly was that individual peasant households recognised the system as a way to regain control of land their families had farmed for generations. They might only get twenty-year licences (later extended to thirty years[16]), but village leaders – and the peasants themselves – knew which land plots were due to them despite nearly three decades of collectivisation. Many still retained property titles from the imperial and republican governments, as Li Bozhong of Tsinghua University has shown.[17] As peasants regained their former land, met their contracts and sold free surpluses on the market, production climbed by 8 per cent between 1979 and 1984, and the land was farmed much more economically than it had been under the communal system. Agricultural productivity rose steeply, on some estimates by as much 8 per cent per year. New rice varieties also spread like wildfire.[18] This was the coping-stone of the entire economic reform programme. It supported the rural savings that would be deployed for huge investment, and it helped reduce poverty in rural China. There would be difficulties ahead: for one thing, the typical peasant plot was far too small to be the basis of a highly productive agricultural sector in the long term. However, the immediate result was a much-needed uplift.

The fragmentation of the commune system and the return of the peasants to their plots posed a problem for village and local government leaders. What to do with the small-scale factories that every Maoist commune had begun, and which produced everything from bicycle parts to buttons and zips? Now that the communes no longer made organisational sense, and in any case were formally abolished in 1983, who was to own and manage these factories? They could not be privatised because Beijing was sending a steady stream of ideological rhetoric against private business and bourgeois capitalism, reinforced by the prohibition of the four newly established state banks (created by breaking up Mao's unitary state bank) lending to private companies. But the factories provided work and were an important source of local supplies. The answer was pragmatic; towns and villages would take them over, manage them and reinvest the profit in the business or invest it in the community.

'Red hat' capitalists

The boom in 'town and village enterprises' (TVEs) took everyone by surprise. Deng, acknowledging that they were 'our greatest success', said they had just developed spontaneously: 'This result was not anything that I or any of the other comrades had foreseen; it just came out of the blue.'[19] They are certainly integral to Chinese development; in 1978 collective enterprise was part of the commune system, but by 1993 TVEs were employing fifty-two million people – 58 per cent of all employment in rural industry.[20] By the end of 2005 they employed 135 million people.

These are rural China's metal bashers and suppliers of building materials, clothes and packaged food, the backbone of the rural economy. Without them rural unemployment and poverty would be disastrous. Yet, according to Western economic textbooks, they should not be so successful. Their property rights and legal standing are and were uncertain; for years they were outside the plan and had to scramble for raw materials and supplies. They do not have profit-maximising shareholders who are willing to risk capital and who want to drive them forward. The result should be indiscipline and waste. Their owners – local governments – should plunder the profits and should have no incentive to make the enterprise grow.

Yet the enterprises have grown, although much faster in southern China than inland and in the north-east, which are more heavily populated with state-owned enterprise. Despite their disadvantages, they had the ace of being given their equity capital free, and they had strong local franchises. The 'tilted playing field'[21] was an incentive to become agile and adaptable. They have been a vehicle for the rapid growth of rural employment, and also a rich source of revenue to fund housing, schools and hospitals.

For the first fifteen years of the reform programme they were helped enormously by a tax system that encouraged them to keep their surpluses and reinvest these in their own growth and finance the provision of local public facilities.[22] In the south and along the coast, where Mao had shunned investing in industry because it would be the first to fall in any invasion, local communities were on their own, with little or no industrial base. Professor Edward Steinfeld of MIT argues that if local officials in these areas did not help their communities nobody else would. The development of the TVE was a matter of life and death, the only route to economic development and to the provision of local 'public goods'. It was also an avenue to personal enrichment (by means of a little local corruption).[23] Local communities were made to 'eat from a single kitchen', as the Chinese say, and were on their mettle rather than 'eating from one big pot'.

In other parts of China, with more state-owned enterprises (SOEs), the 'big pot' tradition could be maintained. Local officials could hold the SOEs to ransom, confident that, whatever the trading deficit, the national banking system would come to their aid. In these areas there was less incentive to build TVEs because officials could plunder the existing state enterprises to build the social infrastructure. In other words, what was emerging was not a new form of capitalist altruism spearheaded by enlightened local government, as some star-struck commentators have argued.[24] Rather, when local governments had their back to the wall, they responded creatively; otherwise they reverted to type, milking state-owned enterprises.

In their heyday TVEs were also a cloak behind which local entrepreneurs – 'red hat' capitalists – could hide their private ambitions right up to the late 1990s, when banks were finally allowed to lend to private companies and entrepreneurs could 'come out'. Typically the entrepreneur would make a deal with the TVE, which would shelter him from party investigation for being a capitalist. For example, the first Chinese company to be quoted on NASDAQ in 2002, Qiaoxing Enterprise Group, spent its first ten years as a supposed TVE in Fujian. Its founder and chief executive, Wu Ruilin, was a classic 'red hat' capitalist; the TVE structure disguised what he was really doing.

However, after 1994 TVEs began a transmutation. In the first place, the tax breaks that supported them were withdrawn as the government recentralised taxation: local government became less interested in their development. The TVEs began to turn themselves into much more conventional private firms with only nominal ownership by local government, although achieving that in a Chinese framework without clear property, legal and incorporation rights remains highly problematic. For the past seven or eight years they have been in an institutional no man's land. They proved to be a brilliant institution of transition, but not, unless the party chooses to loosen its political grip, of ongoing economic development.

Economic reform has been uneven. In the older industrial provinces dominated by SOEs, the state continued to lead the economy. In the southern province of Guangdong, however, it was inward investment from Hong Kong and small firms that drove higher growth. And Zhejiang, a province across the straits from Taiwan, has emerged as the private-sector capital of China and one of its fastest-growing provinces. Zhejiang was the first Chinese province in 1998 to report that half its industrial output was produced by the pure private sector. Its Wenzhou prefecture has been both a showcase and trouble spot, insisting on developing whatever it takes to industrialise and thumbing its nose at party rules. Other provinces want to reproduce its success.

It is a dramatic example of the reaction to the break-up of the Maoist communes in a dirt-poor part of China. Mao's strategic ban on investment applied to Wenzhou because of its proximity to Taiwan and its consequent vulnerability to bombardment in the event of a war. For the prefecture, the end of the communes meant that without institutional innovation everyone faced poverty or worse.

There had to be a conceptual leap. There was no institutional apparatus whatsoever in Wenzhou in 1979, except that of the indifferent, far-away state and, apart from kinship and *guanxi* networks, no civil society. Wenzhou had to create its own structures, all the time kowtowing to the line that its inventions conformed to the rules about 'collective enterprise'. Nor could 'banks' be created, even though in a region as poor as this development cannot happen unless there is access to credit; state banks were forbidden to lend to anything but state-owned or bona fide collective enterprise.

So entrepreneurs in Wenzhou adopted the 'red hat' strategy of associating themselves with TVEs or SOEs more aggressively than anywhere else and, more importantly, inventing private banking institutions but calling them 'money houses' rather than banks. In the early years of reform Wenzhou was home to an increasing number of tiny family businesses. Because Marx had said that the threshold for the exploitative capitalist firm was eight people, the party was happy in the early years of the reform programme to permit private enterprise only up to that limit. Between 1979 and 1987 Wenzhou registered an amazing 190,000 businesses with no more than eight staff members. If entrepreneurs wanted a business to grow, they would need to exceed the eight-person limit; with company formation banned, the only possible route was some form of affiliation with a TVE.

The forms of affiliation that were invented to solve the problem were and are bewildering. They include both artificial 'red hat' TVEs and genuine 'stock-holding cooperatives'. In the latter, entrepreneurs would put up capital in an overt cooperative partnership with their workers, who would automatically receive a quarter of the profits as a dividend. In exchange the cooperative would grow beyond Marx's limit of eight. These cooperatives were a halfway house between capitalism and socialism in which workers and shareholders co-owned the company and profits. This was the kind of organisational structure once proposed by the Nobel laureate Professor James Meade to create companies as partnerships of labour and capital with equal rights to dividends. Meade thought he had invented a building block in what he called liberal socialism, combining the dynamism of profit-seeking capital with the collaborative instincts of socialism. The people of Wenzhou, although they are unlikely to have heard of Meade, might agree.

By 1990 two-fifths of Wenzhou's industrial output was produced by stock-holding cooperatives. As Meade predicted, the workers were just as eager to grow, innovate and invest as the entrepreneurs. Around Wenzhou eighteen satellite townships had increased to 110, a tribute to the pace of industrialisation.[25] Kellee Tsai of Johns Hopkins University, who spent two years in the field researching China's informal banking system, reports that this growth would have been impossible without credit.[26] Wenzhou therefore allowed private 'money houses' – adaptations of rural cooperative credit institutions and even mutated NGOs, all posing as collective enterprises, even if in reality they were private – to get into the credit business. Neglected by Beijing, Wenzhou's officials, local leaders and entrepreneurs took full advantage of Mao's legacy of decentralisation and Deng's remedies: they would take responsibility; they would make practice the sole criterion of truth; and they would glory in getting rich.[27]

Beijing finally forced Wenzhou to close the 'money houses' in the late 1980s, but it could not prevent the appetite for innovation, whetted by what was becoming one of the biggest industrial clusters of small firms in China. By 2003 Beijing relinquished its suspicions, and the People's Bank of China designated the city of Wenzhou an official experimental district for financial and banking reforms. Wenzhou, now one of China's richest cities, whose small business *guanxi* networks and quasi-cooperatives could not be more different from the declining industrial cities of the north-east dominated by SOEs, had proved both the strength and the weakness of Chinese reform. It was dynamic, but in an institutional, legal and social vacuum. Sooner or later, if they were to progress further, Wenzhou and Zhejiang would need the full institutional infrastructure that supports capitalism.

Phase two: 'made in China'

By late 1991 China's reformers had a significant record of achievement. Rural industry was booming in the form of TVEs; agricultural production was rising; state-owned enterprises were beginning, albeit slowly and belatedly, to improve their performance as a result of the responsibility system; and investment in infrastructure was substantial. But Tiananmen had proved a landmark moment. The conservative crackdown – freezing the reform programme, clamping down on the movement of people, renewing hostility toward private business, imposing martial law and slowing down the economy – had unnerved the country.

Tens of millions of peasants had left the land to find work in the cities during the 1980s, and there was no sign that this migration was abating. The evidence from the previous decade was that non-state enterprise drove economic growth, and thus should be further supported. Yet the formal ban on private enterprises with more than eight employees remained in force, inefficient SOEs still dominated industrial output and prices were not yet fully liberalised. Foreign direct investment had stopped growing, and in any case it cumulatively totalled a mere $25 billion since 1979. Elsewhere Thailand, Malaysia, the Philippines and Indonesia were now repeating the success trail-blazed by Japan, South Korea, Hong Kong, Taiwan and Singapore – a sign of what was possible. Communism had collapsed in Eastern Europe and was collapsing in Russia. Unless China could maintain or accelerate the pace of economic development, the writing was on the wall.

So it was that Deng, now eighty-eight years old, made his last significant intervention. In January 1992, weeks after the demise of the Soviet Union and Gorbachev's resignation, he chose to take a 'vacation' in seedy, fast-growing Shenzhen, home of China's first stock market and its first special economic zone. This was the beginning of what became known as the southern tour, a self-conscious reference to Mao's so-called tours, with Deng travelling in a specially equipped train. He told successive audiences that, without development and accelerated reform, the Communist Party was lost. He accused the opponents of reform, echoing a favourite phrase of Mao's, of being like women with bound feet. Reform might mean a little 'spiritual pollution' of communist values, Deng said, but whenever you open a window you let in flies. His presence in Shenzhen, China's foremost capitalist fly, showed that he thought the window should be opened wider. Foreign investment and private enterprise served the cause of development as well as education and scientific research, he declared; China even had to accept that in a race for riches some people would emerge as winners before others. He challenged officials to say where they stood – and Guangdong, one of the pace-setting provinces in the south that already had been exploiting its proximity to Hong Kong and Macao to grow rapidly, needed little prompting. The party secretary of Guangdong, Xie Fie, replied that with the right policies his province could catch up with the Asian tigers by 2010. Deng approved; little did either know how accurate that prediction would prove to be.

It was a galvanising political moment. Up until then reform had been considered in terms of responsibility, contracting, price liberalisation and allowing markets only at the margin of the plan.

Conservatives had been reluctant, but had been mollified because the party was still against private property and private business: state banks were forbidden to lend to private companies in all but exceptional circumstances. The welcome to foreign investment had been guarded; outside the four special economic zones – a fifth was added only in 1988 – foreign investors had to partner Chinese enterprises if they wanted to establish a plant in China. The opening of the coastal strip in the 1980s to even limited joint ventures revived such painful memories of the infamous nineteenth-century treaty ports that the party found itself driving the policy through the National People's Congress with seven hundred abstentions and three hundred opposed – an unprecedented degree of dissent. Without Deng and his prestige, progress would have been glacial.

However, the old man now wanted to accelerate the pace of reform, and he got it. The new general secretary of the party, Jiang Zemin, seized the opportunity and transformed the party's objective from building a 'planned socialist commodity economy', the outcome of the landmark Eleventh Party Congress in 1978, to building a 'socialist market economy', which was agreed on in 1993 at the Third Plenum of the Fourteenth Party Congress. During 1992 the number of industrial and agricultural products whose prices were regulated was slashed. In 1993 production, economic growth and inflation soared. It was the year of what the Chinese called the five fevers – investment, stock market, real estate, government cadres getting into business and fast growth.[28] And it proved the trigger of the retrenchment and overhaul of state structures that I describe in more detail in the next chapter.

In 1997 a decision was made to 'hold on to the big but let go of the small' state enterprise. This has led to a whirlwind of consolidation and redundancy among SOEs. Although Western commentators sometimes call 'letting go' 'privatisation', it was no such thing, and the Communist Party was careful not to call it that. Even when 'let go', management is still beholden to the

Communist Party, which continues to make senior appointments, and cash for investment is generated internally or
borrowed from state-owned banks. As I explore in more detail
later, this is 'autonomisation' or corporatisation, rather than privatisation, and it takes place within a framework of political
control and direction.

For while TVEs and SOEs may be directed by their management teams, ultimately they still dance to the state's tune. Also,
although truly private firms that have been founded by entrepreneurs are the dynamic sector in China, the researcher Yasheng
Huang of MIT found that during the 1990s their average size
hardly grew from around sixty or seventy employees, and those
that did grow larger only did so with access to legal and financial
structures in Hong Kong.[29] There is still prejudice against lending
to private firms, despite the formal relaxations introduced in 1998.
The entire structure of ownership, corporate control and unclear
property rights constitutes a strong bias against building a business as understood in the West.

Chasing the dragon

The pace of reform has been much more impressive in terms of
opening up to the outside world. In December 2001 China
joined the World Trade Organization, a further tribute to the
liberalisation initiated by Deng. Average tariffs on imported
manufactured goods stood at 43 per cent in 1992; by 2001 they
had been reduced to 15 per cent, with virtually all licences and
quantitative import controls eliminated.[30]

The trickle of foreign direct investment has turned into a flood.
It nearly tripled to $11 billion in 1992 after Deng's southern tour,
tripled again to $34 billion in 1994 and doubled to $61 billion by
2004. In 1992 alone, more than 8500 new investment zones were
created; before Deng's tour there had been only one hundred.

Once the Chinese had signalled that they wanted foreign investment on far less restrictive terms, entrepreneurs in Hong Kong
and Taiwan, who had been leading the way since 1979, were
joined by Western multinationals. There was a rekindling of the
'China dream', the lure of a market of one billion consumers. The
English writer Joe Studwell, editor of the *China Economic
Quarterly*, and author of *The China Dream*, highlights the long tradition of Western capitalists who have been captivated by the
prospect of China as a market. 'If only we could persuade every
person in China to lengthen his shirttail by a foot,' wrote one
nineteenth-century English industrialist, 'we could keep the mills
of Lancashire working round the clock.'[31]

Deng's speech and Jiang's reaction sparked an enormous bull-
ishness about China's prospects. This attitude had been waiting to
be reignited ever since Deng took over – and suddenly China
did seem to be a new Klondike. In the first half of 1992 the
Shanghai stock market rose 1200 per cent. In the autumn of 1993
a group of Wall Street fund managers spent a week in China;
Barton Biggs, founder and chairman of Morgan Stanley Asset
Management, said, 'after eight days in China I'm tuned in, over-
fed and maximum bullish.'[32] He spoke for hundreds of others.
Western investment money began to flow into China seriously,
but almost everyone was to be disappointed. China might continue on growing, but making profits would prove elusive. The
Shanghai stock market has yet to fully recover from those heady
early days.

The 'China play' suddenly became the talk of corporate
America, Japan and Europe. The strategy: locate production
capacity in a tax-free zone in China; employ its literate workers at
up to one-thirtieth of the cost of workers in the United States or
Europe; coordinate activity by Information and Communication
Technology (ICT); ship the products on a modern container in
a modern freeway to a modern port.[33] And sell them in the West
for a colossal margin. Exports would do for now; there was a

domestic market that would come on-stream and the advantage would fall to the first mover who could redirect products from the export to the home market when the time came.

A big China deal would reliably move the share price upwards – and companies as disparate as General Motors and Microsoft scrambled to be among the first to make such a deal. Production and, increasingly, research in China are key components of most multinationals' strategy; some, like Microsoft, have signalled that they intend research in China to be cutting-edge. *Business Week* estimates that, by the end of 2005, fifty thousand United States firms were doing business of some sort in China.[34]

Nearly 90 per cent of foreign investment has been directed to the coastal provinces, particularly in the south, and two-thirds has been in manufacturing. China's extraordinary growth in exports has been propelled overwhelmingly by foreign companies. According to the Paris-based Organisation for Economic Cooperation and Development (OECD), 55 per cent of China's exports are made by foreigners; and, generally, the more high-tech the industry, the higher the foreigners' share. More than 80 per cent of electronic and telecommunications exports are made by foreigners, as are 70 per cent of plastics, and 60 per cent of electrical goods.[35] Taiwan and Indonesia are an intriguing comparison; both relied much less on foreign direct investment (FDI) for exports at a similar stage in their development. Only 20 per cent of Taiwan's and 29 per cent of Indonesia's manufacturing exports were foreign-made.[36]

It should be no surprise that a growing number of Western retailers import from China. In the United States Wal-Mart (see Chapter 1), Home Depot and Gap all have a growing proportion of sales from exports made in China. Britain's Kingfisher and Tesco, and France's Carrefour, are other examples, to name but a few.

This avalanche of foreign investment has made China the world's workshop, or at least mass assembler, of choice and by

2010 will make it the world's leading exporter (see Chapter 1). A huge number of consumer products have labels saying 'made in China'. By 1999 foreign plants and companies already employed over twenty million people. The growth in imports is no less spectacular; one feature of China's development since 1992 is the emphasis on openness to both exports and imports – with many of the imports being brought in by foreign investors, reprocessed and then exported.[37]

The concern within China is that this is a sign of weakness. Wu Jinglian, a researcher at China's State Council of Development Research who is close to the government, represents the internal debate. He observes that when Britain, the United States and Japan dominated world manufacturing they had developed and owned the intellectual property of the products they exported. They generated global brands.[38] Japan, after a generation of development, had built up international companies and brands such as Toyota and Sony. China is not in that position today. In 2003 China had no companies in Morgan Stanley Dean Witter's list of the world's top 250 'competitive edge' companies; it had not one company in *Business Week*'s list of the world's top hundred brands for 2005–6; and only one company in the world's top three hundred companies ranked by R & D expenditure.[39] Excitable commentators like the *Sunday Times*' David Smith, who cite the fact that China has twenty companies ranked by turnover in the Fortune 500 as evidence of China's imminent economic threat, overlook that they are all state-owned enterprises, many of them loss-making or barely profitable. China, despite its economic size, growth and export performance, has not one genuine private multinational in the top 500 ranked by profits. Two leading China-watchers – Peter Nolan at the University of Cambridge and Edward Steinfeld at MIT – argue that the way the current international economic and trading system operates makes it very difficult for Chinese companies to catch up. If foreign multinationals can produce at the same cost by operating in China, and if all the obstacles cited above make it hard for Chinese entrepreneurs to grow, then China's place in the world economy is, increasingly, as a dependent part of the supply chain rather than as a player in its own right. This is not what the Chinese want; nor is it a stable platform for economic growth.

This is certainly the view of Yasheng Huang, who, in his book *Selling China*, argues that the flood of foreign direct investment has become a vital source of equity and technology, compensating for the weaknesses in China's own financial and innovation system.[40] China has no system for generating venture capital and its stock markets in Shenzhen and Shanghai (founded in 1990 and 1991 respectively) are organised not to raise equity capital for new enterprises but, as I will explore in more detail in Chapter 5, to offer tame investment to cash-strapped SOEs. FDI offers the prospect of equity capital that otherwise is not forthcoming, especially in the cities; it also closes the gap in an otherwise dismal record of technological innovation and development. We should be looking at the reasons for the FDI boom and we should be growing concerned.

So the balance sheet is mixed. There is growth, rising living standards and a remarkable decrease in poverty; China has managed the reform process with skill. On the other hand, economy-wide productivity is poor and growing only moderately. China has an estimated 150 million migrant workers living in its cities (the official figure is 112 million), and at least another 200 million more are ready to leave its vast agricultural hinterland. Inequality is growing. Every time the party has let Chinese civil society express itself – whether in Tiananmen, at the 'Democracy Wall' or as Mao allowing a hundred flowers to bloom – the reaction has been criticism and complaint. Deng's gradualism and opportunism, preserving the vanguard role of the Communist Party, have taken China this far. The same approach will work much less well in future. Indeed, it may not work at all.

5

The State They're In

The Chinese economy and the Chinese Communist Party are in an unstable halfway house – an economy that is neither socialist nor properly capitalist, run by a party that is neither revolutionary nor subject to the normal constitutional checks and balances of even China's own Confucian past, let alone the Asian or Western present.[1] The achievement thus far is impressive: an average annual growth rate of 9 per cent over twenty-five years (nearer 10 per cent over the last fifteen years), per capita incomes that have increased six times and 400 million people pulled out of poverty. But despite this, the strains are becoming more evident. Some are economic, such as the capacity to continue to save at high levels, or the cost of acquiring foreign-exchange reserves at the current rate. But at least as worrying for the party are the social strains. The great gains in China's reduction in poverty took place twenty years ago, after the communes were scrapped. Since then, inequality has been growing consistently. The World Bank estimates that if the growth in income in rural China had kept up with the growth in the cities, China's poverty rate would now be a quarter of the current level.[2] Chinese peasants do not know the numbers, but they must live with the consequences – and unrest, disaffection and anger are steadily mounting.

A proponent of the Communist Party would argue that we are watching a new economic and political model emerge, the so-called 'Beijing Consensus'.[3] This is a commitment to pragmatic development policies in contrast to an ideological commitment to markets and privatisation. In this optimistic interpretation, the Communist Party is becoming an amalgam of a contemporary Confucian elite upholding a developing Chinese rule of law and a typical Asian nationalist party experimenting with the first elements of Chinese democracy. My own more sober assessment is that economic contradictions, structural defects and sheer economic waste will ultimately lead to a worsening decline in the growth rate, which in turn will set off a chain reaction of change in China's economic and political structures. Communism is a doctrine of revolution, class war and authoritarianism. It has only a very limited ability to abandon the party-state and Leninist corporatism so as to become a successful bureaucratic party accepting constitutional constraints – but that is what must happen. How it will be achieved is the story of the decades ahead.

Progress has been significant. The days of the mass terror of the Cultural Revolution are over; and as urban incomes and employment have grown, so have economic freedom, social mobility and people's sense of possibility. In 1989 the party justified its action in Tiananmen as a necessary response to a counter-revolutionary riot, clamped down on private business development and excluded private businesspeople from party membership. Ten years later, in a constitutional amendment, the party accepted 'private and individual business' as 'an important component' of China's future and was enlisting entrepreneurs as members. Jiang Zemin assumed the general secretaryship of the party in 1989 after the Committee of Elders and Deng Xiaoping dismissed his predecessor, Zhao Ziyang, in the immediate after-math of Tiananmen. Every general secretary until then had been forcibly deposed by a coup, a purge or political intervention. But in 2002, as a sign of more orderly times, Jiang stepped down vol-untarily, in accordance with a new rule that senior leaders should not renew five-year terms once they were over seventy. Jiang handed power over to a successor, Hu Jintao, who had been chosen by a constitutional party process. This was a milestone: power had been transferred seamlessly, peacefully and according to constitutional rules.

These twin developments have prompted the most urgent current debate in political economy. The Chinese Communist Party has made the Chinese state more efficient and financially sound with ambitions better to regulate the economy that it has created. Also, as Hu Jintao's appointment signified, a constitu-tionalism is emerging that tries to maintain the predictable rule of communist law, even if in practice the most predictable feature is that the party gets its way. Jiang himself said in 2001, 'Our party, as the party in power, must pay close attention to the relationship between the party and the masses, and the feelings of the people. Whether the people are for or against it is the basic factor deciding the rise and fall of a political party or a political power.'[4] Hu Jintao has been equally aware of this political truth; the party must deliver economically and it must have a plausible explanation of why it legitimately holds sole power – or else the people will no longer consent to its rule. Hu therefore emphasises 'harmonious development' as one of the three harmonies (the other two are harmony with the world and harmony with Taiwan). This deliberate combination of communism and Confucianism recognises a need to respond to grass-roots concerns about inequality and corruption, and presents Hu as a humane sage-emperor. The formula might work as long as the economy works, but how much longer can the party continue to deliver economi-cally? When will its explanation no longer be good enough?

These two questions are linked. As discussed in Chapter 4, China has become a $2-trillion economy because, for a generation, the state has channelled freakishly huge savings into investment and because, over the past decade, the country has made itself the world's greatest assembler and manufacturing subcontractor by giving Hong Kong, Taiwanese and – increasingly – Western multinationals privileges for which no Chinese company could hope. This has created the world's most sustained and most enormous export boom, based on cheap labour and a first-world infrastructure. But the primacy of politics and party over state, economy and society puts Chinese indigenous enterprise, and thus the long-term efficiency of the domestic economy, in a cage. Economic progress so far has been achieved despite this impediment, but China is approaching a tipping point. Enterprise must be let off the leash and allowed to move into self-sustaining entrepreneurial maturity, or else there will be a sharp and destabilising deceleration in the growth rate.

Despite the talk of economic reform, liberalisation and state modernisation, the party-state remains the grand economic puppeteer. Its enterprise marionettes are only allowed longer and longer strings to the extent they are considered less strategic – but for everyone the strings are never cut, just lengthened. All of them, from the management buyout of a state enterprise to the company bought by a foreign investment bank, are ultimately manipulated by the party-state. It could not be otherwise. The party runs the state, and the state retains discretionary power to do what it chooses and override any challenge or complaint from any non-state actor – or indeed from state actors if they cross the will of the party. The distortions are obvious and unsustainable – now becoming evident in sharply rising inflation – and must be corrected if China is to maintain the growth rate it needs, but this will entail the party's losing control of the state. To analyse China's choices today, we need first to examine how Jiang Zemin responded to the crisis of 1993.

Saving the party-state

Tiananmen forced a recognition that the party was facing a crisis of legitimacy. The dizzying inflation of 1992 and 1993, in reaction to Deng's southern tour, was no less shocking a reminder of the weakness of China's economic structures. In fifteen years China had moved from a command and control economy, in which every production unit was part of the state plan, to an anarchic network of autonomous provincial governments, local TVEs and SOEs that, in effect, were accountable to no one. These autonomous entities could spend and borrow much as they liked, could rig and protect local markets as they chose and could fix the court system to get the required decisions; moreover, local communist cadres and officials could help themselves to what they wanted. It made Caligula's Rome look like a vicar's tea party.

Beijing had no means of calibrating an economic tempo that was not the generalised clampdown on which it had insisted after Tiananmen, or the complete free-for-all that succeeded it. There were no institutions in government or in the intermediate public domain that could put budget constraints on provincial governments with ambitions to build new infrastructure, or on SOEs and TVEs determined to expand, mindless of the financial consequences. There were no independent shareholders who would be concerned about organisational over-ambition and over-stretching; there were no independent auditors to expose excessive indebtedness, or imprudent overlending by banks; there was no independent press to report on generalised excess, corruption and market rigging; no powerful central bank; and there was no central system of tax collection or national audit.

Instead, the state banks, with their provincial headquarters, and the provincial development banks did the bidding of the local communist hierarchy and the enterprises it directed. The People's Bank of China had an office in every provincial capital that was simply co-opted for the local cause.[5] Provincial governments were and are jealous of their autonomy and protective of local interests; there were de facto trade wars between provinces. Enterprises and courts were told to favour local interests and ignore claims from outside the province. Markets, as I have argued earlier, are social constructions with contours and dynamics framed by government regulation and law. Their spontaneity has to be shaped; otherwise, they degrade. The United States can look back over its own history of bank failures and growth of federal regulation to find evidence of this long-standing truth. China in 1993 was another example of this logic playing itself out.

In this Gadarene rush for growth, exploiting the lack of discipline, investment in state assets jumped by 48.1 per cent in 1992 and by 44.1 per cent in 1993 – in effect doubling over a two-year period. In the first half of 1993 industrial production was up 25 per cent; inflation averaged 17.4 per cent over the same period, reaching 21 per cent in June.[6] Depositors were withdrawing their money from banks while bank lending was growing at an unparalleled rate, threatening a financial crisis. Arbitrarily deducting money from workers' pay to invest in government bonds – forced saving – was no longer adequate to finance the government debt. There were more strikes in factories, and there was unrest in the rural areas, where incomes were not keeping pace with inflation. When Jiang Zemin visited Mao's birthplace he was jostled by crowds of farmers petitioning him for relief.[7] An additional cause for protest was the increasing number of central and provincial government agencies that arbitrarily levied fees on villages and enterprises; nearly ten thousand had emerged in Beijing alone. The toxic mix of inflation, inequality and growing popular resentment of communist corruption was once again threatening the stability of the regime.

The collapse of communism in the Soviet Union seemed to foretell its inevitable collapse in China. After all, inflation had been an important factor in the popular revolts against the Nationalists in 1948 and the communists in 1989; now it was back with a vengeance. Revolt against communist rule in some provinces seemed certain. In Japan Kenichi Ohmae predicted that eleven Chinese republics would emerge from China's inevitable break-up and form a new 'Federal Republic of China'. The Pentagon's Office of Net Assessment assembled a thirteen-member task force to analyse China, and a majority of the members predicted China's disintegration.[8] It seemed all over for China.

But during 1993 Jiang Zemin and his tough-minded prime minister Zhu Rongji worked on a reform programme to save the party-state. As Jiang declared in December, the party had to 'take forceful measures to maintain social and political stability'.[9] The inability to check the economy during 1993, when the old techniques – instructing banks to recall loans and instructing provincial governments to freeze infrastructure spending – were both widely ignored. Something new had to happen fast. Discipline would have to be imposed, but not by increasing the watchdog powers of the network of intermediate public institutions, which might endanger the hegemony of the party. Rather, it would be necessary to re-empower the centralised state. The approach was three-pronged: (1) devise tax-raising powers and processes that would slow the economy and inflation immediately while giving central government more management and spending power; (2) reorganise the financial and legal systems while retaining party control; and (3) give the Communist Party more political authority by reclaiming its power over the provinces, rehabilitating it ideologically and demonstrably tackling corruption.

The first requirement was for the central government to establish its own nationwide tax base rather than rely on the 'contracting system' in which it negotiated with provincial governments for revenue. Under the contracting system its revenue had plunged to around one-fifth of all state revenues during the previous decade. If the trend had continued, Chen Yuan, deputy governor of the People's Bank of China, warned, China risked 'a further loss of economic control and even disintegration'.[10] In early 1994 a nationwide value-added tax was introduced to replace the plethora of local product taxes; taxes were earmarked for the centre; a new institution was established to oversee tax collection; and broad new powers were given to the National Audit Office to investigate fraud and evasion. The impact was immediate; in 1994 the central government's share of total budgetary revenue jumped to 56 per cent, where it remains. Moreover, the long slide in central government revenues as a proportion of GDP – from about 30 per cent in 1978 to 10.7 per cent in 1995 – was reversed; in 2002 the proportion was 18 per cent. A modest increase, but it was enough to avert the disintegration of the Chinese state.

To keep the powerful provinces content, Jiang promised that sufficient cash would be rebated to ensure that their baseline budgets would not be cut in 1994. Then in 1995 he introduced a new system for appointing, promoting and screening senior party officials that put Beijing unambiguously in charge, trying to limit the existing incestuous spoils and favours system. Interestingly, the Communist Party found itself reintroducing the old Confucian system of avoidance; as in the imperial era, senior officials are not allowed to govern their home town or home province, and they are regularly rotated out of an office after a maximum of ten years. There are also more inter-provincial transfers: according to Zhiyue Bo, chair of the Department of International Studies at St John Fisher College in Rochester, New York, every province has had a party secretary, deputy secretary, governor or vice-governor transferred either to another province or to Beijing.[11] By 2001, when a new round of appointments to the Central Committee began, the Organisation Department of the Communist Party controlled a national system of recruitment from China's provinces, departments and key SOEs, with the final selection made by the Standing Committee of the Politburo. Beijing's centralised mastery of the party was becoming complete.

The losing battle against corruption

Jiang set the party on its current course – to shed its revolutionary skin and become a governing party attempting to be bound by rules and focused on economic development and the people's welfare. The first practical consequence was that the party should no longer be in business itself. Since the early 1940s the Maoist doctrine of self-sufficiency had meant that not just the army but also many organs of government had become producers and profit centres, opening up vast scope for corruption. In the early 1980s the need to develop had been so desperate that no stone could be left unturned. Deng Xiaoping had wanted the People's Liberation Army (PLA) to deploy the massive production resources it had developed to help support growth, but what this had meant in practice was that the army, and many of its generals, had become, in effect, full-time businessmen, using their privileges for self-enrichment. Apart from the factories it owned to produce its own supplies, the PLA ran coal mines, airlines, telecommunications companies and hotels. So did the police, government departments and parts of the judicial system. Nearly all prospered through rigged prices and uncontested procurement contracts, and were proof positive that the Communist Party was both corrupt and corrupting. In 1998 Jiang Zemin ruled that they should all divest themselves of their businesses. 'The military must no longer be in business,' he declared. 'Otherwise, this tool of proletarian dictatorship will collapse, and the socialist state power will change colour.' Within twelve months more than thirty thousand trading enterprises run directly by arms of government were either closed or taken over by third parties, although in truth unravelling relationships in a party-state and making them genuinely arm's-length is almost impossible.

This was the first step of an attempted professionalisation, and a preoccupation with corruption, that increased in Jiang's last five years in office. 'If we do not crack down on corruption, the flesh-and-blood ties between the party and the people will suffer a lot and the party will be in danger of losing its ruling position, or possibly heading for self-destruction,' Jiang declared in 2002, in his last political report to the National Congress. High-level officials were arrested and imprisoned for embezzlement and racketeering; they included the party secretary and mayor of Beijing, Chen Xitong, a member of the Politburo. Cheng Kejie, vice-chairman of the Standing Committee of the National People's Congress, was executed for taking $5 million in kickbacks for arranging land deals and contracts for private business. In the financial system the highest-profile casualties have been three of Prime Minister Zhu Rongji's hand-picked 'can-do commanders'. Wang Xuebing, former president of the Bank of China and an alternating member of the Central Committee, and Zhu Xiaohua, vice-governor of the People's Bank of China, were arrested and jailed for banking fraud. Li Fuxiang, director of China's State Administration of Foreign Exchange (SAFE), leaped to his death from the seventh floor of Beijing's Hospital 304 while under investigation for involvement in illegal exports of foreign exchange. On July 10 2007 Zheng Xiaoyu, former head of the State Food and Drug Administration, was executed for allegedly taking $800,000 bribes to approve fake and sub-standard drugs from eight pharmaceutical companies. To put this in a British or American context, it is as if, within the past five years, the mayors of London and New York, the speakers of the House of Commons and House of Representatives and the chief executives of Goldman Sachs, Citibank and HSBC, along with governors of the Federal Reserve and Bank of England, were all imprisoned for fraud and one committed suicide, with the execution of the head of the Food Standards Agency. Add to this convicted high-court judges and state governors and the scale of the problem becomes clear.

The anti-corruption and Orwellian-sounding Central Discipline Inspection Committee has been strengthened; punishments have been increased; tougher anti-graft laws have been introduced, with the burden of proof of innocence now on the defendant; officials have been forced to take responsibility for the behaviour of their families and are forbidden to engage in business relationships with family members; rectification campaigns have begun; and audits have been introduced so that officials leaving office or being promoted have to pass anti-corruption screenings.[12] But, for all that, corruption remains deeply embedded. If there are signs that petty corruption is levelling off, reports Sun Yan in *Current History*, large-scale corruption is mounting. The average 'take' in the 1980s was $5000; now it is over $250,000. The number of arrests of senior cadre members above the county level quadrupled between 1992 and 2001.[13] Two examples are particularly significant. In 2005 it was disclosed that a cool $1 billion had been misappropriated or embezzled in Gansu, one of China's poorest provinces, by a ring of forty or more officials. As further evidence of the growing scale of corruption and the seniority of the offenders, four provincial governors and one provincial party secretary have recently been charged, not to mention the sacking of Cheng Liangyu, the head of the Shanghai Communist Party (the most important outside Beijing) for corruption in September 2006.

The economist Hu Angang in his trailblazing book *Great Transformations in China: Challenges and Opportunities* cites evidence provided by government departments that the annual economic loss between 1999 and 2001 due to corruption averaged 14.5 to 14.9 per cent of GDP. His own estimated range, as quoted in Chapter 1, is between 13.3 and 16.9 per cent of GDP over the late 1990s alone. Every incident of corruption – smuggling, embezzlement, theft, swindling, bribery – arises in the first place from the unchallengeable power of communist officials and the lack of any reliable, independent system of accountability and scrutiny. There is some truth in the view that in the early years of the reform programme the corruptibility of officials gave some necessary flexibility to what was otherwise a highly bureaucratic and monopolistic system, and so might even have contributed to the growth. As Samuel Huntingdon has put it, the only thing worse than a rigid, over-centralised corrupt bureaucracy is a rigid, over-centralised honest bureaucracy.[14] But Hu Angang's computations, and the evidence of the depth of corruption at the apex of government, business and finance, mean that any paradoxical usefulness has long since been surpassed. Corruption to this extent is chronically dysfunctional and even threatens the integrity of the state.

Is corruption endemic?

Lu Xiaobo, director of the East Asian Institute at Columbia University, takes the analysis even farther. In *Cadres and Corruption*, he argues that a post-revolutionary revolutionary party is trapped between its need to become a bureaucracy bound by rules, and its revolutionary purpose – to break rules and bureaucracies.[15] As judge and jury for its own cases, abjuring any external scrutiny, communism cannot easily police its own deviant party members. But that is not the only reason corruption is difficult to eradicate. The organisation itself is driven into deviance because, once the revolution is over, there is an unbridgeable inconsistency between revolutionary rhetoric and the compromises of non-revolutionary practice. The morality of revolution – that the ends justify the means – becomes a morality that justifies corruption. And when as many as 40 per cent of officials are not paid regularly they seek self-preservation in a morally ambiguous political climate. This reality, coupled with the growing opportunity for corruption, has characterised China's development. The deviant officials of the deviant party-state can prey on wealth with no ideological discomfort because of the ambiguity over where the state ends and private life begins.

Lu's argument is similar to my own. China has a well-developed concept of the state, but communism cannot permit the conception of an intermediate public domain between state and civil society. In this respect it is the faithful heir to the Confucian tradition of governance with systemic corruption. Absolute power, along with moral exhortation to its official class to refrain from plundering the people, is preferred to offering institutional, legal or ideological protection from the mendacious official. There is always a tendency towards corruption in authoritarian states; but, founded on the doctrines of communist revolution, officials are more powerful and more psychologically predisposed to corruption in a communist one-party state than in any other. I have argued in earlier articles[16] that corruption flourishes where social norms that might induce a sense of shame are weak, where there is a widespread belief that a high income results not from effort or merit but from effectively working the system and where there is a belief that corruption is victimless – crime involves someone else's money. In China all three inducements to corruption exist in spades. Add the peculiarities of communism and it is not difficult to understand why corruption is so dominant and so hard to root out.

James Kynge, a former Beijing bureau chief of the *Financial Times*, writes in *China Shakes the World* that in China 'trust is a commodity constantly under siege. Poverty and competition for scarce resources impinge upon it. The ideological vacuum that replaced communism undermines it. The daily diet of propaganda disorientates it. The venality of officials devalues it. The ascendancy of a value system dominated by money hollows it out. What is left is a society in which describing someone as "honest" can just as easily be a gentle criticism as a compliment.'[17]

The costs of this mistrustful, corrupt environment can be very high. Kynge describes a crooked blood bank scheme in Henan in the 1980s that was run with the full knowledge of corrupt local officials. Donors received blood back, minus its plasma, from a general blood pool that had been infected by HIV-positive blood. This scheme seems to have left as many as one hundred thousand children orphaned. Yet the enriched officials have arrested Aids activists, shut down orphanages and harassed journalists. In another scandal, officials allowed companies to sell fake and poisonous milk powder that caused disfigurement and even deaths; even though officials have been imprisoned, the product has reappeared on the market.[18]

Corruption is part of the system's DNA. Jiang and his successor Hu Jintao have thus been disabled, despite their rhetoric and their attempted actions. Legislative injunctions have to be implemented and policed by the very system which is corrupt and which disallows any external independent agencies because they would challenge the party's political hegemony. The party begins successive 'rectification' campaigns and inquiries, but these are compromised by the fact that the investigators are themselves corrupt and becoming more so. The climate of psychological warfare creates an atmosphere of fear and uncertainty: corrupt individuals demand even higher bribes because the risks are higher.[19]

Keeping control

The party's approach to the legal and judicial system is a further illustration of how the logic of its position deforms China's institutions.[20] The judicial apparatus is politicised from top to bottom. Every president and vice-president of a court is appointed by the party and as the courts are funded by provincial governments they are thus mindful of the need to keep their patrons sweet. The court bureaucracy works on the same basis as the rest of the government bureaucracy, with a party committee system superintending each rung of the court hierarchy. Judges often make decisions at the instruction of the committee or government independently of the legal merits of the case; according to one unnamed judge in Shandong, as much as 70 per cent of his caseload was influenced by directives from local government and Communist Party officials.[21] Many judges still have no formal legal training – the majority are retired army officers only too ready to do the party's bidding. Jiang Zemin's and Hu Jintao's attempts to professionalise the system and bring some objective legal principles into court judgements have made little progress; in any case the preferred route has been Confucian-style moral exhortation and top-down investigations rather than wholesale reform.

The scale of the exposed corruption is stunning. In 2003, 794 judges were tried for corruption (out of a national total of two hundred thousand). In 2003 and 2004 the presidents of the provincial high courts of Guangdong and Hunan were both found guilty of corruption.[22] Progress towards establishing the 'rule of law', despite official reaffirmation of the intention, is faltering.

When the party does not or cannot influence the judgement in a case it can use its influence over the police system to decide whether to slow down or not enforce the judgment. Enforcement rates in China are lamentable; for example, only 40 per cent of provincial high-court decisions are enforced.[23] Provinces are notoriously protectionist, insisting on cumbersome procedures for enforcement by courts outside their jurisdiction; the lack of a clear system of property rights, with the party-state claiming particular privileges, can make debt enforcement against state organisations close to impossible. The judicial system is an accomplice to the party, compromising the commitment to justice, but underwriting political hegemony. Interestingly, there is evidence that the Chinese themselves are increasingly disillusioned, as Minxin Pei of the Carnegie Endowment for International Peace argues.[24] Since the late 1990s the number of administrative litigation cases brought by Chinese citizens has decreased, which has been mirrored by a dramatic decrease in the success rate of litigation cases against the government to about 20 per cent. The Chinese are voting with their feet.

As Beijing has sought to control provincial parties and what it considers the strategic areas of the economy, it has also tried to control the plethora of national and local social organisations that have developed since 1978. Then, China had one hundred national and some six thousand local-level social organisations. Today there are over 1700 national social organisations, like the All-China Women's Federation and the China Charity Federation, and 140,000 local ones. It has more than 125,000 so-called private non-enterprise units so that altogether there are more than 250,000 non-governmental organisations.[25] Yet under the Regulations of the Registration and Management of Social Organisation introduced in 1998, every single one must have a government or party unit supervising its day-to-day operation.

This policy spills into rural China.[26] The obligation of villages to elect their leaders is portrayed by the party and some observers as a move toward democracy, but the process is managed so that in reality it tightens party control. The village councils from whom the candidates are drawn consist almost wholly of party members screened by the party; campaigning is not allowed, and ballots are less than secret. Party secretaries sit on village councils and are encouraged to put themselves up for village chairs, with the result that overwhelmingly the local party boss also becomes the village chair. Formal power is therefore vested in one person, the party representative now generally legitimised by a vote. It is true that peasants have developed a taste for voting, and that village chairs may find themselves torn between what the party wants and what their constituents want. But the party's intention is clear – to legitimise and intensify its control. Crucially, voting has not been extended to townships and cities.

Control extends to the media. China now has more than two thousand newspapers, two thousand television channels, nine thousand magazines and 450 radio stations, but they are all under the watchful eye of the party in Beijing or provincial propaganda departments. These authorities issue daily instructions on what may and may not be reported; journalists who digress will be suspended from working, or even imprisoned. China is estimated to have imprisoned forty-two journalists, the highest number in the world. Editors know roughly how much slack they have but recently, under Hu Jintao, there has been a tightening of the leash. The right to *yidi baodao* – to travel independently and report from a non-local city – had allowed more aggressive reporting of corruption, but it has been rescinded. Some prominent editors have been fired. For instance, Yang Bin, editor of China's most forceful tabloid, the *Beijing News*, was dismissed in December 2005 for reporting village protests against unfair confiscation of land. Other journalists have been prohibited from publishing.[27] The Committee to Protect Journalists, in its report of 2005 on repression of the media, quotes the government-run *People's Daily:* '[During 2004] censorship agencies permanently shut down 338 publications for printing "internal" information, closed 202 branch offices of newspapers and punished seventy-three organisations for illegally "engaging in news activities".'

Foreign broadcasters' plans for expansion have been frozen, and as much as $800 million has been spent on screening the Internet and blocking websites that contain prohibited words (including 'democracy') or stories (90 per cent of sites with the words 'Tiananmen massacre' were blocked).[28] The party has managed this not by owning media itself – it now funds only a couple of national newspapers, including the *People's Daily*, and one newspaper per province – but by exercising raw directional power. The party's instinct is to monopolise the flow of information, relenting only under extreme presssure. In early April 2003 the Chinese health authorities knew they were experiencing an epidemic of SARS, but the media faithfully parroted the line that there were only a few cases. The official response did not change until seventy-two-year-old doctor Jiang Yanyong contacted the foreign media, and the World Health Organization investigated. Two weeks later the Chinese government had fired the health minister and the mayor of Beijing, dramatically raised its estimate of deaths and started a nationwide campaign alerting the Chinese to the dangers – receiving universal praise for responding quickly![29] Emboldened by his success, Jiang Yanyong wrote to the National People's Congress suggesting that it was now time for Tiananmen to be re-evaluated – as I commented in Chapter 1, one of the most controversial claims in China. He was arrested and 're-educated', and has not made a public comment since.

The hope that after SARS China might take a more enlightened attitude to the reporting, at least of disease, has been dashed. China has fourteen billion poultry, one-fifth of the world's total, and is a potential centre of avian flu. But when in July 2005 the journal *Nature* published evidence from a Chinese laboratory that avian flu had spread from poultry to migratory birds the laboratory's work was stopped. Six Chinese journalists who wanted to cover the outbreak were detained and forbidden to continue reporting. Information about infectious disease is classified as a state secret; a journalist who reveals it is deemed to have committed treason – a crime for which the minimum penalty is re-education, and the maximum death.[30] More recently, following concerns over product safety and a spate of Chinese export recalls, an undercover journalist secretly filmed in July 2007 a restaurant making meatballs using chemically-treated cardboard; he was sentenced to one year in prison. Hu Jintao has appealed to reporters to follow the precepts of 'Marxist journalism' in the run-up to the 2008 Beijing Olympics. This approach is attracting criticism, and the tremors have reached the West. In February 2006 three of China's most distinguished elders – Li Rui, a former aide to Mao Zedong, Hu Jiwei, former editor of the *People's Daily*, and Zhu Houze, a former party propaganda chief – published a letter condemning the approach: 'History demonstrates that only a totalitarian system needs news censorship, out of the delusion that it can keep the public locked in ignorance,' they wrote. Far from ensuring stability, they continued, such media repression would 'sow the seeds of disaster'.[31]

The desire to control and direct extends across all the structures of the state. Since 1998 the party has tried simultaneously to remodel, rationalise and streamline the state. The purpose is only partly to save money. In the main, the party wants to equip the state with structures better suited to regulate and monitor those parts of China's economy, which it no longer directly owns or plans. The giant Soviet ministries, each responsible for an industry, have been abolished and their functions divided. Ownership and direction are now delivered by the State-owned Assets Supervision and Administration Commission (SASAC), and a new network of generic regulatory agencies has been created to superintend areas such as environmental protection, intellectual property rights and workplace safety. Between 1998 and 2002 staff in central, provincial and municipal government have been halved, reflecting the new emphasis on light-touch setting of strategic targets and regulation rather than detailed, daily, hands-on management.

Thus Hu Jintao now presides over a state that is better organised, more centralised and better funded than the China of 1993, which was on the point of disintegration. To the extent that bureaucratic centralisation can solve the China dilemma it has been partly achieved. Economic management is focused in the Ministry of Finance, the People's Bank of China, the streamlined State Development and Reform Commission (significantly, 'planning' was dropped from its title) and SASAC. The party in Beijing is in better control of its provincial branches and governments, runs the judicial system and closely superintends the media and the millions of social organisations. With its direction of police, military and security services its monopoly of state power is complete. It even, as I was completing the first edition of this book in July 2006, had required private companies to establish their own internal Communist Party committees as state-owned enterprises are obliged.

Ideological quicksands

Yet despite budgetary discipline and the more streamlined state structures, the Chinese political system remains haunted by the ambiguities of communism becoming a post-revolutionary party running a post-revolutionary society and an economy in transition to a form of capitalism. The quest is for legitimacy – in Jiang's words, maintaining 'flesh and blood ties with the people' – and for continuing to justify communist one-party rule. The Chinese state is not the first among a network of equal public institutions through which, along with competitive elections, civil society could hold it and the Communist Party to account. It is the Leviathan; at once the executive, legislative and judicial arms of government; policy-maker, law-maker and implementer; and judge and jury for all its own actions. Even in 2007 the excuse for this is that the party is the sole legitimate trustee for the victory of the Chinese masses in the revolution of 1949. The rationale is a simple Marxist syllogism: Chinese socialist democracy is a democracy of the masses won in the revolution; the Communist Party, as the champion of the masses, thus democratically controls the state alone to further their interests; and those interests are to build socialism around the canonical thought of Marx, Lenin and Mao Zedong.

When Deng began his reform programme he insisted that he was conforming to what he described as the four cardinal principles of communism: socialist democracy; the Communist Party state; building socialism; and conformity with Marxist–Leninist–Maoist thought. As reform progressed, it became ever more of an ideological stretch to describe how what was happening in reality conformed to the four principles. Socialism was attenuated to include the idea of the socialist market, with every new accommodation justified by Mao's pragmatic insistence that practice had to be the judge of theory. It took all of Deng's prestige to get away with it.

By 2000, as China headed towards full membership in the World Trade Organization, thus accepting by treaty that private business was an important component of the future, the party could no longer pretend that it was implementing the four principles as they might have been conceived in 1978, let alone in 1949. There would have to be an ideological overhaul, not least because by 2001 some one hundred thousand private business-people had joined the party. It could no longer claim that its reason for being was only to represent the worker and peasant masses. On the other hand, it would somehow have to stay in touch with the four principles; otherwise, the line of legitimacy leading back to 1949 would be lost.

Jiang Zemin's answer – his last legacy – was the consolidation in the constitution of the 'three represents' in November 2002 (see Chapter 1). In effect, the party declared ideologically that it intends to represent all China, not just the worker and peasant masses, as a kind of national party, while unashamedly creating a variant of a market economy. As a short-term political necessity the 'three represents' were critical modifications. They have allowed the party unapologetically to recruit the once-hated capitalists as members, and to confirm the direction of economic reform. A twenty-first-century variant of the old Confucian gentry is being recreated, but now reinvented as a class of communist officials, managers of SOEs and private businesspeople who are members of the party whose interests, like those of the Confucian gentry, are bound up with those of the centralised state and who are clearly seen as a crucial pillar of communist support. There are some six million owners of private firms in China; about two-thirds are former state officials.[32] In the other direction, about one-fifth of registered entrepreneurs have now become party members – one survey reported a proportion as high as 30 per cent, about six times the percentage in the population at large.[33] According to an author-itative survey of private businesspeople who were not members, one-fourth said they wanted to join, and half of those had already applied.[34] In other words, the party is inventing a new class of former officials and party members who are running private busi-nesses but who depend on the party and state networks for work, and who understand and benefit from the new ideology. The new Communist Party committees in private business complete the picture. The evidence is all around. In the National People's

Congress (NPC), workers' and peasants' representation declined from 27 per cent and 21 per cent respectively in the early 1980s to 11 per cent and 8 per cent in the late 1990s.[35] As reform deepens, the bedrock of communist rule is changing. Communist interests are increasingly intertwined with business on the Asian model; and the communists' roots in the villages and farms are dwindling.

The 'three represents', like economic reform, are a form of groping for stones to cross a treacherous ideological river. But whatever short-term relief the concept has brought, in the longer term it has created a dilemma of legitimacy. The justification for one-party rule is that communism represents the democracy of the masses who have won a class war against capitalists and land-lords. Thereafter socialism, involving collective ownership and planning, is to be constructed by the party-state embodying the democratic collective – and justified because the masses are the fountainhead of wealth. But if the party is representing the 'broad masses', and in its repudiation of class war is de facto recognising that wealth comes from capitalists as much as from workers and peasants, it is not building collective socialism and has smashed the coherence of its own ideology. It has no intellectual or ideo-logical defence against those who argue that there should be more formal pluralist political representation and more plural public institutions. In these new circumstances, why not? After all, the former general secretary of the party, Zhao Ziyang, had openly called for such a development at the Thirteenth Party Congress in 1987. 'Different people have different interests and views,' Zhao said, 'they need opportunities for the exchange of views.'[36] The argument is much more powerful today.

Without institutionalised channels to manage tension, there is growing restlessness, and even conflict, as people begin to take matters into their own hands. Since 1978 there has been mount-ing turbulence underneath apparent conformity. For example, during Tiananmen one-third of the leaders of the National People's Congress, supposedly a rubber stamp, signed a motion asking its Standing Committee to oppose martial law. Throughout the 1990s the party has consistently failed to get its preferred slate of candidates through the provincial elections for the NPC. At the village level, there are vigorous protests when town or provincial officials impose unfair taxes or do not compensate owners properly for land purchased for development. The number of protests is rising sharply within the workplace and beyond. But so is the number of illegal land seizures against which to protest.[37] In November 2003 the Ministry of Land and Resources reported more than 168,000 cases of illegal land seizure, twice as many as in all of 2002. In 2003 2 per cent of China's total farmland was lost to development, and the pace of loss has been accelerating.[38]

Criticism is levelled against corrupt village, county and provincial governments that have allowed peasants to be fleeced. The more one interacts with government, the more disillusioned one tends to be. To date, distant Beijing has been understood to want to make the system fairer, and it escapes the general censure. Beijing is where citizens go for redress. The *Washington Post* reports one party scholar saying that the number seeking redress has doubled in recent years.[39] But this raises expectations that will not be met; the inevitable disappointment will leave the people feeling that there is no arbiter on their behalf.

In 1989 Deng Xiaoping could rely on his reputation as a revolutionary hero, the respect of the army and the standing of the Committee of Elders to drive through the repression of the Tiananmen protesters, the imposition of martial law and the dismissal of Zhao Ziyang. Otherwise, he would have been unable to override the army's uncertainty about firing on Chinese citizens and carry out the repression. Hu Jintao is working hard to build up similar relationships, appointing children of the revolutionary leadership to key positions in the PLA and strictly enforcing to the letter China's tight censorship of the media. But Hu did not fight in the 1940s for the revolution, and so he cannot command the same prestige as Deng. The next generation of leaders will be even more distant from the revolution.

Similarly, communist doctrines are incomparably weaker after nearly twenty years of economic reform driven by concepts mostly overtly hostile to state ownership and planning. Although the *Falun Gong* is regarded in the West as a harmless creed that should not be persecuted, its attraction and threat must not be under-estimated. It is seen by both the party and many of its own adherents as offering an idealism that the party lacks; as one indicator, even the former director of the 301st Army Hospital in Beijing has been advising cadre members to join.[40] If the weaknesses of the system ever threatened economic growth, with consequential large-scale protests about its legitimacy, there can be no certainty that the apparatus of state and army – used only reluctantly in 1989 – could be applied with the same force again.

All this weakens the state's capacity. In the World Bank's listing of 199 strong and weak states China was ranked very low. In 2002, it was number 186 on voice and accountability, 116 on regulatory quality, 111 on control of corruption and ninety-four on rule of law. Only in governmental effectiveness did it score modestly well, ranking seventy-first.[41] And on all measures the trend has been downward since 1998, and, except for regulatory quality and a fractional improvement in rule of law, has slipped further in the 2006 rankings. The party is keenly aware of the collapse in idealism, the inability to make communism live as an ideology and the consequences for the state. In 2002, 80 per cent of the cadre members polled at Beijing's Central Party School (whose graduates are destined to become members of the Chinese elite, rather like graduates of Harvard, Oxbridge and the École Nationale d'Administration) declared that lack of progress in political reform was the most important constraint on China's development. Other polls at the school consistently confirm this result. The viewpoint of Zhao Ziyang lives on, and occasionally bubbles up into public view. Li Rui, whose letter I cited earlier, spoke out at the Sixteenth Congress in November 2002: 'Chinese and foreign histories prove that autocracy is the source of political turmoil. As the collapse of the Soviet Union shows, the root cause is autocracy. Modernisation is possible only through democratisation. This is the trend in the world in the twentieth century, especially since the Second World War. Those who follow this trend will thrive; those who fight against this trend will perish. This rule applies to every country – and every party.'[42]

The Central Committee is familiar with both the unease and the debate. In 2004 it acknowledged that reform had reached a critical stage and that the party's 'ruling status will not last for ever if the party does nothing to safeguard it'.[43] Meanwhile Hu Jintao himself has reasserted that the party 'takes a dominant role and coordinates all sectors. Party members and party organisations in government departments should be brought into full play – so as to realise the party's leadership over state affairs.'[44] In other words, Jiang's formula for strengthening the party and its control over the party-state is to be applied with redoubled zeal as a response to the new complexity and diversity of China and, deploying the 'three represents', the party's legitimacy in claiming sole rule is unchanged. In 2005 the party issued a 'white paper on democracy' making this claim explicit – but the very fact that the party chose to write such a paper, and that it was so intellectually barren, shows how precarious the ideological halfway house has become. Yet the party needs some justification for its control, whether of village elections or the media. All that stands between it and its own demise is its capacity to deliver economic growth and its control of the army and police. These are thin reeds on which to build long-term hegemony, especially as the economy is beset by the same weaknesses of the halfway house as the polity.

6

The Economic Impossibility of the Halfway House

The emergence of China as a $2-trillion economy from such inauspicious beginnings only twenty-five years ago is such a giddy accomplishment that even the best can suspend their better judgement. The consensus is that China proves conclusively that liberalisation, privatisation, market freedoms and the embrace of globalisation are the only route to prosperity. For example, Martin Wolf, chief economic commentator for the *Financial Times*, writes in his book *Why Globalisation Works* that China is successful because it is the biggest liberaliser, and 'all else is commentary'.[1] China has made the transition from a planned economy to a more market-based economy, has joined the World Trade Organization and is so obviously successful that the magic ingredient must be its commitment to markets, the profit motive and private property. Its intention to continue in the same vein is also obvious. Intellectuals, analysts and diplomats, therefore, should discard their reservations about why China has achieved all this, discard any concerns about its future and recognise it as a full market economy as soon as possible.

The reality is more complex. If you doubt that, consider Hu Jintao's remarks at the end of Chapter 5. This is an economy and society over which the party seeks and so far has maintained extensive direct and indirect control despite a broad liberalisation of prices, a rollback of planning, a boom in foreign direct investment and the granting of substantial autonomy to all forms of enterprise. Both the OECD and World Bank, in their recent reports on China, tread a fine line between acknowledging its impressive transition and expressing serious concern about how much more still has to be done before China becomes a full market economy. The World Bank is particularly hard-hitting.

For the party's approach to the economy has reflected its approach to the political system. The streamlining of government structures discussed in Chapter 5, a process that involved halving the workforce, has been reproduced in SOEs. The number of SOEs has been halved, from three hundred thousand in 1995 to 150,000 in 2005,[2] in pursuit of 'holding on to the big while letting go of the small'. This is a dramatic transformation that seems to point in the direction of privatisation and a reduction in the SOEs' share of GDP. But the SOEs' share of value-added has fallen scarcely at all. About 10 per cent have gone bankrupt, and there have been mergers, leasing deals, management buyouts and reorganisations as 'shareholding companies'.[3] In almost every such case the resulting shareholding structure of the 'let-go' SOEs has been carefully devised, as I wrote in Chapter 4, to maintain the state's controlling interest. Moreover, in an economy where the only effective source of external capital is bank finance and where only 25 per cent of the shares of banks can be owned by non-state shareholders, there are further limits on the ability of even 'let-go' small SOEs to operate outside the boundaries set by the party-state.

The party is performing a balancing act. It knows that as a

general rule the more autonomy an enterprise possesses the greater its productivity; and it knows that China's success as an exporter has been built on the technological, branding and distribution networks of foreign multinationals whose expertise and skills China will need to reproduce in order to be a global player. Indeed, the party has repeatedly reaffirmed its ambition to build as many as fifty globally competitive enterprises by 2010.[4] Ever since the amendment to the constitution favouring business in 1999 and Jiang Zemin's 'three represents' of 2002, the atmosphere favouring the private sector has been improving. But only to the extent the party still retains control. China is half-pregnant; and that is the way the party intends to keep it.[5]

Leninist corporatisation

China's approach to creating firms owned and backed by shareholders – the heart of any concept of capitalism – exemplifies the primacy of political control over private ownership. The 'Standard Opinion' delivered in 1992, notwithstanding subsequent Company Acts, remains the foundation document for the formation of companies. It is wholly concerned with how SOEs are transmuted into corporations; there is no detailed provision for a private company to issue tradable shares. It establishes four essential classes of shares: (1) state shares owned by the state or its agencies; (2) 'legal person' shares owned by state-authorised social groups, enterprises or institutions; (3) individual shares owned by Chinese investors or employees; (4) foreign shares owned by foreigners up to an aggregate maximum of $10 billion (raised from $4 billion in 2005). How these shares are traded, and to what assets and profits respective classes of shareowners are entitled, are closely regulated. Until the end of 2006 the 63 per cent of shares owned directly by the state (state and legal person shares) could not even be bought and sold on the stock market, but a new rule allows them to be traded from the beginning of 2007, as long as the buyer is another state or legal person. Only individual 'A' shares can be freely traded by Chinese public investors within China; in addition, this is the only class of share which investors can build up as strategic stakes, and then only on the promise they hold the shares themselves for three years. Equally, foreign-held 'special' and 'B' shares can be transferred only if the buyer meets state provisions: H and N foreign-held shares are more freely tradable: some sixty Chinese enterprises, for example, have issued H shares that are actively traded in Hong Kong.[6]

The relaxation of trading rules, however, has been carefully organised to ensure that the state retains effective control – guaranteed by the way the way state and legal person shareholders are the only permissible owners of fixed assets. China's unique accounting structure requires different and discrete funds for fixed, current and special assets. Foreign shareholders are not entitled to ownership of any of the fixed assets, and individual shareholders have only a limited entitlement. Fixed assets, in effect, are to be owned only by state and legal person shareholders. As a result, share valuations on the stock market have depended on the transactions between A, B and H shareholders who have the same claims on the current profits and cash (but at the discretion of majority state and legal person shareholders) but no claim or only a limited claim on the companies' fixed assets. In any case, non-state shareholders constitute a majority of the shareholding, as we shall see, in only a tiny fraction of China's listed firms. Moreover, only half of China's listed companies have ever paid dividends. Thus it is easy to understand the persistent weakness of the Shenzhen and Shanghai stock markets as allocators and providers of capital and to understand perennially ailing share prices; between 2001 and 2005 share prices halved as disillusioned investors shunned the rigged markets despite the booming economy.[7] The trebling of prices over the subsequent two years has not been because of a change in the underlying dynamics; rather it is a direct consequence of the unsustainable build-up of liquidity within the Chinese financial system. It is part of a generalised asset price bubble driven by gambling (there are now over 100 million retail accounts opened to trade in shares) and easy money, with the valuation of Chinese shares carried to absurd levels. This will, however, be a source of future destabilisation. The brute reality, despite the reforms and the 2006–7 boom, is that the Chinese stock market is the creature of the state.

The point of the exercise has been to retain control of the former SOEs now listed on the stock market, while giving them more managerial autonomy and some capacity to raise new capital. The World Bank cites a study of 1105 listed Chinese enterprises in 2001, in which at first sight it seemed that the state had relinquished control of more than 90 per cent. However, once the labyrinth of the share structure had been unravelled the opposite was the case: the state had de facto control of 84 per cent of the listed companies. In 2005 it still retained control of 81 per cent.[8] There is evidence that some holders of legal person shares, notably provincial governments, are becoming frustrated by the lack of dividends and selling to de facto private interests. If so, surrogate private ownership may be higher than a straightforward reading of the numbers suggests. Nonetheless, after more than a decade of stock market development this $2-trillion economy has succeeded in creating fewer than two hundred genuine private companies, according to the economists Guy Liu and Pei Sun, who conducted the study reported by the World Bank.[9] Whatever else this may mean, it is hardly a triumph of privatisation. Martin Wolf may be right about the direction of travel, but is it 'commentary' to imagine that this is happening any faster than at a snail's pace – or that the party has any other end in mind than retaining its own control?

The process should more correctly be described as 'corporatisation', and it sharply redefines the manner in which the Chinese economy should be conceptualised. In collaboration with China's National Bureau of Statistics, the OECD carefully analysed the

2003 survey of 180,000 industrial firms with turnovers in excess of five million renminbi ($600,000), which together make up 35 per cent of Chinese GDP. Of these, 47.7 per cent were state-owned or collectively controlled, only 13.3 per cent were unambiguously private and 12 per cent were foreign-owned companies. The OECD generously identifies the balance of 27 per cent as privately controlled. For example, it counts legal person shares as non-state and de facto private, although this is factually and legally incorrect, and it interprets majority control by foreign investors of most joint ventures as meaning that the private sector controls the venture, though this too is unrealistic. Two-thirds of new foreign direct investment is now done as a wholly owned foreign enterprise (WOFE) because foreign investors are not prepared to have a contracting relationship with a minority Chinese partner who provides little of the capital but exerts de facto, and frequently counterproductive, control. It is doubtful that more than one-third of the 27 per cent the OECD deems as privately controlled would stand up to such a definition under close scrutiny. More probably, about two-thirds of China's largest 180,000 enterprises are de facto state-controlled. This conclusion is broadly in line with the results of the study by the World Bank of listed companies cited above.

China's approach to private ownership means that attempting to assess how much of China is public and how much private is a fool's errand because it cannot capture how the party is trying to develop Leninist corporatism. The party-state is at the centre of a spider's web of control. Political direction is matched by direct control of those parts of the economy that the party considers strategic – telecommunications, energy, transport, iron, steel and metal production, automobiles, etc. To build an international presence it is encouraging the creation of fifty-seven 'business groups' as strategic 'pillars' of the Chinese economy – a Chinese version of South Korean *chaebol* or Japanese *keiretsu*. Each group has its own house bank. The two largest groups are in petrochemicals

(Donglian and Qilu Petrochemical Groups), and the third largest is steel (Baosteel). The party exerts direct control over the strategic groups. The less strategic the party considers a sector or enterprise, the more it is prepared to loosen its control; but the shareholder and accounting structure is such that at any time the party can regain control if it is necessary. The genuine private sector has been growing and is the most dynamic part of the economy with the highest productivity, but in the party-state every private company exists under sufferance. As noted earlier, state-owned banks control the flow of credit; every entrepreneur knows that this flow can be turned off if he (or the occasional she) does not fulfil the party's wishes – and now each will have an enterprise-based Communist Party committee on top.

The spider's web

The evidence of the spider's web of control is all around. This control is locking China into a low-productivity, low-innovation economy with a disproportionate number of small-scale enterprises that do not and cannot make the commercial weather. In the World Economic Forum's Business Competitiveness Index of 116 countries, China has slid from forty-second when it was first launched in 1998 to sixty-fourth in 2006. Not only is China's absolute performance worse than that of other middle-income developing countries like Brazil and India, but is also deteriorating faster.[10]

Broadly, the more politicised a Chinese enterprise is, the lower its productivity and performance. The performance of China's SOEs, which control two-thirds of industrial assets, has been lamentable, only improving slowly during twenty years of reform. One in three of their workforces is estimated to be structurally idle.[11] Revenues are heavily skewed to the top ten; the bulk of the rest are on a financial cliff-edge and are barely profitable. According to one influential estimate, even the tiniest upward movement in interest rates or the slightest decline in sales would mean that between 40 and 60 per cent of their enormous bank debts would not be serviced, rendering the entire Chinese banking system bankrupt.[12] They are overdiversified and unfocused. They spend a trivial proportion of their sales revenue on research and development. Their labour productivity, on average, is 4 per cent of that of the United States. Three-quarters of SOEs employ fewer than five hundred people.[13] They are commercial and business disaster areas.

The drive to corporatise and consolidate SOEs was meant to address these problems and to reduce the financial drain on the state. The problem is that, organisationally and culturally, even after reform they are not structured to be as efficient as companies in the Western national market economies of thirty or forty years ago, let alone companies in today's fast-moving conditions. SOEs were conceived as self-sufficient industrial communes that would provide workers and families with an 'iron rice bowl' of support from cradle to grave – nurseries, schools, housing, doctors and pensions. In many parts of China SOEs remain the sole reliable source of welfare. The huge lay-offs of the past five years – involving more than sixteen million workers – were politically possible only because in some cities and provinces there is now a rudimentary system of social insurance, even if it extends to only one-third of most urban dwellers and about 3 per cent of migrant workers.[14] The many provinces and cities with no social insurance system go to any lengths to sustain SOE employment in order to avert widespread social unrest. Better to have a basket-case SOE subsidised with state bank credits that employs people and provides their families with welfare than no employer at all.

And the party has the means. State, provincial and municipal governments own state shares and direct legal person shares, and every SOE has a Communist Party committee to ensure that it does the party's bidding. The system is used ruthlessly, despite the recent moves towards corporatisation. The vast majority of

SOEs that have been restructured into shareholding corporations retain their party committees. According to Minxin Pei, the same person is both party secretary and chair in about half of the firms, and in more than 70 per cent of restructured SOEs party committee members have joined the board of directors.[15] Moreover, the State-owned Assets Supervision and Administration Commission, which runs the 196 largest SOEs in conjunction with the party's organisation department, decides who will manage which SOE. The SOEs' supervisory boards do not make this decision. In the recent past the CEOs of China Telecom, Netcom, Mobile and Unicom were arbitrarily swapped around because the party was concerned that the companies were becoming too competitive and wanted to encourage a more collaborative culture.[16]

This is not unusual. Edward Steinfeld provides case studies of the politicisation of decision making in three steel-industry SOEs in his extraordinary book *Forging Reform in China*.[17] Enron famously made profits by inventing sales; similarly, Chinese SOEs invent sales by lending credit to buyers – in effect, the company is borrowing to purchase its sales. One company, Magang Steel, was floated on the Hong Kong stock market but the party still controlled the company through its shareholdings and the party committee. Magang, after its listing, simply bought sales in the time-honoured way, expecting its parent holding company to lend it the wherewithal but, of course, not paying the parent any dividends or interest in return. Twelve months later the holding company went bust and had to be bailed out with bank loans. This is a system not of wealth creation but of wealth destruction.

Productivity is 40 to 70 per cent higher for enterprises controlled only indirectly by the state and for town and village enterprises (TVEs) and for private companies, where control is more distant from the party, productivity is more than twice as high.[18] Problematically, SOEs have to fund the infrastructure of welfare for their employees; the statistics make a partial adjustment for this. More crucially, once an enterprise under any ownership reaches a reasonable scale it is inevitably drawn into a universe where business judgements are compromised by political direction. The TVEs and private companies have higher productivity because they are small, but their size means that their contribution to economy-wide innovation is also small.

A private sector like no other

Bureaucrats and party officials make the decisions not only for the medium- and large-scale SOEs they control directly, but also for large private companies. Davin Mackenzie, managing director of Peak Capital, which is based in Beijing, says that almost no private company, however well run, wants to leave the opaque, informal world of *guanxi* personal relationships in which the main aim is to hide revenue, cash and profits from outsiders' eyes and from potential political direction.[19] Only 1 per cent of private Chinese companies subject themselves to independent audit, he claims, and only then because they want a listing. The vast majority focus on staying below the radar, under-reporting their sales and over-invoicing abroad to keep money overseas or simply, as he puts it, running even large companies from the 'cash box in the back of the Mercedes'. Most Chinese companies have three sets of accounts – one for the banks, one for the tax authorities and one for the management. Outsiders can never believe what they are told, so banks lend only on the basis of hard collateral. Most private firms do not last long; the average duration is about three years. The law of the jungle prevails: you do what you can get away with. China is the counterfeiter's paradise, where intellectual property rights are neither respected nor enforced. Between 15 and 20 per cent of all well-known brands in China are fake; two-thirds of the imports confiscated by United States customs as fakes were made in China. Counterfeiting is estimated to represent 8 per cent of GDP – eloquent testimony to Chinese business strategies and the ineffectiveness of the Chinese legal system.

Inevitably, the private sector devotes much of its strategy to currying favour with the party and key officials who, as we have seen, are only too willing to trade privileges for bribes. Private companies cannot stand aside from the politicisation and corruption, and have no choice but to do official bidding, even when it is financially and strategically ludicrous. In one famous case, a provincial government twisted the arm of Sichuan Changhong Electric and forced it to sell television sets to a financially suspect distribution company in California. The transaction cost Sichuan Changhong $500 million.

Another case involved the downfall of China's leading refrigerator manufacturer, Kelon Electrical Holdings. By the late 1990s its flair for design and production had carried it from its beginnings as a TVE in Guangdong to $1 billion in turnover, giving the appearance of partial privatisation with H shares quoted in Hong Kong and A shares quoted in Shenzhen. Today it has ceased production after charges of embezzlement and rigging its balance sheet. Despite its share quotes and entrepreneurship, de facto control remained with the Guangdong authorities, who, in the late 1990s, forced it to buy an SOE manufacturer of air conditioners that was operating at a loss. The only way, it seems, that Kelon could manage the shotgun marriage and keep its head financially above water was to manipulate its accounts within China's cavalier financial and political environment. But the Bank of China, smelling a rat, froze new lending in 2004. By August 2005 the end had come for Kelon.[20] An inadequate soft public infrastructure of auditing, banking and corporate governance had interacted with the dynamics of Leninist corporatism and de facto state control; the result was the company's downfall.

Kelon is but one of many examples; the risks extend even to China's showcase companies. Haier, based in the coastal city of Qingdao, is one of China's leading white-goods firms. The government delegated management to Zhang Ruimin at the beginning of the reform process and he has now built Haier into a $5-billion multinational business, with H shares in Hong Kong and operations in more than twenty countries. Zhang, one of China's favoured businessmen, is the most influential private entrepreneur to have joined the Central Committee. But even he could not prevent SASAC from ruling in 2004 that, despite everything, apparently including significant shareholding by its employees, this former SOE remained controlled by the state. Like Kelon, it once had to take over a company that was making a loss – in this case a drug business – but so far that has not brought Haier down and Zhang has used his influence to resist other forced marriages. The question remains how much longer it will be before Haier, too, succumbs to the same endemic weaknesses. The economist Yasheng Huang of MIT is quoted by *The Economist*: 'Government shareholders may be passive at first, but once a company succeeds, they interfere. Countless Chinese firms have been driven to bankruptcy or failed to grow big because local governments decided to exercise their legal claims on ownership.'[21]

The Chinese companies that can focus on their business undistracted are those whose majority ownership is in the private sector. Huawei is a privately owned multinational that is emerging as a fast-growing manufacturer of wireless equipment and software with a strong commitment to R & D. But even it is not free from the long arm of the party-state. It operates with a $10-billion line of credit from the China Development Bank; has close links with the People's Liberation Army; and, to win business in China's protected telecoms markets, it is reported to have given controlling shares to the provincial telecoms companies with which it trades.[22] But without transparency, nobody knows where de facto control resides. So far the combination of committed long-term bank finance, visionary leadership and a passion for technology has brought it prosperity, and Huawei is one of the main beneficiaries of China's boom in mobile phones. But George Gilboy of MIT, a long-time senior executive in Beijing, details how political interference has profoundly damaged a successful rival, Julong Technologies.[23] The same fate could lie in wait for Huawei.

China does not have a dense network of research-oriented, innovative companies, so it cannot afford to be this careless of the examples it does have. Gilboy contrasts China's meagre effort to import technology into its production with the experience of the South Koreans and the Japanese. When they were trying to catch up with the West in the 1970s and 1980s they spent two or three times the cost of imported high-tech equipment in buying the licences and training key staff members in order to 'indigenise' the technology. Today Chinese industrial groups spend less than 10 per cent of the value of imported high-tech goods on technological 'indigenisation'.

Companies' innovation is focused on lowering costs. Edward Steinfeld reports on the World Bank Survey of 2001, in which a mere 7 per cent of 1500 Chinese high-tech enterprises declared that they provided customers with R & D, and only 15 per cent designed parts for overseas customers.[24] The rest broadly manufactured products to specifications, designs or licences set by foreigners, and mostly sold them to customers within their own cities. Their average size was just over six hundred employees. These responses eloquently captured the provincialism, technological dependence and emphasis on competing at low costs that define much Chinese private enterprise.[25] Another study[26] reports that localism is, if anything, rising; 72 per cent of goods consumed in any Chinese province tend to be produced within that province, and the proportion has recently risen. Sandra Poncet, the author of that study, remarks: 'Barriers to trade between Chinese provinces appear to be closer in magnitude to that on international trade than that on trade flow within a single country. Chinese domestic market integration is low . . . This evolution underlines the failure of reforms to promote domestic market integration and the growing division of the Chinese domestic market into cellular submarkets.'[27]

I have met one of the officials in Guangzhou who is trying to create a single market on the scale of the European Union in China's nine southern provinces plus Macao and Hong Kong (the so-called 'nine plus two'). Intriguingly the differences between provinces are so great that the obstacles to harmonisation rival those of the European Union: the talks are hopelessly bogged down. As long as the state sector continues to loom large and provincial authorities feel compelled to shelter it from competition, there is little prospect of any change.

No less inevitably China's R & D is led by the Leninist state. Two-thirds of China's eight hundred thousand research scientists and researchers work in government laboratories, a trend that is likely to intensify with the adoption of about ten to twenty 'megaprojects' of up to $1 billion each under China's National Middle to Long Term Plan (MLP). When China spends heavily it tends to get results, whether in stem cells or underwater robots, and is rapidly rising up the science citation index. But two leading Chinese scientists – Yi Rao, who is co-director of the Shanghai Institute for Advanced Studies and a professor at Washington University, and Bai Lu, who gives scientific advice to the Ministry of Science and Technology of China and is a senior investigator at the National Institutes of Health – have complained publicly that politics, as everywhere in China, looms too large. They characterise Chinese research as 'rule-by-man' rather than 'rule-by-merit'.[28] Top-down research determined by the Ministry of Science and Technology is wasteful, does not engage researchers' hearts and minds and does not foster the serendipity and creativity of great science. Less state direction here, as in enterprise more generally, would unbottle a great upsurge of energy.

In the West Chinese science and technology are portrayed as a juggernaut that will sweep all before them. The headlines about China's research effort are well known: China spent $30 billion on R & D in 2005 at current exchange rates to make it the sixth biggest spender in the world; the ratio of R & D spend to GDP doubled in a decade to 1.3 per cent in 2005; the country ranks only behind the United States in total numbers of researchers; and the number of patents lodged at the World Intellectual Property Organisation is doubling every two years. It would seem a formidable and challenging litany of achievement.

It masks the reality. On patents, for example, the OECD has developed a measure to assess the internationality and thus originality of an invention, avoiding the home bias in applying for patents, by identifying whether a patent is part of a 'patent family' registered in Europe, Japan and the United States. In 2003 the United States held 36.4 per cent of such triadic patent families, Europe 30.3 per cent and Japan 25.7 per cent. China held a meagre 0.3 per cent. The problem, as identified by Yi Rao and Bai Lu and supported by a 2007 OECD study which argued that 'a high technology myopia' pervades the Chinese R & D effort, is that China spends too much on experimental development and too little on basic research – and in any case the whole exercise is systemically weak. Comparisons with India make salutary reading. From 1981 to 1995 China had 537 scientists and engineers in R & D per 1 million, compared with India's 151. China also led India in personal computers three to one and in Internet usage by four to one. Yet in 2001 India produced one-fourth more software, of which three-quarters was exported – despite having a much smaller economy than China's. Not only did China produce less software, but less than 10 per cent was exported, so, despite massive investment, it trailed far behind India.[29] The missing link is the soft institutional infrastructure.

China's problems all stem from this incapacity to let the puppet enterprises off the puppeteers' strings and provide them with the institutional network that would permit more creative pluralism and endogenous accountability. The lack of such a network is also the chief cause of China's environmental crisis.[30] The pace of desertification has doubled over twenty years, in a country where 25 per cent of the land area is already desert.[31] Air pollution kills four hundred thousand people a year prematurely.[32] Energy is habitually wasted.

But the worst problem is water. One-fifth of China's 660 cities face extreme water shortages and as many as 90 per cent have problems of water pollution; 53 per cent of the water in major waterways is unfit for human consumption.[33] As a result, 500 million rural Chinese still do not have access to safe drinking water. Illegal and rampant polluting, a severe shortage of sewage treatment facilities and chemical pollutants continue to degrade China's waterways. In the autumn of 2005 two major cities – Harbin and Guangzhou – had their water supplies cut off for days because their river sources had acute chemical spills and leakages from SOE plants.

Enterprises are accountable to no one but the Communist Party for their actions; there is no network of civil society, plural public institutions like a free press or representative government and property rights to create pressure for enterprises to become more environmentally efficient. Pollution, unless it exists in an international city or a coastal region trying to attract foreign investors, is in effect cost-free; to constrain it would slow down development. Local officials, as Elizabeth Economy describes, want and need growth; enterprise does their bidding; and environmental degradation keeps costs down. But the wider costs are huge: on some estimates ranging up to 12 per cent of GDP.[34] Indeed, it is the same constraint-free commitment to economic growth by provincial local officials, who will suffer no consequence for over-investment and only benefit, that contributed to the severe overheating of the economy in 2006. China's environmental crisis, like this crisis in its enterprise and legal systems, is an outgrowth of Leninist corporatism.

So if it's so bad, how come it's so good?

In the face of all these problems, how has China managed to grow so fast? The World Bank provides the answers. It estimates that between 1990 and 1998 China's high rate of investment added 6.4

per cent to the annual growth rate; migration of workers from rural areas has added around 2.1 per cent. The increase in the labour force brought the growth rate up to 9 per cent. The proportional contributions to growth were very similar in the 1980s. As the World Bank remarks dryly, China is gaining relatively little benefit from technological progress by its urban enterprises. They add a mere 0.5 per cent to the growth rate – almost nothing.[35] To put it another way, China's growth is pretty much guaranteed by state-driven capital accumulation in the cities financed by state-owned banks using China's vast pool of savings, together with migration from the land. The answer is as simple as that.

At the end of 2005, after a generation of aggressive lending, bank lending stood at 130 per cent of GDP and bank deposits some 200 per cent of GDP – among the highest in the world. The debt is almost entirely lent by state-owned banks, and the four state-owned commercial banks account for half of it. Nearly all the lending is to support industrial activity. Two-thirds of all lending is focused on SOEs, which raise virtually all their required external finance from the banks.

To put it bluntly, the banking system is the essential and indispensable tool of the Leninist party-state.[36] Some argue that since the late 1990s there has been a significant rise in corporate profitability and thus saving as being apparently evident in China's national accounts – a view associated for example with the World Bank – and that as a result the role of banks is becoming less significant. This is wishful thinking that dangerously misunderstands the nature of the Chinese economic model, conflating flows of cash with saving. As Weijian Shan, managing partner of Newbridge Capital in Hong King argues, if these claims were true there would be a decline in the amount of debt held by companies, both absolutely and proportionally.[37] There is none. Chinese firms generate cash from their excessive investment but much lower profits after depreciation and tax; the cash is lodged with the banks as the quid pro quo for another round of lending – usually on the basis that every 100 renminbi of new lending is financed in part by 50 renminbi of the borrowers' own deposits. The banking system remains the driver of growth and gives the party the ability to pay its bills whatever the level of productivity, performance and profit of the enterprises it supports, and despite any shortfall in tax revenues. The bail-out of Magang Steel, for example, is a typical use of the banks. Without control of the banking system both the position of the Communist Party and the structure of the economy would collapse. It should therefore be no surprise that the government has made plain its intention to continue to control the banking system. The maximum stake foreign shareholders are permitted is 25 per cent; the maximum any single non-state shareholder is allowed is 20 per cent. As for a private or foreign company considering starting a bank of its own in competition, capital requirements to open a branch network are set prohibitively high.

When the Chinese economy was relatively small it did not matter much that the basic disciplines of banking – assessing the creditworthiness of borrowers, pricing for risk and insisting on collateral – did not exist. Nor did it matter much that bankruptcy law was rudimentary and that the politically directed court system prevented predictable enforcement of loan contracts and payment of bad debts. What mattered was ensuring a steady flow of cheap finance to support investment, much of which – for bridges, reservoirs, railways, motorways and steel and cement making – was so obviously needed that complex rate-of-return calculations and pricing for risk were hardly necessary. The SOEs would request a loan and the party would make sure it was granted.

The resulting Chinese growth rate has come at the price of escalating bad debts and non-performing loans in the banking system, and business recipients who have never had to be serious about putting together a business case for credit, sticking to it and suffering the consequences if they did not achieve the expected outcome.[38] The lack of hard budget constraints or incentives to make a profit has had dire consequences. China has a 'non-payment' culture: interest on loans, dividends on shares and the servicing of debt are seen as optional extras rather than business necessities.

The Asian financial crisis in 1997 and 1998 laid bare the scarcely believable nature of the mismanagement of the banking system. Two of Guangdong's leading banks went belly-up as their racy customers in Hong Kong, where they had expanded their business, got into financial difficulties. This exposed a morass of non-performing lending the banks had made to the 'red chip' state-owned enterprises floated on the Hong Kong stock market. Suddenly the viability of the banking system became an object of close scrutiny. In 1998 the government officially estimated that non-performing loans stood at $205 billion – 25 per cent of all bank lending, and about 30 per cent of China's then GDP. The unofficial estimates of non-performing loans were double that.[39] To put the crisis in context, consider that the bad debts in the American savings and loan in the 1980s, the worst financial crisis in the United States since the Second World War, were significantly smaller and its economy much larger. Essentially, the capital at the core of the Chinese banking system had been eliminated; Chinese banks were bust. Nor did they make any profits on their operations that would allow them to rebuild their balance sheets. Without radical action, the party was about to lose its principal economic prop.

The response was prompt. Four asset-management companies were set up to which the government transferred $168 billion of non-performing loans and whose task was to recover as high a proportion of the debt as possible. To date the government has injected more than $260 billion directly into the banks and asset-management companies.[40] The banks were simply instructed to stop lending to over two hundred business areas deemed to have too much industrial capacity. By 2002 non-performing loans had officially stabilised at around $255 billion, and as lending soared dizzily they fell below 10 per cent of all lending in 2005.

The crisis had been forestalled, or at least deferred. To help the banks restore their balance sheets, they were allowed to start lending on commercial terms to consumers and private businesses – up until 1998 banks could lend only to SOEs on the narrowest of margins. Today about one-fourth of new lending is directed profitably for car purchases, mortgages and education and has grown rapidly. However, private companies still get very little access to bank credit. To encourage some basic discipline, banks have been required to become more sophisticated in their loan appraisal techniques, accounting has become much stricter and the banks are policed by a newly established regulator. Even more extraordinarily, foreigners have been allowed to take stakes, including stakes in three of the four big state-owned commercial banks, both to raise money and to bolster the pitifully poor management. The China Construction Bank floated 12 per cent of its shares in Hong Kong in October 2005 for $8 billion, which valued it as one the largest banks in the world. This was followed by $11.2 billion raised by the Bank of China for 11 per cent of its shares in June 2006 and a stunning $22 billion raised by the Industrial & Commercial Bank of China for 14.8 per cent of its shares in October 2006 – the largest Initial Public Offering ever. Corruption remains endemic. Readers will recall that the chairman of the China Construction Bank had been arrested for bribery five months earlier.

All this seems like a genuine attempt at structural improvement. Yet the scale of the challenge remains enormous. The China Construction Bank, for example, has over fourteen thousand branches and three hundred thousand employees, all of whom have to be trained in basic banking techniques even as all the old incentives for corruption and direction of lending remain in place. According to a leaked report from the China Banking Regulatory Commission, banks commonly ignore the regulations and understate bad loans, a practice that is made worse by poor accounting.[41] The Communist Party, not a bank's board, appoints the chief executive and makes other key appointments. Richard Podpiera, in a paper for the International Monetary Fund, acknowledges the significance of what the party has tried to do in cleaning up the banks, but reports that so far it has made very little difference to the way business is done. Bank officers do not price risk or take profitability into account when lending, Podpiera says; they simply lend when money is available to be lent, and alarmingly – despite the foreign shareholdings in three of the state-owned banks – their share of lending to more profitable enterprises in the provinces has fallen. Rather, they have lent to sectors like steel, cement and construction, which have chronic overcapacity and poor profitability. The idea that bad debts have fallen from 45 per cent before 2000 to 2 per cent after 2000 is too good to be true. Podpiera is sceptical about whether so much can have changed so dramatically in such a short time.[42] Moreover, there are signs that the zeal for allowing foreign shareholdings is diminishing: Citibank only managed to buy 20 per cent of the acutely bad-debted Guangdong Development Bank in 2006 rather than the planned 40 per cent. Despite the de facto bankruptcy of the bank, the Communist Party would not relax overarching rules; Citibank had to pay $3 billion for the privilege of purchasing the bank, with no guarantee of being able to exert managerial control.

The possibility of another bank crisis is obvious. The scarcely profitable SOE sector remains the principal recipient of this avalanche of lending, which is hardly better managed. The SOEs owe China's banks more than $2 trillion, and the World Bank's projections suggest anything up to $1.2 trillion would not be serviced if interest rates rose or sales fell even marginally. Each year the banks add at least another $500 billion to the stock of debt. Now that China is the world's fourth-largest economy it cannot dare to repeat the crisis of the late 1990s. Officially China's non-performing loans amount to about $300 billion; unofficially they are double that. Indeed, one recent report by the accountants Ernst and Young estimated that in 2005 the real total non-performing loans of the banking system stood at $900 billion, of which the four big state-owned banks accounted for $358 billion – twice the official estimate.[43] The report was withdrawn after the Chinese government protested it was 'ridiculous and barely understandable',[44] itself testimony to the way China is run. Simple arithmetic implies that in a weaker economic climate the total of non-performing loans could easily pass $1 trillion and climb toward $2 trillion. In November 2006 Fitch Ratings calculated that total non-realised losses in the banking system exceeded capital and reserves by more than a third. Even China, with its $1.3 trillion of foreign-exchange reserves, could not afford to restructure and pay off bad debts of that magnitude. It would be overwhelmed, the growth process would stall and social unrest could rise to unmanageable proportions.

The unmistakable message is that China dare not stop growing. For although the banking reforms are welcome, they fall short of what is needed. Only a profitable enterprise sector and an end to political interference and corruption can in the medium term guarantee the health of the banking sector. And these are what China does not possess.

The ticking clock

Today China needs $5.4 of extra investment to produce an extra $1 of output, a proportion vastly higher than that in developed economies like Britain or the United States. But twenty years ago China needed just $4 to deliver the same result.[45] In other words, an already gravely inefficient economy has become even more inefficient. China's national accounts tell the same grim story. China had to increase its capital stock by 9 per cent every year in the 1980s to produce a 9.8 per cent growth rate, but by the late 1990s it had to increase capital stock by 12 per cent to produce a lower growth rate of 8.2 per cent. Hu Angang calculates that China is now back to the Mao years in term of the inefficiency with which it uses capital to generate growth.[46]

This astonishing wastefulness is confirmed by Qu Hongbin and

Sophia Ma Xiaoping of HSBC Bank.[47] They also calculate that the additional output produced by investing the incremental dollar is now below what it was in the late Mao years. Comparisons with other countries at a similar stage of their development are equally unflattering. Korea and Taiwan between 1970 and 1980, Japan between 1965 and 1975 and the United States between 1890 and 1910 were all urbanising and industrialising at about the same rate as China was between 1998 and 2004. China, however, has needed at least one-third more investment than Japan and twice as much as Taiwan and Korea to achieve the same result.[48] However you look at it, the numbers tell the same baleful story. A visitor riding into Shanghai from Shanghai Airport on the new, virtually empty train will recognise the phenomenon: the project was so expensive that it will take 160 years to pay for itself.[49]

The clock is ticking. How much longer can China's current approach to economic development last? One pressure point is the internal economic structure; another is external – China traps every penny of Chinese saving inside China because it needs the pool to be as high as possible to fund its high investment at the lowest possible interest rate. It also wants to keep the renminbi as competitive as possible to promote exports – even while China earns a current account surplus that in 2007 is expected to exceed 10 per cent of GDP and receives about $60 billion a year as foreign direct investment. The People's Bank of China buys dollars to manage the exchange rate, so there is an explosive rise in China's foreign-exchange reserves, which in the first six months of 2007 rose by $266 billion, more than for all of 2006. The more China moves into the black, the higher its foreign-exchange reserves become.

The consensus is that the renminbi is between 15 and 40 per cent undervalued against the dollar.[50] To put this another way, China's exports are artificially cheap compared with those of other middle-income developing countries, even allowing for its cheap wages. Thus, if the Chinese authorities ever allowed the renminbi to respond to pure demand and supply – to float – it would rise rapidly and substantially against the dollar; conversely, that would mean the dollar would fall against the renminbi. China thus would be faced with the elimination of $300 billion of its foreign-currency assets (30 per cent of $1 trillion of reserves) in currency losses. Olivier Blanchard and Francesco Giavazzi of MIT calculate in an important paper that every year that China adds between $200 billion and $250 billion to its reserves it runs the risk that those reserves will fall by between $60 billion and $75 billion, or about 3.5 per cent of GDP, when the renminbi eventually revalues.[51]

Blanchard and Giavazzi calculate that the undervaluation of the renminbi by 30 per cent adds 0.45 of a percentage point to China's growth rate because of additional export growth. Therefore, in any given year, while the People's Bank of China risks losing 3.5 per cent of GDP from a potential revaluation, it is adding to the growth rate by 0.45 per cent – a good rate of return until the whole fabric unravels. But there is another contribution to growth from the current policy. China is keeping its savings bottled up internally as a crucial part of its growth strategy. If it yielded to pressure from the United States and agreed to float the renminbi freely it would want to stop its currency from rising. The best way to do that would be to allow Chinese savers to take their money abroad, supplying the renminbi that the world's markets want. But how much would leave China? Blanchard and Giavazzi estimate that about one-fourth would go abroad. Owing to the structure of the Chinese banking system that amount would reduce the growth of its deposit base by one-fourth, and thus its capacity to lend at today's low interest rates. Using the World Bank's numbers, that would reduce growth from investment by one-fourth – about 1.6 per cent per year. In other words, capital controls and reserve accumulation are worth about 2 per cent to China's growth rate every year – more if you believe that savers would move proportionately more assets into higher-earning overseas assets than Blanchard and Giavazzi estimate.

Nor is that the only consequence. If the renminbi rises, then Chinese agricultural prices that are now keyed to world market prices will fall. As the renminbi gains in buying power, so the world market price translates into lower domestic prices and lower domestic rural incomes. Abysmally low levels of agricultural productivity mean that rural incomes are barely above the subsistence level. A revalued renminbi would thus trigger a crisis: for example, in 2000 value added per person per year averaged a mere $490 compared to $1040 in the Philippines and $4851 in Malaysia. This would immediately accelerate the movement of the pool of 300 million agricultural labourers to the cities in search of work, and lower rural savings still further. A revaluation of the renminbi is something the party treats, properly, with great care.

In these terms Chinese resistance to the intense pressure from the United States to revalue its currency in a one-off 30 per cent jump, as Congress is demanding, has made sense – except that the monetary and inflationary domestic consequences of acquiring foreign-exchange reserves equivalent to 25 per cent of GDP every year as the price of targeting the renminbi are becoming overwhelming. Inflation in the summer of 2007 had risen to around 6 per cent, with 8 per cent or more predicted by some over 2008. The boom in the stock market and the property price bubbles in Beijing and Shanghai are part of the same story. And, as noted in Chapter 1, inflation in China, particularly with such high saving, is a source of potential political instability.

Administrative measures to contain the impact on the growth of domestic credit are plainly reaching the limits of their effectiveness. When the Chinese Central Banks sells renminbi to Chinese organisations at its target exchange rate in return for the dollars they have earned from exports, necessarily more renminbi are created, potentially adding to the Chinese supply of money and credit. To try to stop the cash from entering circulation Chinese banks are required to buy government bonds to 'sterilise' the cash inflows so they are not lent. Already the banks own more than $700 billion of such bonds – an amazing figure – but that directly hurts their already poor profitability; the interest they get on bonds is lower than they would receive from commercial loans. The incentive is to lend even more aggressively to compensate. In any case the policy is not working. The People's Bank of China also requires banks to lodge a growing part of their assets on account with the Bank as so-called reserve requirements, again a form of monetary sterilisation. Reserve requirements have been increased an unprecedented nine times since 2006 so that 12 per cent of banks' assets have to be lodged with the People's Bank. In addition interest rates have been lifted five times, even though, at 7 per cent, base lending rates are hardly onerous for an economy growing at close to 11 per cent with a near 6 per cent inflation rate. Despite everything, Chinese money supply is increasing at very nearly 20 per cent a year, with obvious implications.

As Michael Pettis, director of New York-based Galileo Global Horizons argues, China finds itself in a deepening monetary trap.[52] The result of the interaction between its banking system, administered monetary policy and economic structure, which is so export-dependent, is to create an unmanageable monster. The more foreign exchange reserves are created, the greater the capacity to lend, and thus more investment, export capacity and trade surpluses – which only make matters worse. Meanwhile the threat of inflation, along with ever-greater non-performing loans and an eventual credit crunch as the banking system implodes, grows all the time.

Foreign exchange reserves must grow less rapidly – but even that is hard to achieve. In the summer of 2005 the Chinese government did give way, offering the concession of a managed float and a tiny upward revaluation with the implicit promise of more to come. In the event the currency has been allowed to appreciate by some 7 per cent against the dollar – but foreign exchange reserve acquisition has accelerated. In a sign of mounting desperation, from 2008 individuals will be allowed to buy securities overseas to promote some currency outflows to try to relieve the upward pressure – but this will lower the savings pool at any given interest rate. It is testimony to the scale of the monetary trap in which China finds itself that such a pivotal building block in the old Dengist growth model has been shaken. A more traditional statist tool, creating a strategic $200 billion fund to invest in overseas assets (beginning with buying a 9.9 per cent stake in the United States' Blackstone Group, one the world's largest private equity companies), is also being deployed to create some crucially needed downward pressure on foreign exchange reserve growth.

The domestic pressures are matched by growing foreign restiveness. The capacity of the rest of the world to absorb China's export growth is being tested to the limit. The protests about the surge of textiles exported to Europe and the United States in mid-2005 were a storm warning. Chinese exports to Europe in 2007 now match export volumes to the United States, and are growing at a mind-boggling 35 per cent per year compared to just 18 per cent growth to the United States – reflecting in part the different path of the respective exchange rates. While the renminbi has appreciated against the dollar, it has fallen by more than 4 per cent against the euro – a differential movement that has already caught the eye of incoming French President Nicolas Sarkozy and which he wants to reverse. Western economies need time to adjust to the avalanche of cheap Chinese exports.

The financial message is unambiguous. China must stop acquiring foreign-exchange reserves at this rate, must allow the renminbi to float and must allow Chinese savers to move their money abroad so that the potential upward movement of the currency can be slowed. Only thus can China bring down the growth of its domestic money supply, head off the risk of inflation and slow the momentum of its exports. But this will lower the rate of its economic growth, the rate of saving and investment and rural incomes – and if nothing changes greatly it will increase the risk of social protest. Every year the decision is deferred for another year, in which foreign-exchange reserves soar upwards, increases the risk of a huge loss when the revaluation ultimately comes. It's a no-win situation: float and accept a deceleration of growth, or don't float and accept a deceleration of growth, if not immediately then eventually. Any deceleration of growth will inevitably expose the weaknesses in the banking system, which will force a further deceleration of growth. This is similar to what Japan experienced as a result of banking weakness in the 1990s.

One way or another, China's economic model is certain to begin to change some time in the next five to ten years. The rest of the world cannot indefinitely absorb Chinese exports growing at their current rate. China cannot continue acquiring foreign-exchange reserves at its current rate. Living standards in rural China cannot be allowed to fall much farther below those in urban China, for both social and economic reasons. The larger the urban economy grows, the more rural savings it must have to keep on growing – but the rural economy is shrinking proportionately every year.

China must become a more normal economy, with higher consumption, lower saving and more efficient enterprises. But that will demand major changes in Leninist corporatism. The Chinese Communist Party is faced with a second no-win situation. It can relax its political control to allow the economic reform process to be completed. Or it can retain political control, watch the economic contradictions build and so create the social tension that may force loss of political control. The party's instinct is to muddle through. The force of events, I suspect, will force more radicalism. Nobody can say with certainty. What you can say is that these choices are approaching – and fast.

Breaking China – can the change be made?

China needs to take the pressure off investment and exports as the drivers of economic development. It needs to become a more normal economy in which private consumption, now a mere 37 per cent of GDP, rises significantly and does more of the work of propelling the economy, and so relieve the impossible strains described above. A major report commissioned by the Chinese government from a panel of front-rank Chinese and foreign economists concluded that consumption had to rise towards 60 per cent.[53] Note for comparison that consumption is 70 per cent of GDP in the United States, around 60 per cent in India and some 57 per cent in Japan. So much is common ground. The issue is how. The problem is that persuading the Chinese to save less, consume more and to make enterprise more productive are not just technical issues. They go to the heart of Leninist corporatism.

The problem in raising consumption is that the habit of saving is very deeply embedded, largely because China's health, pensions and social security systems are so shockingly weak. As discussed in Chapter 4, the chief explanation of high personal saving is the interaction of China's chronically poor, patchy welfare system with the one-child policy; saving is needed for health, income in old age and education, and there is no wider support available from either family or welfare. The intention of the next five-year plan – to improve rural incomes, welfare and health care – is hard to fault, but it starts from so low a base that it is hardly a plausible solution. For example, until the 1970s health care in rural China was provided by the communes and covered 90 per cent of rural areas. When the communes collapsed, so did rural health care, which by the late 1980s covered only 5 per cent of rural areas. The government has made no serious effort to compensate; only 15 per cent of the health budget is allocated to rural China even though this is where 900 million people – 70 per cent of the population – live.[54] Worse, the only way health care could be sustained in the countryside is for doctors who used to work for the communes to charge fees, but peasants do not have the money to pay. The quality of health care has nosedived. In 2001 a study of four hundred village clinics found that two-thirds did not keep medical records and that only half of the surgical equipment was sterilised.[55]

Even with costs and thus prices cut to the bone, the National Health Service survey conducted by the Ministry of Health in 1998 conceded that 37 per cent of farmers who fell sick could not afford medical treatment, and 65 per cent of peasants were refused admission to hospitals because of their inability to pay.[56] The system is better in the towns, but still far from comprehensive. Only 12 per cent of individuals in rural China are insured, and the proportion in urban China rises only slightly above half, to 54 per cent.[57] In the World Health Organization's report for 2000, the overall performance of China's health care system in 1997 ranked 144th, placing China behind India, Indonesia and Bangladesh. For 'fairness' China was ranked only 188th (by contrast, India was forty-second). So it is understandable that peasants save so aggressively.[58]

The story is similar with regard to education. Much of China's improvement in literacy and numeracy is a legacy of the Mao years, and progress has largely stopped. China, having made great strides between 1949 and 1976, will not meet UNESCO's goal for literacy in 2015.[59] As with health, the central government has not stepped in to make good the loss of the 'iron rice bowl', the system of care formerly provided by the communes and the state-owned enterprises. Townships foot four-fifths of the education bill, obtaining the money from a mix of fees, taxes and charges. In rural areas the schools have to charge fees, with the inevitable result that the poorer the area, the poorer the education. Low-income countries spend on average about 3.4 per cent of GDP on education; China spends only 2 per cent, forcing large areas of the country to make do as best they can.[60] Peasant families save for their children's education because they must.

Also, China's population is ageing. Ten per cent of today's population is over sixty, and by 2015 the proportion will have risen to 14 per cent. Yet there is no national pension system. Children have been legally required to take responsibility for their ageing parents; most families have only one child, so the potential burden is considerable. Fear of what will happen to them in old age impels urban and rural Chinese alike to save intensely. And with the one-child policy the ratio of elderly people to the working population can only rise. In the seventy years between 1970 and 2040, China will have gone from a country where every 'elder' over sixty was outnumbered six to one by young people, to one where there are twice as many 'elders' as children.[61] It is a phenomenal switch, and the Chinese are reacting by saving.

Then there is the lack of property rights, and the complex linkage with saving and spending rates. Consumers in Western societies have lower savings in part because they borrow against the collateral in their housing assets. This happens more in Britain, the United States and Scandinavian countries than in Germany and France, but the trend is apparent everywhere. Communist China still makes private property a contingent right. Houses and flats in towns are available on seventy-year leases, renewable with the Communist Party's agreement, but typically rural smallholdings are available only on thirty-year leases, if at all. China also lacks a national land registry, and this situation aggravates the unclear property structure. Chinese consumers thus have no backing from their property and face life's hazards – ageing, poor health, unemployment and educating children – largely on their own. What has aggravated these realities is that household incomes – wages, investment income and government transfers – have been falling since the 1990s with an obvious downward consequential impact on consumption. Government transfers are paltry, and even recent government efforts to boost rural incomes with tax concessions and urban incomes with a minimum wage have had a tiny effect; the tax concessions are minimal, worth little more than 0.1 per cent of GDP, and the discretion given to local authorities in setting the minimum wage (in any case a quarter to a fifth of average wages) means that in practice it is close to valueless. Negative real interest rates and intermittent dividend payments imply that there is little compensation from rising investment income, despite high personal saving.

Nor can Chinese workers look to a trade union to advance their interests, protect them from arbitrary lay-offs or secure real wage increases.[62] The unions are directed by the All-China Federation of Trade Unions, and are creatures of the party, so another piece of China's soft infrastructure is lacking. Recent moves to allow collective wage contracts and give unions a role in arbitrating disputes may be welcome but, as David Metcalf and Jianwei Li of the London School of Economics report, collective contracts are not collective bargaining. China's workers are not effectively represented and remain at the mercy of their managements.[63] To form an independent union is punishable by a prison sentence of up to ten years. Small wonder that saving is so high.

To move to a lower-saving, higher-spending economy requires solving these conundrums. Solutions will necessarily involve the party in having to concede property rights, allow independent labour unions and introduce the taxes needed to finance a more comprehensive welfare system. But the party does not dare move on any front. To permit private property is to empower Chinese civil society as well as to repudiate the ideological base of communism. To permit independent labour unions is to lose control of the workforce and create a base for ideological competition. And to raise taxation is to invite taxpayers to want to hold the government that spends their money to account. As Montesquieu notoriously observed, the compensation for despotism is modest taxes. In the same way that the Chinese business sector needs an Enlightenment soft infrastructure to move to higher levels of productivity, so Chinese society needs it to save less and spend more. Welfare systems, freedom of association, representative government and enforceable property rights are not simply pleasant options. They are central to the capacity of a capitalist economy to grow to maturity. Without them China will be condemned to live with its economic contradictions. Indeed, the dangerously overheating economy in 2007, refusing to slow down despite interest rate increases and Beijing's exhortation, pleading and instructions, shows how difficult it is to manage an economy where normal constraints do not apply and the independent institutional power to enforce what we would consider normal accountabilities is non-existent. China is in a very similar dilemma to the one Jiang Zemin confronted in 1993. Sooner or later the contradictions and dilemmas will become unsustainable. Why that should be so is what we examine next.

7

The Democratic Graces

Twenty years ago Reaganism and Thatcherism were at their peak in the United States and Britain; they were responses to the perceived economic and social dead-end into which these countries had plunged in the 1970s. What these creeds sought to accelerate was more animalistic, go-getting individualism, more personal responsibility, more personal reward and less dependence on the state. Their critique was similar. Western capitalism had become too soft; it was too influenced by trade unions, state subsidies and regulatory busybodies. Above all, the state got in the way of private property owners, businesses and entrepreneurs, forcibly exerting their proprietorial and managerial rights to create wealth. Inflation and slow economic growth were symptoms of a deeper malaise. Prometheus had to be unbound. Workers and citizens alike had to realise that there were hard budget constraints and hard choices. To revive Western economies, profits would have to be higher, incentives greater, prices and wages more flexible and the scope of personal ownership enlarged. In particular, in Britain the privatisation of nationalised industries and weakening of trade unions were to open the way to greater productivity and growth.

Chinese reform had similar antecedents. By the end of the 1970s there was an analogous impatience with the state as an agent of economic development, even if the Chinese state was a model apart from anything in the West. China's pro-market reforms of the past thirty years have taken much the same direction; China has now arrived at a corresponding fork in the road. Everywhere applied experience and severe intellectual examination are making the explanation of capitalist success more complicated and nuanced than the simple account advanced in the 1980s. Just as the West, as I shall argue, is rethinking what works and why, so the challenges to policy and institutional challenges in China are moving beyond Deng's brave but simple concepts about loosening planning and celebrating markets and wealth.

The free-market economic propositions that made such advances in the 1980s under the penumbra of Reaganism and Thatcherism are being challenged and modified. To make the case that perfectly competitive markets would arrive at a perfect point of balance, the so-called neo-classical free marketeers had to make some highly doubtful assumptions about human behaviour and attributes: for example, that people process information and assess risk with scientific precision and form preferences as if in a state of nature, uninfluenced by culture, history or each other. As soon as the utopian free-market economic model is peopled by human beings, each possessing different amounts of information and making false guesses about the unknowable future, i.e. real people – it quickly becomes obvious that, even in theory, markets cannot be left to their own devices. They reflect the universal human tendency to undervalue future costs and benefits and overvalue the immediate; in short, they are myopic. They do not automatically create public goods. There are externalities – external consequences of private activity, ranging from environmental costs to traffic congestion, that the price mechanism does not automatically capture. Equally, there are spillover benefits from private activity, such as undertaking R & D, which the price mechanism also does not capture. Markets create winner-take-all and loser-take-all effects that increase inequality. In sum, human beings are far too fallible and unreliable in identifying their own best interests for price signals in markets to be the only means of coordinating what they do.

Moreover, unlike the predictions of the free-market textbooks, economic life is saturated with the truth that the more one does, the more accomplished one becomes and the more one learns. This cumulative learning and raising of skills then translates into a capacity to produce at lower cost. The larger the scale at which a firm produces, the more its returns tend to increase and the easier it becomes for it to monopolise its market. Unless counteracted, there is, in short, an inevitable tendency to monopolies in market economies with all the unfair and inefficient political and social power thus implied. The best argument for markets is not the argument of the 1980s – that they are unimprovable and always deliver best outcomes – rather, it is that they are the best way to sustain plural societies and economies. However, it is an interpretation that requires much more complexity in how markets are to be conceived and governed than that offered by free-market theorists.

If the debate among economists has become more sophisticated, so the debate has among practitioners – who have had twenty years' experience trying to make free-market solutions work in what came to be known as the Washington Consensus. There have been successes; arguably, globalisation, the intensification of trade flows, the rise of Asia and the great reductions in poverty are attributable to a better understanding, and an embrace, of market solutions. But there have also been failures. In too many countries, for example, privatisation has been tantamount to embezzlement: handing over state assets to political cronies and insiders at bargain prices. The most scandalous example was the creation of the Russian oligarchs. Financial deregulation has too often meant little more than allowing the financial system to lend freely while paying few of the costs in terms of wider credit growth, reduced savings or clashes with other policy objectives. The proximate cause of the Asian financial crisis, for example, was rapid credit growth (in turn caused by financial deregulation) colliding with the policy objective of lowering inflation by pegging currencies to the dollar. Mountainous speculation, another feature of deregulated financial markets, caused devaluation and economic retrenchment: GDP fell by 13 per cent in Indonesia, by 10 per cent in Thailand and by 7 per cent in South Korea. Some adjustment might have been necessary, but this speed and this ferocity almost certainly were not.

Even the economic development process has been rethought because of weaknesses in application of the theory. When the Washington Consensus was in its glorious pomp at the time of the collapse of the Soviet Union, the view was that the underdeveloped world stayed underdeveloped because of its attachment to statism and its resistance to the magic of markets. As a result there was an unfocused, universal belief in liberalisation, privatisation, price stability and deregulation whatever the particular circumstances of any country, and with little interest in how specific policies were sequenced. In some countries it might be human-capital constraints that were limiting growth; in others, weaknesses in the physical infrastructure; in still others, high real interest rates caused by high investment demand and low saving. No such differentiation counted. As the Harvard economist Dani Rodrik argues, instead of a forensic examination of what the particular diagnostic signals were saying, the Washington Consensus became a kind of spray gun in which everything was tried, in the hope that a generalised movement towards markets would be beneficial.[1]

Today there is a new sobriety. In the first place there is recognition that, for example, geography, climate and disease constrain development, and that more careful analysis is required. In *Guns*,

Germs and Steel, Jared Diamond observed that, historically, innovations that worked in temperate Europe and northern Asia did not travel to Africa; even the animals and crops could not be reproduced.[2] Other analysts have shown that disease severely limits the scope for gains in agricultural productivity.[3] Similar drawbacks exist today. Achieving basic levels of education and health, and accepting the necessary public expenditure, may have better payoffs than market liberalisation. In these contexts, just unleashing markets is hardly likely to start the development process. And for many landlocked poor economies such as Bolivia in South America, Burundi and Rwanda in Africa and Laos and Mongolia in Asia, their own physical isolation and low demand from neighbouring countries limit their growth options.[4] Profits from long-distance trade, as discussed in Chapter 2, are important to development, but such profits presuppose both goods and partners with which to trade. Invocations of free markets that neglect the hard truths of geography are of no help to anyone.

The emerging consensus takes this into account. In particular, it is now understood that the quality of a country's institutions is as important to development as the strength and diversity of its market processes. John Williamson, the man most closely identified with formulating the Washington Consensus, regretfully acknowledges the mistakes of the 1990s: '[My] emphasis would have been different; I would have focused much more generally on institutions . . . The major advance of the 1990s stemmed from recognition that the central task of the transition from communism to market-based economies involved building the institutional infrastructure of a market economy. This realisation was complemented by a growing recognition that bad institutions can sabotage good policies.'[5] It is a recognition that the reliable weathervane of the international consensus, the well-intentioned but self-regarding World Economic Forum, accurately reflects. It produces an annual Global Competitiveness Index in which businesspeople rank more than one hundred countries. Market efficiency and macro-economic rigour, once the conservative revolution, are now only two of nine 'pillars of competitiveness'. The other seven are the quality of public institutions, the quality of infrastructure, health and primary education, higher education and training, technological readiness, business sophistication and innovation.[6] Reaganism and Thatcherism, it may be objected, never overtly dismissed these other pillars; on the other hand, neither philosophy stressed them. The Reaganites and Thatcherites held that individuals, entrepreneurs, businesses and managers must be empowered; markets were magic; and the state must, as far as possible, stand aside.

No such simplicity is available today. The new stress on the role of institutions in development and growth may seem to widen the argument and deepen our understanding, but in truth it muddies the waters. Generally institutions are regarded in one of two ways. First, they may be said to support growth because they undergird a particular type of Anglo-Saxon capitalism – e.g. tradable property rights enforced in independent courts, powerful stock markets or 'light' regulation that does not inhibit market efficiency. Second, they may be collapsed into a list of desirable 'good' institutions, with little sense of whether they are the cause or the outcome of successful development. Are independent media, a good transport infrastructure, a strong innovation system and even efficient, transparent government causes or effects of development? And if any of these are causes, how and to what degree can they be created?

We alternate between a catch-all view of institutions, because they all count, and the view that, because the American business model is presumably best, any developing or developed country had better create institutions like those in the United States as part of a general commitment to 'liberalise'. This thinking comes close to being a circular, non-falsifiable argument: markets are best, so institutions that support and complement markets are obviously crucial. This wishful reasoning, typical of the Washington Consensus or the World Economic Forum, may certainly be more sophisticated today than in the past, but it still falls short of the rigorous non-circular logic we need.

Which institutions matter, and why?

Dani Rodrik is one of the creative thinkers about the role of non-market institutions in the effective functioning of a market economy. He identifies a wide range of non-market institutions, such as trade unions and social insurance systems, which help the market to function better even though that is not their primary purpose.[7] Rodrik is on the right road, but we need to go further. Efficient markets require complementary market and non-market institutions. In fact, sustainable, legitimate and high-growth capitalism needs institutions whose values and mission are in tension with, and sometimes opposed to, markets and market values in order to keep the markets honest. They are non-market institutions precisely because they have different values, different mechanisms of accountability and different purposes. Their clashes with the values of markets are not technical, but are felt passionately and arise from a clash of vocations.

Consider the values and origins of the distinct network of institutions with a public vocation whose purpose is not capitalist success, but which play an indispensable role in driving capitalism forward. Justice and the rule of law are grounded in the insistence that right and wrong have their roots in reasoned justification in the light of evidence judged before universally applicable principles enshrined in law. Justice cannot be bought and sold. Another example is the university, an institution committed to the acquisition and dissemination of knowledge; scholarship has to follow reason and truth rather than commercial advantage. Even the media, although they may need to make a profit, have an independent vocation to report and comment on

objectively observed reality. They are an indispensable component of transparency and accountability in both the private and
the public sphere. Nor were welfare systems ever conceived as
'market supporting'; rather, they were created as instruments of
social solidarity, basic insurance against the risks of life and the
means of securing equal opportunity. Welfare may help to manage
social conflict and protests when firms are involved in tumultuous
competition and technological change, but its moral force comes
from a different wellspring. Trade unions want a voice in the
workplace and better working conditions, and have proved a crucial mechanism in making workplaces less exploitative, more
humane and frequently more productive; yet the right to strike,
and even the unions' right to exist, resulted from a prolonged
political battle. The tension as much as the complementarity
between hard market processes and such non-market institutions
impels capitalist development and growth.

Non-market institutions are direct or indirect descendants of
the Enlightenment – a result of at least two centuries of historical
development. They create and sustain accountability, transparency, the process of justification, the acquisition of knowledge
and the capacity of ordinary citizens to participate in social and
public life. One way or another they make up the concept of
'publicness' and the public sphere. If they are crucial to the functioning of the capitalist economy they are no less crucial to the
functioning of representative government. Charles Taylor of
Northwestern University, McGill and Oxford – one of the most
influential philosophers in the English-speaking world – identifies, in *Modern Social Imaginaries*, the separation of public sphere
and government as a fundamental quality of an effective democracy. The public sphere is where 'society can come to a common
mind about important matters', he writes; because the debate is
not just sounding off, but rather an attempt to arrive at a reasoned
collective judgement, the government ought to listen and
respond. This is where a sovereign people think out loud; the

public sphere is self-consciously outside power and does not exercise power itself – rather, it is listened to and plays a crucial role in defining the limits of governmental action. This legacy of the Enlightenment underpins not just representative government but the institutional pluralism that in turn underpins the good economy and society. To describe these values and the institutions they have created as 'non-market' is to denude them of their lifeblood, rob them of their historical context and accord them a technocratic, instead of a moral and political, foundation. China, as I have argued, needs the gamut of such non-market institutions. But getting them is not a matter of organising a technocratic transplant or copying. It is a matter of revolutionising Chinese non-market spheres and, in particular, accepting the idea of a public sphere that is independent of the state and the Communist Party.

This is where the political and the individual are conjoined. Communism purports to enlarge individual choices and enrich individual lives through collective action. Mao believed the communist proposition that underpinned the Great Leap Forward: the creation of communes would enfranchise peasants and, more importantly, expand their imagination. It would give them the chance, for example, to write poetry, an opportunity that they had never experienced before. Some did, notwithstanding the wider inhumanities and mass deaths. But the experience of the past forty years of reform has shown the Chinese that expanding the imagination does not necessitate the suffocating daily compliance with an all encompassing ideology. Nobel laureate and economist Amartya Sen, echoing Mao but proposing very different means to achieve the same end, has declared that the objective of development is not just material wealth but the substantive freedom and capability 'to choose a life that one has reason to value'.[8] This is a common urge among all peoples, rich and developed or poor and undeveloped.

So here is a mechanism – plural public institutions – and here is a consequence – human happiness. Enlightenment institutions need Enlightenment people to breathe life into them; modernity has to be won by real people prepared to imagine a life that they themselves want to make and are prepared to act on that concept, leaving behind the universe in which preferences are inherited and fixed. Nick Stern, a former World Bank adviser who is now chief economic adviser to the British government, argues that this involves a mental shift from the traditional to the modern.[9] What societies have to demand and governments supply are the tools to do the job, and that first requires even better proof of why and how pluralism works.

The pluralist advantage

The Great Leap Forward was admitted to be a disaster, an utopian top-down master plan for China forced on a civil society that was powerless to resist. So was the aggressive implementation of the Washington Consensus and financial liberalisation that was forced on much of the world. Latin America's protracted stagnation in the 1990s,[10] Asia's financial crisis later in the decade and Russia's reform programme imposed severe but avoidable costs on one-third of the world's land area. When utopian grand ideas do not respect the complexity of real human communities there is serious trouble.

James Scott of Yale University, in his book *Seeing Like a State*, discussed the twentieth century's debacles, ranging from Soviet agricultural collectivisation to Le Corbusier's schemes for new urban communities such as Brasília. He argues that they have in common an overriding of the wisdom and practice of many actors in favour of a grand plan.[11] In a way, this is obvious; what is intriguing about Scott's analysis is his demonstration that the disasters have similar pathologies. First, grand-plan thinking needs stylised aggregated facts so that complex reality becomes standardised.

Also, the planners have a passionate confidence in what Scott calls 'high modernist ideology' – the idea that science and rationality, by revealing how nature and human society work, allow them to be mastered. Le Corbusier, the introducers of calamitous Western agricultural techniques into Tanzania under President Nyerere, the authors of the Washington Consensus and Mao himself are linked by the same golden thread. But the combination of modernist ideology and stylised facts becomes deadly when they are in the hands of an authoritarian state willing to coerce its subjects, and when there is a prostrate civil society unable to resist the plans. China's tragedy, as with collectivisation in the Soviet Union, was that communism was uniquely powerful and coercive in implementing its modernist ideology and civil society was uniquely weak. The result was murderous havoc. Mao recognised that the lack of accurate feedback from the local communes allowed the Great Leap Forward to continue unchanged for too long, and in his own terms he did want better socialist democracy to inform the planners so that the centre could be more responsive. Scott's retort is that the problem is more than faulty design; it is inherent to the grand designers' way of thinking about the world.

Scott argues that states have to respect what he calls 'metis' – the fabric of institutions, knowledge and practice that societies have developed to solve problems, live together and propel their economies. He describes this as a wide array of 'practical skills and acquired intelligence in responding to the constantly changing natural human environment'. Scott is thinking along the right lines, but if his idea is taken to the extremes it is a de facto prohibition on government action. For governments have to act as well, and are necessarily imperfect; as much as we may deplore Maoism, Sovietisation or the clumsy implementation of the Washington Consensus, these philosophies were responding to genuine economic and social concerns that had reached a crisis. What was wrong (over and above the obvious intellectual mistakes) was the arbitrary ideological intervention and, in the case of communism, the totalitarian imposition. We can acknowledge this and still accept that society, while respecting 'metis' and the plural institutions that create it, has to find some way of acting collectively in order to capture the benefits of public good and avoid the expensive externalities of some private actions. The holy grail is to combine them, in order to re-achieve social coherence consistent with plural actions.

Even birth control is better controlled democratically

Even a policy that at first sight seems best implemented by an authoritarian state will, on closer examination, be seen to work best if the system respects pluralism and 'metis', and so wins cultural ownership of ideas. An intriguing example is the contrast between the Chinese approach to birth control and the approach taken by India. Fertility in China has certainly fallen since the one-child policy was introduced in 1982, and the target of stabilising the population has been broadly achieved. However, there have been terrible costs: abortion, female infanticide and gross imbalance between the sexes. (Chinese couples want a boy rather than a girl, and the manipulation means there are 120 male births for every one hundred female births.) With an illegal trade growing in prostitutes and forced brides, there are increasing question marks about the sustainability of the policy. In 2004, President Hu Jintao asked 250 senior Chinese demographers to study whether the one-child policy should be revised.[12] The projection is that by 2020 as many forty million men could be unmarried. In the past, such a situation has been a source of economic and social instability, and the regime fears that this could happen again.[13]

The one-child policy may be reaching the limits of administrative sustainability. Systematic intrusion into the intimacy of hundreds of millions of couples is even beyond the capacities of the Chinese state; the quality of the four hundred thousand-member birth control bureaucracy is patchy, and the policy of bulldozing or dynamiting the homes of couples with more than one child is gradually being abandoned because of its brutality and lack of legitimacy. Instead, China has been moving away from coercion towards a policy based more on fines, tax penalties, exhortation and education about birth control.[14] However, it does not dare abandon coercion altogether, because there is so little cultural ownership of the need for small families. Despite rising prosperity and female empowerment, the birth rate might bounce upwards again. Nor is there any prospect of the distrusted bureaucracy and distrusted organs of state propaganda winning such cultural ownership; nor of plural communities in civil society doing the same job, because they are so weak. Coercion finds itself at a dead-end.[15]

In fact, as Amartya Sen has argued, the fall in China's birth rate might have been expected anyway, given the rising per capita income, the education of women and rising literacy. (These are all the best predictors of fertility.) Sen discusses how the birth rate in the literate, rapidly developing Indian state of Kerala, where women are increasingly as well educated as men, has actually fallen faster than the rate in China since 1979.[16] The plural communities of Kerala – schools, women's birth control advocacy groups, expanding companies and families themselves – have voluntarily and spontaneously constructed a culture of greater female empowerment that, along with higher living standards, has motivated women to have fewer children. Also, Sen points out, there is no evidence of increased abortion of female foetuses or murder of infant girls, as there is in China. The intervention in Kerala has been less heavy-handed from the beginning, working with the grain of Kerala's civil society, so it has won ownership of the notion that families should be smaller while respecting the pluralism of its society. The outcome is both better and more stable than China's.[17]

This is tribute to the advantages of democratic pluralism in the broad sense I have used throughout this book: not just voting, but the entire network of institutions and processes in which representative government nests. The obvious case for democracy is that it delivers sovereign government of the people, by the people and for the people, and, despite all its problems of implementation, it is the least bad way of guaranteeing liberty. In fact, the case is more profound. In *Why People Obey the Law*, Tom Tyler, professor of psychology at New York University, marshals evidence that the more people have participated in forming the law, the more likely they are to accept its rulings, even if they disagree with a particular outcome. Process matters. People want to participate; they want procedures to be neutral and consistent; they want to be treated with dignity and respect; and they want to be sure that the law-makers have considered their needs and concerns.[18] China's birth control policy fails to meet all four criteria, so its illegitimacy is guaranteed – and the many attempts at evasion are inevitable. In Kerala, by contrast, birth control was felt to be more legitimate.

The economic case for democratic pluralism

There is growing statistical proof that democracy and economic advantage are closely associated. Consider *The Democracy Advantage: How Democracies Promote Prosperity and Peace*, written by Morton Halperin of the Open Society Institute, together with Joseph T. Siegle and Michael M. Weinstein.[19] They argue that democracies, understood as states with a network of democratic institutions constituting a public realm rather than just representative government, tend to have more interests involved in government decision-making, to be more open and to have more accountability. The democratic institutions may be rudimentary and incomplete, but over a period of decades democracies tend to manage their resources more effectively and accommodate themselves better to necessary economic and social changes. Halperin and his colleagues test the thesis as rigorously as possible.[20] They find, for example, that since 1960 poor democracies have grown 50 per cent more rapidly on average, so that the Baltic countries, Botswana, Costa Rica, Ghana and Senegal have done much better than, say, Angola, Syria, Uzbekistan or Zimbabwe. The social dimensions of development – access to drinking water, girls' literacy, health care – are better in democracies. Life expectancy is typically nine years longer in poor democracies than in poor autocracies; the likelihood of finishing secondary school is 40 per cent higher; infant mortality rates are 25 per cent lower; agricultural yields are about 25 per cent higher. According to Halperin and his colleagues, '95 per cent of the worst economic performances over the past forty years were overseen by non-democratic governments'.[21]

The numbers are hard to dispute. Democratising countries are less vulnerable to both internal and external conflict. In sub-Saharan Africa, one of the world's conflict black spots, democratisers have been only half as likely to experience civil conflict as others.[22] The only exception to this worldwide rule is in parts of Asia, where authoritarian Singapore and China have been successful. By contrast, democratic Japan, Thailand and now India exemplify the thesis – and Singapore, like Hong Kong, has the British legacy of an independent judiciary. South Korea and Taiwan, even in their authoritarian periods, were significantly pluralist. As for China, the next phase of its growth will probably be accompanied by more pluralism.

The process at work here is often inadequate and always imperfect, but more frequently than not fosters better government, more pluralism and better decisions. Herd behaviour, groupthink and conformism all menace the quality of decision-making in government or private-sector organisations. The more diverse the interests that are represented at the table, the less likely it is that groups will commit themselves to a decision or conform with an approach that is self-defeating or plain wrong. Cass Sunstein, a professor of jurisprudence at the University of Chicago, argues in *Why Societies Need Dissent*[23] that societal pressure to conform stifles the multiplicity of voices that are needed to articulate views other than the group norm – and that groups tend to reach lowest common denominator decisions acceptable to all that are either second best or downright wrong. Democratic systems make fewer such mistakes than others, but even so are prone to the same biases.

Sunstein's list of bad decisions attributable to conformist thinking includes Neville Chamberlain's appeasement of Hitler, the fiasco at the Bay of Pigs, the infamous corporate debacles of the early 2000s – Enron, WorldCom and Tyco. He also includes the Nazis' invasion of the Soviet Union, NASA's failure to stop the launch of the *Challenger* space shuttle, the Watergate cover-up and Ford's ill-fated Edsel. In every case the decision-makers maintained a course of action that was wrong, ignoring the dissenters. These are two powerful forces that reinforce each other to create such conformity, Sunstein argues: cascade effects and the tendency of groups to polarise around more extreme decisions. Because information is costly to obtain, once a few individuals have agreed that a particular course of action is right other participants in the process either have to be very confident or have to know a great deal more in order to challenge them; there is a cascade of alignment behind the core decision-makers motivated by a fear of being ostracised by other group members. Sunstein posits, for example, that many Republicans voted for Bill Clinton's impeachment not because they thought it was right but because by falling behind their leadership they would not be penalised.

Similarly, one paradoxical consequence of deliberative discussions is that the group gets persuaded by argument to coalesce around not just a favoured course of action but its most extreme form. There is a race among broadly like-minded people to demonstrate that they are not cowardly and are committed to the same cause. The more persuasive the leading proponents, the more these dynamics move the group to an extreme position. This concept makes the development of Islamic fundamentalist terror more understandable; the group is moved to an extreme position because everyone competes to demonstrate a commitment to Islam.

Decision-making needs the grit in the oyster – the passionate dissenter who, with institutional safeguards, can oppose an emerging consensus and force the group to re-evaluate what it is doing. It needs, in short, genuine pluralism. This point is made by James Surowiecki, who seized on the intriguing and apparently contrary insight that the average of aggregated individual decisions is often right and, consequently, called his book *The Wisdom of Crowds*.[24] Building on the 'Jury Theorem' developed by the French mathematician Condorcet, he shows how such averaged decisions prove to be astonishingly accurate when those expressing an opinion have independently made up their minds – whether about the weight of a cow or the location of a sunken submarine. The wisdom of crowds emerges from comprehending the universe of possible outcomes in all their original diversity and then averaging them.

Pluralism thus improves the quality of deliberative decision-making; as a process it also provides crucial safeguards for the whole system by offering insurance against mistakes. Decisions are made in a context of uncertainty, fallibility and complexity, which grows more uncertain and unpredictable when consequences depend on events in the distant future. Some decisions have nearly immediate consequences, others may take years to prove their worth, but decisions all require delicate judgements about whether the supporting conditions will hold, or whether and how the world might change to alter them. The value of plural decision-making from the point of view of the whole economy and society is that although one individual decision is almost certain to be wrong, one decision among a multiplicity is likely to produce the right answer. One famous example from the business world was the rivalry between Sony's Betamax and JVC's VHS.[25] It was not obvious that the VHS would triumph as a video technology over the technically superior Betamax; each company perforce had to back its own technology and JVC outmanoeuvred Sony by allowing other producers to licence VHS, 'going plural' even if it suffered some loss of revenue. Sony emerged as the relative loser. This was bad for Sony but good for the whole system because experimentation took place, which ensured that the technology capable of faster diffusion would dominate. The problem with authoritarian planning is that necessarily it has to choose which idea to back, so that as a system it lacks the protection of a multiplicity of diverse decision-makers.

The case for pluralism does not stop there. Within the United States, the urban geographer Richard Florida has linked the economic growth of cities to their diversity and thus to the creativity of their populations, using the presence of gay adults as an indicator. Five metropolitan areas with the highest gay population – Washington, DC, San Francisco, Austin, Atlanta and San Diego – are among the fifteen top high-tech cities.[26] Similarly, Stanford Research International has developed the 'waterholing' technique to maximise the creativity of organisations by designing a problem-solving process that rests on diversity. Groups are established whose membership is as diverse as possible – with different talents, genders, ages, sexual orientations and skillsets – to get the most serendipity and thus creativity. Early evidence indicates that this process delivers results.[27] Richard Lester and Michael Piore argue in *The Missing Dimension* that innovation cannot simply be commanded from the top down.[28] They differentiate between goal-oriented analytic research and more discursive, open-ended 'interpretative' research. The latter results from the conceptual thought and unexpected connections that develop when diverse researchers, with diverse minds, come together. It is 'fluid, context-dependent and undetermined', reminiscent, in fact, of Scott's 'metis'. Genuine innovation almost always comes from ambiguity and fluidity – the kind of creativity waterholing principles try to capture – rather than from goal-oriented projects. Goals may be vital in developing the innovative results of interpretative research, but rarely are in themselves a source of innovation. Pluralism works.

The paradox: governing pluralism

Whatever its intellectual and practical advantages, pluralism is not easy to create or sustain. Economists have long been aware that to maintain competitive markets the state has to set limits on monopolies and unfair trading and, critically, has to ensure that new entrants can easily challenge incumbents in markets. The United States government's famous Sherman and Clayton Acts of 1890 and 1914 respectively outlawed monopoly and predatory pricing. This legislation, together with the activism of the Supreme Court and the government, especially during the New Deal, created a climate in which existing American firms are wary of colluding to restrict entry, price unfairly or exploit monopolistic power because they could incur the whole panoply of law suits, fines and governmental intervention. They police their own conduct knowing that if they stray beyond the line they could get badly burned, even although recently the line of restraint has been fraying.

Taking on dense concentrations of private power is politically and technically hazardous; governments have to prove market abuses and spend political capital in wrestling with private companies that protest their innocence and use the courts to defend their interests. Over the past twenty years the United States federal government has been more indulgent of concentrations of corporate power; apart from the famous case against Microsoft, there has been much less activism than in the first sixty years of the twentieth century. Between 1945 and 1960, for example, the federal government demanded that over one hundred leading corporations license patents they had acquired in order to get the technology into the marketplace. Little such activism is evident today in the United States, although interestingly the European Union has begun to flex its muscles, albeit from a low base.[29]

Indeed pluralism is more generally under assault, and one of its most dangerous enemies is the market process and market values. Enforcing competition is crucial to the vitality of the market economy, but giving privileges to markets and incentives over every other aspect of a plural economy and society is paradoxically an anti-competitive act to which economists seem curiously blind. The media, education, research, law and politics, for example, are all spheres where non-market values need to be nurtured if these functions are to stand in tension with capitalism, keeping it honest, and sustain the accountability and justification processes that lie at the heart of great companies. For example, according to Lester and Piore, United States corporations, under pressure from Wall Street, are so hungry for profits that they insist on goal-oriented, commercialised research. This commercial research is killing off interpretative research, which requires time and different structures. A good example is the once great Bell Labs, now part of AT&T. The new hegemony of markets and corporate values is driving Bell Labs towards groupthink, homogeneity and sterility, and away from pluralist research thought. Innovative research needs the protection of the university, with its Enlightenment vocation of creating and disseminating knowledge, if the advantages of pluralism are to be captured.

The media in Western societies is crucial to the accountability process. It gathers and disseminates the information without which public debate and the accountability of private and public actors is impossible. However, throughout the West, and especially in the United States, the media has been increasingly adopting entertainment as its transcendent value. Its defenders say that this makes news more accessible and appealing, but the transformation in the content of news, documentary and current affairs programmes, the scheduling and the declining budgets suggest a different agenda. In a quantitative study of media content, John Zaller observes that between the 1970s and 1990s, the proportion of material about government, education and politics in local news programmes in Pennsylvania (which he considered representative of the United States) had fallen from 54 per cent in 1976 to 15 per cent in 1992. Over the same period, programmes he describes as 'sensationalistic' or human-interest rose from 25 per cent to 48 per cent. There has been further deterioration in news programmes since the early 1990s. In Britain, the regulator Ofcom found that political content had fallen by a quarter in the ten years up to 2005, while a survey in 1999 by the British Film Institute found that 52 per cent of those working in news and current affairs felt the need to distort contributors' views or the truth to make their programmes more exciting and watchable.[30] Human-interest stories on television have always been a way to attract viewers; but now we have reached a tipping point in which such stories are crowding out information that public-spirited citizens need to know. During the United States' presidential campaign of 1968, candidates could expect to speak on camera for an average of forty seconds without interruption. Two decades later, the average was just nine seconds.[31]

It seems obvious that the government must respond to these challenges to pluralism. But this is not easy in a culture where 'government' is seen as inherently bad. Nor is it obvious how to respond, because the forces at work are very complex and the government does not want to lower pluralism by an intervention aimed at increasing it. The media is a classic example, because one determinant of its content is internal pluralist competition, aided by new delivery platforms such as the Internet and satellite and cable television. However, another determinant is a less pluralistic trend: increasing concentration of media ownership and the demand by today's capital markets for ever-increasing profits, which forces private media to adopt aggressive commercialisation just to stay alive. Wearing one hat, the government wants competition; wearing another, it wants a vigorous public realm; wearing still another it wants any intervention to leave the media independent and plural. One way or another, ideas must be developed and a view has to be taken about how the balance is to be regained. Simply praising competition or pluralism is not enough.

In an important paper Andrew Dunsire of the University of York conceptualises government action in a plural society as continually tipping the balance. He draws a useful analogy: the various institutions, actors and communities in an economy and society are held together in tension, rather as the rigging of a yacht holds masts and sails together. If one part becomes too strong or too weak it puts the whole system of interdependent checked and balanced tension out of kilter. The state, as the custodian of the whole, must do something that is corrective but is not so interventionist that it will destroy the capacity of the system to function by itself again once the balance has been re-tipped.[32] Dunsire lists a variety of interventions available to government, ranging from straightforward subsidy through law to 'light-touch' rebalancing of power. There is no a priori 'right' way for the state to respond except, if it wants to sustain social pluralism and the interdependent tension, to proceed cautiously and not damage the communities whose interaction are part of the society's health.

The strictures I have made against authoritarian government should not be interpreted as a generalised attack on all government. Rather, government in a pluralist society must respect the governed, not coerce them or subject them to top-down plans. The possible solutions to the issue of the media thus include, for example, increasing grants and revenues to public service broadcasters like the BBC, or PBS in the United States; reintroducing the American 'fairness rule' abolished in the 1980s, under which broadcasters ensured that individual programmes were fair and adapting to Britain's current context; reducing concentrations of ownership within the media sector; and placing a regulatory obligation on newspapers to report within certain guidelines. How the government should respond will depend on politics and on its own ideology; there are many options. The larger point is that pluralism does not just happen; it is a precious quality that has to be protected and nurtured. China has a long way to travel.

8

The Soft Infrastructure of Capitalism

Pluralism is not guaranteed. Its enemies are public and private monopolies. Its ally is the variety of pressures, lobbies and interest groups that come from a vigorous, independent civil society. The underpinning of such a civil society is not only a state that understands the need to keep rebalancing forces, but the empowerment of ordinary citizens with the minimal necessary material living and educational standards to give them the capacity and coinage to participate actively and sustain the pressure to stay plural. Poverty and ignorance drain pluralism of its support. As Western societies gave their citizens the franchise in the nineteenth century, the citizens used it to insist on more social and educational spending – which in turn helped the economies to become richer, with more vigorous civil societies, which in their turn sustained the growth of pluralism.

To get to that point, however, there had to be a number of preconditions. One was the Enlightenment's creation of the public realm and its commitment to an egalitarian enfranchisement of citizens. Citizens became infected, as leading social theorist Arjun Appadurai argues, with a 'capacity to aspire'.[1] This is a complex phenomenon. The capacity to aspire is rooted in material and intellectual capability. One reason that widespread property ownership is important – and was an early advantage of the United States – is that it confers a sense of autonomy and allows control over a minimum level of personal material well-being. This is also why universal education is important: it endows individuals with the intellectual capability to turn aspiration into reality – and to become vigilant citizens.

Something equally important is afoot today. Economic and social dynamism originates, as the economist and theorist of risk Robert Schiller has insisted, with individuals who are prepared to take risks. And risk-taking is more likely when there is a material cushion to guard against the consequences if the risk goes wrong. If there is insufficient protection people become wary and conservative: 'Fearing to venture out into the rapids where the real achievement is possible, brilliant careers go untried because of the fear of economic setback. [Instead] we tend to work cynically, treading water, staying in an unsatisfactory job, pretending to achieve.'[2] This is not just about welfare systems, education and property ownership. It reaches into the marrow of a society. Lack of protection penalises risk-takers; protection encourages them. For example, the United States has a lenient approach to bankruptcy.[3] The more a society permits a fresh start, the more genuinely it allows risk and dynamism. There is nothing mystical or culturally unique about the United States per se that endows American culture with its strong 'can-do' ethic; that ethic evolved from a combination of property ownership with the egalitarian spirit of the Enlightenment – and from the way the United States underwrites and encourages risk.

One pillar of this spirit is private property. The urge for the

security of individual property ownership and for the fair distribution of land is a universal instinct; and has been an issue in all
civilisations. More notably, it is a precursor for rapid economic
development. In Asia after the Second World War, Japan, South
Korea and Taiwan all benefited from major programmes of land
redistribution. In Japan the programme was led by the United
States military authorities; in Taiwan by the fleeing Nationalists;
and in South Korea it was made possible by the retreat of Japan as
a colonising power. In all three countries the combination of equi-
table land reform and a strong commitment to education
reproduced the foundations of the growth experienced in the
United States a century earlier.[4] Interestingly, China found its
way to a similar position in the early 1980s when peasants
regained de facto control of their plots of land and were much
better educated after the massive Maoist investment in radically
improving their literacy and numeracy. China, in this respect, has
two of the preconditions for a plural society: a long tradition of private property ownership and a powerful cultural commitment to
education. But it lacked, and continues to lack, Enlightenment
values and institutions.

Property rights are thus crucial in transforming peasant societies into self-sustaining modern plural societies – not just
economically but also psychologically. This is an insight developed by Hernando de Soto, the Peruvian economist, who has
argued that the best means of giving peasants a material and psychological impetus to challenge tradition and stop accepting
poverty is to give them formal control over their informal property
rights, and then construct financial institutions that will offer
credit with the property as collateral.[5] He estimates that throughout the undeveloped world $9.3 trillion of 'dead' capital is locked
up in squatted land and *favelas* over which the occupier has de
facto but not legal property rights. If this estimate is accurate, the
amount is twenty times greater than all of the cumulative foreign
direct investment since 1989.[6] In countries as disparate as Peru

and Egypt, the assets of eight out of ten people play no part in the formal economy. If governments could find ways of legally defining occupiers' rights, a new vista would open up. Peasants would own property and have collateral against which to borrow. They would even have the simple asset of a reliable address, so there would be a greater likelihood that utilities could get their bills paid; this would make the economics of extending power and water to peasant cities more favourable. Registering voters, the indispensable precondition for democracy, becomes easier and more reliable. Property, economics and political enfranchisement go hand in hand.[7]

However, de Soto needs to go further, as his more recent writing concedes. Property rights are a necessary condition but, on their own, are not a sufficient condition for sustained development and a plural society. For example, without independent courts and a body of law, property rights are stillborn. And courts and laws require, as we have seen, a process of legitimisation in which some form of deliberative and representative democracy is essential. Nor is the legal system just about courts and judges; if these are to work they have to be part of a wider culture which understands that clashes of interests are best adjudicated using general principles such as justice and objective evidence. This process – the idea of justification – lies at the core of a successful, active legal system.[8] It is where the Enlightenment ideal of reason and pluralist practice intersect: I may have disputes and conflicts with my rival, competitor, family or neighbour, but I am prepared to seek justice within what I understand to be an independent and objective framework. More profoundly, my acceptance implies reciprocity; we are playing by the same rules, and each of us has faith that the other will respect them.

Justification and reciprocity, and collaboration in creating shared rules, are thus crucial to pluralism. They cannot just be imported into underdeveloped countries. Each country has to learn them by resolving its own pluralist conflicts and building up its own institutions to incorporate these values. Seen through this prism, however, the scale of the challenge facing communist China becomes apparent. China has relied on communism to bull-doze the country to economic modernity – justification and reciprocity did not enter the picture. Now they must.

Understanding the human proclivity for cooperation, equality and justice

Learning, adaptation and creation processes are the sine qua non of a pluralist society. These sustain competition, propel empower-ment and continually repopulate the plural economy and society. To adapt and create require social interaction within and between institutions, firms and actors. Learning is not just a matter of individuals responding to material incentives in markets – the vision of the neo-classical economists. It is a matter of commu-nication between macro and micro communities: each must be able understand what is being said, to process it and to act. For example, a firm whose products are selling badly needs to be able to interrogate its customers and workers for an expla-nation, process what it has heard and then decide on a course of action.

A firm, like other institutions, can never be conceptualised merely as a bundle of transactions, which is the curious common ground between communist and free-market theorists. The firm is neither the black box of the communist planners' imagination, turning inputs automatically into outputs according to a techno-logical blueprint, nor the Pavlovian institution of the free marketeer's imagination, responding slavishly to price signals. Rather, adaptation and responsiveness in the marketplace depend on the mutual trust among those delivering information, those processing it and those who will later act differently because of it. Firms are sites of social acts and social exchange which depend on reciprocity and mutual respect, operating within processes that are understood to embody those values. A firm can no more escape the reality of its social make-up than any other social actor. Neither communist theory nor free-market theory comes close to comprehending this insight.

Of course the better the process of social exchange, the better its quality, pleasurability and effectiveness. So far so good. But there is an umbilical link between effective process and equality, and it has to do with an elemental human characteristic: the pleasure that we take in the well-being and happiness of others. We have what the economist Adam Smith called moral sentiments: a desire to reciprocate and collaborate with an understanding that general well-being is a collective good from which we all benefit materially and psychically.[9] We want the regard of other human beings, a shared sense of purpose and the pleasures of friendship. The underpinning of a good social process requires the acknowledgement of these truths, which is easier the readier we are to reciprocate; our readiness in turn is more likely when there is less social distance between the parties – which, in turn, happens more when the parties to the process are equal. Social distance makes reciprocity harder. Professor Richard Wilkinson of Nottingham University argues that the more inequality, the more feelings of dominance and subordination, superiority and inferiority become prevalent.[10] Human beings want respect, but are not in a position, materially or psychologically, to earn it if the economic and social gap between them becomes too wide. Equality and reciprocity are thus mutually reinforcing. If they are in short supply it becomes impossible to construct well-functioning communities, and pluralism is diminished.

This is the heart of the conundrum over values facing a pluralist society. Of course there is a need for individualism, materialism and response to incentives; firms are trying to make money, and so are their directors and employees. But if adapting, learning and cooperating are to take place, then the opposing values of reciprocity, trust and altruism must also co-exist. This is a matter of economic efficiency. If, for example, firms have to monitor and enforce every aspect of every contract, then the transaction costs will overwhelm them. This is not liberal hand wringing, but part of the gospel of one of the toughest advocates of free markets. Alan Greenspan is former chairman of the United States Federal Reserve. In the aftermath of Enron, he observed: 'In virtually all transactions, we rely on the word of those with whom we do business. A reputation for honest dealings with a business or financial corporation is critical for effective corporate governance. Reputation and trust were valued assets in freewheeling nineteenth century America. I hope and anticipate that trust and integrity again will be amply rewarded in the marketplace as they were in previous generations. There is no better antidote for the business and financial transgression of recent years.'[11] This is not just a question of trust between firms; it is also about trust within them. Firms have to trust their employees with secrets, with ideas and even with having the best interests of the firm at heart: employees have to trust each other and also their employer. This social capital exists beside the professional competence the firm must possess if it is to succeed; the better it can talk and communicate with itself, the more productive it will be.

This may seem to challenge the received wisdom of decades of economics in which the core assumption is that individual self-interest is the only reliable guide to action. In fact, new interdisciplinary thinking has begun to support the view that human beings are more than simple prosecutors of self-interest. This thinking combines insights from social and evolutionary psychology about how human beings really behave with more sophisticated models of economic interaction, especially game theory.[12] Humans are not hardwired to calculate only their own advantage, distrust others and cheat if they can in the pursuit of self-interest; they are more complex. We are neither the economically self-interested beings of classic economics, nor the altruists and co-operators imagined by Jean-Jacques Rousseau or Karl

Marx, frustrated by the shortcomings of the wider economic and social system. Banally, we are a combination of both. We are wary cooperators because we understand the rewards, but our cooperation is conditional on reciprocation by others, whom we are ready to punish if they cheat.

Some behavioural psychologists and economic theorists specialise in setting up 'games' between individuals to see which strategies the players adopt in a variety of settings. These analysts tend to agree that it is best to think of human beings as conditional reciprocators.[13] Essentially, cooperation pays off, in part because it meets other human needs, and in part because it guards against the risk that we may need help at some time in an unknowable future. Moreover, if we want others to cooperate with us, we have to be fair. This adherence to fairness is observed in experiments such as the 'ultimate game'. In this game, two individuals are shown £10, and one has to make an offer to the other about how the money should be shared. If this offer is accepted, they both keep the money. Typically the proposer suggests an even split, £5 each. Typically responders reject anything less than £4 because it is unfair – even though both then end up getting nothing.[14] The 'tit for tat' strategy in game theory, outlined by the economist Robert Axelrod, leads to very similar results.[15] Essentially, if I apply 'tit for tat' I respond cooperatively with you until you defect, and then I punish you by defecting. Because both sides know this is likely to happen, they continue cooperating.

Some behavioural psychologists argue that humans are inclined to cooperate because of the structure and cognitive complexity of the brain. The orbitofrontal cortex, the temporal cortex and the amygdala, which allow us to estimate time, recall reputation, delay gratification and detect cheaters, both separate out human beings from other animals and give humans a proclivity to cooperate.[16] Other behavioural psychologists, notably Samuel Bowles and Herbert Gintis, believe that human emotions have a 'prosocial' bias to make cooperation more likely.[17] Contempt, anger and disgust, for example, prompt individuals to punish free-riders; gratitude and honour incline us to reward altruists; sympathy, compassion and empathy encourage contributions towards the public good; other emotions such as guilt, shame and embarrassment persuade us to avoid cheating or to repair its effects.[18] The era of the hunter-gatherers lasted from a hundred thousand years ago until the beginning of the agricultural age, less than twelve thousand years ago, which, in evolutionary terms, is scarcely the blink of an eye. Biological evolution is a slow process, the evolutionary behavioural psychologists remind us, and many of our cognitive and emotional functions were extraordinarily useful when human beings would perish without cooperation. Even the most skilled hunter could return from an expedition with only a few kills, or none at all, because of bad luck; this possibility made pooling the yield from any one hunt more rational. Equally, in the fluid world of population collapses, sudden disease or the need to move on, human beings had to have cooperative skills to manage their encounters with the strangers they would inevitably meet, and with whom they would want to collaborate.[19]

Dan Kahan of the Yale Law School builds on these insights to show that too much stress on individualism is counterproductive, imperilling the benefits of the cooperation for which we instinctively quest.[20] When group members believe that others are behaving cooperatively they are more likely to be motivated by honour and altruism, and more likely to contribute to the public good, even without material incentives. But if they believe that someone else is shirking or cheating they relapse back into individualism. For example, an incentive can itself become an organisational cue signalling that at least some members are not inclined to cooperate voluntarily: if everyone were inclined to cooperate, the incentive would be unnecessary. Thus incentives can crowd out altruism by making it impossible for individuals to show that they would have behaved altruistically regardless of an incentive. What makes people fill in their tax forms honestly, says Kahan, is not exhortation or an advertising campaign; on the contrary, the more people are alerted to the opportunity to cheat, the more they will do so assuming that others will. The best predictor of honesty is thus interaction with others who plan to behave honestly.

Interaction is greater when equality is greater. Wilkinson traces the close link between deteriorating social relations and unequal societies. These societies tend to have lower levels of trust, more violence, less involvement in community life, lower turnout in elections and more discrimination against women and minorities. He cites more than fifty studies showing that rates of violent crime and homicide are higher where income inequalities are greater – in some places there is a ten-fold difference in homicide rates related to inequality. From Robert Putnam's *Bowling Alone* to Ichiro Kawachi and Bruce Kennedy's study ('Social Capital, Income Inequality and Mortality'), the evidence in the United States is unambiguous: the more equal the state, the more trust. In the most equal of states, Kawachi and Kennedy found, only 10 to 15 per cent of the population feel they cannot trust others; in the more unequal states, the proportion rises to 35 to 40 per cent.[21]

This impacts on economic performance. William Easterly, Jo Ritzen and Michael Woolcock maintain that too much income inequality in less developed countries leads to poorly designed, malfunctioning economic and political institutions, which in turn lead to lower economic growth.[22] They argue that even well-intentioned politicians in fractured, unequal societies cannot easily build coalitions for reform. This is because people have to trust governments to deliver long-term benefits to offset inevitable short-term costs – and the lower the social cohesion, the harder it is to persuade losers that there will be long-term benefits. Rich and poor alike try to avoid taxation. Poverty and inequality, in short, tend to beget more poverty and inequality.

Social cohesion and social capital turn out to have strong economic payoffs – a result confirmed in numerous articles and statistical tests.[23]

The charge that inequality is offensive morally, socially, economically and in human terms thus takes on new life. The foundation of human association is the idea that human life has equal worth and human beings are equally entitled to political, economic and social rights which will allow them to choose a life they have reason to value. But without powerful countervailing forces, the accident of birth will always predict the rights to which one effectively has access, and thus one's capacity to choose a life one values. The issue is to what degree. In most Western societies, social mobility is declining, as it is in most less developed countries. That makes it more urgent to reach some agreement on the minimum entitlements and capabilities society will guarantee to offset the increasing importance of birth. The philosopher John Rawls and economist Amartya Sen agree on the need for a social safety net to ensure a basic standard of living, basic human rights, equality of opportunity and the accountability of political decision-makers. Most moral and political philosophers will accept that society has such obligations in the broad areas identified by Sen and Rawls. The questions are to what degree these obligations exist and how to persuade the better-off members of society that it is in their interests to acquiesce in the redistribution of income and opportunity in order to provide what Rawls calls an 'infrastructure of justice'. These questions need to be asked everywhere.

The answers are brutal, if subtle. Inequality is the enemy of pluralism, and pluralism is the friend of the good economy and society. Wilkinson cites the first page of Alexis de Tocqueville's *Democracy in America* and the 'enormous influence' of what Tocqueville called the 'equality of conditions' on the workings of American society. It influenced law-makers, governors and the governed; beyond that, 'its empire expands over civil society as well as government: it creates opinions, gives rise to sentiments, inspires customs and modifies everything it does not produce'.[24] Tocqueville hit the nail on the head: equality of conditions is crucial to pluralism. China and the West neglect it at their peril.

Justification and the classic idea of the company

The company animates the plural economy. Companies are a necessary (though not a sufficient) condition for successful capitalism, but a company is a complicated mechanism. It is at once a profit-seeking machine, necessarily ruthless in eliminating obstacles, and a living community peopled by complex, simultaneously self-interested and altruistic human beings. When people walk into their place of employment they do not leave behind their sense of fairness or their responsiveness to being respected and trusted. Companies have to accommodate these sentiments and respond to their expression; indeed, the highest-performance companies are those that manage to combine the hard and soft dimensions of successful business.

A high-performing company, whether in the United States, Asia or Europe, has to find a way of creating the social capital and trust that allows its employees to share a language, respond flexibly and quickly to daily business challenges and understand what the company is trying to do. In *Built to Last*, their best-selling study of seventeen 'visionary' American companies and one Japanese company, Jim Collins and Jerry Porras found that companies which endure over time, pick themselves up after setbacks and successfully take over other companies and integrate them into their own, have a strong sense of organisational purpose. Collins and Porras call this a 'reason-to-be'. What is important about GE's success, for example, has been its powerful sense of shared purpose and its strong 'core ideology', as much as Jack Welch's legendarily aggressive leadership in pursuit of rising quarterly profits.[25]

The notion that a company has a purpose or vocation is not

new. It was the cornerstone of the original idea of the company. A group of companions would come together to share risk in an enterprise and would petition the crown for a licence to trade. The licence would set out the function or purpose of the company, and its accompanying obligations to the crown, which represented civil society. Companies, as I explained in Chapter 2, were first routinely established in England and the Netherlands as organisations that would exist over time to solve the problem of how to create the infrastructure for long-distance trade – but they were more than that. In 1600 the East India Company received a monopoly licence to undertake England's trade in Asia, but it accepted as a quid pro quo that it would carry the cargoes in English vessels, undertake their defence, expand England's political and commercial influence and pay duties to the crown. The right to trade was accompanied by obligations – the core notion of what we would now describe as corporate responsibility. And the company had an explicit purpose, which was not in the first instance to maximise profits. In the case of the East India Company, the purpose was to trade in Asia, and it would seek to maximise profits from that trade. This is a subtle distinction, but it is enormously important in how the company is conceptualised and how it constructs its internal and external relationships. The company builds its internal social capital and external reputation and brand around its declared purpose, to which discharging its mission accountably and publicly is central.

For most of the following three hundred years, incorporation in Britain, America and Europe required the company's founders to declare what the function of the company would be, and faithfully follow it. This principle has been weakened in the United States and Britain since the so-called shareholder-value revolution of the 1980s, which asserted that the sole purpose of a company is to maximise profits. Still, what the great Western and Asian companies have in common remains a commitment to what they do. Boeing, for example, was founded to build airplanes, and although this ethos has been strained by the shareholder-value revolution it continues to exist.[26] Unilever was founded to build great 'everyday things for people everywhere'.[27] Sony was founded to establish a place of work where engineers can 'feel the joy of technological innovation and be aware of their mission to society, to apply advanced technology to the life of the general public.'[28] Incorporation reinforced the purpose and the accompanying ethos, and provided a compass to help the leaders navigate varying technological and market challenges.

From the beginning, the company would issue an annual written public statement of its activities, and this would be held accountable for its actions by shareholders and public authorities. With the introduction of regular audits to provide accounts for bankers and other creditors, the process became more formalised. It becomes still more formalised when companies' shares were listed on public stock exchanges and companies earned the privilege of limited liability. Investors wanted an accurate, comparable and verifiable flow of information on which to base investment decisions; the quid quo pro for directors being offered limited liability for corporate debts was that they provided accurate information about the companies' affairs to the public authorities. Companies, in short, are and were at the heart of an iterative justification process providing evidence on which they were to be publicly judged – hence the notion of a public company.

The public company, in the business domain, accepts that it must justify itself to its investors and the wider public; democratic justification becomes a unifying element in the world of markets and democracy alike. Public companies, therefore, are both market and non-market institutions. In their external affairs this should now be obvious, because the company continually interacts with the key constituencies that will determine its future, notably government and shareholders, and of course it will be constantly processing information from the marketplace about the strengths and weaknesses of its offering. But the description of companies as

markets and non-market entities also extends to internal relationships. For example, wages do not capture the entire relationship
between employer and employee as they would if the company
were wholly economic and market-based. The other dimension is
how the employee is motivated, communicated with and adopts the
company's objectives as his or her own. Workers hold management
accountable for keeping their internal promises. This can be done
formally, through collective bargaining and information and consul-
tation – the *raison d'être* of trade unions – or it can be done
informally through one-on-one conversations or whatever structures
the company provides for such exchanges. High staff turnover is
often a sign not only of dissatisfaction with any particular market
wage but also that management has been unable to manage the
non-wage, psychological part of the employment contracts.

Channels for such interaction and justification vary with history, culture and nationality, but whatever the channel, the larger
point is that the company deliberates with its own staff and its
external shareholders and stakeholders. In Germany the process
may be organised with union members, bank creditors and large
investors formally represented on company boards. In the United
States the process may be largely through transparent disclosure of
information to the capital markets. But, one way or another, there
is a deliberate two-way flow of debate involving judgements about
the appropriateness of the chosen means to achieve the declared
ends. The process involves collecting and assimilating evidence
and, as far as possible, reasoning to form a collective judgement
about how to proceed. In other words, the idea of justification – the
exposure of reasoned judgements to other reasoning in an attempt
to get the best and most correct answer – which is at the heart of
deliberative democracy, independent media and justice, also turns
out to be at the core of the classic concept of the company.

Because the process cannot begin without a shared idea of what
the company is trying to do, the great companies are those that,
over time, maintain a clear concept of their reason-to-be. They do

this by managing the relationship with their shareholders and stakeholders so successfully that all parties to the deliberation understand what is to be achieved and contribute to that goal. Danger arises when companies overemphasise any particular dimension of their operations. Porras and Collins' objection to maximising shareholder value is not that companies should avoid it; plainly, the pursuit of profit is a key corporate goal. Rather, their objection is that profit may displace the corporate reason-to-be, so that the company neglects its own function and becomes merely a profit seeker. This may work in the short run, but it never works for long, according to Porras and Collins. A great company that makes airplanes, automobiles or soft drinks has a vocation to be in its particular business. Once it admits that it is indifferent to its line of business, and that its only criterion is short-term profit, in effect it torches its justification process, its social capital and the unique capabilities it has developed over time. It is on the road to perdition.

The Work Foundation (declaration of interest: I am the chief executive), an independent, not-for-dividend British business think tank and consultancy, has found in a survey of some three thousand companies that what drives business success is the capacity to blend five key clusters of business activity.[29] Companies need to engage their employees, satisfy their shareholders, manage their external networks responsibly, innovate and respond to the market. In other words, they have to respect market and non-market impulses simultaneously and holistically. Companies that can perform this balancing act have measurable and significantly higher performance than those that cannot – a British validation of Collins and Porras' insights. Successful companies have powerful processes of justification and accountability, but those cannot exist if the company does not declare a purpose by which to be held to account – and that purpose has to be more than simple profit maximisation. In the right conditions, companies are sophisticated, subtle and moral organisations. Small wonder China has found it difficult to create enduring ones.

Asia is no different

In the early 1990s Mahathir Mohamad of Malaysia and Lee Kuan Yew of Singapore were passionate advocates of the notion that Asia's economic success had its roots in distinctive Asian values – a blend of Confucianism and Buddhism. In Asia, authoritarian government was different from elsewhere in the world, they argued; it used its power to promote general economic and social welfare, in keeping with the Confucian tradition, and overrode sectional, pluralist interest groups that might obstruct the general good. Democracy got in the way of this disciplined mobilisation of resources. The Asian belief in the family allowed the development of high-trust, long-term business groupings that aimed to build enterprises over time. This belief also meant that Asia could spend less on welfare systems, because the family undertook many of the welfare responsibilities provided by the state in the West. A Confucian work ethic and belief in self-development contributed to a strong impulse to educate and train, and to work hard after training. Thus the Asian model consisted of low taxes, low welfare, high education, high savings, high investment, business-building, entrepreneurialism and authoritarian, Confucian-minded government. In the Bangkok Declaration of 1993, Asian governments supported the notion that Asia was different; its stance on human rights had to be judged by Asian standards and culture.

After the Asian financial crisis and the retirement of both Mahathir Mohammad and Lee Kuan Yew from active office, the case for Asian values both lost its chief champions and part of its underlying justification.[30] Confucian authoritarian states, just like any others, could make policy mistakes that led to economic calamities; these mistakes could work their way through the economic system with noticeable similarity as well. Family capitalism, which had looked like an asset before the Asian financial crisis, looked remarkably like crony capitalism afterwards. The argument then became subtly different. It is not that Asian values implied a radically alternative approach to capitalism; rather, Asia has variants of democracy, law, human rights and capitalism.[31]

The desire to assert 'Asian difference' is understandable. The new countries established after European decolonisation wanted to declare their nationhood and identity – and to declare that, while they might borrow from the West, they still retained an Asian core. Amartya Sen, in his new book *Identity and Violence*, describes this desire as the product of the 'dialectic of the colonised mind': it becomes tragically impossible to see past the grievances and resentments of colonisation to recognise any intrinsic worth in Western values and institutions – or of any analogous function played by their Asian counterparts. There were also reasons of practical politics. In particular, Singapore needed to establish a personality distinct from Malaysia, of which it had been part, and to justify oneman rule. Similarly, Malaysia needed to assert its identity. China, associating itself with the movement, was also anxious to show that Western-style democracy was foreign to Asia. Interestingly, one of the most vigorous critics of this theory of Asian values is Kim Dae-Jung, the democratic victor in South Korea, who says that distinct pro-authoritarian Asian values are a myth. His view is also taken by Taiwan's Lee Teng-Hui of Taiwan.[32] Democracy and capitalism, they argue, have the same essential attributes and appeal everywhere. What defines Asia is its diversity in moving towards these qualities, rather than its denial of their usefulness.

The trouble with this debate is that it sets up two straw men. Western culture is much too complex to be diagnosed simply as individualist and materialist. For a start, as I have argued throughout this book, it incorporates the Enlightenment tradition of the public realm. But that rationality co-exists with a strong religious Christian and collectivist socialist tradition that proponents of Asian values ignore or underestimate. Nor are Western societies hostile to the ideas of social capital and community. Arguably, they have succeeded because of their ability to create the social capital that sustains economic and social pluralism. Equally, values embodied in Confucianism have cross-cutting trends: it can be as accommodating to individualism as Western philosophies. Asian family dominance can be too strong and *guanxi* family networks corrupt and closed. Cultures in all civilisations reflect the same tension between hard and soft, individualistic and altruistic. Look more closely at Asia, and you will see universal rules in operation.

For example, the heart of Japan's post-war economy, like China's, was its capacity – for more than thirty years – to mobilise very high savings for infrastructure and manufacturing investment. A large proportion of the output was then exported to the United States, prepared to have an otherwise unacceptable trade deficit for the sake of strategic ends. Of the three great principles of successful capitalism – pluralism, building individual capabilities and creating justification processes – Japan had weak pluralist institutions and weak justification but, as mentioned earlier, land reform and a long tradition of the importance of education had produced citizens readier to think and act for themselves after 1945. Japan wanted to leave authoritarian militarism behind and start anew. The industrial mobilisation was organised by the Ministry of International Trade and Industry (MITI), which ensured that chosen or 'guided' industrial groups received the technology, finance, grants and freedom from competition to invest on an enormous scale. Between 1960 and 1970 Japan's national income doubled, as had been planned.

Yet Japanese firms were never wholly creatures of government, however close the relationship with the government might be. Also, although Japanese banks made long-term loans to permit investment on a scale rarely matched in the West, they were also highly activist in ensuring that a company pursued the growth strategies it promised – and they would ruthlessly replace any management team that failed. The justification process to external shareholders, government and the public might be weak, and transparency effectively non-existent, but inside the *keiretsu* or *kigyo shudan*, networks of interlocking cross-shareholdings between banks and group members, companies were and are held accountable for the success of their strategies. Moreover, the company was and is recognised as a core, autonomous social unit, not just a network of transactional market contracts – a community of employees ambitious for themselves and their company, overtly committed to promoting corporate goals. This is a far cry from today's Chinese companies, and much closer to a variant of the classic Western company. Indeed Japan's success has forced a re-examination in the West about what it means to be a company and organise high-performance production.

The Japanese economic boom went on until it reached a climax during the late 1980s, with record levels of bank lending to construction and property, sky-high share and property prices and the emergence of overcapacity in key industrial sectors such as consumer electronics and automobiles. The lack of proper accountability in the banking system, the insider crony networks of lenders and borrowers, the intimate and frequently corrupt involvement of the government bureaucracy in so much of the economy – in short, a lack of economic and political pluralism, together with weak accountability – finally undermined the Japanese miracle. As the yen appreciated, growth slowed down and share and property prices collapsed. The Japanese banking system was essentially bust, holding at least 43 trillion yen of non-performing loans ($325 billion, but government estimates range up to $650 billion) that it should never have made.[33] Fifteen years of negligible growth followed, as the financial system wrestled with its titanic losses (no fewer than six insurance companies have collapsed, and banks have merged and restructured). There have also been fifteen years of small-scale reforms, which cumulatively have begun to create a plural soft institutional infrastructure and better legal and justification processes. Bank and stock market regulation has been beefed up and made more independent of the central bureaucracy.

Prime Minister Koizumi was re-elected in 2005 by appealing directly to voters over the heads of the governing party's faction leaders. He asked for support in taking on vested interests, and he has been part of a strengthening of Japan's process of democratic accountability. Freedom of public information, unheard of in the early 1980s, was established nationally in 1999, although it does not include Japan's notorious public enterprises, which continue to have privileged access to government funding and are subject to little scrutiny.[34] Shareholders' rights have been augmented. Official guidance of public companies has been constrained. The legal system is being reformed; trial by jury has been established for criminal cases; there is a two-year time limit on first-instance criminal and civil trials; and the number of trained lawyers is being doubled, with a third expected to be women. Some twenty thousand NGOs have been established under a new law permitting their formation.[35]

Gradually, Japan is developing the sinews of economic and political pluralism. Company accounts are more detailed, banks more careful and aloof in their lending and regulation is more transparent. Hard processes have been addressed alongside the soft processes. The labour market has also been less closely regulated. Lifetime employment has receded and 'non-regular' workers without the same entitlements and costs now constitute 30 per cent of all Japanese employment – up from 18 per cent in 1990.[36] Japan remains authentically Japanese; the political system is in thrall to one party and to the malfunctions and systemic corruption that flow from this reality. But as an imperfect and incomplete pluralism begins to take hold, Japan looks more like an Asian country expressing a need to develop its people's capabilities, establish justification and accountability and create soft Enlightenment pluralist institutions, than a country which is a paradigm apart from the West. The first sign of accelerating economic growth is testimony to the success of the transformation.

There is a similar story in India, Asia's other giant. Since the early 1990s India's growth has averaged more than 6 per cent, even though its investment levels are half of those in China. In other words, India's fast-growing companies – such as Infosys in software, Ranbaxy in pharmaceuticals, Bajaj Auto in automobile components and Mahindra in car assembly, succeed in getting more growth per dollar of investment than their Chinese counterparts. If companies are not held to account by the 130-year-old stock market – many are unquoted and private – then a more independent banking system, with new powers to enforce loan covenants, does the job. India has inherited from the British an independent judiciary with a strong culture of upholding the rule of law. Its argumentative tradition, identified by Amartya Sen as a major strength, can be traced back to the Rig Veda, India's oldest sacred text, which questions the very existence of a divine entity.[37] Sanskrit 'has a larger volume of agnostic or atheistic writings than in any other classical language'.[38] This tradition combines with the British-style legal system to give India strong justification and accountability processes. India's corporate governance is among the best in Asia.[39] In a survey by the *Far Eastern Economic Review*, India had more companies ranked for their leadership performance than any other Asian country.[40]

India has a democratic political system as well as genuine changes in government, which, given its one billion people, twenty-nine independently minded states and six religions, is a remarkable achievement.[41] Its left-wing parties are closer to 'old Labour' in Britain than to Asian communists, and have tended to be more strongly committed to promoting social welfare and alleviating rural poverty than to engaging in class war and expropriating private property. As a result of Nehru's foresight in developing the Indian Institutes of Technology and Management, Bangalore has more IT engineers than Silicon Valley, and India's universities produce 3.1 million graduates a year. Unlike China it has the opposite of an ageing population – it is youthful, with a rapidly expanding labour force. It has an independent media and a lively public sphere. In short, this is an Asian country with embedded economic and political pluralism, an educated middle class and a strong tradition of justification.

Still, two fundamental problems are its lack of openness and its weakness in developing its people's capabilities, in part because of the caste system. Its tariffs average 22 per cent; its $4 billion of foreign direct investment is only a small fraction of China's; its exports are one-eighth of China's and growing less rapidly. The long decades of attempted autarchy after independence in 1947 have left their mark, together with a legacy of clumsy state regulation, stubborn fiscal deficits and rickety public infrastructure. Also, the level of illiteracy in rural India remains appalling. Forty-four per cent of Indian workers are illiterate; 55 per cent of Indian women are illiterate, compared with just 13 per cent of Chinese women. India is, however, making an overdue attempt at female education.[42] Although the Indian constitution forbids discrimination on the basis of caste, between 150 million and 200 million untouchables continue to live mostly on the margins of society – and in rural areas literally on the margins of the villages.[43] Old prejudices die hard, and the development of a genuine labour market encompassing every Indian remains elusive. Service-sector employment is proportionally lower than in comparable countries, and India has focused skill development on a narrow cohort of acceptable castes.

Is India an embodiment of Asian values as its pace of industrialisation accelerates? Is its development attributable to principles different from those identified in this chapter and Chapter 7? Hardly. Capitalist success entails managing the interplay between hard capitalist processes and soft institutional processes. A country can avoid this for as long as a generation, but ultimately reality will emerge. India and Japan are plotting a more pluralist future. China will inevitably follow suit.

Yet the view persists that Asia is special. For instance, Joshua Cooper Ramo, a consultant based in Beijing, argues that China represents a new 'Beijing Consensus' about how to pursue development. There are three key factors, according to Ramo. First, China has embraced technological innovation rather than basing its growth on cheap labour. Second, it stresses equity and sustainability in its growth priorities. Third, it has been prepared to strike out on its own with its own experiments, true to its own Chinese destiny, rather than adopt Western examples and rules as necessarily better. China, Ramo says, is admired throughout the less developed world because its ideas about how growth can be organised offer a viable alternative to the Washington Consensus.[44]

Ramo is right in saying that the Chinese leaders now stress technology, equity and sustainability in their rhetorical declarations of their aims for the economy and society. But in reality indigenous Chinese enterprise has competed largely on the basis of low wages, has copied technology and has disregarded environmental costs throughout the reform period. Moving to an alternative model without substantial institutional reform will be beyond it. Any other narrative is implausible, whatever the official goals declared for the future may be. China has been innovative in managing its gradual transition from communism, and, although inequality has grown dramatically, the commitment to universal education, including women, has had economic benefits. And China does insist that its jurisdiction as a self-determining nation-state should be respected – an insistence which has given it the self-confidence to make its own way.

This does not constitute a new consensus or a refutation of the need for economic and political pluralism. Ramo's claims, like those of Lee Kuan Yew or Mahathir, cannot survive close scrutiny. The more we examine the post-war Asian miracle and today's China, the more obvious it becomes that economic development, and in particular the evolution of successful firms and financial systems, follows universal rules, even though housed in the particularities of individual states.

Western capitalism succeeds because its institutional framework permits more such companies; the weakness of China's Leninist corporatism is that it can hardly get to first base. There is no constitutional framework to allow China's companies to develop their own corporate identity; there is no tradition of justification that companies can build on as a process to strengthen themselves; there are no institutions through which such values could be created or expressed. China's weaknesses, however, expose the current dangers in the Western system. The Western consensus still does not acknowledge the subtlety of company building, the crucial role of the wider institutional complex and the danger of consecrating companies to the sole cause of maximising shareholder value. Neither the Beijing Consensus nor the Washington Consensus has a real grip on the dynamics of successful capitalism.

9

Of War and Peace

No country is an island. Communism in China would not have begun without the rise of communism in the rest of the world; its subsequent success was part of a worldwide communist advance over the first half of the twentieth century. Similarly, the last twenty-five years of successful Leninist corporatism would never have taken place without the special character of globalisation, opening up unparalleled opportunities for foreign direct investment, transfer of technology, growth of trade and economic development without ever challenging China's right of peaceful sovereign self-determination – in other words, communist authoritarian rule – within its frontiers. Deng accurately saw the character of the emergent international system and how it could be turned to China's advantage. 'Peace and development,' he pronounced, 'seem to be the trend of the times.'[1] China could play the same economic cards as the rest of rapidly growing East Asia and use the consequent growth, ironically, to entrench and legitimise communist rule which the rest of the world would not challenge. Openness in the current climate would not mean de facto colonisation and humiliation as it had in the past; rather, it would be a way to make up the time lost during the Mao years. Deng was right.

He was nonetheless careful to present openness as essentially nationalistic. He told the Twelfth National Congress of the Communist Party in 1982 that opening was not only indispensable for economic modernisation, but also would achieve two other aims: strengthening China so that it could challenge the hegemony of foreign powers, notably the United States, and furthering the cause of bringing Taiwan back to the 'motherland'.[2] China's identity would not be changed by engaging with foreign multinationals and technology, but its capacity to meet its destiny would be vastly enhanced. Like other reformers in China's history – such as Li Hongzhang, who masterminded the abortive self-strengthening movement between the 1860s and 1890s[3] – Deng believed that China could adopt Western forms of modernisation (*yong*) without having to import the culture and essence (*ti*) of them. Communist China would remain communist China, but in turn it would require a foreign policy that did not disturb the international system from which it intended to profit.

Deng's advice after Tiananmen was that China should 'observe developments soberly, maintain our position, meet challenges calmly, hide our capacities and bide our time, remain free of ambition, never claim leadership.'[4] China should not attempt to be a hegemon, it should never practise power politics and it should never pose a threat to its neighbours or to world peace. These are mantras that Chinese officials continue to repeat. China's foreign policy, as Foreign Minister Li Zhaoxing has declared, is designed first and foremost to serve economic development, following Deng's injunction.[5] Moreover, its rise is to be peaceful, in the famous formulation by Zheng Bijian, chair of the China Reform Forum.[6] But rising peacefully did not imply that China would forgo its proper interests; rather, it would seek to pursue and resolve them peacefully. Thus, although China has felt the need both to sound and to act more aggressively nationalistic in the years after the collapse of international communism, it has operated within Deng's maxims and the doctrine of the peaceful rise. So after the accidental bombing of the Chinese embassy in Belgrade by the United States in 1999, and later the mid-air collision between a United States EP-3 spy plane and a Chinese fighter in the South China Sea in 2001, China allowed an upsurge in nationalist street protests to accompany its own diplomatic response, but quickly curbed the protests when they threatened to get out of hand. The communist leadership did not believe that either issue damaged Chinese interests seriously enough to be worth threatening China's basic foreign policy. The objective is to be sufficiently nationalist to assuage domestic opinion and legitimise communist rule; to pursue carefully calculated national interests, and not to challenge an international system that is fundamentally friendly to China's development.

This is a tightrope that is increasingly difficult to walk as China becomes larger. The United States, as a hegemonic power, cannot be certain what China means by eventually regaining its 'rightful place' in the world, however unmenacingly it tries to behave at any moment. In the view of a realist like John J. Mearsheimer, a professor of political science at the University of Chicago, China and the United States are destined to clash militarily, and the United States' interest is to do all it can to forestall China becoming economically rich enough to challenge it. He draws an analogy with the Germany of Kaiser Wilhelm II and imperial Japan just before Pearl Harbor. They were rising powers whose developing might precipitated war, and war with China is similarly inevitable.[7] Others, such as Professor Avery Goldstein at the University of Pennsylvania, argue that China is different because – unlike Germany under Wilhelm or imperial Japan – it is not part of a wider coalition of states ready to challenge the United States. Also, there are areas of collaboration as well as competition between the

United States and China; an international system based on open markets makes war less necessary to secure vital interests. Comparisons with the nineteenth century omit a key difference: in an era of nuclear weapons, rising states have to be a great deal more circumspect in how they challenge the hegemonic power militarily. The United States has formidable hard and soft power compared with China, whose regime might collapse if any potential conflict – even one in Taiwan – went wrong. Goldstein concludes that the United States should remain watchful while holding China accountable for continuing to improve its international behaviour.[8]

China is keenly aware of the American debate; its best strategy is to pursue its national interests in a way that makes Mearsheimer look wrong, while striking a suitably nationalist note for domestic ears. So far both sides have managed the relationship, but there are vast possibilities for mistakes and miscalculations; furthermore, the party could lose control of the nationalist sympathies it has unleashed. As a good international citizen, China became a signatory of the Comprehensive Test Ban Treaty in 1996, condemned India and Pakistan for testing nuclear weapons, did not devalue the renminbi during the Asian financial crisis, has put pressure on North Korea to freeze its nuclear missile programme as a member of the 'six-party talks' and is establishing the ASEAN-China free-trade zone. It has used its veto in the UN Security Council only five times, and two of those vetoes were over Taiwan. All to the good, and all consistent with the doctrine of peaceful rise. China even dispatched $60 million of relief to the victims of the Tsunami and publicly demoted Major General Zhu Chenghu after his unwise warning to the Americans that China could and would aim missiles with nuclear warheads at its cities.[9]

On the other hand, China's size, economic growth, hunger for resources and military build-up can hardly be ignored. Its ambition to reintegrate Taiwan into China is undimmed. It is suspicious of Japan's intentions and of the Japanese alliance with the United States. Its anti-Japanese rhetoric is unrelenting. Moreover, China's good citizenship stops at the issue of human rights. It has assembled a majority coalition in the UN to prevent the Western powers from making motions condemning its actions. It has portrayed itself as a victim whose internal frictions – characteristic of any state – are being exaggerated by the West and described as systemic violations of human rights so that Westerners can infringe on its right of self-determination. To give way would be to hand the United States a propaganda coup, and would serve as a precedent for further incursions into states' freedom of action and sovereignty across the third world in the name of human rights.

This is a stance that many authoritarian third world leaders, such as Robert Mugabe of Zimbabwe, find congenial, excusing them from making the economic and political reforms the West urges. When the European Union and the United States made representations to the UN Security Council about Mugabe's slum clearance programme of 2005, which left hundreds of thousands homeless, China left the room. Mugabe has been fêted in Beijing and is now an honorary professor at the Foreign Affairs University there. Zimbabwe gets Chinese arms; China gets favourable mining concessions from Zimbabwe. The African Union expelled François Bozizé of the Central African Republic from membership in 2003 after a violent coup; China gave him a $2.5-million interest-free loan and welcomed him on an official visit.[10] China's championing of 'Asian values' is part of the same crusade; communism, far from being aberrant, is one more way that different Asian values express themselves and is thus excusable.

Western governments and business have largely let China off the hook. American business is anxious to have a foothold in China for low-cost production, to protect its international competitive position and to build its share in what is already one of the world's largest markets. It has urged successive United States administrations to look at China's problems through the eyes of the Chinese communist rulers and not to push issues of democracy and human rights too far. The businesspeople argue that the first priority is to feed China's hundreds of millions; human rights and democratic freedoms will evolve later, and are in any case the preserve of the Chinese people, not of outsiders. This, for example, was the consistent argument of Maurice R. Greenburg, chairman of American International Group, which is one of the world's largest insurance companies and was an early well-connected front runner in developing its Chinese business interests. British business echoed the argument in the period before the handover of Hong Kong to China in 1997. When Governor Chris Patten opened up the appointed legislative assembly to universal suffrage, China saw this (correctly) as putting it in a very difficult position after the handover. Either it would have to abolish the council, to a predicable storm of international criticism, or it would have to accept the council and the explicit challenge to China's concept of socialist democracy. British business, a powerful faction within the British Foreign Office, and the communist government put intense pressure on Britain to reverse Patten's position; Prime Minister John Major – to his credit – resisted and supported Patten.[11] The democratised Legislative Council was preserved.

In the grand scheme of things, this was only one, albeit significant, reverse amid a general advance. Its importance is that it suggests a lack of sustainability in China's position. China accepts pluralism, the rule of law and accountability abroad, however imperfectly expressed, while denying them at home, a position it has formalised with regard to Hong Kong. Moreover, since the fall of the Soviet Union democracy has become the new international gold standard – the desirable political structure to which more and more states are moving and which is the best way of exploiting globalisation. In 1988 two-thirds of states were non-democratic; today two-thirds are democratic.[12] China is increasingly an outlier. The more it grows and the more economically powerful it becomes, the more its identity as a one-party authoritarian state intent on remaining complicit with the international system – because that system serves its interests rather than builds and upholds it – will become ambiguous and difficult to manage.

The writing on the wall

So far China has defused tension and exploited the system of which, arguably, it is one of the biggest beneficiaries. China's problem is that its objective interest is to buttress the international system from which it benefits; but this means associating itself with values, institutions and processes that directly challenge what it practises at home. Yahoo, Microsoft and Google are part of the cultural yeast of globalisation, yet each has been at the receiving end of China's Internet firewall of censorship that, whatever security advantages it might bring, has been a severe propaganda setback. Equally, no trading partner can afford subsidies like those China gives to its state-owned enterprises. The larger China becomes, the more it will be subject to intense scrutiny about its trading practices.

Nor is the democratic question going to become easier to finesse. It is no accident that globalisation has been so closely associated with the spread of democracy. If states want the benefits of trade, foreign investment, transfer of technology, access to saving and reciprocal rights for their own enterprises to enjoy the same benefits, then they have to accept that there are attendant rules. Moreover, a dynamic is set in train. It can seem very attractive, for example, partially to privatise a state-owned enterprise to foreign investors; but afterwards there are demands for higher standards of transparency and accountability – part of the democratising agenda.

This process, for example, is now indirectly at work as China seeks foreign shareholdings in its banking system. China wants Western banking know-how and better banking standards because it is trying to avoid the high proportion of non-performing loans that it had in the 1990s – such loans would now be unfinanceable and would threaten the entire economy with a meltdown of the financial system. But that means accepting much higher standards of corporate governance and reporting, together with constraints on using the banking system to further the ends of the nation-state. China certainly obtains foreign investment in its financial system, hard currency and skills in an asymmetric deal heavily loaded in its favour, but it has had to concede a degree of transparency and accountability that is more consistent with democratic capitalism than Leninist corporatism. I repeat one crucial argument: to raise the productivity of Chinese enterprises and rebalance the Chinese economy towards more normal levels of consumption, saving and investment while maintaining current rates of economic growth vital to generating jobs and ensuring social stability, China will have to accept more economic and political pluralism, and the processes of justification and accountability that go with it. Deng's assumption, like Li Hongzhang's, that China can enjoy the economic advantages of the West without accepting the substantive processes that create them, will prove to be wrong.

China is thus a cockpit, both for the emergence of democratic pressures and for resistance against them. The West needs to judge over what time period, how smoothly and how inevitably China will march towards the distinctive mix of capitalism and democracy that is emerging in parts of Asia like India and Japan, and how to use its small leverage to advance the process. The danger is that China is now a $2-trillion economy. Although currently the world's fourth largest economy, it could have – on current trends – overtaken Germany by 2007 to become number three. It therefore has options for autonomous action to shape globalisation that might suit its interests but not those of the West. Chinese communism

and Chinese nationalism are an uneasy coalition; the more nationalism gains an upper hand in an authoritarian state, the more China
will want to behave according to its own criteria. China is perfectly capable, for example, of invading Taiwan, obstructing any
international action concerning Iran, or refusing to accept international protocols regarding climate change. The power it will
necessarily confront above any other is the United States. The
hope and aim must be that the story has a happy ending; but there
is plenty of scope for it to turn out otherwise.

Flashpoint 1: trade and finance

The United States is the anchor and driver of globalisation, but its
domestic coalition favouring globalisation is becoming ever more
fragile. The question is whether the avalanche of Chinese exports
which dwarfs any of the flows from China's predecessors, but
without any of the strategic necessity that justified free trade in
the past, is going to force the United States away from its free-
trade, open-market policy. After all, China, unlike Europe or
Japan, is communist. In 2006, the United States had the largest
bilateral trade deficit of any country in history. It imported about
$288 billion of goods from China and exported a mere $55 billion
back, so the trade deficit was $232 billion. This represents a ratio
of five to one. C. Fred Bergsten, director of Washington's Institute
for International Economics, points out that the ratio is twice
as bad as the ratio at the peak of concern about Japan's export
flood in the 1980s.[13] And with Chinese exports continuing to grow
faster than its imports from the United States, there is little sign
that the ratio – or the deficit – will do anything but get worse.

Six industries have lobbied Congress and won special protection – textiles, clothes, wooden furniture, colour televisions,
semiconductors and Louisiana shrimpers. They are harbingers of
more to come; the Department of Commerce has begun some

seventy anti-dumping proceedings against Chinese imports. Seizures of Chinese counterfeit goods are increasing dramatically. Pressure has been growing steadily in Congress. In the summer of 2005 Senator Charles Schumer of New York managed to get a two-to-one majority on a procedural vote calling for a 27.5 per cent tariff on all Chinese imports unless the Chinese revalued the renminbi. The Chinese conceded the 2 per cent upward movement in July 2005, together with a more flexible framework for making revaluations; few expect more than small annual movements, for the reason I have set out – the risk of a destabilising economic and social shock from a sharp revaluation is too high.[14] However, cumulatively by the summer of 2007 there had been a 7 per cent revaluation. On his state visit to Beijing in the autumn of 2005, George W. Bush received a promise from President Hu Jintao that China would eliminate its trade deficit. The problem is that without a dollar devaluation against the renminbi of about 30 per cent (see Chapter 6) there is not the remotest chance of such a correction. In May 2006, when Hu Jintao came to Washington on a visit that deliberately was not described as a state visit, the deficit was higher and the renminbi was unaltered. As identified in Chapter 1, the Senate Finance Committee's 20–1 support for a bill requiring action from the United States government against countries with a persistently 'misaligned' currency looks like the precursor of sabre-rattling translating into real legislation in the run-up to the United States presidential election in November 2008.

A formidable institutional apparatus is being constructed, whose interest is to oppose the growth of Chinese imports. A warning of the congressional mood has been the five annual reports of the cross-party United States China Economic and Security Review Commission, established as part of the deal to allow China into the World Trade Organization. It has used its position to put together an impressive body of analytic evidence supporting its basic stance: that, as it said in its report of 2005, 'over the last year, on balance, the trends in the United States-

China relationship have negative implications for our long-term national economic and security interests'.[15] China, it argues, is pursuing a twenty-first-century mercantilist policy as part of its ambition to be a great power with commensurate military capacity, boosting its high-technology sector through huge government spending and subsidising export growth and foreign direct investment – the centrepiece of which is the persistent undervaluation of the renminbi. Cumulatively, the United States has lost 1.5 million jobs between 1989 and 2003 because of China, it claims; a further study reported that some one hundred thousand jobs were lost in 2004 from Chinese exports.[16] Interestingly, neither study makes any effort to estimate compensating growth of employment in the United States' service and knowledge industries, resulting in turn from higher consumer spending and lower interest rates as a result of cheap Chinese import prices. In the commission's universe the traffic is all one-way. There should be an across-the-board tariff on Chinese imports if China does not revalue the renminbi, and the commission warns of the strategic dangers if China acquires United States companies. In its 2007 report it went further, observing that currency reform alone would be insufficient to rebalance the deficit because 'the disadvantages are compounded by China's other unfair trading practices'. It called for 'coordinated actions in the World Trade Organization against unfair industrial subsides and restriction on workers' rights'.

Five years ago the commission represented the hawkish wing of American views of China, but it has increasingly become more mainstream. Democrats are concerned about blue-collar jobs and human rights; everybody is concerned about the strategic threat; and everybody opposes China's acquiring any but the most innocuous companies. *The Economist* reports Gary Clyde Hufbauer of the Institute for International Economics as saying that there are twenty draft anti-China bills in the congressional hopper, among which the most menacing would rescind China's 'permanent normal trading status', which was the precondition for its membership in the World Trade Organization.[17] Actually, a unilateral attempt by the United States to suspend China's membership of the World Trade Organization would be illegal. But that has not deterred its two sponsors, Byron Dorgan of North Dakota and Lindsey Graham of South Carolina. In February 2006 the Bush administration created a China enforcement task force within the United States' Trade Representative's Office to monitor the growth of Chinese imports – something that never happened at the height of the hysteria over Japanese imports in the 1980s. The administration warned darkly of counter-measures and anti-dumping suits if China did not heed American concerns. In April 2006 Timothy Stratford, assistant United States trade representative, said that the trade relationship with China lacked 'equity, durability, and balance in the opportunities it provides'.[18] The United States reserves the right under the Omnibus Trade and Competitiveness Act of 1988 to initiate, either alone or with the International Monetary Fund, action to force a country to readjust its currency if this has been manipulated to produce a material trade imbalance. So far the United States Treasury has ruled that China is not manipulating its currency, but it is under intense pressure to change its ruling. Every Democrat candidate for the presidential nomination has taken a get-tough approach to China and there is a consistent carelessness about whether the United States should operate unilaterally or within World Trade Organization protocols. A Democrat President and Congress in 2009 would be hard put not to turn campaign rhetoric into policy – the potential trigger for a full-scale trade and financial war.

China's problem in formulating a response is threefold. First, a revaluation of the renminbi on the timescale and magnitude of United States' demands has profound economic and social consequences. Second, without a broad move to Western and the best Asian standards of corporate governance, transparency and accountability, China will never be able to prove before the World Trade Organization's investigations that it is not subsidising state-owned enterprises through its banking system, or that its allegedly private corporations are not puppets of the Communist Party – accusations that will stand because they are substantially true. When China was smaller it could escape international censure, but as the emergent world's number-one exporter it will have to comply with the rules of transparency in order to show that it is competing fairly. The attempt to draw the sting of criticism because so many of its exports are produced by foreign companies is working less and less successfully; American politicians do not make this distinction. Third, even if China manages these two problems, its last problem is insoluble: it is formally communist.

It is this that will make China's attempts to repeat what the Europeans and Japanese have done – buy American companies – so toxic. For a generation the United States has financed its monumental trade deficit by allowing foreigners to buy its assets – Hollywood studios, Ben and Jerry's ice cream and Sohio. Foreigners have $1.5 trillion invested in the United States, and until recently this fact has created a surprisingly small political backlash. Europeans and even the Japanese have been seen as surrogate Americans who, ultimately, are not challenging American interests and who in any case allow reciprocal purchases in their own countries by Americans. China, following the doctrine of peaceful rise, has so far held the mountain of dollar foreign-exchange reserves it is acquiring through its trade surplus and rigging its currency in United States treasury bills, but the risk-to-reward ratio is looking increasingly silly from its point of view. It receives a derisory interest rate and risks a capital loss as the renminbi is revalued; it badly needs to acquire American companies and assets, both in the United States and throughout the world, that will offer better returns and better protection against currency movements. Yet China's total stock of overseas foreign direct investment was $44.7 billion at the end of 2004 – about 5 per cent of its current stock of foreign-exchange reserves.[19]

Cumulatively, Chinese investors have bought perhaps nine hundred small United States companies worth, in all, $1 billion; Lenovo bought IBM for $1.25 billion.[20] It is doubtful that the total value of Chinese-owned American companies is more than $3 billion.

It was already difficult enough for China to buy into the United States before 9/11. But now, with the intensely hostile reaction to Dubai Ports World acquiring a management interest in six United States ports, it is close to impossible. If CNOOC's bid for Unocal aroused security concerns, the threshold has become very low. According to the Congressional Research Service, Unocal accounted for only 0.8 per cent of the United States' production of crude oil and natural gas liquids, and 0.3 per cent of United States consumption; it is hard to characterise the potential change of ownership as 'threatening the national security of the United States', as the blocking of the bid was rationalised. On the other hand, CNOOC could top Chevron's bid of $17.7 billion only because it had access to cheap credit from a state-owned banking system that was indifferent to the underlying strength or weakness of its balance sheet. And there is no escaping the fact that the ultimate owner of an American oil asset would have been the Chinese Communist Party. Dubai Ports World and CNOOC are the advance guard of a new trend in global finance: funds run by governments and which take stakes, or even take over, companies in Western countries. Sovereign funds, which Morgan Stanley estimate could grow to $12 trillion by 2015, have the capacity to politicise investment. China's overseas investment ambitions are likely to become the flashpoint for generalised American resistance to foreign governments owning wholly or in part American corporate, property or equity assets.

For the United States is becoming increasingly nationalist about foreigners. The Exon-Florio amendment of 1988 authorises the president to block foreign takeovers if they threaten national security; between 2003 and 2006 there were six reviews and five withdrawals under threat of review – more than in the previous ten years combined. China's companies are not like BP, VW or Sony: they are the arms of a communist authoritarian state, or are intensely influenced by it. If China came shopping for companies and assets in the United States in a major way, the reaction would be ferocious. And, unless China changes, such a reaction would be partly justified.

Flashpoint 2: resource wars

The arrival of an oil price of $50 per barrel in 2004 and its rise to over $70 during 2006 and some $90 in 2007 is more than a cyclical upward spike after which the oil trade will return to normal. The emergence of China as the world's second-largest oil importer with the most rapid growth of oil demand underlines a long-term change in the imbalance of oil demand and supply, of which the latest oil price rise has been the most significant manifestation. The world is making a transition to a period when oil and gas are more likely to be expensive, with alarming moments when they may become very expensive indeed. At a time of international terrorism, when oil pipelines and trans-shipment ports are targets, shocks to prices can come as much from unexpected fall-offs in supply as from demand. The investment banking firm Goldman Sachs, for example, warns that oil could experience a 'superspike', rising to up to $105 a barrel, some time over the next few years.[21] Oil prices at these levels, driven by demand rather than by artificial limits on supply (such as those imposed by OPEC at the time of the Yom Kippur war in 1973), sound the tocsin about how much longer finite oil reserves can last, given the present rates of demand and energy efficiency. After another thirty or forty years there simply will not be enough identified, readily accessible oil under the ground to meet the United States' current and anticipated demand for oil, together with the surge in demand coming from China in particular and, if growth continues, from India and the rest of the world. By 2030 China will import as much oil as the United States. The United States Geological Survey takes the Panglossian view that there is sufficient oil to meet demand, at least until 2040, when production will peak; other observers, such as the International Energy Agency, concede that peak production could come as early as 2017.[22] But whether one is an optimist or a pessimist, the end is in sight. Chevron's warning that the era of cheap, plentiful oil is over[23] is shared by most senior analysts and industry watchers.

The importance of the politically unstable Islamic Middle East as an oil supplier is going to grow. Today two-thirds of the world's oil reserves are in the Middle East, but the rapidity with which oil is being exploited in Africa, Russia, the United States, the North Sea and South America means that by 2020 the proportion of global oil reserves in the Middle East will have grown to 83 per cent.[24] Moreover, much of this oil passes through the Strait of Hormuz between the Gulf of Oman and the Persian Gulf. The strait is twenty-one miles wide at its narrowest point, and the Iranian island of Abu Musa is near its entrance – manned by Iranian Revolutionary Guards reportedly equipped with Silkworm anti-ship missiles.[25] Even today they could wreak havoc on world oil supplies and prices: 17 million barrels of oil flow through the strait every day. By 2020 Iran, or any committed terrorist group, would be in an even stronger position.

The threat is live. Al-Qaeda's leaders Osama bin Laden and Ayman Al-Zawahiri have said that the Saudi Arabian oil infrastructure is a target. The Abqaiq oil processing facility in Saudi Arabia, the massive complex that removes impurities from two-thirds of the kingdom's oil production before it is pumped to the coast, has already been the object of an unsuccessful suicide-bombing mission in February 2005. A former CIA operative, Robert Baer, estimates that the facility's output of 6.8 million barrels per day could be reduced to one million in the event of a 'moderate to severe attack'.[26] Nor is the Suez Canal any less vulnerable. About 1.3 million barrels of oil move through daily and it is three hundred yards wide at its narrowest point. Terrorists have so far restricted their attacks to Egyptian holiday resorts; an attack on the Suez Canal would produce much more damage for the West.

Also, there is evidence that higher oil prices and revenues are likely politically to freeze the oil-producing states with authoritarian, repressive political regimes. Michael Lewin Ross studied 113 countries between 1971 and 1997 and found that the oil producers were more resistant to democracy.[27] An authoritarian government with significant oil revenues has more revenue to pay for internal repression; it has less need to justify its actions to its citizens because it does not have to tax them; and by having a less developed, less diversified economy it experiences less pressure to open up to the forces of economic and political pluralism. This phenomenon is observable from Indonesia to Nigeria. Ross's findings dovetail with research by Jeffrey Sachs and Andrew Warner; resource wealth, they find, holds back the process of industrialisation and modernisation because the spillover effects into the rest of the economy are much lower from exporting oil than exporting manufactures.[28] Other research, examining forty-seven civil wars between 1965 and 1999, found that once an economy hit a threshold where around one-quarter of its GDP originated in a commodity like oil there was an irresistible tendency for rival groups to fight for control of the spoils. Civil war became much more likely.[29]

Oil, in short, is something of a curse. And, as Iran is vividly demonstrating, it has plenty of destabilising implications for power relationships within the international system. Iran wants to build nuclear reactors; the United States is opposed because these would give Iran the possibility of developing a military nuclear capacity. Iran's delegate to the International Energy Agency, Ali Asghar Soltanieh, has described Tehran's view: 'The United

States has the power to cause harm and pain,' he said in March 2006, 'but the United States is also susceptible to harm and pain. So if that is the path that the United States wishes to choose, let the ball roll.'[30] The logic is merciless. Global demand for oil is currently about eighty-five million barrels a day; global supply at maximum production is only slightly higher. Iranian oil exports – some 2.7 million barrels a day – are a crucial swing factor. If, for any reason, they were suspended the price of oil would rise sharply. If the United States attacks Iranian nuclear installations, and Iran retaliates by either stopping its exports or attacking oil tankers in the Strait of Hormuz, the United States and the West would be in the middle of oil mayhem. Fortified by this knowledge, and China's support, Tehran is happy to face down almost any threat from Washington.

Because of these challenges, Chinese and American leaders have become alert to the risks and to the need to develop energy policy at the highest level. There is well-established precedent. Few British readers will have been alive when the United Kingdom grabbed the oil-rich parts of the former Ottoman Empire after the First World War in order to make sure it had secure oil supplies for its oil-dependent fleet. More recently the United States led an operation to liberate Kuwait from the Iraqi invasion in 1989, in part because of concerns that Iraq would control too much of the world's oil reserves. The open question is whether states will revert to historical type, or will they continue to rely on the global market system?

The auguries are not good. In May 2005 China established a new State Energy Office that reports directly to the State Council, the highest executive body in the country. President Bush, in his State of the Union address of 2006, declared that one strategic objective was to lower the United States' dependence on imported Middle Eastern oil. His intervention followed a simulation called 'Oil Shockwave', chaired by Senators Richard Lugar (Indiana) and Joe Lieberman (Connecticut). It purpose was to assess what the

United States could do to mitigate the price and supply effects of a small interruption in oil supplies due to, say, a terrorist attack on a major Middle Eastern supplier. The answer was almost nothing. Robbie Diamond of Securing America's Future Energy (SAFE), one of the chief sponsors of the event, declared: 'This simulation serves as a clear warning that even relatively small reductions in oil supply will result in tremendous national security and economic problems for the country. The issue deserves immediate attention.'[31]

China is of the same opinion – and its diplomacy is increasingly driven by the need to make sure that it has dependable, diversified, secure oil reserves and the means to get them to China. As the deputy chief of the Chinese general staff, General Xiong Guangkai, acknowledged just before his retirement in 2006, the competition for oil has become 'fiercer': Xiong argues that China's energy problem needs to be taken 'seriously and dealt with strategically'.[32] That means less reliance on the Middle East,[33] less transportation of oil via sea-lanes policed by the United States' navy, more capacity for the Chinese navy to protect Chinese tankers and more oil brought overland by pipeline from central Asia. The American build-up of its naval base at Changi in Singapore, allowing it to patrol the Strait of Malacca between Malaysia and Indonesia, through which 80 per cent of China's imported oil moves, is regarded with particular suspicion. The channel is five hundred miles long, and less than two miles wide at its narrowest point. With India modernising its military facilities on the Andaman and Nicobar Islands at the northern end of the strait, China feels sandwiched in and strategically vulnerable. Hu Jintao has referred a number of times to what he describes as the Malacca dilemma. 'Certain powers,' he has declared, 'have all along encroached on and tried to control the navigation through the strait.'[34] There is no mistaking whom he means.

For decades the doctrine of peaceful rise has meant that China has tried to secure energy and raw materials without confronting the United States and the West. China's long-standing willingness to deal with states that the West regards as pariahs is in part a practical and ideological refusal to make judgements about countries' domestic policy. (That is their concern, and China is not going to set a precedent for closer scrutiny of its own internal arrangements.) It is also in part a recognition that dealing with Sudan, Angola, Iran or Uzbekistan allows China to avoid direct confrontation with Western interests. Indeed, the United States has tacitly considered China's readiness to access oil from pariah states helpful. However, the larger China has become, the sheer scale of its needs has forced it more and more to intrude into areas that the United States regards as its own sphere of influence. China has also moved from non-committal engagement with pariah states to openly supporting them. The relationship with the West, therefore, is becoming steadily tenser.

Examples abound. Consider China's courtship of Canada. In April 2005 Petro China and Enbridge signed a memorandum of understanding to build a $2-billion 'gateway' pipeline to move oil from Alberta to the Pacific Coast. Yet only four years earlier Dick Cheney, the United States' vice-president, had declared that Canada's tar sands were part of the United States' energy security. Venezuela in South America sells 60 per cent of its oil to the United States: President Hugo Chávez, in Beijing in December 2004, declared that he now wanted to put Venezuelan oil 'at the disposal of the great Chinese fatherland' after a hundred years of American domination; in 2005 he signed deals to allow the Chinese to explore for oil and gas. Like the Canadians, the Venezuelans want to build a pipeline to the Pacific coast, which in their case they reach via Colombia. They reached an agreement in principle with Colombia in July 2004. Conspiracy theorists can portray the two moves as China darkly intruding into Uncle Sam's backyard; the fair-minded can see that Canada and Venezuela, as major oil exporters, need to be able to offer their Asian customers the opportunity to load their tankers inexpensively on the Pacific coast. Both stories are congruent with the facts.

Saudi Arabia, holder of the world's largest oil reserves, supplies 16 per cent of China's imports and is an object of assiduous Chinese courtship – again, a direct challenge to the United States' traditional sphere of influence. In 2004 Chinese companies were given exploration rights, and China has reciprocated by offering the Saudis preferential partnership rights to build oil refineries in China that can refine heavier Arabian crude. For the moment Saudi Arabia knows that its long-term security and its defence interests lie with the United States. But Islamic militancy is increasing, and Saudi Arabia has its own strict Wahhabi sect, which is now in total control of the Saudi education system. The Saudis are facing explosive growth in the numbers of young people seeking work (Saudi Arabia has one of the highest birth rates in the world) and are having difficulty meeting this demand. For such reasons, it might one day make sense for the Saudis to align with a power that is less controversial in Islamic eyes. That reality has already begun to mean that China has diplomatic opportunities to confront the United States which were not available even five years ago.

In Iran, the Chinese have been given rights to exploit the giant Yadavaran oil field and are examining the feasibility of a pipeline project to link the transport of Iranian oil to pipelines from central Asia. As I have discussed, Iran is particularly problematic. China has used its veto in the UN Security Council to block attempts to bring Iran's nuclear programme under the United States Inspection regime, and has sold C-801 and C-802 anti-ship cruise missiles to Iran – which could be used against American naval vessels in the Persian Gulf. Suddenly China's foreign policy looks less benign – perhaps indicating that its moves in the Americas should be reinterpreted. In Sudan, China has persistently obstructed international efforts to sanction the government over the genocide in Darfur, which has killed some two hundred thousand people. In Uzbekistan, China has refused to allow an international investigation of President Karimov's bloody suppression of dissent. Thus an ominous picture emerges of China developing a foreign policy that is actively hostile to human rights and to international law: all it wants is oil. Deputy Foreign Minister Zhou Wenzhong (now China's ambassador to Washington) said, when asked about genocide in Darfur: 'Business is business. We try to separate politics from business, and in any case the internal position of Sudan is an internal affair, and we are not in a position to influence them.'[35]

If this is the state of affairs in 2007, tension is only going to rise. China's trade with Africa has quadrupled since 2000. In November 2006 Hu Jintao held a summit for 48 African leaders pledging $5 billion in assistance for Africa, cumulatively providing $20 billion in infrastructure spending and trade financing between 2007 and 2010. The main target has been oil from the Sudan, Angola, Nigeria and Somalia. But China has also been in the African market to secure supplies of platinum from Zimbabwe (hence the relationship with Mugabe discussed earlier), copper from Zambia, tropical timber from Congo-Brazzaville and iron ore from South Africa. China has bought natural-resource companies in Australia and Canada; gold mines in Bolivia and coal mines in the Philippines; and it is developing soy production in Brazil. Australia, ally of the United States in Asia – the United States' deputy sheriff in East Asia, as George W. Bush characterised it – is sedulously courted. Australia even acknowledges that its support could not be automatically assumed in any resistance led by the United States against a potential Chinese invasion of Taiwan.[36]

All this is congruent with a peacefully rising economic power. The interdependencies of trade foster the interpenetration of the world economy, and although China may be boosting its secure sources of energy and raw materials it is also massively benefiting the world by lifting prices and itself providing an enormous market for imports. Those are not the concerns. Rather, the worry is that China will – sometimes consciously, and sometimes just because of its sheer bulk and its authoritarian character – find itself undermining the framework in which globalisation has taken place. This is partly a willingness to have all states share minimum common norms regarding the rule of law, and partly a willingness to accept that security is provided by the United States. China chafes under these constraints already; it watches the United States picking and choosing which international laws to obey, and it sees no reason not to copy. The world issue will come if the chafing ever transmutes into an active challenge.

Flashpoint 3: strategy and defence

There are plenty of running sores and territorial disputes in Asia, but the most potentially dangerous is Taiwan. Captured as a Japanese colony in 1895, it was repossessed by the Nationalists in 1945 and was where they fled after their defeat by Mao. China has never accepted Taiwan's claim to the status of a sovereign state, and has effectively blocked its international recognition ever since 1949. Chiang Kai-shek ran Taiwan as a militarised authoritarian state. He died in 1975, a year before Mao, and after that there was a democratic unfreezing as part of a Nationalist strategy to create a Taiwanese identity and unity in defiance of Beijing. In 2000 the opposition party, the Democratic Progressive Party (DPP), founded in 1986 as part of the democratising process, won the election. It has been in power ever since.

Taiwan has not been controlled by Beijing for more than a hundred years, and now it is run as a Chinese democracy – two facts that madden the communist government. In its view, Taiwan is an integral part of the People's Republic of China. Its flourishing as a democratic, capitalist territory that dares to call itself the Republic of China is a constant reminder that the revolution is not yet complete; that there is a rival and successful alternative economic and social model for dissident mainland Chinese to compare and copy in their critique of communism; and that the century of humiliation is not yet completely revenged. Hong Kong has been returned by the British, and Macao by the Portuguese, but because Taiwan was a Japanese colony during China's period of weakness the foundation was laid for today's regime and no prospect of a handover is in sight. If an invasion did not risk impelling the United States to intervene on the side of Taiwan, it would have been made long ago.

The Taiwanese, meanwhile, are increasingly frustrated by its semi-statehood. The DPP is committed to fight for the completion of Taiwanese democracy in a fully fledged Taiwanese state. The party has been the beneficiary of Taiwan's steady move towards economic and political pluralism – freedom of the press, a two-party democratic system and the rule of law. In 2004 President Chen proposed two referenda – one on strengthening Taiwan's defences and the other on opening talks with China. If passed, they would have laid the basis for a larger referendum on Taiwan's independence. China regarded the proposals with deep dismay and as a provocation. However a boycott by the Nationalists and opposition from the United States meant that the necessary 50 per cent quorum was not reached. But the episode reinforced Beijing's belief that a movement towards full statehood is under way in Taiwan and, if unopposed, will gather momentum. Beijing is newly alarmed that Mr Chen's putative successor, Frank Hsiek, has received his party's nomination for the presidential elections in March 2008 only by pledging another referendum on reconstituting the constitution and asserting sovereign independence. In 1992 only 17.3 per cent of the population regarded themselves as Taiwanese, but by 2003 the figure had jumped to 43.2 per cent. This trend too confirms Beijing in its view that the relaxation begun in the mid-1980s could easily lead to Taiwan's declaring statehood, even if only 10 per cent of the Taiwanese want independence 'as soon as possible'.[37] Another sophisticated poll of the Taiwanese found a substantial increase in those prepared to risk independence even if it implied war, with only 27 per cent supporting reunification with China.[38] The use of the local Minnan dialect has soared, effectively displacing Mandarin. The Examination Yuan, the government's top examination agency, has omitted Chinese history and geography from future civil service exams.[39] The cultural changes are profound. If Taiwan ever succeeded in winning consent for independence within its own democratic rules, it would be very difficult for the world to withhold recognition. That would be a severe diplomatic and political reverse for Beijing.

Beijing is using every tool it can find to resist. It encourages cross-strait trade and investment, so that Taiwan has a growing stake in the mainland: China has now supplanted the United States as the number-one destination for Taiwanese exports. It supports those forces in Taiwanese politics that favour the status quo, such as the mayor of Taipei, and future Nationalist presidential candidate Ma Ying-Jeou. In 2005 it passed an anti-secession law in which it reminded Taiwan that it would regard a claim for statehood as secession, which it reserved the right to resist militarily. It consistently builds up its military forces. Rear Admiral Eric A. McVadon, a seasoned China-watcher who is the current director of Asia-Pacific studies at the Institute for Foreign Policy Analysis in Washington, argues that there is only one way to interpret China's priorities for defence spending. China is not seeking to become a rival superpower, but rather is seeking to reclaim Taiwan and repel any Japanese and American reaction.[40] McVadon explains the military 'concept' that China's investment supports: it will use short-range and medium-range ballistic missiles, in particular the mobile DF-21, to overwhelm Taiwan's air defences and offensive missile capacity. It concentrates on accurate medium-range missiles because it wants to attack United States carrier groups and surface vessels at sea, which it expects would be sent to support Taiwan. China is investing in sub-marines, particularly those of the Russian Kilo Class and their lethal weapon system the SS-N-22 missiles, because it wants to be able to deploy anti-ship cruise missiles against the United States from submarines in addition to its land-based efforts. The naval and air force investment, again, makes sense only as essentially second-wave operations after the missile systems have done their work, and again in the context of expected retaliation by the United States.

This is a formidable and growing armoury. Even so, an attack on Taiwan, together with pre-emptive attacks on potential American and Japanese retaliation, would be a huge logistical challenge; although China has engaged in fourteen joint exercises since 2000, according to the Pentagon, it is still a long way from the kind of coordination that the United States achieved in Iraq. Indeed, the Pentagon Report of 2005 on China's Military Capacity[41] endorses McVadon's analysis: although it acknowledges that China is building up long-range, road-mobile intercontinental missile systems – the DF-31 – it nonetheless describes China's posture as essentially 'active defence' focused primarily on Taiwan. However, the scale of this more limited build-up is increasingly impressive. In the Pentagon's words: 'The pace and scope of China's military build-up are, already, such as to put regional military balances at risk. Current trends in China's military modernization could provide China with a force capable of prosecuting a range of military options in Asia – well beyond Taiwan – potentially posing a credible threat to modern militaries operating in the region.'[42]

The question is whether China will act. From the Chinese point of view, to regain Taiwan would be a great boost to domestic legitimacy, would remove a potential ideological threat and would also open up military options not present at the moment. The Pentagon quotes General Wen Zongren, political commissar of the elite PLA Academy of Military Science, as saying that resolving the issue of Taiwan is of 'far-reaching significance to breaking international forces' blockade against China's maritime security . . . Only when we break this blockade shall we be able to talk about China's rise . . . [T]o rise suddenly, China must pass through oceans and go out of the oceans in its future development.'

On the other hand, an attack on Taiwan would be a massive risk. Taiwan has a well-equipped substantial air force with nearly three hundred modern fourth-generation fighter planes including 146 F16s and over fifty Mirages (on a similar scale to the British RAF). The Chinese air force may be more than one thousand planes strong, but it can field fewer than one hundred fourth-generation planes. The airspace over Taiwan permits operational airspace for around three hundred aircraft; Taiwan would give a good account of itself, especially as it could expect assistance from Japan and the United States.[43] An amphibious attack on Taiwan would also be fraught with hazard. In 2001, the International Institute for Strategic Studies observed that 'it would take around eight hundred to one thousand large landing craft nearly two weeks to transport the required thirty infantry divisions to Taiwan. At present, the Chinese Navy could move one, perhaps two divisions.'[44] The landing craft would have to run the gauntlet of the Hsiung Feng III, a highly sophisticated supersonic anti-ship missile. But while the balance of military risk and advantage suggests that China would not dare an invasion at present, it is outspending Taiwan by ten to one on arms. Taiwan is actually reducing its spending – confident that China will not invade and that it can rely on the United States. After all, an unsuccessful Chinese invasion would probably constitute a lethal blow to the Communist's Party standing and prestige. It would also be a green light to other restless parts of China – Tibet, Xinjiang and Inner Mongolia. They too could then try their luck against a diminished regime.

Even if an invasion of Taiwan succeeded, the change in the world's perception of China would be decisive. China could no longer pretend to be engaged in a 'peaceful rise', and some of its moral authority as a challenger to the United States would be lost. Nor could it be certain that it would win a long war against a broad Asian alliance, including the United States and Japan, aimed at the restoration of Taiwan's status. Such a defeat would represent a more extended and dramatic humiliation than failing to take the island. The best strategy for China, if it wants to reintegrate Taiwan, is to do so within a democratic, pluralist China based on the rule of law – the very structure opposed by the Communist Party. But what may be best is not necessarily what will be pursued. Indeed, a Communist Party with its back against the wall could decide that invasion was one way out of its troubles.

What should America do?

American diplomacy in Asia should be aimed at keeping the temperature down, keeping the lines of communication open and constructing an unthreatening environment in which China can move in a pluralist direction. Instead, it does the opposite. It over-accentuates its preoccupation with bilateral military and security relationships, underplays its commitment to fostering strong multilateral regional groupings, which it almost casually neglects, and incites fierce nationalistic rivalry between Japan and China. As a result, whatever its warm words about 'engagement' or inviting China to be a 'responsible stakeholder' in the international system,[45] China believes that the real aims of the United States are containment, encirclement and blocking China's rise. China is, of course, partly right. The United States cannot make up its mind whether to contain or engage China, and by default it has found itself applying a foreign policy more in keeping with the nineteenth-century German statesmen Bismarck than with the enlightened United States that created the post-war international settlement and supported the formation of today's European Union.[46] This is an historic mistake that could all too easily topple the United States into a conflict it does not want, and does not need. Allowing the Pentagon to define the interests of the United States and the West will inevitably mean that the focus is on defence and security, bilateral alliances and coalitions of the willing. Whether having a spat with South Korea's president Roh Moo Hyun, or showering favours on Japan's prime minister Junichiro Koizumi, President Bush shows that United States approbation will be conferred on those who do his exact bidding.[47] Regional security, regional alliances and multilateralism are seen as the soft option. This view could not be more wrong.

The management of the United States' relationship with Japan, and thus with China, is fraught with difficulty. Japan is a capitalist democracy that is deepening its commitment to pluralism and the rule of law; it has apologised twenty-one times for what it did in China between 1931 and 1945. Within Japan the state is receding in importance, and increasingly there is a genuine marketplace of ideas and opinions. The coalition in favour of freezing defence expenditure at 1 per cent of GDP is very powerful. However, Japan is a key regional actor, and the second biggest economy in the world; there is every reason why it should adapt its constitution to permit more overseas activism and offer greater input to global security initiatives, especially within the United Nations. Over the past two years Japan has begun to flex its muscles. In February 2005 a joint statement by Washington and Tokyo explicitly linked, for the first time, the alliance's interests with peace in the Taiwan Strait. After Prime Minister Koizumi won the election in October 2005, the governing LDP has proposed retaining Japan's permanent renunciation of war as a constitutional obligation but amending it to allow Japan's Self-Defence Force to join collective efforts at defence beyond Japan. The United States broadly supports the initiative; it wants Japan's support in its international adventures, and it will need Japan's Special Defence Force if it ever has to intervene in the Taiwan Strait.

Asians regard these moves with suspicion. For China's communists they prove that Japanese militarism is just below the surface. China even objected to Japan's participation in sending six hundred non-combat soldiers for support operations in Iraq. Lee Kuan Yew of Singapore has likened the idea of Japan's participation in peace-keeping operations supervised by the UN to giving liqueur-laced chocolate to a reforming alcoholic: a needless lure which could entice Japan back to bad old habits.[48] And Japan does not help its own case. In the spring of 2005, when China and Japan were squaring up over the Senkaku Islands (see Chapter 1), tension also mounted between South Korea and Japan over the Dokdo (or, in Japanese, Takeshima) Islands: about 0.08 of a square mile, or fifty acres of land. Heavily armed Japanese and Korean naval vessels were sent to an ocean face-off. The dispute is still unresolved.

Japan is more and more self-assertively nationalistic, confident of the United States' defensive nuclear umbrella. Koizumi's annual visit to the Yasukuni shrine to commemorate 2.5 million dead Japanese soldiers, unfortunately including fourteen convicted war criminals, was hardly an act of emollience, notwithstanding his protest that the visit is private and that it is wrong to distinguish among the dead. Even within Japan the visit provoked outspoken criticism. Japan's war record – of comfort women, slave labour, the notorious Unit 731, where human experiments were undertaken, and the slaughter at Nanjing – is still not accepted or confronted by some on the nationalist right, whose textbooks (in particular, *Atarashii Rekishi Kyokasho*) omit these crimes.[49] All is grist to the mill of the Chinese Communist Party, which is looking for evidence of growing Japanese militarism and nationalism.

From China's perspective, the United States' bilateral military alliances with Japan and India and its network of military bases do not look like 'engagement'. When Defence Secretary Donald Rumsfeld said in Singapore in 2005 that he did not understand which enemy China thought it had in mind to justify its growing military spending, it was disingenuousness of the highest order. Readers only have to cast their eyes back over the various quotations from Chinese officials in this chapter to get a sense of how China feels. Although it promotes ASEAN + 3 (the ten members of the Association of South East Asian Nations plus China, Japan and South Korea[50]) as a multilateral regional economic and security forum, China can hardly fail to notice Washington's reluctance over any form of multilateralism except the Association for Pacific Economic Cooperation (APEC), which the United States leads and which is little more than a talking shop. And when China collaborates in the 'six-party talks' (United States, North Korea, South Korea, China, Japan and Russia) to address the issue of North Korea's nuclear capacity it observes the United States' double standard, because the United States takes an accommodating approach to India's civil nuclear programme. Concerning North Korea, the United States is careful not to institutionalise any mechanism that would give China a formal international role. If America wants to play Bismarckian politics, why should not China?

The answer is that for the time being China gets too much out of the international system to rock the boat. China carefully appraises the advantages. It keeps a close watch on how its 'comprehensive national power' is developing – a term the Chinese Military Academy defines as 'organic integration of capacities of subsistence, development, and coordination'.[51] Each year there is a detailed appraisal of the Chinese coordination system, assessing the ability of the Chinese political leadership to unify and coordinate; and of China's 'hardware', including all its physical factors, and then its software – its 'ideational ethos' and intelligence. This is a conscious analysis of the totality of China's power capacity.

Chinese nationalism is, if anything, growing, as a consequence of massive domestic propaganda. In September 1994 the Central Committee of the Chinese Communist Party, advised by the Central Propaganda Department, issued an 'Outline for Conducting

Patriotic Education'. The outline established patriotic education from the nursery schools to the university as a key party aim, and it has been delivered with scant regard for historical truth. Zhao Suisheng argues that Chinese history has been over-simplified and that inconvenient truths – such as the expansion of the Qing dynasty, the violence of the Boxers and Chinese atrocities during the war against Japan – are downplayed or ignored.[52] There is no mention of China's recent wars. There is almost hysterical paranoia and distrust of foreign intentions. Beijing's failure to be chosen as the site of the 2000 Olympics was depicted as an anti-Chinese plot – though this is conveniently forgotten as the Beijing Olympics of 2008 approach. The message is unambiguous. China has to be on permanent guard against its enemies. It must avoid disunity at home, and its interests must be protected abroad by a vigilant communist government.

Patriotic education has built on a proclivity ever present in the population at large: defiance aimed against the allegedly predatory foreigner. This attitude is rooted in a lack of confidence in China, its culture and its achievements. The *China Can Say No* books of the 1990s were bestsellers with little official inducement. In August 2005 China presented an e-signature petition with forty-six million names to UN Secretary-General Kofi Annan, opposing Japan's being offered a permanent seat on the Security Council, a reform that the Chinese government implacably opposes.[53] Communist leaders know that General Secretary Hu Yaobang's championing of reconciliation with Japan in the 1980s contributed to his ousting, and even Mao is sometimes accused of having been too soft on Japan.[54] Yet this genuine nationalist feeling, together with the party's own nationalist rhetoric, locks it in a foreign policy trap. It cannot give ground or change a stance, even when doing so may be in its own objective interest. All this makes the conventions of normal diplomacy very difficult. For instance, Jiang Zemin's state visit to Japan in 1998 was, in Japanese terms, a public relations disaster: Jiang felt obliged to hector Japan on its conduct, only to be criticised at home for being insufficiently tough.

The consequence is that as Japan becomes China's largest trading partner diplomatic relations are – to repeat – very difficult, with both populations in a cycle of deepening mistrust. China believes it has a rightful, proud place in the world and that its destiny is to recover this place. Its leaders, however, having chosen to ride the nationalist tiger, could easily find that it rounds on them – forcing them or their successors into warlike actions to match their words. The single most important counterweight is the United States. The least good way to respond is to go head to head with China and thus vindicate and exacerbate its paranoia. The United States needs to wean itself from the 'seductive but nonetheless destructive simplicity' on which it is currently set.[55] The smarter policy is to build China into the world system and genuinely offer it the possibility of co-managing the system for mutual benefit. Assessing the likelihood of that is where we turn next.

10

It's the Enlightenment, Stupid

The United States is not an obvious candidate to be the anchor of an open-world trading and financial system, even if it has been an enormous beneficiary in terms of lower interest rates, cheaper goods, vast inward flows of savings, smarter organisation of production and higher living standards. The problem is not only that those who lose by any dislocation from imports are more obvious and shout louder than those who gain – the latter being diffused through the entire population – or that the United States has a long-standing and powerful protectionist tradition. Rather, the problem is that at the heart of the United States' relationship with the rest of the world is an ambivalence that has deepened since the collapse of the Soviet Union. The pursuit of its national interests involves preaching multilateral openness in trade and finance, and simultaneously claiming the scope to act unilaterally with regard to security, the military and diplomatic relations. Economic openness may be a strategic necessity; it sits uneasily beside America's protectionist instincts and traditions – all against a background of fears of a mounting economic squeeze on its middle class and its opportunities declining.

The United States is not alone in its ambivalent attitude to trade. An open trading system tempts every country to pursue strategic trade policies that are much more mercantilist in their rationale than their rhetorical obeisance to free markets and openness would suggest. The United States' strategic interest is to keep the system open in order for its multinationals to sustain their global brand leadership and growth prospects. China, by pegging its exchange rate to the dollar and being open to foreign investment, is strategically boosting its export sector and thus the momentum of industrialisation. Japan's prosperity depends on having a large manufacturing sector that needs strategic access to Chinese, American and European markets. Nor are members of the European Union innocent. France, for example, has established ten strategic sectors in which it refuses to allow foreign takeovers. All genuflect to the rules-based openness of the trading system as regulated by the World Trade Organization. But they believe in it more because it is the means to secure their strategic, mercantilist aims than because of any desire to create gains from which everyone would share. Thus the suspension in July 2006 of the Doha Round of World Trade talks – an ominous moment for the world system.

The United States now finds that its own strategic trade policy – openness – is being exploited by a potential superpower rival that is using its growing economic strength to support communism or, more accurately, authoritarianism. Deng's policy of opening to reinforce the legitimacy of the Chinese Communist Party is working precisely as he anticipated. The United States is beginning to re-examine whether the pursuit of its national interest should mean remaining strategically open, or whether it should revert to the system of the nineteenth century. This latter option is a real and growing temptation, and the more communist China seems to benefit, the more urgently the question will be asked. That the United States could escape back to its nineteenth-century protected laager is the siren call: it does not have to engage with the world. But if Deng and the Chinese seem to have won the first round, this is a much longer-term contest. The United States needs to have more confidence in the fact that its democratic Enlightenment institutions are vital to growth. If it can stay open it will be rewarded by the ultimate achievement of transforming communist China and growing richer at the same time. Openness works, and protection was never the real reason why the United States grew – indeed, protectionism may have restrained growth. To embrace that proposition, the United States will need to have a better understanding of its own past as well as the present.

American trade nationalism was ever thus

The United States is a country on a continental scale. Whatever the differences among the founding fathers of the United States, what united them was their keen awareness that the new country could and should declare independence from more than George III. The New World should operate according to different principles from the Old World, and one of its principles would be that a single continental economy had prospects and options that no single European national economy had. For a start, the United States had nearly inexhaustible fresh land to settle. It was not just the farmer on his homestead who could be self-sufficient and independent; so could the country. Protectionism is but one by-product of a wider belief in the particular and providential destiny of the United States. America was big enough to go its own way. It could declare independence from British free-trade policies, if it chose, and still prosper.

American protectionists never made the case for generalised governmental or state intervention in the economy. They were on the side of the private sector and an American internal market. They observed that Britain had been protectionist in the eighteenth century, and its growing commitment to free trade in the nineteenth was no more than a self-interested attempt to kick away the ladder by which it had reached economic strength. If other countries could not protect their industries, then the first-mover advantage would always lie with British companies – which, in effect, could never be challenged. Protection was a way of simultaneously financing the federal government at the expense of foreign producers and giving American producers a jump-start. There was an implicit understanding that, as the United States grew in area, eventually its multiple industrial producers would have the advantage of continent-wide production on a scale at least equal to that of the British. They would have a parallel opportunity to specialise in what they were good at. There would be plenty of American competition and incentives to become efficient. Protection would not create expensive, sleepy monopolies. The United States could be committed to free-market principles internally, but it could afford to be pragmatic about whether those same market principles worked for it abroad.

Up until the war with the British between 1812 and 1814, the young United States was broadly liberal in its attitude towards trade. But the burning of Washington in the British–American war; the flooding of the United States' market by cheap British industrial goods; and the British Corn Laws, which imposed a high tax on imported grain, were wake-up calls. In 1816 the United States introduced its first hefty tariffs; in 1824 it transmuted them into a generalised tariff on imported industrial goods. That tax averaged 35 per cent and would stay in place until the disastrous 1930 Smoot-Hawley Tariff Act, which averaged 48 per cent and precipitated the Great Depression. No other industrialised or industrialising country has ever had such high tariffs for so long. German and French tariffs during the nineteenth century never topped more than 15 per cent, and Japanese tariffs even in the 1930s did not go above 30 per cent.[1] Historically the United States was the undisputed king of protectionism.

A passionate advocate of protectionism was Henry Clay. In 1824, as speaker of the House, Clay gave a famous six-and-a-half-hour address in favour of protectionism when arguing for the generalised tariff. 'The measure of the wealth of a nation is indicated by the measure of its protection of its industry,' he said.[2] He argued that the United States' vast and fertile lands offered security against too much power falling to manufacturers. The diversity of a country as large as the United States would also allow everyone to benefit from the construction of a genuinely American system. The agricultural south might benefit from free trade, but it could not be allowed to call the shots for the whole country.[3]

Protection lasted throughout the nineteenth century, and because it and rapid growth happened together it has been difficult to challenge the idea that one caused the other. In fact, a close examination of the economic data, as economist Douglas Irwin demonstrates, undermines the protectionist cause. American productivity growth between 1870 and 1914 grew no faster than in free-trade Britain, and the fastest growth of all was in the service sector where employment rose from 30 per cent of the workforce in 1870 to 43 per cent in 1910 – but where there was neither protection nor foreign trade. What drove the high growth in American GDP was massive population growth, fuelled by immigration, and high investment. Indeed, thinks Irwin, protection had the perverse effect of making capital goods more expensive in the industrial and service sector alike, so slowing down productivity growth and meaning that America got less bang for any single buck of capital investment. Protection almost certainly damaged the United States more than it helped.

Indeed by the turn of the century this was beginning to be the view of contemporaries. As the continental economy linked up, the frontier closed down. The great factories in New England and the Midwest carried on spewing out their products as if the helter-skelter expansion of the previous two centuries was continuing undimmed, but the American consumer could not keep up with the pace of potential production. The proposition that prosperity and well-being lay in self-sufficiency, protectionism and looking inward began to be more aggressively challenged. According to an emerging intellectual consensus, unless America could find a new way to continue the frontier tradition and harness the energies of its people, social upheaval might result. Frederick Jackson Turner caught the mood in his famous essay 'The Significance of the Frontier'. He argued that to sustain a concept of space and ambition, which was at the root of the American sensibility, the frontier now had to be extended overseas. Foreign trade should replace land as the spatial anchor of the republic. Turner's ideas became influential; even Theodore Roosevelt expressed his indebtedness.[4] American expansionism, however, would be distinct from European expansionism. The aim was not to create an overseas empire, but to export the American idea – and a fervent belief in Christianity. The United States would create a commercial network overseas that, as the British historian Niall Ferguson puts it, would create dependence on the United States rather than domination by the United States. Its trading partners would benefit by having access to American goods, values and ideas.[5] Following historian Charles Maier, the ascendancy the United States sought (and seeks) is part-territorial – 'to project power, exert influence and enjoy prestige far beyond traditionally founded jurisdiction'.[6] America's open-door policy for China would of course benefit the United States, but the growing wave of American missionaries genuinely hoped to bring benefits to the Chinese as well.

The expansion of American trade would also entail a broad expansion in its merchant and military navies. Alfred Thayer Mahan's *Influence of Sea Power upon History*, another influential work of the 1890s, insisted that the United States now had to develop the sinews of its naval power if it wanted to exercise influence overseas.[7] The lesson was heeded. In the 1880s the United States was a trivial naval power, but by 1907 its intense naval building programme had carried it to second in the world, after the British. The United States had to protect its vital sea-lanes as it began to look outward. Thus, as protectionism reached its apogee, it was already being challenged as the best means of developing America: the young republic should start to look outward – a strategic reorientation that would ultimately change the United States' trade policy. Even President William McKinley, who was responsible for the highest tariffs in the nineteenth century, had begun to argue that there might be a case for lowering tariffs if other countries reciprocated. American industry no longer needed protecting. This was the theme of his last speech before he was shot in 1901.

When the Democrats won the presidency in 1932 they blamed protectionism for the disaster that had befallen America – developing an economic and political argument that had been gestating for more than forty years. Although their argument in favour of reciprocal tariff cuts fell short of calling for a full free-trade system, there was nonetheless a recognition that protection had led nowhere. The strategic interest, now that United States companies were clearly among the most innovative and productive in the world, was to develop a policy of reciprocal tariff cuts to help them boost their overseas sales. The Reciprocal Trade Agreements Act (RTAA) of 1934 empowered the United States government to cut tariffs by 50 per cent if the trading partner reciprocated; by the end of the Second World War bilateral agreements had been agreed with twenty-five countries. The United States' policy was changing.

Like Britain before it, the United States was gaining enough confidence in its industrial strength to drop its long commitment to protection. The way was being paved for the settlement that would be created after the Second World War. Britain, meanwhile, as its share of world trade slipped to 14 per cent in 1913 compared with 24 per cent in 1870, found itself more willing to accept the protectionist case. The leading Conservative politician Joseph Chamberlain had first made the case for imperial preference in the early 1900s. In 1933 the British government, presiding over a network of small to medium-size producers in the hard-pressed traditional industrial sectors, finally gave way and started a system of tariff protection within the British Empire. Britain, having kicked away the ladder for others in the 1840s and 1850s when it insisted on low tariffs for all, was now rediscovering the virtues of protectionism as it became industrially weaker – just as the United States was becoming strong enough to abandon it. Strategic interests came first for both.[8]

The golden era of free trade

After the Second World War the United States' first reaction was to try to make sure that German and Japanese reconstruction was as limited as possible. Essentially both countries would be ruralised and their capacity to wage war would be removed for ever. But the march of events turned the tide. The Soviet Union's ambitions to extend communism were obvious, and Chinese communism was getting the better of the tired Nationalist armies. It was becoming a strategic imperative for the United States to ensure that Western Europe and the rest of East Asia did not fall under communist rule. There was a real prospect in the immediate post-war years that most of the Eurasian land mass and the newly independent nation-states emerging from European decolonisation would constitute a communist bloc, whose economic and military power could challenge the United States. As it was, the Soviet Union and communist China constituted a formidable prospect, and there were strong communist parties in Italy, France and southern Europe.

The United States' response was, in some respects, chosen for it. It had to pre-empt any direct military challenge by promising mutually assured destruction through nuclear retaliation. It would fight local wars, like those in Vietnam, to limit communist gains and buy time, and it would organise and support the build-up of Europe, Japan and other Asian powers into robust capitalist democracies not prone to communist temptations. For nearly thirty years, from 1947 to the Trade Act of 1974, the United States embraced free trade as whole-heartedly as nineteenth-century Britain had.

The decisive year was 1947. In March the United States decided to reverse the ruralisation strategy in occupied Japan and began to develop the Japanese economy along with the economies of Korea, the Philippines and, eventually, French Indochina, as part of an Asian capitalist bulwark against communism.[9] In June the Marshall Plan was initiated to reconstruct a prostrate Western Europe (in today's prices, more than $100 billion was sent) and provide it with vital convertible currency to pay for imports. In July George Kennan wrote a famous essay in *Foreign Affairs* (under the pseudonym X) urging a policy of 'containment' of the Soviet Union.[10] And in October the last piece of the jigsaw puzzle was put into place with the establishment of the General Agreement on Tariffs and Trade (GATT), in which every signatory agreed to extend bilaterally whatever reciprocal tariff arrangements it had agreed on to every other signatory. The signatories also agreed to an across-the-board 20 per cent reduction in tariffs as a down payment on their future intentions. In effect, the reciprocal agreements under the United States' RTAA would be extended multilaterally and new signatories such as Japan and Germany would be able to shelter under the United States' trade umbrella. The GATT was the trade tool that would deliver the economic dimension of the geopolitical strategy.

Yet even at this high-water mark of the strategic case for free trade, the United States Congress ferociously resisted proposals to set up an international trade organisation as an autonomous body to police the GATT. Arthur Vandenberg, the most senior Republican on the Senate Foreign Relations Committee, had already told

Truman that the only way to get congressional agreement for the Marshall Plan was 'to make a speech and scare the hell out of the country'.[11] To reverse more than a hundred years of protection and establish an international organisation to regulate the new trade system was a leap too far. Congress could accept conditionally extending the RTAA as long as the United States reserved the right to retaliate against unfair trade. It could not accept a commitment to free trade that entailed abiding by the objective rulings of an international body in trade disputes. It wanted the United States to have the right to act independently and in its own interests.

Still, the evident superiority of United States industry made free trade easier to sell. John Foster Dulles opined that while the Japanese might be able to export shirts, pyjamas and 'perhaps cocktail napkins' to the United States market, little else was possible for them.[12] So it was that until the mid-1970s the United States refrained from using the leeway that a suspicious Congress had insisted on in 1947. It indulged both Japan and Europe. Japan was allowed to peg the yen at a super-competitive level against the dollar, thereby boosting its exports. Until 1975 the United States government supported Japan in every claim against it by individual American companies complaining that they had been damaged by unfair Japanese competition. The United States even allowed Japan to protect its market against foreign imports, and Japan was allowed to use forty-two thousand Western technology patents without challenge.[13] The story was similar in Europe. Article XXIV of the GATT permitted the formation of customs unions and regional free-trade areas if other states allowed them, and the United States indulged the formation of the European Iron and Steel Community in 1952. Subsequently, it approved the initiation of the quintessential expression, a regional trade bloc, the European Economic Community (EEC). American negotiators, during the 'Kennedy Round', which sought cuts in industrial tariffs of about 35 per cent, accepted that the EEC could maintain the Common Agricultural Policy. They also accepted that fifty-eight developing countries could continue to rig their domestic markets and still have access, under the terms of the GATT, to the United States market.

American policy was more successful than even its most ardent proponents could have hoped. In 1950 European output per person-hour worked was about half of American output. By the mid-1970s the gap was rapidly closing, and by the mid-1990s it had almost closed. The situation was similar in Japan. Rapid economic growth, rising employment and booming trade brought an ideological legitimisation of capitalism that reversed its delegitimisation in the inter-war period. Communist parties in Western Europe were in retreat. In Asia, by the end of the Vietnam War the 'tiger economies' of Singapore, South Korea, Hong Kong, Taiwan and the Philippines proved that open trade and pro-market economic structures were the precondition for a rate of economic growth that was plainly faster than the rate in the communist world. The ideological tectonic plates were shifting – of which one was the rise to power of Deng Xiaoping.

The era of rising trade tensions

In the mid-1970s the United States suffered from the first oil shock. The growing competitiveness of Europe and Japan was now reflected in a stubbornly large United States trade deficit, which meant that it was becoming increasingly onerous to allow a growing number of foreign holders of dollars to exert their right to convert dollars into gold. Economic growth slowed down. Inflation soared. Unemployment rose. In Washington the post-war consensus began to break down. The Republicans, smelling an opportunity to reverse what the Democrats had done in 1932, argued that the United States had to return to more self-interested economic policies. It should move away from trying to create a global commons abroad, and retreat to calculate its narrow interests while challenging the liberal consensus at home.

Not that the United States had ever wholly repudiated protectionism. The Buy America Act of 1933, insisting that federal and state government place orders for key supplies with American producers, had never been repealed. Indeed, it was under this act that the Pentagon had justified focusing its post-war spending wholly on United States industry. The United States closely monitored exports of any high-technology goods that might be incorporated into the defence industries of the communist bloc, even through third parties. And for some years there had been a growing consensus that the burden of maintaining the dollar as the world's anchor currency, linked to gold, was placing too much strain on the United States economy. The United States should float the dollar and manage its economy just as it chose.

The year 1974 was a watershed. Convertibility into gold had been formally abandoned in 1971 and the United States had walked away from the so-called Bretton Woods system, with exchange rates pegged to a predictable value of the dollar in turn pegged to gold. Now the United States abandoned all the capital controls that had been intended to support the dollar's role as the linchpin of the international financial system. The value of the dollar would henceforth be set by the markets, and the United States would be free to pursue whatever economic policy it thought best rather than be hamstrung by international obligations. The Trade Act of 1974 backed up the move to a supposed new hardheadedness, as if the former policy of attempting to boost liberal capitalist democracy worldwide by being generous was soft. The United States empowered itself unilaterally to reinstate tariffs if imports from any country suddenly rose. Under Section 301, if United States exporters complained of any discrimination against them the United States reserved the right to take unilateral punitive action. This move was a destructive challenge to the concept of multilateral reciprocity that is at the heart of the world's free trade. If the United States chooses, it can act by itself.

The change of direction has persisted with growing intensity.

Japan, once cosseted, over the 1980s became an object of intense American pressure to revalue its currency and open its markets. Under the Structural Impediments Initiative of 1989 the United States required Japan to consider every aspect of its economic structure – from the retail distribution system to the supply chains of firms – as essentially reformable. The goal was to increase the reciprocal access of American goods to the Japanese market. By the early 1990s the combination of United States trade hawkishness and the imposition of a sharply rising yen were the most important contribution to ending the long post-war Japanese boom.

Financial liberalisation was another area where the United States demonstrated its new focus on its own strategic interests. Here it had the wit and vision to see that manufacturing, which had been regarded as the heart of the process of creating wealth, was giving way to services. This was an embrace of the future that some commentators have called a 'revolution in social ontology'.[14] Opening up the world to American financial institutions and telecommunications companies might seem obvious now, but then it was a leap in the dark. Nonetheless, the United States pushed for their liberalisation and deregulation as hard as it could. In 1982 Citibank and Federal Express founded the Coalition of Services Industries, which consistently pressed the United States Department of Commerce and United States trade negotiators to liberalise world service industries to competition from American business. Between 1972 and 1985 the thousand largest United States banks increased their dedicated spending on telecommunications from 5 to 13 per cent of their operating expenses. The progressive liberalisation of both permitted the development of twenty-four-hour global financial networks. By 1985 Citibank had linked its offices in ninety-four countries and was trading $200 billion daily in the foreign-exchange markets. The company needed telecoms deregulation as much as capital-market deregulation to pull off the coup.[15]

For the multilateral trade institutions the choice was stark; if they did not accommodate the United States' strategic trade ambitions, then the United States would achieve its ends without them – so it was better to keep some multilateralism than none at all. The GATT could not launch a round of tariff reduction negotiations without support from the United States. When the 'Uruguay Round' of reducing tariffs and opening markets began in 1986 the United States insisted that intellectual property rights, service-sector trade and, in particular, telecommunications were on the agenda. The strategy was to bypass what the Reaganites saw as the statist International Telecommunications Union (ITU), the inter-governmental agency that regulated international telecoms business. Four years later the ITU submitted to the GATT talks, recognising the reality that the United States was going to drive through liberalisation of telecoms and that its only chance of saving even minimal regulation was to work through the GATT.

In 1990 the GATT ruled that American multinationals should, in principle, have access to all the service markets of its signatories. Four years later the United States used the GATT to force the European Union to agree to open all its voice communications (post, telephone and telegraph) to competition. In 1995 the United States forced through a framework agreement (trade-related intellectual property, TRIP) that subsumed all earlier treaties in order to enlarge the enforcement of intellectual property rights. In effect, the United States Patent Office – as the gatekeeper of exercising patents in the world's largest market – would become the world regulator of patents in the information age, and American rules would become the global standard. This was an extraordinary achievement; according to John Braithwaite and Peter Drahos, it resulted from the coordinated lobbying of fifty key American executives and was a tribute to the capacity of American business to get the United States government to act in its interests, and of United States trade diplomacy to fulfil its mission.[16] In April 1996 the United States delegation walked out of talks held by the World Trade Organization (the successor of the GATT), insisting that telecoms liberalisation should become global. A year later the World Trade Organization gave in and opened up seventy countries to United States telecoms companies on the United States' terms. With the World Bank and the International Monetary Fund insisting on telecoms deregulation as the price of every structural adjustment programme, the United States was succeeding at deregulating global telecoms in the 1990s, just as it had deregulated finance during the 1970s and 1980s. In 2005, the value of United States service exports amounted to $323 billion, nearly 40 per cent of the value of merchandise exports and generating a surplus of some $65 billion.

At home there has been rising hawkishness over dumping, the practice of exporting products into other markets at below economic cost. Since 1980 the United States has led the world in the number of anti-dumping suits brought against foreign exporters.[17] And ever since 1980, as Bruce Blonigen has pointed out,[18] the average fine has been increasing by 2.5 percentage points a year. In the early 1980s fines averaged 15.5 per cent of the imputed difference between a 'fair' price and the actual price, and by 2000 they had quadrupled to more than 60 per cent. Not only that; the United States International Trade Commission is increasingly likely to find injury – the rate is up from 45 per cent in the early 1980s to 60 per cent in 2000. The United States' trading partners are becoming increasingly vociferous at the one-sidedness, injustice and mounting costs of the United States' approach and wanted to put this issue on the table in the now-abandoned 'Doha Round' of trade talks begun in 2001. The House of Representatives voted 410 to four before the first meeting to insist that the president should not agree to any major revisions of the anti-dumping practice.

That vote is of a piece with the wider American approach. The United States, like Britain preceding 'imperial preference', is finding that, as its relative economic power wanes, sustaining a coalition in favour of trade openness becomes harder. So the debate over trade increasingly focuses on security. Industries considered crucial to national security – semiconductors, high-definition television screens, steel and supercomputers – are strategically supported by the Pentagon.[19] Amendments have been proposed (the Shelby and Inhofe amendments) to expand the definition of national security under the Exon-Florio amendment, which gives the United States president the power to block foreigners buying American companies if they are judged to impair United States national security, and is supported by the administration. Foreign ships are forbidden to move from one American port to another, even in extreme conditions like the hurricane in New Orleans. And so on. Security, to paraphrase Samuel Johnson, is the last refuge of the protectionist scoundrel.

The United States, more economically challenged and genuinely concerned about terrorism, feels weaker and less able to make unilateral concessions for the common good. As the trade expert Jagdish Bhagwati argues, free trade has to be increasingly justified by reference to reciprocity and fairness.[20] The United States is ratcheting up its demands for reciprocity; the Structural Impediment Initiative against Japan is a classic example. It demands not so much reciprocal cutting of trade tariffs as sweeping, across-the-board economic change. This is twenty-first-century reciprocity, in which the United States wants to demand that its trading partners have economic and social structures like its own if they want the right to trade with it.

In short, trade is becoming more politicised and more dominated by one-sided concerns to maximise immediate strategic advantages. American law-makers are doing no more than following United States public opinion. According to a recent survey, 84 per cent of the public wants the United States' top foreign policy objective to be the protection of American jobs.[21] In this atmosphere, China's cheap labour is seen not as a natural advantage from which both sides benefit but as an unfair excuse to dump goods in the United States. It's the same story everywhere. If the United States is going to allow free trade, then there has to be an overt strategic reason, as in the creation of the North American Free Trade

Agreement (NAFTA) in 1993. That initiative, bringing Canada and Mexico under the same free-trade umbrella, consolidated North America into a strong regional trading bloc in a world of blocs. Even in 1993 this was a knife-edge decision requiring the lobbying effort of four American presidents (Clinton, Reagan, Bush and Carter) together with an enormous effort by American business to overcome the protectionist lobby and win a very tight vote. And if a country does not play ball – if New Zealand does not allow United States ships carrying nuclear weapons to dock at its ports, or if Chile does not back the UN resolution to go to war with Iraq – it finds itself threatened with, or even paying, trade penalties.

Today the coalition in favour of NAFTA would be impossible to assemble. American business and much of the political class may understand the benefits of free trade to the American business model and to the wider American public, but they are also wary of being on the wrong side of a new anti-foreign populism. Populist feeling is reaching unexpected heights. Fifty-eight per cent of Americans agreed that Congress acted correctly in opposing the acquisition of six United States port terminals by Dubai, with 41 per cent saying they watched it closely – only 2 per cent less than watched the Iraq war closely.[22] This episode ranked seventh among political stories attracting most interest since the mid-1980s, exceeded only by such controversial issues as court rulings on the pledge of allegiance (2002), the debates surrounding Clinton's health care plan (1993) and whether to lift the ban on gays in the military (1993).[23] American commitment to a rules-bound, open trading system based on free trade is weakening. The old-time religion of protection is making a comeback.

The Enlightenment legacy

Yet it was never protectionism that stimulated America, but rather the nation's pluralism and its Enlightenment institutions. The difficulty is that even Americans find it hard to discern the truth, which is buried under the country's celebration – almost deification – of liberty. Liberty, in the American narrative, is the sun under which everything flourishes. Liberty permits individual hard work, courage and the scope to produce wealth and happiness. Government should not get in the way; nor should it tax the fruits of hard work. If unfair foreign competition puts otherwise hard-working Americans at a disadvantage, then it should be stopped. Liberty and the American Dream are linked; they make for a pleasingly coherent story because the United States is so successful. The great conservative counter-revolution of the past thirty years has been grounded in its brilliant capacity to exploit these cultural icons to support its own cause.

Liberty is indeed crucial to the American story, but not in the way the story is conventionally told. American liberty has been advanced within a highly sophisticated Enlightenment political infrastructure. The danger from excessive private power has been as well understood as the danger from excessive public power.[24] The founding fathers' concept of checks and balances in government has been an essential guarantor of pluralism; the right to free speech and the rule of law have embedded argument, debate and justification in the warp and woof of United States institutions and culture. Moreover, the United States has cherished a deep conviction that all men and women are born equal. In reality, the United States has always been an unequal society, but as professor Benjamin Friedman of Harvard argues in *The Moral Consequences of Economic Growth*, there has been, until recently, sufficient prospect of mobility and change to construct a conceptual equality – a belief that even if my circumstances are inferior to yours there is a very good chance that our children might change places.[25] It is not a belief that is widespread in Britain.

But the young republic was lucky that for three or four generations after its founding there was almost limitless free land. The economic and social reality was that settlers could get an equal stake, with all that implied for a sense of individual empowerment; there was a real chance of moving upwards. The Louisiana Purchase, the acquisition of Florida, the annexation of Texas and the securing of Oregon, all between 1800 and 1850, added two million square miles of land to the country. Whether with the decision in 1785 to grant land ownership absolutely 'fee simple', so that the ownership was unqualified, or with the Homestead Act of 1862 entitling any settler to claim ownership after five years' tenure, the United States' approach has been that everyone has a right to property. It has been a crucial social safety valve.

Look at the United States through the same lens with which I have analysed China, and you see an economy and society characterised by pluralism, diversity and investment in individual capabilities. Every nook and cranny is characterised by accountability, scrutiny and justification. Whether in the crystallisation of the concept of the company, the acceptance of the rule of law, the commitment to education or the normative acceptance of the need for a free press, this country is the living embodiment of the links between the Enlightenment and economic growth – the proposition at the heart of this book. It is true that in the first decade of the twenty-first century these institutions are atrophying through neglect and wilful disparagement of their importance, in particular by American conservatives. But it is hard to imagine that they will never be rediscovered.

I have already mentioned that Alexis de Tocqueville, touring the young republic in the mid-1830s and trying to understand the particular forces in its dynamics, identified what he described as 'equality of conditions' as the central feature animating its economy and society. American egalitarianism, even in the 1830s, never had the levelling-down character that European egalitarianism would assume. Rather, it was an aspirational egalitarianism in which all citizens felt so equipped by property ownership, education and the enfranchisement conferred by the Constitution that they could aim equally high. Americans had both the mind-set – the willingness to embrace the modern and abandon tradition, imagining a life they would construct for themselves – and the capacities to act upon their will. The Enlightenment public sphere was the essential component of this culture, enfranchising everyone and entitling everyone, as Tocqueville wrote, to participate in public debate and deliberation. That, in turn, imparted a sense of self-esteem and self-confidence in the pursuit of one's private affairs. Public engagement and never-ending argument leavened what otherwise might have been a culture of egoism, argued Tocqueville, and transmuted it into a culture in which egalitarianism and individualism enriched each other. Self-interest was not only a matter of bettering oneself; it was also a matter of ensuring that there would be a vigorous public life and opportunity for others. American intellectuals, for example, whether natural-rights republicans, Jeffersonian liberals or land reformers, have simultaneously championed the right of an individual to own property and wanted to see property fairly distributed.[26] This same impulse – wanting the best for oneself and for others – prompts much of American civic activism.

Commitment to education was also intimately connected with egalitarian culture. In 1830, for example, nineteen of the then twenty-four states in the Union had given every man the vote, and each made education a high priority. As early as 1874 school districts were allowed to raise public funds for not just primary but also secondary education.[27] Universities were established in every state, generously endowed with hundreds of thousands of acres – an act of far-sightedness and commitment to higher education from which the United States is gaining ever greater dividends. The proportion of GDP going to tertiary education is currently twice that of the European Union.[28] Egalitarianism went into the marrow of what was taught and how it was examined. Claudia Goldin of Harvard, the leading authority on the history of the United States education system, notes: 'If the American system is characterized as open, infinitely forgiving, lacking universal standards, and academic yet

practical, the European system was closed, unforgiving, with uniform standards, and academic for some and industrial for others.
One was egalitarian; one was elite.'[29]

By 1900 the educational gap between the United States and the
rest of the industrialised world was yawning, but so was the extent
of the franchise. European countries came to democracy later, and
to mass education later. The United States had mass secondary
education for both boys and girls, and the curricula and exams
were structured so that every child had an opportunity to find a
subject in which he or she could at least pass, if not excel. Its
pupils fed a mass college system that also had no parallel, and its
universities were emerging as intellectually pre-eminent. When
Truman signed the GI Bill in 1944, giving every GI the right to a
college education, Britain was just about to enact its own education
bill which gave each British teenager the access to secondary education that was already fifty years old in the United States.

This investment in individual capability led the world, and it
drove growth in productivity first in agriculture and then later in
industry. American industrialists – the Carnegies, Pullmans, Fords
and Rockefellers – could organise and coordinate production on a
scale unknown in Europe because, as a precondition, they had the
people with the skills and educational background capable of
engineering and managing the often complex logistics. On top
came the development of the company. Without corporate organisation of production the scale of output could not have happened.
But the speed and facility with which the American corporation
developed as an organisational, financial and legal entity also
sprang from the Enlightenment infrastructure of the United
States. Within a generation of the signing of the United States'
Constitution the corporation was a common part of American life;
entrepreneurs were petitioning states to form corporations with a
declared purpose and formal rights for investors because, under
the Constitution, companies had the same legal rights as individuals to own land and develop their business.

To produce on the enormous scale that the United States' internal market permitted meant raising vast amounts of risk capital and loans. Doing so in turn required transparent financial accounts, management and processes in which governments, banks and investors could be confident. The corporation, with its complex accountability networks, solved the problem. In other words, this expression of capitalism was rooted in the United States' Enlightenment approach to accountability, the rule of law and justification. Shareholders could pursue their rights under the law. Companies had to deliver what they promised, or explain why not.

Nobody would or could pretend that industrialisation in the United States was anything other than turbulent and, often, brutal. This, after all, was the era of the robber barons and vast private fortunes. But another Enlightenment principle informed it throughout – a deep belief in the pluralist requirement to set up countervailing power to limit monopoly and check arbitrary private power. The twenty-nine-year quest to break up the Standard Oil Trust, which had been founded in 1882 with a virtual monopoly of United States oil and refinery production, finally succeeded in 1911. This was a result of Enlightenment institutions and culture in action: application of the law in the Sherman Antitrust Act and the Supreme Court's final judgement; the muckraking, campaigning journalism of a free press that exposed Standard Oil's nefarious practices and blatant profiteering; the instinctive sense that private monopoly was as problematic as state power; the insistence that notwithstanding its private character the company is nonetheless a public actor; and, of course, the belief in competition. All contributed to the spectacular break-up, one of the most celebrated in American corporate history.

The growth of vigorous independent journalism in the United States during the second half of the nineteenth century and into the twentieth century played an indispensable role in keeping the system more honest and creating American successes.[30] The number of independent newspapers quintupled between 1870

and 1910. The press in New York challenged Tammany's control of
the city and state. And it was the muckraking tradition, along with
Upton Sinclair's novel *The Jungle*, which gave the United States its
first proper regulation of food and medicine in the Food and Drug
Act of 1906. The press was the arm of the citizen in holding private
and public power to account, an irreplaceable watchdog policing
scandal and corruption alike. It developed singularly high standards for evidence, and for balance. The Radio Act of 1927,
reflecting the Enlightenment culture, required licences to be distributed on the basis that licensees served the 'public convenience,
interest, or necessity'. In 1949 the Federal Communications
Commission adopted the doctrine as a formal rule.

Pluralism works

All these forces combined to share in, guide and foster the emergence of an astonishingly vigorous capitalism and propel it in the
direction of serving a wider interest. Thus the Interstate
Commerce Act of 1887 set out to ensure that trusts and corporations did not abuse their power across state lines, in particular in
the setting of rail prices. In 1903 Theodore Roosevelt persuaded
Congress to establish the Department of Commerce and Labor to
ensure better regulation; a separate Department of Labor was
created in 1913. Rail regulation was introduced by the Hepburn
Act of 1906. The Federal Trade Commission was created in 1911
to prevent fraud and misleading practices. The Federal Reserve
Act of 1913 aimed to bring stability to the banking system. The
Clayton Antitrust Act of 1914 outlawed monopoly and unfair price
discrimination. Private power had to be institutionally challenged
and regulated in order to try to make the pluralist system regulate
itself more effectively – a concept that even extended to labour
law. By 1896 Pullman and Carnegie had broken strikes, and Pullman
had introduced yellow-dog contracts under which workers promised

not to join a union. But despite this in *Veghelan v. Gunther* in 1896, Justice Holmes wrote: 'Combination on the one side is potent and powerful. Combination on the other is the necessary and desirable counterpart, if the battle is to be carried out in a fair and equal way.'[31] In other words, trade unions were also a legitimate part of American pluralism – and indeed the Clayton Act explicitly excluded trade unions from its definition of anti-competitive combinations.

The corporation, whose rise Alfred Chandler charts in his book *The Visible Hand*, thus had antecedents in this Enlightenment architecture.[32] Companies were developing and multiplying in Britain and Europe, but it was in the United States that they most rapidly developed their public character and scale. In 1832 the McLane report found only 106 manufacturing firms with assets greater than $100,000; by 1917 there existed more than 278 firms, each with more than $20 million in assets.[33] The twentieth-century American corporation would prove to be the most restless and dynamic driver of capitalism so far devised.

The United States had created a sophisticated system of justification and accountability, without which the modern company could not have developed. Systematic audits, for example, promised integrity of financial affairs so that ownership could be dispersed among external investors and traded in company shares. That in turn allowed companies to operate at scale, coordinating production and distribution all over the United States. By the early 1930s, when Adolph Berle and Gardiner Means first observed that the management of a company and those who owned it were now divorced and separate functions, the modern company was truly born.[34] Shareholders now held management to account for the stewardship of a company's assets, its trading prospects and the pursuit of its goals. This would lay the foundations for future problems when shareholders insisted their only aim was short-term profit maximisation, but at the time it was a revolution. An Enlightenment principle of accountability was at the heart of the capitalist process. The company had come of age.

Until the early 1970s the economic history of the United States is a story of this turbulent interaction between its Enlightenment architecture and associated culture mingling with egalitarianism and liberty on the one hand, and the driving energy of dynamic capitalism on the other. Episodes such as the suing of IBM and AT&T by the Department of Justice for abuse of their market position, and Franklin D. Roosevelt's overhaul of banking and securities regulation after the Wall Street crash, were ongoing efforts to maintain economic pluralism and keep private power accountable. Roosevelt's New Deal, Truman's Fair Deal and Johnson's Great Society were presidential initiatives to sustain the educational opportunities and stake in society that free land and basic education had provided in the previous century. In the nineteenth century the Army Corps of Engineers had been vital in creating the national transport infrastructure, which was the precondition for mass production; in the twentieth century the tradition was carried on by fifty thousand infrastructure projects begun under the New Deal and the post-war construction of the interstate highway system.[35] And no story of the Internet or the array of recent innovations such as nanotechnologies and magnetic resonance imaging is complete without reference to government funding.[36]

The United States had not arrived at its pre-eminent position by an exercise of pure liberty as the conservative Reaganite counter-revolutionaries and later neo-conservatives have argued. Rather, liberty had been exercised within an Enlightenment constitutional framework that always included conceptual egalitarianism, which provided the tension between the ambition and appetites of the propertied rich and their accountability to society. This is not the egalitarianism of income or opportunity; rather, it is the equality of self-esteem, self-worth and possibility. My circumstances in life might be different from yours today, but there is no obstacle of title, birth, accent or social rank that would prevent my children from occupying the same place as you, or a higher place, because the constitution and the expansive geography put us on the same footing and offer us the same possibilities. It was never markets and the price mechanism alone that created the United States: it was their fecund interaction with its Enlightenment infrastructure and the culture that flowed from it that formed the American genius. And it is that which is in peril today.

The American condition

Imagine a twenty-four-hour parade of all Americans with their height corresponding to their income. For the first four hours and fifteen minutes the spectators would see very short people of five feet or less – those with incomes no more than $20,000. Over the next nine hours there would be a progressive doubling in height, and over the following seven and three-quarter hours another doubling. You would have watched for twenty-one hours before you saw twenty-foot giants, people with incomes of $80,000. Another two and a quarter hours would pass before you saw another doubling in height. In the last forty-five minutes the rate of increases in height would start to accelerate. Fifteen minutes before midnight individuals two hundred feet high would be walking by, representing incomes of $400,000. In the last ninety seconds of the parade there would be individuals four hundred feet tall and then, in the last seconds, America's richest would pass by – a cool 21,750 feet tall. They would be Himalayan beside the earlier molehills.[37]

This is what is implied by inequality – and inequality in the United States is not just a matter of income, but today it also involves opportunity, life chances, neighbourhood and the experience of work. It is over work that the fears and anxieties of ordinary Americans are becoming most acute – and this is where their experience has been most rapidly changing. Over the past twenty years, according to an analysis by Louis Uchitelle in *The Disposable American*, thirty million American workers have lost their jobs because of downsizing and economic restructuring. As many as thirty million more have taken early retirement or left the labour market, never to return, for the same reason.[38]

Nor is that the only adverse impact on them. There has been a collapse in the value of pension benefits, as corporations wind up the old defined benefit pension, which gives retired workers a fixed proportion of their final salary, and replaced it with 401k plans which, with either no or much reduced company contributions, pay out much less. It may be true that with rising life expectancy, low interest rates and a stagnating stock market the defined benefit pension was insupportably expensive, but from the point of view of the average American worker this is a lowering of his or her lifetime income. According to one calculation, every man, woman and child in the United States would need an additional $28,000 of assets to compensate for the lower income in retirement.[39] Then there is the fact that forty-five million Americans do not have health care coverage.[40] And we should not overlook the thirty-four million people who work full-time for less than $8.70 an hour, the hourly wage necessary for a family of four to rise above the poverty level.

Nor is the middle class excluded from concern. There is a growing national preoccupation with the disappearing middle: the income of the typical two-child couple is hardly rising in real terms, and the number of middle-income households is steadily shrinking.[41] It is a toxic brew. While the great American middle class is under siege, a tiny elite of plutocrats prosper. As Thomas Piketty, director of studies at the École des Hautes Études en Sciences Sociales (EHESS) in Paris and Emmanuel Saez of the University of California Berkeley have shown in a path-breaking work, income distribution is slowly but surely returning to levels not seen except during the 'gilded age' around the turn of the nineteenth century.[42] Economists use a measure of inequality called the Gini coefficient – the proportion of income earned by the top 10 per cent of the income distribution over the bottom 10 per cent – to compare inequality between countries. At 0.41 the Gini index of the United States outstrips that of Japan and Europe (0.25 and 0.32 respectively), and is only fractionally lower than China's 0.45.[43]

The growth of inequality is matched by a decline in social mobility: Americans are less likely today than a generation ago to move out of the socio-economic group into which they were born. For example, boys from the bottom three-quarters of the socio-economic scale were less likely to move up in the 1990s than in the 1960s. By 1998, the *Wall Street Journal* reports, only 10 per cent of sons of fathers in the bottom quarter (defined by income, education and occupation) had moved into the top quarter. Twenty-five years earlier more than double that proportion – 23 per cent of lower-class sons – had managed the move.[44] The exit rates from poverty tell the same story. Families with children are much more likely to stay poor in the United States than in Europe. The economist Gøsta Esping-Anderson estimates that after three years American poor families are five times more likely to stay poor than their British, German, French or Spanish counterparts.[45]

And there is a racist aspect to the figures. Seventeen per cent of the children of poor white parents, but 42 per cent of the children of poor black parents, stay at the bottom.[46] As I reported in *The World We're In*, access to college is becoming ever more unequal. In 1979 a student whose family was in the top quarter of the income distribution was four times more likely to get a college degree than someone from the bottom quarter; by 1994 the likelihood had grown to ten times more. Whether exit rates from poverty, the chance of moving upwards from one's family or the change of going to college, the United States has become a more immobile, sclerotic society.

Americans expect better. Seventy per cent of Americans believe that the poor have a good chance of escaping poverty; only 29 per cent believe that they are trapped there. By contrast, Europeans, living in more socially fluid societies, are nonetheless much more pessimistic about the chances of mobility. Only 40 per cent believe the poor can escape their fate, and 60 per cent believe they are trapped.[47] The utopian ideal of America – that through hard work you can achieve your place in the sun – is being confounded by daily experience. Benjamin Franklin was born the fifteenth son of a candle maker and retired at forty-two with enough of a fortune to comfortably pursue a life of politics and scientific inquiry. The opportunity for such mobility is retreating, and this is beginning to affect not just American society but the American imagination.

The wheel turns full circle

Against this background it is hardly surprising that the impact of globalisation on the United States is regarded with growing alarm and has become widely debated. Lou Dobbs devotes part of his CNN show, *Lou Dobbs Tonight*, to a fight against the export of American jobs. The claim is that four or five hundred thousand jobs a year are lost to outsourcing and relocation of production – and he likes to name the corporations and state governments that are guilty.[48] Meanwhile *American Prospect*, the magazine of the intellectual left, carries a polemic by a former candidate for the Democratic presidential nomination, Ernest Hollings, in favour of reviving the American protectionist tradition.[49] The columnist Tom Friedman of the *New York Times* titled his recent book *The World is Flat*. But unlike Lou Dobbs or Ernest Hollings, Friedman is not a protectionist. Rather, he is an apostle of the new order. Protectionism would be self-defeating, he argues, damaging to the rest of the world and only a short-term escape from reality.

The best response is to embrace change as an opportunity, to 'upskill' and to concentrate on industries whose advantage is based on brainpower, agility and high value-added, rather than those based on low wages.

I am on the same side of this argument as Friedman, but I think the entire exchange should be cooled down. The impact of globalisation is vastly exaggerated, by him as much as by Dobbs and Hollings. It is true that the future of Western economies – Britain and Europe as much as the United States – will be much more biased towards 'knowledge industries' (broadly defined to include high-tech manufacturing, education and the creative and cultural industries) and the service industries associated with them. It is also true that education and skills are going to be more important in the future, but that is because of important trends within our economies, driven by the usual forces of technological change, which are changing consumers' tastes, leading to higher disposable incomes and the secular growth of knowledge-based goods and services. It is alarmist, counter-productive and intellectually wrong to associate the ills of Western industrialised societies with globalisation and with foreigners. Look more closely at what has been happening, especially in the United States, and the proposition begins to seem more ragged.

First of all industrial production in the United States is prospering, up by a third in the decade 1996–2006 to new record highs. What has fallen is employment, but again this needs to be placed in context. Every week the United States loses and creates half a million jobs. In any given year about one-fifth of the country's jobs have been eliminated, but another one-fifth have been created. Some of this is due to the march of technological change; some is a result of restructuring to be better equipped to meet new tastes and preferences; some, as in manufacturing, is because it takes fewer people to produce the same output. It was ever thus and it is comparatively small changes in these very large numbers that can change the United States' economic conditions from being job-rich to job-poor. But foreign trade has a minuscule impact. The most exhaustive and impartial inquiry into the impact of foreign trade on American jobs estimates that 226,000 jobs are lost annually – and the authors of the study believe that it is a high estimate.[50] As for China, calculations using the model built by the Economic Policy Institute, which is very hawkish on trade, can attribute only 2.24 million lost job opportunities to Chinese imports between 1989 and 2005. That is little more than one hundred thousand a year.[51] As for offshoring, its impact is even smaller. The Bureau of Labor survey in 2005 identified 884,356 job losses from mass lay-offs; only 12,030 jobs moved abroad.[52] British figures tell an almost identical story. In the forty months from April 2003 to July 2006 Britain lost, cumulatively, 390,000 jobs (including 140,000 intended redundancies announced by Chancellor Gordon Brown in his pre-election spending review) according to the European Restructuring Monitor; however only 19,000 were attributable to corporate and organisational decisions to locate abroad. Adjusting for the greater openness of the British economy, that almost exactly reproduces the American experience.[53]

Globalisation and the trade deficit do have an impact on the pattern of employment in the United States, and there may be a greater impact from offshoring in the future. But trade effects cannot begin to explain the totality of what has happened in the recent past – and certainly not the sixty million job losses attributable to downsizing and restructuring between 1984 and 2004 cited by Louis Uchitelle.[54] Chinese imports, after all, constituted 2.2 per cent of United States GDP in 2006, Indian imports 0.2 per cent of GDP: proportions on this scale can hardly explain the wanton damage that is alleged. Nor does the avalanche of gloomy material about the impact of trade on United States employment mention the improvements in efficiency that derive from trade. The economists Scott Bradford, Paul Grieco and Gary Clyde Hufbauer, who have used four different models for estimating trade effects, believe that $1 trillion of

American GDP is the result of global integration.[55] Also, the United States has enjoyed a sustained consumer boom for most of the past twenty years, with only shallow recessions. We cannot explain that boom without recognising the importance of sustained low interest rates and strong capital inflows – features of globalisation that work to the advantage of the United States. They also work powerfully to the advantage of Britain.

The relative rise of services and relative decline in manufacturing as a share of GDP (even if output rises absolutely) is inexorable, with or without trade. According to the Current Population Survey provided by the United States government, blue-collar and administrative support workers fell from 56 per cent of all adult workers in 1969 to 39 per cent in 1999.[56] The biggest compensating jump in employment was recorded for professional, managerial and technical occupations, up from 22 per cent to 32 per cent over the same period. That rise reflects the growing importance of applying cognitive and judgement skills in an increasingly complex workplace. The growth in sales jobs – up to 12 per cent from 8 per cent – reflects not just a growth in American consumption but a growth in more complex and multiple products for which consumers seek sales advice. The increase in pure service occupations – up to nearly 14 per cent from 11.6 per cent – also reflects the reality that some categories of jobs are physically rooted in place. It is structural change that is creating these changes, and trade is only a relatively small part of the story.

Nor is the divergence of wages and incomes within these fast-growing occupations due to the fact that the market values certain kinds of skill more highly in an era of globalisation. If that were true one would expect a rise in inequality to be associated with rising productivity. In fact, the opposite is the case. The most rapid growth in inequality in the United States was between the late 1970s and the mid-1990s, when growth in productivity was falling. Skill was having little impact on underlying productivity in those years, but there was still a growth in inequality. If it were true that skills are driving income differentials, then we would expect the earnings of skilled workers to rise. But, as Ian Dew-Becker and Robert Gordon of Northwestern University show,[57] between 1989 and 1997 (the latest date for which we have figures) the earnings of computer scientists and mathematicians rose by 4.8 per cent, those of engineers dropped by 1.4 per cent and those of CEOs rose by 100 per cent. What has driven the growth of inequality over the past thirty years is not the wage and salary income of the top 10 per cent as a whole, which has grown hardly faster than the average, but that of the top 1 per cent. The dramatic gains have been won by a tiny number at the very top. Income at the 99th percentile rose 87 per cent between 1971 and 2002, they estimate; at the 99.9th percentile it rose 181 per cent; and at the 99.99th percentile it rose 497 per cent. Paul Krugman, writing in the *New York Times*, estimates that the last 0.001 per cent are now earning more than $6 million on average.[58]

What has been taking place is a redistribution of income from the bottom 99 per cent to the top 1 per cent. This is not about skills and the development of the knowledge economy driving income disparities in an era of globalisation. It is about market power, failures of corporate governance and the increasing capacity of winners in today's society to take all. 'Virtuous circle' effects are now so quick to be established, in industries as disparate as investment banking and football, and have such dramatic impacts on sales and profits, that those considered responsible can name their remuneration.

In short, it is not possible to offer a satisfactory account of job insecurity, rising inequality and the acceleration of downsizing without recognising the substantive changes that have taken place in the United States' own economic structures, institutions and processes over the past twenty-five years. Those include the decline in trade union membership, the new priority given to maximising shareholder value, the decline in impartial news media and malfunctions in the political system. The circuit breakers and systems that used to stand in tension with the American market system, and so provided forward momentum, creativity and underlying legitimacy for ordinary people, have been systematically undermined and scrapped. The embedded checks and balances in the economy, society and polity have grown weaker as the United States has neglected its Enlightenment tradition. America's blues are largely home-grown.

11

Born in the USA

The retreat from the American Enlightenment tradition is a world event to rival the emergence of China. What began in the 1970s as a conservative campaign to revitalise American capitalism has grown into an all-devouring monster. Arguably American capitalism by the late 1970s did need rebalancing, away from the structures that had grown up over the previous thirty years, but today even some of the conservative authors of the revolution have themselves become dismayed as they watch the flight from Enlightenment values. The former neo-conservative Francis Fukuyama recently argued that, over the long term, multilateralism and the rule of law are better ways of securing American interests than pre-emptive unilateralism. Former Federal Reserve chairman Alan Greenspan is concerned about the scale of the budget deficits that have emerged courtesy of tax cuts and extravagant spending. Nancy Reagan, widow of President Ronald Reagan, has spoken out against cuts in stem cell research spending by the Federal government. Milton Friedman, the originator of monetarism and a leading exponent of free-market economics, reminds us that liberty was never meant to be understood as licence. Conservative columnist William Safire inveighs against the vast scope of government material that is now routinely classified as outside the purview of the Freedom of Information Act because of supposed security concerns. All, one way or another, find themselves representing a tradition in American life that is being eroded and derided.

The unravelling began in the 1970s, the decade whose disasters seemed to testify to America's growing vulnerability. There was defeat in the Vietnam War, Watergate and an escalating trade deficit. In 1974 inflation broached 12 per cent, the worst in United States peacetime history, while unemployment in 1975 touched 7.5 per cent. All of these seemed proof that America must change direction. The fact the Vietnam War was unwinnable did not take the sting out of what, by any standards, was a humanitarian and tactical disaster. It was scant relief that America's trade deficit might be testimony to the emerging economic strength of Europe and Japan, and thus to the success of the United States-driven post-war policy of stimulating their economic development. There were two unsuccessful attempts to assassinate President Ford. The Soviet Union invaded Afghanistan. The United States felt on the brink of relative economic, social and even military decline. The confident Enlightenment centre of American politics that had encompassed Eisenhower Republicans and Truman Democrats, the twin architects of the astonishingly successful post-war settlement at home and abroad, was now held responsible for failure by the ideological wings of both parties.

For the centrists in the Democratic party the decisive issue was Vietnam. Even today it is difficult for a Democrat to mount an argument that the original intent of the war was justifiable (communism was a threat and the war did buy a crucial fifteen years in which democracy and capitalism became rooted in Asia), without being decried as an amoral warmonger. Nor could the Democrats cohere around a programme for the use of government, regulation

and the role of welfare while taking a credible position on inflation.
The Enlightenment core of the party became overwhelmed by the
left, by single-issue crusaders and by proponents of the cultural
war against the right. Meanwhile the Enlightenment centrists in
the Republican party could not find a way of defending the role of
government, regulation, the legitimacy of taxation and the redis-
tributive fairness of welfare before the coalition of libertarians,
free-market fundamentalists and anti-statists – and they in turn
became overwhelmed. A political coalition initially founded as an
economic argument transmuted into a socially conservative movement centred on cultural propositions concerning the family,
abortion, the desirability of school prayers, religion and resistance
to the ramifications of the sexual revolution. The extremism of
these positions has left the Enlightenment tradition in the
Republican Party as weakened as it is in the Democratic Party.
The American Enlightenment centre has been unable to hold.
For thirty years the dynamic element in United States politics has
been an aggressive conservatism allying itself with a radicalised
evangelical movement

The story is complex. While broad strands of opinion in the
public at large have remained stable, there has been an increased
unwillingness to look for common ground, with an ideological
crystallisation especially on the right. In part this is a reflection of
growing inequality in American society (which I discuss later), as
Nolan McCarty, Keith Poole and Howard Rosenthal explain in
Polarized America: The Dance of Ideology and Unequal Riches. And,
in part, it is a reflection of the United States' new political geography, as its centre of economic gravity – and population
growth – has migrated from the north-east, with its heavy
reliance on blue-collar manufacturing work, to the south and
west and the new service industries. Between 1959 and 1989
the eight states enjoying the fastest economic growth all
belonged to the Confederacy.[1] In these more naturally conservative parts of the country 'frontier values' hold more sway: those

of self-help, voluntarism and distrust of government – readier audiences for the arguments of the intellectual right. A cultural suspicion of the 'elite' liberal positions on social issues has grown. The south and the west are also home to a disproportionate number of the just under ninety million evangelical Protestants who, over the past twenty years, have become progressively radicalised. As late as 1987 they split virtually fifty-fifty into Republican and Democrat camps. Now they are more than two to one in favour of Republicans.[2] As political scientists William Galston and Elaine Kamarck argue in 'The Politics of Polarization', religiosity has become a newly important driver of political identification.[3]

What has propelled this change is the politicisation of evangelical religion, which has become ever more ready to pick fights and oppose what it considers to be anti-faith, anti-American values. The causes are multiple. The American evangelical movement boasts a superabundance of denominations: the United States in 1996 had nineteen separate Presbyterian denominations, thirty-two Lutheran, thirty-six Methodist, thirty-seven Episcopal or Anglican, sixty Baptist and 241 Pentecostal, according to one source[4] – and they compete for congregations aggressively by outdoing each other in the intensity of the religious experience they offer. There is a form of evangelical bidding war. Sixteen per cent of Americans have changed their faith,[5] and one study reported that half the pastors in the United States' megachurches had themselves come from another denomination. The Republican Party has been effective in harnessing the power of the evangelical right to its political advantage, organising in the churches and introducing an evangelical discourse into its campaigns.

It is this recruitment of the evangelical right into the Republican base, with little effective resistance from within mainstream Republican ranks, that has propelled the party's increasingly anti-Enlightenment stance. The Enlightenment centre has not managed to marshal an effective counter-argument or majority coalition. American politics and culture have become polarised between a militantly ideological and dominant right, characterised by a fervent anti-Enlightenment religiosity, and a more fragmented and less coherent coalition of liberals and centrists who remain loyal to American Enlightenment values and who have reconciled their religious beliefs with modernity. The *National Journal* mapped the ideological loyalties of Democrats and Republicans in 1999 and found, for the first time, no crossover: the most conservative Democrat was more liberal than the most liberal Republican.[6]

The consequence has been a general diminution of Enlightenment values and processes. Whether the rise of biased new shows in the media, the collapse in trade unionism or the emasculation of the institutions that regulated monopoly, price-rigging, accountancy and corporate governance, the effect in all cases has been the same. The tensions between the Enlightenment and the market that with varying intensity have characterised the United States for all of its history up until the 1980s have been firmly resolved in favour of the market, property and the rich. It is this that has given the United States its particular character over the past twenty years.

The economic vicious circle

The United States has evolved a new business culture. The answer to why wages, downsizing, inequality and social mobility have performed as they have is staring the United States, and the many critics of free trade, in the face if they care to look. American managements have become decisively more transactional and hawkish in their approach to managing the companies under their stewardship. Over the past twenty-five years they have reconceived their purpose, not as building a business but rather maximising the immediate financial returns to their shareholders.

They transact, cut, restructure and downsize rigorously to achieve that objective. The culture of the first half of the twentieth century, with professional management teams dedicated to creating companies focused around investment, innovation and R & D, and with a compact between labour and management, has become a financial engineering culture. Raising the share price has become the dominant objective of the CEO, the board and the wider management team. A new logic holds sway: shareholders own the corporation and put their money at risk and, because the sole purpose of ownership it to maximise profits, the only strategic purpose of the corporation is to maximise the financial returns to shareholders. The share price is God. Everything is consecrated to raising it.

While this thesis may have attractions in theory – it provides direction and what is good for the company must be good for the share price – in practice it leads to a destructive short-termism. Individual savings are increasingly concentrated in funds managed by professional asset managers. The top hundred managers control $6.8 trillion worth of shares – 52 per cent of the value of the United States stock market.[7] These professional managers have become ever more peripatetic in their quest for higher financial returns. The average annual turnover of shares in a portfolio has jumped from 15 per cent of the portfolio in the mid-1960s to 100 per cent today.[8] Short-term profit is what will drive the buying or selling decision of the average fund manager. This is true even though, as analyst and founder of the Vanguard mutual fund group John Bogle (named by *Fortune* as one of the four investment giants of the twentieth century) has pointed out, high-turnover equity mutual funds yield lower financial returns than lower turnover funds.[9] Fixation with short-term share price movements not only destroys investment performance, it destroys value creation in business and biases management towards short-term cost strategies rather than long-term growth.

Downsizing and rationalisation may be the best avenue to

produce one-off gains through cost reduction, which pleases short-termist fund managers, but sustained growth in productivity is always associated with sustained growth in output and employment. In a revealing paper Martin Baily and John Haltiwanger, together with Eric Bartelsman for the National Bureau of Economic Research, prove this point by examining the experience of no fewer than 140,000 American manufacturing plants. Theirs is one of the largest analyses of its type.[10] Productivity increased in the plants that expanded output and employment; those that were downsizing experienced mostly decreased growth in productivity. It is the oldest and hoariest truth in economics and business. There is a virtuous circle of growth in output, growth in employment and growth in productivity; there is a vicious circle of stagnation in output and employment, together with falling productivity.

The takeover of another business, the transaction above any other that offers the apparently certain route to rationalisation, reorganisation and cost minimisation, in reality generally moves companies from the virtuous to the vicious circle. The scale of mergers, acquisitions and takeovers in the United States is breathtaking. In the 1960s and 1970s acquisitions ran at between 2 and 4 per cent of GDP. Over the past ten years they have averaged some 10 per cent of GDP, spiking up to over 15 per cent of GDP in the late 1990s, when the stock market was in full bullish charge. In hard cash the cumulative value of deals between 1995 and 2005 was $9 trillion, with $4 trillion between 1998 and 2001 alone.[11] In other words, over the past decade such deals have been cumulatively equivalent to nearly 100 per cent of United States GDP. This is the origin of so much downsizing in America.

Mergers and acquisitions have proved not to be the route to the promised improvement of either the share price or the efficiency of the underlying assets. *Business Week* conducted a study of 302 deals of more than $500 million between 1995 and 2001.[12] It found that 61 per cent of the deals delivered a 25 per cent lower rate of return to shareholders than the industry average: buyers consistently overpaid for the companies they bought, over-estimated the synergies, systematically found marrying two disparate businesses very difficult and obsessed over trying to cut costs to justify the takeover rather than make the business grow. Bringing together two living social organisms – two companies – is fantasti-cally difficult, as is paying a price that represents a realistic chance of success. The few successful takeovers in the study could not compensate for the scale of overall losses. Nor is the *Business Week* study unusual; every other study of mergers comes to similar conclusions. The management consultant McKinsey, for exam-ple, reviewing 160 mergers between 1992 and 1999, discovered that only twelve of the merged groups succeeded in lifting organic growth above the trends that existed before the merger; the other 148 failed.[13] Another management consultancy, KPMG, found in a survey of over seven hundred cross-border mergers between 1996 and 1998 that only 17 per cent of all mergers added value, while as many as 53 per cent actually destroyed share-holder value, with the remaining 30 per cent of deals making no difference.[14]

The merger of AOL with Time Warner in January 2001 has become legendary as an example of both why takeovers happen and why they go wrong. On the one hand there was AOL, the Internet company, where the share price had become 'the group's mission, a sacred trust'.[15] As became obvious after the merger, AOL had sacrificed everything, including business probity, to maintain growth in quarterly earnings. On the other side, the venerable Time Warner celebrated the Enlightenment value: a free press, the '*Time* culture'. The two organisations could not be more different, but that did not prevent either CEO from extolling the synergies to be had from the merger of the best of the new economy with the best of the old. Twelve months later Gerald Levin, Time Warner's CEO, had been forced from office because of the culture clash. He had put journalistic standards before cost-cutting, declaring in one e-mail after 9/11 that *Time* had a 'fundamental moral responsibility' to the twin ideals of journalistic independence and democratic dialogue.[16] However, within another twelve months nearly all the senior AOL team had also left, with the AOL business under a cloud because of accounting irregularities. The synergy that had promised to be so impressive in fact proved non-existent. Thirty months after a merger that had been launched with such a fanfare, the organisation took $99 billion of write-offs, paid a $300-million fine to the Securities and Exchange Commission for accounting improprieties and was facing $3 billion in payments to settle a class action suit. The fall in the share price from about $100 to $11 represented a $200-billion loss for shareholders.

What motivates the orgy of deal making is that it is the CEO's easiest answer to the question from shareholders and boards alike about how he plans to deliver above-average growth. Of course, the deal will usually have the happy consequence of sharply increasing his own remuneration. Robert Bruner, professor at Darden Business School and author of *Deals from Hell* – a catalogue of American mergers that have gone wrong – says that he talks a lot with senior executives in the course of his research. 'They all tell stories about how they are charged with maintaining earnings growth,' he says. 'They can only get to 5 to 6 per cent growth organically, yet the CEO has set a target that is much more ambitious, and they make up the difference by acquisitions.'[17] The deal will presumably provide synergy; will provide the opportunity for cost cutting to eliminate irrational duplication of activity; will propel the company to higher market share; and thus will confer the capacity to control prices and margins better. The argument is always a variant of one or all of these points, and it is extraordinarily persuasive – as AOL's Stephen Case and Time Warner's Gerald Levin can ruefully testify. Nor is this new business culture confined to the United States. Since I wrote *The State We're In* ten years ago, criticising the impact of financial short-termism and extravagant expectations of returns on British business, the phenomena has got worse. Britain is as exposed to irrational takeover, poor deals and excessive preoccupation with shareholder value as the United States.

What turns mere persuasiveness into action, despite the evidence that most deals will end in tears, is a set of interlocking perverse incentives that have no countervailing checks and balances. There are three preconditions for the epidemic. First, most companies no longer have widespread, diverse ownership consisting of millions of shareholders who are committed to the company for the long term and whom any predator will find difficult, time-consuming and expensive to convert to his cause. Financial institutions now account for half of all company shares, and they are addicted to deals because as sellers it helps their investment performance. Persuade a dozen of them of your case and you have a deal. Second, today's banks have a hugely enhanced capacity to raise large sums of cash that can be lent to pay for takeovers by predator companies. And third, as Lucian Bebchuk and Jesse Fried argue, as CEOs have become more powerful because of the weak corporate governance system in the United States their pay no longer depends on their performance.[18] What matters to a CEO is not whether the deal will succeed but whether it gives him a story to tell about how he will drive up profit; the resulting success or failure does not matter to his remuneration. Failure means a golden goodbye; success means more share options. Either way it is win-win. Add the investment bankers, who broker the deals for a handsome commission, and the story is complete.

Nor are these developments simply accidental. They are part of the retreat from the Enlightenment tradition and its associated belief that enterprise is a mission best pursued by a team of managers and workers who share goals, values and beliefs. The duty of care for the whole organisation has been abandoned; the only duty is to shareholders. The aim has been to create all-powerful CEOs who want to boost the share price; thus the generous allocations of share options that have increased more than ten times over the past decade.[19] Despite some notable recent efforts, there has been little or no preoccupation with how corporations are governed, how directors are selected and held to account and how shareholders can constitutionally challenge the powers of CEOs.

John Bogle reports that the thousands of publicly traded firms faced an average of just eleven challenges per year between 1996 and 2002; for companies with market capitalisation exceeding a mere $200 million the average number of challenges was one. The chances of success for a challenge were close to nil.[20] As a result CEOs have become more able to manipulate companies and corporate strategies to their own advantage.

After the collapse of the American banking system in the 1930s, regulations, checks and balances were imposed to make sure it would never happen again. These have been steadily eroded, culminating in the 1999 repeal of the great 1933 Glass-Steagall Act, which sought to separate commercial and investment banking. Controls on bank mergers, interstate banking and interest rates have all been lifted. As a result the flow of credit to finance takeovers has become an avalanche. Accountants, hungry for lavish fees, have been complicit in presenting company accounts in the kindest of lights. Meanwhile financial savings institutions, mutual funds and insurance companies have grown pell-mell off the back of tax breaks – but they are treated by the law as if they had no more power than individual shareholders. Unable effectively to control or direct the enterprises they own, they have colluded in demanding that managers simply raise the share price as the overriding goal.

Regulation in general has been allowed to atrophy and to be captured by those it seeks to regulate. When the American Law Institute has attempted to tighten the procedures of corporate governance and the Financial Accounting Standards Board has tried to make companies account for stock options as a cost of running the business, they have been beaten back by business interests, sometimes unashamedly lobbying Congress.[21] The Securities and Exchange Commission, the United States' widely admired and powerful securities regulator, has been allowed to become progressively poorer and enfeebled. After the Enron crisis it wanted to empower shareholders in poorly performing companies to be able to elect two directors to the board to gain information. The powerful Business Roundtable was fiercely against the idea; it lobbied Bush (the members of the roundtable are extremely influential as important sources of campaign funds) and the SEC was made to drop the proposal.[22] The idea of regulation as essential to the health of the American economy has been mocked and derided. Challenges to corporate power, to price rigging and to monopoly have become less and less likely. Corporate America has been encouraged to play the game of takeovers, mergers, monopolies and downsizing. And play it has.

The social vicious circle

The victim in all this has been the people. Corporate leaders pay lip service to the notion that their greatest asset is their workforce, but every action speaks otherwise. Essentially, the injunction is to transact the company to higher profits – by downsizing, by outsourcing, by merging and cutting out duplication and by lowering wage rates per hour worked. Three of the most distinguished economists in the United States – William Baumol, Alan Blinder and Edward Wolff – call this the 'dirty little secret of downsizing'.[23] Looking over the 1990s they find the same phenomenon as Baily, Haltiwanger and Bartelsman: that downsizing has not contributed one iota to growth in productivity. Rather, downsized companies have delivered the same or reduced output, but have succeeded in paying less for any given hour worked. In other words, downsizing is merely an effective way of holding down wages and transferring income from labour to capital.

The principal institutional opponent to downsizing is the trade union. American trade unionism has always struggled to find cultural, legal and social roots, but, even so, as late as the 1970s unions represented a quarter of all American workers, aided by New Deal legislation and the willingness of much of United States business to accept their legitimacy and usefulness as workplace partners. Now in the private sector unions represent only about 8 per cent of the workforce, and representation has also declined, although not so sharply, in the public sector. Part of the decline of unionism is due to the decline of large-scale manufacturing plants and of concentrations of white-collar workers in big offices. It is much harder to recruit and organise in much smaller-scale service-sector workplaces such as hotels, garages and fast-food outlets where the labour force is much more mobile and less inclined to accept unions' traditional appeals for mutual support. Success in this new economic structure demanded an agility and adaptability from the unions that they have notably lacked. Overly bureaucratic and locked in internal power struggles, they have presented an unattractive face to the public. The horror stories of corruption and thuggery have been difficult to live down because they are true. For example, in 1969 United Mine Workers of America (UMW) reformer Jock Yablonski and his family were murdered after he won the union presidency. Not only do potential members recall such acts; potential reformers are afraid of suffering the same fate.

Yet despite these handicaps some forty million workers declare they would like to join a trade union if given the opportunity.[24] Membership is low because of an ideological onslaught against trade unions by American business exploiting the anti-union biases in labour law. The most obstructive feature of this body of law is that a union will be recognised only if a majority of the workforce vote for union representation. Determined employers deploy a host of schemes to deter employees from voting yes. For instance, an employer might threaten to move the workplace, though such threats are nominally illegal. Employers also hire anti-union consultants, an industry that has mushroomed over the past twenty-five years, to make it as difficult as possible for unions to organise. They harass union activists and organisers, and use temporary or contingent workers who are less likely to join a union. Or they might locate in a state with a right-to-work clause that de facto makes organising a trade union close to impossible. And if an employer finds that there is an existing union he or she can use federal courts to appeal decisions by the National Labor Relations Board to adjudicate on disputes (federal courts are felt to be more pro-employer), thus undermining the purpose of union membership. There are any number of avenues open to a hawkish manager who is motivated to maximise shareholder value and who wants to lower costs by having no union to deal with – and all these avenues have been taken in varying degrees. Nor is there any popular or cultural backlash. In the prevailing environment, to defend a union as a source of Enlightenment-style countervailing power in the workplace is to be branded as anti-enterprise and hostile to the individual's right to work.

The new insecurity pervades the work experience. Human Resource Management, for example, is meant to be the organisational discipline responsible for training, developing and nurturing the company's workforce and fostering the high-performance workplace that supports an organisation's goals. But it is a profession in crisis because of the wide gap between its rhetoric and its practice. The high-performance workplace supposedly consists of strongly motivated, self-managed autonomous teams with a high level of education and skills that undergo continual 're-skilling' to adjust for changing market conditions. In both the United States and Britain, where the tradition of vocational training is weak, it is very difficult to embed the culture of the high-performance workplace. Re-skilling has to be done on the job because no wider institutional structure exists for it to be done any differently. Anglo-Saxon managements are permanently tempted to transact their way to short-term cost reduction with a compliant, non-unionised workforce that they direct from the top. Autonomy and high performance are aspirations rather than deliverable reality – hence the crisis in human resources. The trouble is that any countervailing forces – trade unions, workplace regulation or obligations to train that might lean against the trend to transactionalism and low-performance workplaces – are disappearing. The case for low regulation thereby has become self-fulfilling. The United States and Britain lie at the bottom the international league table of labour-market regulation; business interests in both countries insist that regulation must stay that way.

It is hardly surprising, as the social commentator Richard Sennett writes in *The Culture of the New Capitalism*, that employees have become distrustful and cynical of their employers' intentions. Sennett and his researchers interviewed a panel of workers in Britain and America over more than ten years and they found a pervasive and growing sense of uselessness. Employees, from white-collar and skilled workers to less skilled workers, are keenly aware that, even if they work hard and acquire skills, they can be laid off through no fault of their own, but simply as a by-product of a merger or reorganisation dreamed up to tell a story about future profitability. The idea of work as the progressive development of one's skills in order to apply one's craft and do a job well in an organisation that appreciates experience is dissolving. Instead, work becomes a series of episodes rather than an evolving narrative about deepening one's professionalism and skill over one's working life. The new injunction is to discard the past and embrace the new. What counts is not what you have done, but the capacity you are judged to have in adapting to the new. In her book *Bait and Switch*, Barbara Ehrenreich observes that applicants for jobs are advised not to give a job history that extends more than ten years. Experience is considered to be a possible obstruction to one's ability to change and move on.[25]

Calls for workers to re-skill themselves and educate their children are futile in a system which is biased against the poor and unskilled. Disadvantage begins at birth and continues in early childhood, now understood to be a critical period for intellectual and emotional development. It is vital for a child's development either to have an adult parent at home full time, implying forgone income, or alternatively child care, averaging $4500 a year, which is beyond most working families. Neighbourhood determines the wealth of the school because schools are financed by local property taxes. Scores on the Scholastic Aptitude Test (SAT), which is the passport into the higher education system, closely correlate with family income. International comparisons of standard achievement tell the story. Early education remains of high quality; American fourth graders do well. But eight years later American students have fallen behind their international peers, especially in mathematics and science. And for those who drop out of the educational or standard vocational route to achievement, there is little likelihood of a second chance. In Germany 80 per cent of school drop-outs go on to receive some form of vocational degree; in the United States only 54 per cent do.[26] Twenty-seven million adult working Americans do not have a high-school diploma.

The community college system struggles to carry out its mandate. More than half of its students have full-time jobs; 16 per cent are single parents. Community colleges are democratic and inclusive, but they have increasingly become a second-class system for those who cannot pay their way to academic success. The courses are ill-coordinated with those in the United States' some two thousand so-called corporate universities, and there is no national system to ensure good and rising common standards and curricula. The drop-out rate is high and the standards are increasingly variable. Community colleges fall a long way short of a system that might provide the basis for comprehensive lifelong learning.

In the nineteenth century there was no hesitation about creating a first-class infrastructure of public education for all funded by the tax-payer. But in the twenty-first century such structures are accused of being a wasteful burden and ineffective because they are public. It is no accident that nineteen of America's top twenty world-class universities are private. In the contemporary United States universities have used high fees to put themselves on a virtuous circle; from their point of view these fees enable them to pay for the world's top teachers, researchers and intellectuals.[27] Annual tuition fees above $30,000 are increasingly common, which, together with living expenses, means that students can graduate – even allowing for some college, state and federal grants – with debts in excess of $100,000. Fewer people, especially the struggling middle classes, are entitled to need-based student aid programmes like Pell Grants, which are generally awarded to students whose family incomes are under $40,000. Even the Pell Grants have not kept pace with tuition fees and living costs. They covered 80 per cent of the costs at four-year colleges twenty years ago, compared with just 40 per cent today. Young people from poorer families are, in effect, increasingly barred from attending college. Families whose incomes are below the median account for little more than 10 per cent of students; families in the top quarter for about three-quarters.[28]

Defenders of the system argue that at least the United States is a great job-generating machine. No more. The pace of job creation is dramatically lower in the current economic cycle than in previous cycles.[29] Employment has grown a mere 1.5 per cent in the upturn. In the past, growth has only been this feeble during recessions, near recession and in the famous jobless recovery of 1992 and early 1993.

As Henry Farber of Princeton University discusses, losing a full-time job in the United States is traumatic, despite the good chance of finding new work.[30] Using the Displaced Workers Survey he finds that nearly half of all Americans who lost their jobs between 2001 and 2003 (at the time of writing in July 2006 the survey for 2003–5 had not been published) either had not found work (35 per cent) or only part-time work (13 per cent). Moreover, those who found full-time jobs earned some 13 per cent less than in their old jobs. Those with a college degree lost more earnings than college graduates in the past. Thus for workers in so-called flexible labour markets job loss is not only traumatic but also costly. In this atmosphere it is natural to search for a scapegoat. Chinese imports and the menacing foreigner come easily to hand.

The imploding public realm

A great democracy should be able to organise a public discourse in which these issues and fears are debated, some resolution achieved and remedial action taken. Of course parties, interest groups and individuals still fight hard for their ideas with more or less success. No doubt some conservatives reading these pages will think that the criticism of American democracy as retreating from its Enlightenment legacy is little more than liberal sour grapes. If the roles were reversed and we were living in a period of liberal hegemony and bias, they might ask, would the criticism be so fierce?

I submit that it would. In the first place a core Enlightenment concept is a public space where arguments compete freely for acceptance amid the widest public possible on the basis of objective evidence. Free, independent media with access to good resources are crucial in the construction of such a public space and in the development of shared experience. But this concept is under fire in the contemporary United States, accelerated by the abolition of the Fairness Doctrine, the broadcasters' former obligation to report fairly and objectively. It appeared in 1929 as a voluntary principle; later it was built up through a series of rulings by the Federal Communications Commission and the Supreme Court and came to have the force of law. It was abolished in 1987, however, and now the networks have the right to be partisan. On top of the other deep trends in the media – the intensification of competition and the weakness of advertising revenues in traditional media forms like newspapers and broadcast television that have migrated to new media such as the Internet – this has lead to a dramatic fall-away in former editorial commitments to objectivity in an effort to win audiences by taking a clear editorial line. The most aggressive exponent of the new latitude is Fox News, which for all its liveliness runs a news agenda kindly to conservatism in general and the Republican Party in particular. It may object that it is only exercising its new right, but to claim as it does that its coverage is fair and balanced is a step too far. It is a betrayal of the real values of America's great Enlightenment tradition.

This is more than just a controversial marketing ploy; it signifies the general direction in which American news coverage has been moving for more than a decade.[31] The abolition of the Fairness Doctrine was a turning point. The argument was that individual news and current affairs programmes no longer had to apply a public interest notion of balance, fairness and objectivity. Rather, broadcasting (with the explosion in the number of broadcast media outlets) could be treated in the same way as newspapers, which have no formal obligation to be fair. In the 1920s, when there were few spectra on which to broadcast and necessarily only a few monopolistic broadcasters, it had been right to insist on fairness; however, no more. Listeners and viewers should be allowed to choose the editorial stance they prefer as they do with newspapers, and balance would be achieved through many media outlets offering a multiplicity of views.

But the broadcast media are not like print. Skim over the printed pages of a newspaper and you will see many more stories and commentary than in the sequential episodes in a news broadcast, which is necessarily linear in the way it must be seen or heard. The reader has the opportunity to read outside his or her original choices and to chance on something unexpected or challenging; what we hold in common is broadened. Once the principle of fairness is surrendered in broadcasting, every sequential episode, interview, report or film can come from the same philosophic viewpoint with no contrary or offsetting opinion. What is held in common is narrowed to the prejudices we share with one particular minority. Today Internet news is becoming highly personalised, simultaneously screening out what the user is not interested in and reducing what is held in common. Broadcasting is moving in the same direction.[32]

The sense of media beleaguerment and retreat is palpable. Between 1981 and 2001 the three network news broadcasts lost 40 per cent of their audience; the mission of NBC's *Nightly News*, declared its anchor Tom Brokaw in 2000, had become no more than survival.[33] The threat also affects newspapers whose circulation, editorial self-confidence and sense of their cultural importance are all shrinking. There is a migration to entertainment, as I noted in Chapter 8, and also considerable caution about challenging the prevailing consensus – over the Iraq war, campaign financing, the dot.com miracle during the dot.com bubble or almost any other journalistic subject. The media's owners aid and abet the onslaught. Westinghouse owns CBS, GE owns NBC and Disney owns ABC. The Tribune group of newspapers own, among others, both the *Los Angeles Times* and the *Chicago Tribune*. Institutional shareholders own more than half of the *New York Times* and the *Washington Post*. All adopt the same transactional approach to their media assets as they do to any other asset, seeking to maximise shareholder value, reducing editorial staffs and budgets and refusing to accept that the media has a special vocation. Tribune, having squeezed the editorial budget of the *Los Angeles Times* ever since it acquired the paper, poignantly insisted on losing sixty more reporting jobs after the paper had won five Pulitzer Prizes in 2004. The editor resigned. CBS News used to have a global network that included fourteen major foreign bureaux, ten mini-bureaux and stringers in forty-four countries. Today, CBS has only eight foreign correspondents and three bureaux. Foreign news is increasingly supplied by four of the London-based correspondents voicing over news agency video feeds.[34] And so it goes on. Despite some exceptions, such as the

Pulitzer Prize-winning investigation of federal wire-tapping of the public's phones, the great muckraking journalism of the early twentieth century is a distant memory.

On radio the talk show has become largely the preserve of aggressively conservative hosts, of whom Rush Limbaugh is the best known. Limbaugh's daily three-hour show, whose agenda in the past has been coordinated with the Republican high command, attracts fourteen million listeners. Sean Hannity, who co-hosts *Hannity and Colmes* on Fox News (which has twice the audience of its rival CNN), has an only slightly smaller audience for his daily radio show.

Opinion has become more important than fact, so that many facts that do not fit the a priori thesis are simply not broadcast. Suddenly one of the core attributes of an Enlightenment civilisation – citizens' access to information and evidence upon which to debate reasoned public arguments – is seriously undermined. Too many Americans are consuming one-sided opinionated vitriol rather than actual news. Limbaugh routinely complains that the eternal enemy is liberalism. Air America, a liberal rejoinder, has come to the game too late. It has a tiny audience and hardly redresses the incredible lopsidedness of the coverage. Without the Fairness Doctrine, the Enlightenment tradition is being progressively eroded – and there is a cascade effect on the entire United States media.

The level of ignorance about public affairs, especially among people under forty, is dismaying. As a result public opinion is becoming more and more easy to manipulate. This is how a new common sense has been established, notwithstanding the facts. America's jobs are under siege from China and globalisation, even when they are not. The war in Iraq is a war against the terrorists who were responsible for 9/11, when there was no evidence of any link between Al-Qaeda and Saddam Hussein. There was so much disinformation and so little high-quality journalism about the 2001 and 2003 tax cuts that only half of those polled in 2003 could even recall the tax cut of two years earlier. The more they were informed about tax cuts, the more they opposed any.[35] This is not a media culture that empowers citizens to hold their rulers to account. Rather, it is a media culture that disempowers citizens and empowers the governors.

Unequal politics

At the heart of the crisis of Enlightenment values lies the United States' political system. The Enlightenment concept of democracy rests on four bases: accountability, representativeness, respect for the rule of law and the capacity, through free speech, for debate, exchange and deliberation. By these standards the American system is increasingly compromised. The accountability process is silting up; the spirit, and sometimes the letter, of the law is evaded; the effectiveness of the representation process and the representativeness of elected officials of their electorates' views are declining and the quality of exchange and debate is chronically poor. The capacity of American democracy to hold political decision-makers to account, to represent the people, to contribute to their happiness and to execute their real wishes is becoming enfeebled.

The starting point is voting. Every citizen's vote is technically equal, but some citizens, the wealthier, are more equal than others. Rich people are much more likely to vote than poor people. Because parties and candidates focus on actual voters, the rich have more influence over them than the non-voting poor.[36] In 2000 87 per cent of the richest third of the population voted, compared with only 60 per cent in the poorest third, and the trend has been getting worse.[37] Five million former felons are forbidden to vote for the rest of their lives. The increasing inequality that I mentioned at the end of the last chapter thus extends to voting; the more people there are at the bottom of the income distribution, the lower voter turnout is likely to be – and the more actual voters will be better-off people.

If that were not enough, winning elections has become ever more expensive, so parties have become more reliant on their richer members and business. In 1974 a candidate successfully challenging an incumbent member of the House of Representatives spent $100,000 in real terms; today the average winning challenger spends more than $1.5 million.[38] This is an invitation for richer voters again to increase their influence. In 2000, one-eighth of American households enjoyed annual incomes greater than $100,000, yet these households made up 95 per cent of those who gave $1000 or more to political campaigns that year. Fifty-six per cent of those with incomes of $75,000 or more reported making some form of campaign contribution while only 6 per cent of Americans with incomes under $15,000 contributed.[39] If the campaign contributors are not citizens, they will be local, state or national lobby groups and businesses who expect a payback in access and legislation when their candidate is elected.

This puts candidates more and more in thrall to their electoral base, and that trend is exacerbated in the way increasing inequality in cities and towns is creating polarised districts. Hispanics and blacks, for example, live increasingly in one part of town that becomes a safe Democrat district; well-off white voters live in another that becomes a safe Republican district. Politicians in both parties have been solidifying the boundaries of their electoral districts to reflect the socio-economic character of their base; in effect, they have been choosing their voters to make their district captive for their party. In 1994 ninety-six Congressional races were tight, won by 55 per cent of the vote or less; by 2004 there were only thirty tight races. In 2004, amazingly, three-fifths of the nation's counties gave supermajorities of 60 per cent or more to either presidential candidate. In 1996, only two-fifths did. As Mark Gersh, the Washington director of the National Committee for an Effective Congress, observes, 'No matter how the voters feel, about 90 per cent of the districts are now preordained to go to a certain party.'[40] The most blatant gerrymander was devised by the now disgraced former House majority leader, Tom Delay, in Texas. The system now works so that if the Republicans carry just 45.9 per cent of the Texan state-wide vote they hold a majority in the statehouse. But if they carry 51.9 per cent of the vote they win not only 70 per cent of statehouse seats but twenty-two out of thirty-two Congressional districts – helping to secure a structural Republican majority in the House of Representatives.[41]

In a world of gerrymandered and polarised districts the key to a congressional seat is winning the primary. The key to that is to be ideologically purer than one's opponent to please the base rather than any swing voters. Barry Burden of the University of Wisconsin reports that a primary typically pulls a congressional candidate ten points towards the ideological poles on a scale of 0 to 100.[42] The activists, the interest groups and the talk show hosts create the highly charged ideological atmosphere in which the primary takes place. This would matter less if most Congressional districts were subsequently genuinely contested. The problem is that the ideologically sound candidate is virtually wafted into Congress unchallenged – or without having to defend his or her position in serious public exchange.

This new environment is kinder to Republicans than Democrats. As the Republican Party is more inclined to represent the views, policies and interests of the better-off it finds itself sailing with the political winds. Its rise has coincided with more ideological militancy and coherence from components of the Republican base, and the political system has permitted that trend to have more expression. The Democrats, on the other hand, have faced a harder political task: to find a common programme and a leader who can weld the liberal professional classes increasingly preoccupied with single issues with the traditional blue-collar base into a cohesively organised, disciplined and ideologically focused movement. They have not succeeded. The presidential candidacies of a succession of losing Democrats, Bill Clinton aside, testify to the scale of the difficulty; even Clinton could not hold the coalition together.

The wider national political problem, as the authors of *Off Center* argue, is not that the conservatives control the political agenda; that is the privilege of a winning party and majority body of opinion in a democracy. Rather, the problem is that they give little evidence of reflecting the values and attitudes of the majority who elected them. They seem to reflect instead the values and attitudes of a narrow ideological base that dictates the outcome of the primaries, and those who bankrolled them.

For despite the conservative ascendancy, Americans are no more conservative today than they were thirty years ago. There is no popular groundswell in favour of the notion that government is too powerful. The National Election Survey reports that although 49 per cent of respondents agreed with that proposition in the 1970s the proportion had fallen to only 39 per cent in 2000.[43] Nor is there much popular demand for tax cuts. In 2000 39 per cent of Americans wanted the government to spend more 'even if it means an increase in taxes', compared with 18 per cent who wanted to spend less. Again, if anything the proportion had moved away from the conservative stance since the early 1990s.[44]

Yet the American political system has been transfixed by the politics of tax cuts. On 7 June 2001, Bush signed into law the Economic Growth and Tax Relief Reconciliation Act, which, together with further reductions in 2003, will cumulatively cost more than $4 trillion if extended as the supporters hope; the loss of revenue in 2014 alone will total $373 billion, equivalent to a 45 per cent cut in social security benefit or a 53 per cent cut in Medicare.[45] Yet there was no great popular demand for reductions of such magnitude. There was certainly no popular demand for 36 per cent of the cuts to be directed to the richest 1 per cent of Americans. There will be no popular demand for the cuts in Medicare, social

security and education that will need to be made to close the enormous deficit opening up in the public finances. The cuts made little
economic sense in terms of stimulating either growth or enterprise;
reducing the tax on dividends and capital gains was a much less
effective form of economic stimulus or incentive than more general
tax cuts – and the most effective stimulus of all would have been an
increase in educational and vocational investment.

Yet the cuts went ahead. When Paul O'Neill, the Treasury
Secretary at the time, warned privately in autumn 2002 that the
budget deficit was mounting dangerously and that there was no
case for yet more tax cuts for the wealthy he was rebuffed. Vice-
president Cheney replied tellingly: 'Reagan proved that deficits
don't matter. We won the election. This is our due.'[46] Karl Rove,
then Deputy Chief of Staff, told a wavering president: 'Stick to the
principle' – tax cuts for the better-off. This is not a democratic
process that the founding fathers or the Enlightenment tradition
would recognise. There was no effective debate or exchange by an
informed citizenry, and no attempt to establish what citizens wanted
and what would be in their interest. Rather, the executive and legislative branches were captured by a faction that looks after its own
very particular interest group.

Nor is unwanted policy restricted to tax cuts. Similar arguments
could be made about climate change, the approach to terrorism
and privatising social security. The political centre of gravity is
nowhere near the heartbeat of what remains essentially an
Enlightenment nation. America needs to escape the gathering
drift towards closure and xenophobia and rediscover the values of
openness, tolerance and generosity of spirit.

That will not be easy, as Benjamin Friedman argues, without
evidence of both growing prosperity and a belief that it is shared.
Human beings feel better about themselves and their society
if they feel they themselves are getting ahead compared with
their own past, and if the general gains are not distributed too
unequally. Indeed, it is during periods of growth that people are

less likely to feel the pangs of relative loss of status, because their own circumstances are improving; thus they are more willing to shoulder their share of paying for policies that promote equality. It is during periods of stagnation, when relative positions can become quickly and irrationally different, that people become fearful and inward-looking.[47] In the United States great moral advances such as those of the progressive era (1895–1919) or the civil rights era (1945–73) have tended to accompany prosperity. Periods of moral retreat like the populist era (1880–95) or the backlash of the 1980s and early 1990s have been associated with stagnating incomes. Similar patterns hold for France, Britain and Germany, argues Friedman. If he is right, today's environment of squeezed living standards and insecurity does not augur well.

The risks of a moral retreat are real. Ever since 9/11 there has been a mounting drumbeat that the only way to achieve national security is to be unilateralist, aggressive internationally against states that might harbour terrorists and tough on civil liberties. As with tax cuts, it is not obvious that this stance represents what the majority of Americans want or think advisable, but the political system and the media permit very little argument or challenge to the consensus diagnosis. Now there is a wave of nationalist and protectionist sentiment which is rising unchecked towards hysteria, and which, as I have argued in this chapter, is unjustified by the facts. The Democrats, the beneficiaries of growing disaffection with the Iraq war (see below) and the sheer inefficiency of the Bush presidency, have had to make important concessions to this mood in their attitude to China, trade and the United States' multilateral treaty framework. The democratic process involving the media, the public, intellectuals and politicians through which reality might surface, is grievously enfeebled. Turning America around is a formidable challenge. It must, however, be attempted.

And it has led to Iraq

The repudiation of Enlightenment values and processes reached their disastrous climax in the reaction to 9/11. The United States can no longer depend on deterrence any more, ran and runs the argument. Rather, it must pre-empt potential terrorist threats before they emerge. Declaring that 'the gravest danger to freedom lies at the crossroads of radicalism and technology', Bush's new strategy cautions that 'the United States can no longer rely solely on a reactive posture as we have in the past'. In particular, the new National Security Strategy called for 'anticipatory action to defend ourselves, even if uncertainty remained as to the time and place of the enemy's attack'.[48] Condoleezza Rice, when she was National Security Adviser, admitted in July 2002 that the decision to invade Iraq was made even before the UN was first consulted in August 2002.[49] George W. Bush had decided that Iraq merited the new pre-emptive treatment. The United States was determined to go to war, with or without the authorisation of the United Nations. Bush agreed to attempt to get a second UN resolution in the weeks leading up to the invasion in March 2003 only because Tony Blair wanted to protect his own political position at home – in vain as it turned out. The Bush doctrine of pre-emption was now in full cry.

Enlightenment values and international law are in profound tension with the doctrine of pre-emption: it offers such an open door to lawlessness, arbitrary government, lack of accountability and warlordism. Within a democracy the doctrine of pre-emption gives enormous power to the executive branch of government and the intelligence services charged with establishing whether or not there is a pre-emptive threat; the legislative branch of government is necessarily dependent upon the executive for information and is inherently more manipulable. And because so much depends on judgement there cannot be clear rules about determining when pre-emption is justified – so that justification, one of the key democratic functions, becomes close to impossible. The same difficulty applies internationally. Obtaining international agreement about what constitutes legitimate preemption is impossible because so much of a threat, unless it is obviously and unambiguously imminent, is based upon perception, with enormous potential for exaggeration. Although there are occasions when any state may feel there is an imminent threat against which it must defend itself, there is inevitably more ambiguity and interpretation with regard to terrorism. The truth of the matter, as the Canadian writer and politician Michael Ignatieff writes, is that pre-emption shades into unilateral aggression which is illegitimate abroad and undermines the democratic process at home.[50]

Iraq is an ample and awesome warning of the dangers. The UN Charter embodies the principle of non-aggression. In order to justify a pre-emptive war against Iraq Bush had to characterise Saddam Hussein as presenting 'a grave and gathering danger', as he did in his speech to the UN in September 2002, because Iraq possessed weapons of mass destruction. Many Western intelligence services certainly believed that Iraq did possess such weapons, and UN weapons inspector Hans Blix reveals in his memoirs that he did too, even if it is now clear that Iraq did not.[51] But the justification of a pre-emptive war could not be a matter of belief, suspicion or an informed guess; the stakes were so high that the intelligence had to prove what the United States government wanted. The CIA, like the British MI6, knew in which direction the wind was blowing, as Paul Pillar, a former CIA official, has written, and it knew that unhelpful information would be played down or ignored.[52] A subtle process of politicisation and self-censorship began in which the information that is wanted becomes the information that is available.

Actually the process was not always so subtle. The Policy Counterterrorism Evaluation Group set up by the Pentagon publicly derided the CIA for doubting that there were direct links between Saddam Hussein and Al-Qaeda. In an atmosphere like this, where in Britain Tony Blair has acknowledged that intelligence and policy were 'commingled', intelligence becomes the servant of the executive branch of government – and the justification and accountability process essential to democracy is undermined.[53] Congress and the House of Commons went along with what the executive wanted in both countries; without evidence to trump the executive's evidence, it is almost impossible politically to resist. Who wants to be soft on terrorism and put citizens' lives at risk? With four years' hindsight it is obvious that large parts of the democratic infrastructure in the United States and Britain were gravely distorted. Both the CIA and MI6 have been made to look like fools. Both governments' legal infrastructures have been compromised. Even the armed services, sent to war on a false prospectus, are encountering a crisis of morale: up to one-fifth of American Iraq veterans have suffered some form of psychiatric illness.[54] Six former American generals have combined to criticise the manner in which the United States went to war and the quagmire it is now in.[55] Pre-emption has begun to poison the American state. Democratic institutions depend upon the rule of law; pre-emption subverts and pollutes it.

The result is Iraq. The authors of the United States' foreign policy did not begin to anticipate how the exercise of raw military power – 'to shock and awe' – in a pre-emptive strike unsanctioned by international law would be greeted internationally, and how debilitating the consequences would be in the United States' own terms. The United States would be faced with suffering most of the military casualties and paying the enormously expensive reconstruction costs. The administration had suppressed the debate that might have revealed such obvious problems; with better information and openness either the invasion would not have gone ahead or it would have been better planned when it did happen. Iraqis who opposed invasion and occupation were handed a propaganda coup; the United States has warranted the condemnation of it made in hundreds of Middle Eastern mosques and in the terrorist training camps.

Planners at the Pentagon anticipated that the United States military presence could be scaled back to just twenty-five thousand troops six months after the occupation of Baghdad.[56] More than four years later there are over 150,000 US soldiers in Iraq. The underestimation of what was entailed could scarcely have been worse. By September 2007 approaching 3800 American servicemen and servicewomen have been killed in Iraq and twenty-seven thousand wounded.[57] Civilian Iraqi dead exceed one hundred thousand, and there are 1.3 million displaced people. Already the United States has spent $750 billion cumulatively by August 2007; one estimate forecasts that direct and indirect costs could together reach $2 trillion.[58] An independent audit for the United States government says that tens of millions of dollars have been wasted in bungled reconstruction contracts. The treatment of prisoners in Abu Ghraib and Guantanamo has been a legal and public relations disaster for little or no security advantage.

Within Iraq, barbarism has been transmuted into legitimate acts of war to respond to the illegal invader. Licence has been given for systemic disorder and mayhem. The ordinary Iraqi citizen has come to see democracy as synonymous with rationing, fear, murder and worse living standards than under Saddam Hussein. The economic and security situations are also cloudy. Before the 2003 war Iraq was pumping about 2.8 million to 3 million barrels of oil per day; in the first quarter of 2007 production was 1.95 million barrels a day because of terrorist attacks on exposed oil pipelines, directly contributing to oil prices approaching $90 per barrel.[59] And there has been an increase in terrorist incidents.

If democratic institutions can be established in Iraq over the long term it is likely that the country's economic and social performance will improve. A constitution has been agreed, and eight million Iraqis went to the polls: over five hundred newspapers have been started and trade unions are forming.[60] The hope is that the new government will provide stability and begin to stop the slide to civil war. All this only intensifies the sense of tragedy and lost opportunity. Instituting democracy in Iraq was possible; that was why any intervention had to have the full backing of the international community to ensure its legitimacy, and there needed to be a careful plan of reconstruction to avoid the escalation of violent religious conflict between the Shia and Sunni communities, of which the CIA warned. Yet by invading as it did the United States has set back the cause of Iraqi democracy, set back the potential spread of democracy in the rest of the Middle East, increased the risk of terrorism and weakened its own capacity to act against the emerging danger-state of Iran. It has enfeebled the rule of law within the United States. Failure on this scale demands a fundamental reappraisal of the philosophy that has led the United States into this mess. Enlightenment values count.

Britain is only marginally less compromised. Its reaction to terrorism mirrors that of the United States. Under the Prevention of Terrorism Act (2005) 'control orders' can be imposed on terrorist suspects by the Home Secretary. The accused can be subjected to indefinite house arrest – without the benefit of a trial. Such orders, said Alvaro Gil-Robles, the human rights commissioner for the Council of Europe, were clearly intended to 'substitute the ordinary criminal justice system with a parallel system run by the executive'.[61] All control orders, he advised, should be subject to judicial authorisation and, where necessary, a trial; if the evidence could not be marshalled the orders should be lifted after twelve months.

Even though this meant that Britain was the only European signatory to defect from the European Convention on Human Rights, the measures encountered virtually no resistance. Apart from some members of the judiciary, a few liberal journalists and the House of Lords, there was scant objection from civil society to measures that weakened Britain's commitment to fundamental rights – a commitment that had survived world wars and the murderous engagement with the IRA.

This criticism is not to argue that the United States, Britain and the West should sit idly by in face of the emergence of fundamentalist Islamic terrorism, whose careless and indiscriminate willingness to murder innocents has been exposed not only by the events of 9/11, but the subsequent outrages in London, Madrid, Mumbai and Bali. We need a response. The mistake that has been made is to fashion it outside the Enlightenment framework.

The first error was to characterise the response as war. War is a condition between sovereign states; it is, as Yale's Professor Bruce Ackerman describes, a life and death struggle to secure a state's will over an area of key national interest when foreign, economic and diplomatic policies have failed.[62] There is an identifiable enemy; a settlement can be reached by treaty, armistice or capitulation. War takes place, paradoxically, within a recognised legal framework. Al-Qaeda is a terrorist network whose ideology is to contest any such framework, and who, in any case, is not going to invade the United States and Britain.[63] Even if its current leadership agreed a truce, it could not guarantee to control its members. Terrorism is a technique to which its adherents remain wedded in their pursuit of fundamentalist aims; if agreement was reached with one group it would very probably mutate into another.

Thus the United States and its partner Britain are engaged in a war that cannot be won, deploying policies that are self-defeating while undermining democracy at home. However, this suits both governments, and in particular the Bush administration. They argue that there is a trade-off between security and legality, or as I would put it, Enlightenment values, and that there has to be a rebalancing in favour of security. To do otherwise is to run unnecessary risks – that political trump card.

A more appropriate response, which in the long run holds out genuine prospects of victory, is not to diminish Western commitment to the rule of law. Rather, it is to recognise that the state may need increased powers of surveillance and detention at home, and even greater capacity to act pre-emptively abroad – but that such action must be cast within an Enlightenment, democratic framework. Ackerman suggests that the granting of emergency powers after a terrorist attack must be conceded, but that after a period – certainly within a couple of months and regularly thereafter – the government should be required to ask the legislature to re-authorise its holding of emergency powers. It should then have to secure ever-higher majorities for the powers to be continued, thus forcing – in my terms – an Enlightenment process of justification and deliberation. The media, parliament and the wider public beyond would be forced into a debate about whether the emergency powers continued to be appropriate. The same rules would apply for increased powers of surveillance and imprisonment. In other words, it would be understood that what was happening was provisional in response to an emergency rather than a once and for all rebalancing of power to the state and the security forces.

The same logic applies abroad. There should not be a general rule in favour of pre-emption. Instead the United Nations should accept that pre-emptive action against terrorism may be required, while setting a high bar in terms of proof, and that the particular power taking pre-emptive action has to come back to the United Nations regularly to regain a mandate – forcing a debate about the appropriateness of the action and a chance to reappraise it if it is wrong. The invasion of Afghanistan would thus have to be rejustified and almost certainly would have been revalidated, and no intervention in Iraq would have been possible. Both would have been better outcomes than what we have.

American hawks will say that this ties the hands of the United States. It does. But the greater gain is legitimacy, both within the eyes of the international community and, more importantly, with the citizens of the nation against which pre-emptive action is being taken. The charges of aggressive imperialism will have much less force and American, coalition or NATO troops would be able genuinely to portray themselves as liberators – crucial in the fight for hearts and minds that is the key to any successful action on the ground against insurgents who depend on the good-will of the local people in order to secure safe houses and an infrastructure of support. The aim is to win this struggle, and in ways that are congruent with wider Western goals.

Iraq has been a diplomatic, security, military and economic disaster on an epic scale. Even more dangerously it has legitimised a more generalised aggressive unilateralism in international relations which will make the handling of China and the wider economic tensions much more problematic and hazardous. And China is the most important challenge of our times. The Western interest is for China to supplant communism, build its own Enlightenment institutions because it comes to understand their crucial value, and become a state that actively wants to uphold the values and processes of international governance. To secure this the United States and Britain would be better advised to live their values within the international system founded upon the rule of law, including the fight against terrorism. They have not and as a result the world is a much less safe place than it should be. It is a mistake of the first order.

Conclusion

Globalisation induces something close to hysteria from both its critics and its advocates. The litany of threats is by now familiar. No unskilled or semi-skilled job in the developed world is safe if it is exposed to international competition, and even jobs that are not currently exposed soon will be. Tens of millions of jobs will be sent offshore to India or China. European-style commitment to high levels of welfare can no longer be afforded as the consequent taxation prices Western workers and producers out of globalising markets. Governments must focus solely on education and training. Nothing or nobody is unaffected. This change cannot be resisted, so the only option is to accept one's fate as a pawn in the globalising great game.

We need to be less alarmist and more forensic. As I argued in Chapter 10, globalisation is not a juggernaut threatening to carry us all away either to a free-market nirvana or hades, depending upon your point of view. Indeed, seen from the less developed world – even from China – the challenge is how to compete with the West. Desperately poor, barely educated peasants, even though their numbers run into billions, are hardly in a position to take on Western workers. Actually the rising affluence that globalisation generates gives the 'soft' factors that contribute to economic success a new importance, so that globalisation *accentuates* rather than levels economic differences. The embedded advantages of the advanced economies become more significant, and the benefits and losses from globalisation are skewed disproportionately and asymmetrically towards the West. For Western producers the global economy is full of niches and opportunities that are enlarging, not diminishing.

For the past five years Susan Berger of MIT has led a team interviewing five hundred companies in the United States, Europe and Asia in an exhaustive and systematic assessment of how globalisation works in practice. The main conclusion from her book *How We Compete* is that wage costs are not the be-all and end-all of economic life. A Chinese worker may earn 4 per cent of the wage of an American worker, but is only 4 per cent as productive. What counts are not absolute wage differentials, but the unit wage costs once you have factored in productivity differences. The Americans, Japanese, Germans and British are comparatively highly productive and can still compete against the low-wage Asians. Also, successful companies apply strategies that depend on much, much more than low wage costs. Market responsiveness, for example, means being both physically and culturally close to one's markets and possessing a sufficient productive capacity quickly to respond. Distance inhibits responsiveness.

Berger and her colleagues marshal evidence to prove their point. With regard to productivity, factories are part of the wider economic, social and value system. Within the factory the capacity of team leaders to solve problems, to fix a broken machine or to find an alternative source of supply when a supplier breaks a contract – the kind of issues that beset factory managers daily – are dependent not just on their level of education and training, but on its character and depth. In other words, the quality of schools and vocational training – built up over decades – is central to factory productivity. McKinsey, for example, estimate that only one-fourth of Indian engineers and one-tenth of Chinese engineers are genuinely equipped to work in multinational companies; a study at Duke University reports that Indian and Chinese degrees are significantly less demanding than their Western counterparts.[1] Moreover, leadership in a corporate setting is subtle; without an understanding of justification and accountability, it is very difficult for leaders to listen, communicate, seek information from below and process it effectively – all crucial processes in driving a company forwards. In the electronics industry, for example, the world benchmark for overall equipment effectiveness is to achieve utilisation rates of 95 per cent; even in relatively well-advanced Taiwan the score is only 84 per cent.[2] The gap of 11 per cent is the difference between profitability and losses. Taiwanese workers and managers are not able to manage high-tech machinery as effectively as their counterparts in the developed world.

Nor is workforce quality the only problem in low-wage, less developed countries. Weak legal systems mean that theft of intellectual property is rampant, so that multinationals have to be wary that their technology, designs and processes may be stolen. The lack of density of the local supply chain means that goods have to be imported, so that supply-chain management becomes expensive and time-consuming. Corrupt officials have to be kept sweet, risking intense reputational costs at home. Transport costs remain significant. One study of the global garment industry found that when all these factors are included the total costs of direct labour constitute only 3–4 per cent of the price of a product at the point of being loaded for transport and less than 1 per cent of the retail price.[3] Similar results are confirmed by other studies.

Technology Forecasters, a consulting group, found in sixty case studies that labour averaged a trivial 2 per cent of a project's total cost.[4] McKinsey, in a survey of Californian companies, found that high-tech firms would save 0.6 per cent through offshoring, plastic firms would save 6 per cent and the apparel firm would save 13 per cent.[5] For many apparel firms even 13 per cent is an insufficient saving to offset the cost of not being close to their markets.

Creating value in an age of affluence is much more sophisticated than just disaggregating production and assembling products where wages are lowest. Rising affluence means a demand for customisation of goods and services to suit individual needs which change and evolve quickly; more and more sophisticated technology means that every stage of the value creation process – design, manufacture, distribution and even finance and marketing – is subject to continual reengineering. This is the heart of the knowledge economy, and firms have to be extremely judicious in how they respond to these powerful forces. According to Berger and her associates, strategies for minimising costs are essentially short-termist and self-defeating. Even a company like Dell, which has embraced the outsourcing philosophy very aggressively, is careful to make sure that it retains the ability to customise its equipment with local in-house productive capacity – and its marketing and distribution services are kept very close to its markets. Other electronics companies, such as Texas Instruments, pursue a more mixed strategy, keenly aware that they may need to overhaul any stage in the production and distribution process and if they contract it out they risk losing control of the ability to be responsive.

Product cycles are shortening dramatically. It required six years to take a car from concept to production in 1990; now it requires only two years. This phenomenon is general. One study found that the time it took to launch new products or make substantial product improvements fell from an average of 35.5 months in 1990 to about 23 months in 1995.[6] Firms that outsource too much production too far away from their markets are putting all their eggs in one basket; that is, low wages become the sole determinant of competitiveness.

Such firms risk being outcompeted by firms closer to home who can better exploit new technologies and new patterns of demand.

In the face of these challenges many firms choose to remain integrated. Sony and Toshiba in Japan, Samsung in Korea (Samsung is Asia's largest chip and mobile phone maker) and the clothes manufacturer Zara in Spain are hugely successful companies that have built their performance around keeping part or all of their production in-house and sourcing most of the balance locally. Half of Zara's products come from trusted, local suppliers located in and around its base in La Coruña.[7] When Ford built its flexible factory in Chicago it insisted on having its suppliers physically close to its new plant. The well-known clusters of high-tech firms in California and Boston in the United States and in Cambridge in Britain are testimony that cluster effects can be more important than low wages. In low-tech textiles in Italy small-firm clusters outcompete their rivals despite higher Italian wage costs. Benetton, Safilo, Max Mara, Luxottica, Geox, Tie Rack and Ermenegildo Zegna, for example, are all globally recognised companies whose production base is still firmly anchored in Italy; they form a critical mass of producers with design genius whose collective output and profitability support trade fairs, design schools, training and information about foreign markets – all of which feeds back into the productivity of the firms.[8] In fact, despite their high wages they are short of labour; in Modena, the centre of the Italian garment industry, the Chinese have bought into two hundred of the 3200 garment businesses in order to learn. Low wages, in turns out, are only a small part of the contemporary business economics. This confirms common sense and empirical observation. For on top of the relative lack of importance of low wages to corporate strategies, there are immense cultural, linguistic and even geographical barriers to trade. For example firms in Canada, so very similar to the United States, trade up to twenty times more with each other than with the country the other side of the 49th parallel.[9] The United States is not much different, and firms in a relatively open economy like Britain are much more likely to meet their needs from home than abroad. Trade even within the European Union's single market underperforms what it should be; trade penetration is congruent with tariffs of 37 per cent. Global integration through trade remains very shallow.

Nor is globalisation tearing down the welfare state. Since 1980, according to the University of California Davis' Peter Lindert, social transfers (which he defines as assistance to the poor, the unemployed and pensions for the elderly, together with spending on health and public housing) have continued to rise in the industrialised world.[10] He can find no evidence that this trend, or the taxation to finance it, has had any deleterious effect on economic growth rates or been adversely affected by globalisation. Indeed, there is some evidence that high social spending is good for growth. The critics of social spending make three errors, Lindert argues. First, they bundle it up with all government spending, so that their statistical tests are not targeted enough on what they claim is the significant variable – the relationship between social spending and growth. Second, they assume that governments design and finance welfare states to create disincentives, and that any form of taxation itself is a disincentive. Third, they assume that there can be nothing economically positive about social spending. Lindert demonstrates that they are wrong on all three counts.

First, he separates out social spending from government spending to test the correlation between it and growth; he finds no negative correlation. Second, he shows that countries with high social spending go to great lengths to design the structure of their spending and its financing to avoid disincentives. Indeed, paradoxically countries with a very tight-fisted approach to social spending – countries that use means testing and withdraw benefits aggressively as recipients' circumstances improve – create more disincentives than countries with more generous systems. Nor do countries with high social spending, notably the Nordic states, finance it with confiscatory taxes on capital or high incomes.

They look for broad-based sources of funding such as income tax, social insurance and sales taxes. And they are careful to keep their system economically rational; they encourage unemployed workers to search for work in return for unemployment benefits and they raise the eligibility age for pensions as life expectancy lengthens.

Third, and most important, social spending, rather than being a ball and chain on the economy, has positive economic feedbacks. It enables a steady growth in consumption by the poor, and it has a strong counter-cyclical stabilising influence during recessions. It can also have an amazing effect on employment participation rates and skill levels. Denmark's universal childcare system, for example, produces two economic wins. It allows young mothers to re-enter the labour market quickly, and it also ensures that young children from low-income homes have the kind of emotional, social and intellectual engagement that supports the development of their cognitive skills at a crucial age. All the Nordic countries, with similarly high levels of social spending, report high employment participation rates for both men and women, high levels of educational attainment and a general readiness – because their living standards are ensured – to take risks, retrain and change jobs. The Nordic economies are thus win-win. They enjoy all the benefits of a market-based system of incentives for their dynamic, high-productivity private sectors and they also enjoy the benefits of high social spending which makes it easier rather than harder for workers to accept the sometimes high cost of economic change.[11]

These are pluralist market economies with strong public realms and a commitment to justification; they also enable ordinary people to develop their individual capabilities. In short, they embody contemporary Enlightenment values – as powerful now as two hundred years ago in sustaining the West's economic advantages. If the United States and the rest of the European Union – including Britain – develop the same powerful commitment they too will have nothing to fear from globalisation or China. And everything to gain.

The West mustn't panic – it has the knowledge economy

This is a moment when both Americans and Europeans need to hold their nerve about their economic strength and keep their markets open. The knowledge economy is a concept abused by hype, but it does capture a truth about the trajectory of economies with high per capita incomes. It is banal to observe that the traditional manufacturing and agricultural sectors in advanced industrialised economies now constitute together less than one-fifth of national output and that this proportion will continue to fall. The service sector constitutes the vast preponderance of output and is set to grow yet larger. A less banal observation is that all sectors of the economy in all Western societies are transmuting because ever more sophisticated consumers are interacting with the potential of new technologies supported by ever greater affluence. Essentially, Western economies and societies are moving up Maslow's hierarchy of needs away from basic human needs that can be satisfied by producing uniform goods and services as commodities and towards more complex preferences that require more nuanced responses. Globalisation aids this process but is not its cause.

Harvard Business School's Shoshana Zuboff and her husband James Maxmin have mapped this new geography of demand in their book *The Support Economy*.[12] Contemporary consumers, they say, now want psychological self-determination. Today, requiting core material needs is no longer sufficient for happiness – material consumption is recognised as an inadequate route to well-being. Consumers want their own voice and feel the need for sanctuary. Rewards, argue Zuboff and Maxmin, will fall to those businesses that create value not just from efficiently combining material inputs into outputs, but from also helping consumers navigate their way through complex choices, and finding answers to consumers' questions about attaining psychological well-being.

The choices created by affluence are stunning. From running

shoes to soft drinks, television channels to magazines, the range of new goods and services is growing at a mind-boggling rate. This multiplicity of choice reflects both today's flexible capacity to produce such customised products and the sophistication of demand in richer societies. It also reflects the deeper psychological and emotional needs identified by Zuboff and Maxmin. Ronald Inglehart makes a complementary point when he argues that economic growth and physical security have freed affluent societies from necessity, allowing the emergence of post-material values. The new values emphasise autonomy and heterogeneity over tradition and conformity: 'Post-modern values bring declining confidence in religious, political and even scientific authority; they also bring a growing mass desire for participation and self-expression . . . today, the spiritual emphasis among mass publics is turning from security to significance; from a search for reassurance in the face of existential insecurity to a search for the significance of life.'[13] This is reflected in the quest for spirituality and happiness, but also in the quest for goods and services that meet the exact specifications of particular consumers.

The knowledge economy is the economic response. Soft knowledge is becoming as crucial as hard knowledge in the chain of creating value. By hard knowledge I mean the specific scientific, technological and skill inputs into a particular good or service; hard knowledge, for example, is needed to build a new chip or jet engine, devise a distinctive marketing campaign or invent a new financing vehicle. Soft knowledge refers to the bundle of less tangible production inputs involving leadership, communication, emotional intelligence, the disposition to innovate and the creation of social capital that harnesses hard knowledge and permits its effective embodiment in goods and services and – crucially – its customisation. Their interaction and combination is the heart of the knowledge economy. While some definitions focus narrowly on technology and science, my own extends the conception from high-tech manufacturing to creative industries like advertising and web design, from investment banking to the world of psychoanalysis, and also includes education and health care. On this definition, for example, some 41 per cent of the United Kingdom labour force is now employed in knowledge-based occupations, compared with 30 per cent in 1990, and the proportion is rising rapidly.[14] McKinsey has a higher estimate: 45 per cent of the British workforce deploy what it calls 'tacit interactions' in the workplace – 'the exchange of information, the making of judgements with a need to draw on multifaceted forms of knowledge in exchange with co-workers, customers and suppliers' to solve 'complex, collaborative problems'. It is these soft skills that lie at the heart of the knowledge economy, which in some sectors, such as health care or insurance, are required in more than three-fifths of all jobs.[15]

So it is ironic that the West feels its position is precarious, when in many respects its advantages in terms of institutions and processes that take decades or even centuries to build are ever more marked. These are essential to the infrastructure that supports the knowledge economy and the creation of hard and soft knowledge. As long as the West recognises and nurtures this asset, its economic strength is guaranteed. There should be a reality check, especially in the United States. The fear of job insecurity and the reality of mounting inequality should be placed in the context of an American economy with one of the highest employment participation rates in the world. The United States is the pre-eminent world economic power. Its technological leadership in many frontier sectors, ranging from ICT to biotechnology, is years ahead of its competitors. The strength and depth of its universities are unparalleled. American researchers rank top in terms of papers published and the rate at which those papers are cited by others.[16] American productivity growth is beginning to accelerate again, albeit from a low base. In many respects this is a success story against which the rest of the world benchmarks itself. Britain also, whose exports of knowledge-based services have trebled between 1995 and 2005[17] and whose universities are second only to those of the United States, has reason for confidence if it can develop its own Enlightenment soft infrastructure more aggressively.

The more accurate fear in today's world is the concern of less developed countries that they will be cast as low-knowledge sub-contractors to the knowledge-rich developed world in a new and more subtle form of colonialism. They are at the wrong end of a series of power relationships – ranging from the intellectual property rights regime to having to borrow in hard currency (thus accepting exchange rate risk) – that are loaded against them. For middle-income, less developed countries like Mexico or Thailand the problem is particularly acute. They have neither the low-wage advantage of China nor a sufficiently sophisticated infrastructure to develop a Western-style knowledge economy, and so, caught between a rock and a hard place, their relative per capita incomes have been stagnating.[18] The concern within China about the label 'made in China' rather than 'made by China' – China's reliance on foreign producers to deliver Chinese exports and their own inability to build great Chinese global brands – shows how difficult even China finds breaking through the way globalisation currently operates, low wages or not. Yet despite all the fears an open global system is of proven universal benefit, especially if it was managed more equitably. The West has to be brave enough to believe in it, demon-strate the advantages, live by universal rules and practise what it preaches. What is made can be unmade. If nobody defends globali-sation it will cease to be. The costs for everyone would be devastating.

And then there is China

At first sight it is true that China's explosive growth seems not just challenging, but terrifying; China, apparently, is set to sweep all before it. In the two years between the commissioning of this book in 2004 and the completion of the first edition in July 2006 China's GDP has grown by one-third. Since 2000 China's fixed investment has tripled from $400 billion to $1.3 trillion in 2006. Over the same period its exports have more than quintupled to nearly $1 trillion in 2006. Recall that these head-spinning numbers have been made possible in the time-honoured way.[19] Investment, representing close to half of China's GDP, has been financed by lending by Chinese banks; this lending has increased consistently by some 20 per cent throughout 2006 and 2007. Exports continue to be manufactured largely by foreign companies. The Chinese trade surplus will have more than doubled from $102 billion to some $225 billion in 2007.[20] Foreign-exchange reserves surpassed $1 trillion in 2006 and will exceed $1.5 trillion in 2007. Recall again that the United States has already declared that it is not prepared to let China buy what it considers strategic assets, even though the Chinese will feel more pressure to buy American companies as China's trade surplus and foreign-exchange reserves increase – one of the explicit aims of the newly established $200 billion investment fund. The United States may simply refuse to accept mounting Chinese imports, and may decide to wage a trade war, either by unilaterally imposing tariffs or suspending the privileges China has won in terms of access to the American market through the World Trade Organization. In that case globalisation will be put in question by its leader-in-chief.

One has to marvel at the China boom; in the second quarter of 2007 growth touched 11.9 per cent – a ten-year record. Equally, one has to warn that growth cannot go on at this rate powered by a near-doubling of bank lending to state-owned enterprises every year; the more the Chinese economy grows around gross contradictions and distortions, the greater the potential problems when the situation unravels. In Chapter 1 I argued that the logic of large numbers alone must soon begin to operate. Who imagines that Chinese investment is going to triple again to $4 trillion a year by 2012, or that Chinese exports are going to rise to $5 trillion by 2020 or sooner? Neither Chinese enterprise nor Chinese banks are profitable enough to borrow or lend money on the scale required to achieve such investment levels; nor are the savings of rural China going to be sufficient to provide the financial wherewithal. Nor is it probable that Chinese exports will be three-and-half times higher than the exports from today's leading exporter, Germany, by 2012. Where are the ships that could move such volumes of goods, the ports through which they could be channelled or the markets that could comfortably absorb them? And how is the renminbi, which currently keeps Chinese exports so competitive, to be prevented from rising without acquiring ludicrous levels of foreign-exchange reserves and an associated dramatic and destabilising increase in China's money supply, already creating asset price bubbles in China's leading cities and a sharp rise in inflation?

Yet if China is to create the twenty-four million jobs a year necessary to stop unemployment from soaring, growth rates like those in the recent past have to be supposed with the current economic model continuing to work as it always has worked. My argument is that China is caught in a gigantic dilemma. It cannot continue with the current model, which is beset by mountainous contradictions and which sooner or later will return to earth, provoked either by a banking crisis or simply a crisis of over-investment and excess supply, or some combination of both. The consequent social reaction will provoke a political crisis, with the risk that the party will resort to nationalism, and perhaps a military adventure in Taiwan, to keep the genie of protest bottled up. But equally, to rebalance China's growth on the basis of more normal levels of investment and consumption, together with a fuller participation in the knowledge economy, requires the building of an institutional structure, a welfare system and property rights which China cannot possess and still remain consistent with one-party communist rule.

At present the party has reached the limits of reform without creating a genuinely pluralist capitalist economy and society, but hesitating whether it dare. For example, the reform of the capital and labour markets has reached a tipping point. All shares in

China's enterprises are now to be tradable on China's stock markets, but still the party wants to privilege shares held by the state to give them a special claim over an enterprise's fixed assets – thus creating a two-tier stock market. The next stage is to give all shareholders equivalent ownership rights, but that would imply that finally China's enterprises might be genuinely privatised with the party losing control. Equally, in the labour market trade unions have been given the right to sign collective wage contracts; the next stage is genuine collective bargaining and thus collective worker independence. In both areas, as in many others, the party can either follow the logic of reform or try to freeze it in order to retain political control. Whatever route it takes, China faces convulsions.

The party leadership surveys the scene, keenly aware of the dilemmas. China's Communist Party is not a monolith. The centre of gravity remains firmly Dengist, committed to the view that the only way to legitimise the party is for it to be the successful champion of economic development, and that implies pro-market, pro-globalisation opening to the world. But it is increasingly un-stable, beset by a strengthening conservative wing anxious to reaffirm communist verities, alleviate peasant poverty as a priority, intensify party control and stop the clock on selling even minority shares in state-owned enterprise to the private sector generally and to foreigners in particular. This faction is hostile to what it views as too large a concession to American liberalism, and is sus-picious of American intent. President Hu Jintao has tacked toward the conservatives, with the party increasingly concerned that the mounting social protests and its own corruption face it with a crisis of ideological and political legitimacy. This is a revolutionary party no longer practising revolution, and which has renounced class war; the impact on its ethics and morality is hard to overestimate. Without external sources of accountability to keep party cadres honest, the only weapon to tackle corruption is anti-corruption drives – themselves undermined by the corruption of those leading the initiatives. The party's instincts are to promote those who are effective in making the current system work within its own terms rather than those who have experimented with substantial reform.[21]

The fifth generation of leaders who will succeed President and General Secretary Hu Jintao and his team were chosen at the Seventeenth Communist Party Congress in the October of 2007. Although the entire proceedings were inevitably opaque, the final line-up appointees spoke volumes about the political balancing act that Hu is being forced to perform between continuity, conservatism and accelerating the reform programme. Intriguingly, the 52-year-old Shanghai Party Secretary Xi Jinping (son of the revolutionary Xi Zhongxun) emerged as the front runner to succeed him as President and party secretary, ranking sixth in the Politburo. Despite the assault on the Shanghai party with the sacking of his predecessor Cheng Liangyu for corruption a year earlier, the combination of Jiang Zemin's patronage and the ongoing strength of this tradi-tional stronghold of Dengist reform and representative of China's middle-class proved too hard for even Hu to resist. However, he managed to secure promotions for his own protégés, Liaoning Party Secretary Li Keqiang as number 7 in the Politburo, and Li Yuanchao on the twenty-five-strong Central Committee and as head of the critically important Organisation Department, which has a powerful say over all appointments. Both have backgrounds in the Communist Youth League and records of successful manage-ment of key Chinese provinces; and Li Keqiang in particular leans to the left with his emphasis on building a harmonious society and helping the interior western provinces, where poverty is rife.

It is a measure of the party's crisis that it feels that it is unable to make a more clear-cut commitment to developing institutional reform. In the provinces, and in particular at city and large township level, the party is seen – reminiscent of *Animal Farm* – as turning into the Confucian official class it purported to replace, with even more corruption and with even less opportunity for the redress of wrong. Inequality is conspicous and growing worse. The danger for the party elite in Beijing is that rather as decollectivisation of agriculture came as an unstoppable force from below between 1979 and 1983, there will be an unstoppable insistence by urban citizens that they should have the right to hold officials to account in elections modelled on what has been allowed in the villages. Some form of accountability is the only proven way of tackling corruption and limiting gigantic waste. Yet the shadow of Tiananmen hangs over the country. Everybody knows that if a popular movement for city democracy ever took off it would be very difficult to resist – not least because those who have power privately recognise the legitimacy and validity of the criticism. It was a general secretary of the Communist Party, Zhao Ziyang, who acknowledged this openly in 1989. Be sure there are others today who think the same thing. It was the fifth generation of communist leaders in the Soviet Union who came to the conclusion that the system was no longer sustainable; it is not inconceivable that after the Beijing Olympics in 2008 some of the incoming fifth generation of Chinese leaders, notwithstanding their apparent conservatism, could come to a similar conclusion.

Without political reform the party's only reliable response is thus pre-emption – the reason why media censorship has increased and why the Internet firewall has been erected and policed so intensively – coupled with limited institutional improvement, such as attempts to professionalise the judiciary, that are congruent with continued one-party rule. All the time it has to keep a close eye on a so-far quiescent middle class whose support is contingent on continuing economic success. One falter and the situation could quickly become explosive. The danger is that China's problems are so serious that the only way for the party to maintain control is an authoritarian crackdown at home and nationalist aggression abroad. The evidence of Chinese history, as Professor Roderick MacFarquhar of Harvard argues, is that it is shocks of this type – losing the war of 1894–5 to Japan that anticipated the collapse of the Imperial system or the Cultural Revolution that presaged Deng – that are the precursors to reform.[23] China's path to modernity and Enlightenment institutions is unlikely to be smooth.

The West needs to understand the depth of China's problems and the possibility, if not probability, of an economic and political convulsion as China seeks their resolution. What the West must avoid at all costs is a position where it forces the Chinese leaders' hand and China retreats towards economic isolation and freezing the reform process. The challenge to the global trading and financial system would be profound; not only would an important source of global demand be scaled back, a key source of financing the United States trade deficit would be removed. China's progress would be shaken to its core. The interest of the West is to help China avoid this fate and encourage a peaceful transition to a pluralist China within a legitimate system of accountability; a country that is comfortable with liberal globalisation and the international rule of law. To describe the goal of policy in this way is demanding enough; it will be more demanding still to execute it. The simple extrapolations of China's growth, predicting that it will eventually become a one-party economic colossus, lead to an alarmist climate in which it is easier to justify trade protection or, in the United States, potential military activism. Such responses are naïve. We have to play it long, encourage and help to co-manage the change that must come.

The economic ship of fools

The wider background is the growing risks within the international economic system. Both the United States and Britain are beneficiaries of globalisation. A trillion dollars of the United States' GDP – around 10 per cent – depends upon it; in the UK, a more open economy, the proportion is significantly higher.

This phenomenon could not have occurred without an underlying political consensus: states wanted it to happen. In turn, globalisation demanded their confidence that multilateral institutions and international laws would allow them to prosper and protect their interests even while they surrendered a measure of sovereignty to international markets and companies. On balance, they would benefit from the trade-off. Since the Second World War American foreign policy has cleverly constructed an international system of rules and processes that delivers this result; it is transparent and equal for all states that participate even while, to repeat, the United States is one of the principal beneficiaries. This system of lowered tariffs, security for foreign investment and growing freedom of movement of capital has propelled the world economy's growth, especially since 1990. Foreign direct investment as a share of world GDP has trebled since then; exports of goods and services have increased by half. As I have argued, it was Deng Xiaoping's genius to see that even China could benefit if it entered the system. It has.

But the system is under increasing strain. It depends on unsustainable, freakishly high Chinese savings to finance unsustainable, freakishly low American savings for the indefinite future. The emergence of a low-saving society is a deep-seated trend. Part of the explanation is that widespread property ownership gives American consumers collateral against which to spend and run down their savings. Another part is that rising affluence has undermined self-control and both the desire and incentive to defer gratification – an argument made with great persuasiveness by Oxford University's Avner Offer.[24] Individuals in societies where social norms are weakening feel less constrained in demanding, getting and satiating their wants as soon as they can. Fortunately for the world system, just as this phenomenon of low saving has become highly problematic in terms of macro-economic management, Asia in general and China in particular have emerged to bail the United States out of the consequences – with their own self-interest very much in mind. Some respected commentators argue that the United States is somehow the victim of high Asian savings and has been compelled to become spendthrift to make the international system work, but this argument is perverse.[25] It is obvious to all but the most purblind that Americans' savings would have fallen whether China was part of the international system or not.

Yet both low American saving and China's compensation for it cannot continue indefinitely. Just as the law of large numbers suggests the unsustainability of China's position, so it points to similar conclusions about the United States. The United States' current-account deficit in 2005 was $804 billion (6.4 per cent of GDP) up from $668 billion in 2004; in 2006 it rose to nearly 7 per cent of GDP. Already the United States has net international debts approaching $3 trillion. It has staved off the consequences so far in two ways. First, it receives three times more in income from its investments abroad than it pays out in interest on bonds and treasury bills. That is how the Asians, and especially the Chinese, lend to the United States.[26] However, the scale of its international debts is now eliminating this advantage. Second, China, Japan and other Asian countries want to peg their currencies to the dollar, both to accelerate their exports to the United States and, as importantly, to make their own exchange-rate relationships within Asia more predictable. By buying dollars indefinitely and building up their dollar reserves, in effect they are lending the United States the savings it needs. So far both sides are winners. China's exports to the American market drive China's economic growth; the United States gets cheap imports and the opportunity to live above its means.

But there is an iron law in economics: what is unsustainable is not sustained. I have already argued that China's exports cannot keep growing at their current rate, and that China cannot afford to acquire an extra $500 billion of foreign-exchange reserves every year. The United States is locked in similar impossibilities. The comforting story offered by many economists and conservative pundits is that America can continue to attract savings to finance its sky-high trade deficit because it is a high-productivity country and its many market flexibilities guarantee high rates of return on investments. This a Panglossian doctrine that ignores the logic of the numbers, a point forcibly made by Barry Eichengreen of the University of California.[27] If the United States continues growing and borrowing as it has been doing, eventually its foreign debts will reach 150 per cent of its GDP. Then necessarily foreigners, with the Chinese and Arab investors at the forefront, would own half the United States' capital stock. Given the reaction to Dubai Ports World, this trend would provoke a political storm long before such high proportions were reached. Even if the United States' growth rate doubled, its monumental trade deficit would eventually imply foreign ownership of one-third of its capital stock. This is not a politically feasible outcome.

Nor, Eichengreen argues, does American investment offer such high returns that foreigners would be likely to invest in the United States to such an extent. In any case they invest in American debt rather than productive assets or shares, an improbable destination for their investment if it is productivity that is seducing them into locating their cash in the United States. It is the Chinese and Japanese central banks that are the main providers of foreign saving to the United States, and they do so for the old-fashioned mercantilist reason that it promotes Chinese and Japanese exports. If United States investment was rising as a result of commandeering such a high proportion of world saving, there might be some justification for its stance. Instead the United States is importing savings to maintain its high level of consumer spending.

Here we encounter another set of economic numbers with an impossible logic. The debts of American households, already 125 per cent of annual disposable income, cannot continue to grow three times faster than American national output. In 2005 American household savings went negative as American consumers borrowed or spent in unprecedented volumes against the value of equity in their homes – a process that also cannot continue for ever. In an era of low inflation debts are not inflated away; they are a real and growing burden. The rise in oil prices reduces the growth of real incomes and forces the United States Federal Reserve to have a much more cautious policy on keeping money cheap. In short, the United States cannot carry on being the world's growth engine because there are evident limits to how much American consumers can borrow, and how much international debt the American economy will be allowed to incur. Economics delivers some tough news. There must be a change that is closer to a paradigm shift than a technical correction. The pattern and structure of Chinese and American growth must be rebalanced, as must the interrelationship between these last great powers. That is a given. The question is how this change is to be achieved.

In the mid-1980s, when the United States' current-account deficit was half its present level, American and international policy-makers were keenly aware of the risk that the scale of the emerging imbalances could create mayhem in the international markets. At the Plaza Hotel in New York City on 22 September 1985 Secretary of the Treasury James Baker sealed the results of three months of secret financial diplomacy by getting Britain, France, Germany and Japan to agree that an appreciation of their currencies would be 'desirable' and that action to bring this about would be 'helpful'.[28] Baker was working within the multilateral framework of the International Monetary Fund and what was then the Group of Five leading industrialised countries to get the dollar to fall – which it did spectacularly, on average by 54 per cent from its peak in February 1985 to the end of 1987. In the seven years preceding the Plaza Accord, American exports had shrunk every year by 0.7 per cent; in the eleven years that followed they grew at an average rate of 9.3 per cent, one-third faster than the rate between 1950 and 1971, and manufacturing exports doubled from 21 per cent to 42 per cent of manufacturing value-added.[29] The United States still ran a current-account deficit during the 1990s, but its position was sustainable. For Japan, however, the appreciation of the yen ended the way the country had grown since the early 1950s and precipitated fifteen years of restructuring, economic stagnation and retrenchment that have only recently shown signs of ending. The consequence was a domestic disaster. Stephen Jen of Morgan Stanley concludes that the Plaza Accord of 1985 was one of the greatest policy mistakes Japan has ever made.[30] However, the larger point is that the international system held.

Twenty years later there is no similar shared urgency or agreement about the action needed to keep the international economic system together. Nor is the United States showing any readiness to reinforce, extend or even use the multilateral framework to organise a shared way of distributing the burden of painful adjustment. Instead there is a disturbing, careless willingness to test to destruction the capacity of the international system to absorb imbalances. The excuse is that it will be foreigners who will get hurt by any fallout; that real Americans do not do deals with lesser countries; and that the domestic political consequences of any belt-tightening in terms of increasing taxes or saving energy – the obvious American share of any adjustment – are impossible to contemplate. Whether the issue is trade, carbon-dioxide emissions or energy use the position of the United States government is now overt self-interest to the point of self-hurt; its aim is to squeeze the lemon as hard as it can for its own immediate advantage. The post-war concern to create a range of global agreements from which the United States was the single largest beneficiary but which nevertheless had legitimacy has vanished in a cloud of neo-conservative smoke. This is a dereliction of duty by the United States government, which has an obligation both to its citizens and to these agreements. Its dereliction threatens, sooner or later, to blow up in the face of the United States and the wider world.

The world in turn has learned from the Americans' lesson in how to pursue self-interest. Consider the bargain that is now needed over trade. Since the early 1960s average tariffs on imports into industrialised countries have fallen by half to under 5 per cent; tariffs on developing countries' imports have fallen by two-thirds to just over 10 per cent and China's tariffs have fallen from over 40 per cent in 1992 to just over 5 per cent today. It is a remarkable achievement, and the world now needs the same to happen in agriculture and services to achieve the same build-up of trade, and thus output growth, in these key areas of the economy. Yet the United States, matched by the European Union, is resisting in a game of chicken; nobody wants to be the country that blinked first and began to make concessions without knowing for certain what concessions would be received in return. China, India, Japan, Brazil and Russia follow suit, and so the trade talks have been suspended in a destructive stand-off. For all of them, especially the middle-income, less developed countries, there is also the fear that if they open to China as it is currently organised they could be overwhelmed. The United States is too fragile and China too challenging for a meaningful deal to be done. In the absence of a trade deal the United States continues to pile on ever more anti-dumping suits, ever higher fines and ever more aggressive threats of retaliatory trade action. The great post-war achievement of a rules-bound international trading system on which globalisation depends is in peril – at the same time as the scale of international imbalances is reaching new and untested levels.

Not only is this short-sighted in terms of the self-interest of Asia, Europe and North America but it has consequences for the rest of the world that are even more serious. The Greater Middle East, from Morocco to the Central Asian Republics, has been deglobalised over the past twenty-five years. Between 1979 and 2000 its share of global trade and investment fell by three-quarters, while its population nearly doubled to 600 million. Across the Arab world average per capita incomes fell from $2300 to $1600 between 1980 and 2000 – this is the background to the anger directed against the West.[31] There is a similar, if not quite so dramatic, picture in Latin America – economic stagnation amid the emergence of a leftist authoritarian populism. Four elected presidents have been forced from office since 2000, and Bolivia's nationalisation of its natural gas industry is a signal of where Latin America's politics are heading. If the world trading system breaks down, then the direction of Latin American politics and trajectory of Islamic fundamentalist terrorism are all too obvious.[32]

Alarm bells should be ringing in Washington. The United States is at the centre of a worldwide system of delicate economic interdependencies that could easily topple into economic dislocation. Three countries – China, Canada and Mexico – supply the United States with two-fifths of its imports; another four – Germany, South Korea, Britain and Japan – account for the next one-fifth of imports. All seven are connected through their supply chains to other countries. Nearly 40 per cent of American consumer demand is met by foreign producers; if for any reason that demand stagnates or falls the international, let along the domestic, consequences will be severe. The biggest risk is a precipitate sell-off of the dollar, forcing interest rates to rise with a potentially awesome downward impact on inflated American property prices and bankruptcy for many overextended borrowers. Hedge funds could be unable to settle their debts. Jochen Sanio, president of the Federal Financial Supervisory Authority, has said that the issue is not whether hedge funds, as currently regulated, will cause a disaster; 'the only question is when'.[33] The 'when' is most likely to occur during the financial after-effects of an unexpected sell-off of the dollar, when unregulated and overextended hedge funds finding they are unable to settle their debts will precipitate a first-order financial crisis. Indeed in the September of 2007 the threat had emerged from the so-called 'sub-prime' United States mortgage market, whose hundreds of billions of dollars of mortgages lent to borrowers with no income, employment or assets had been inserted into the global financial system. As American house prices fell it became clear that the mortgages were valueless and the banks and hedge funds that held them might be suffering such substantial losses their solvency could be threatened. Lending within the financial system became seriously impaired; central banks responded with massive injections of liquidity. The interdependencies of the financial system and simultaneous lack of international governance was ruthlessly exposed.

Which brings us back to China. As I have argued, it must be

carefully managed, rather than forced into a retreat from global markets or into a nationalist response. Of course consistent pressure for change needs to be maintained, and an example set of how to behave. But not to the point of hurting ourselves more than them. The United States could find it is simultaneously confronting a war over Taiwan, a financial crisis and economic recession. Pre-emptive unilateralism on terror and a parallel policy with regard to the international economic system will have landed the country and the world in a debacle that was all too foreseeable. But nothing was done in better times to avert the risk.

To conclude

The West needs to stand by its values and institutions at home, and reproduce them internationally to give the rest of the world a genuine opportunity to catch up and to recast its domestic organisation around Enlightenment principles – inevitably a slow task. Yet the international institutions are hardly exemplars of Enlightenment values. The International Monetary Fund, World Bank and World Trade Organization, for example, all have grievous deficiencies in their accountability, representation and mandate. They may be better than nothing; they may be subjected to unrealistic criticism; and at least they have kept the show running so far. But even their defenders have to acknowledge that they too readily resemble a rich men's club and fall far below the standards we would expect of domestic institutions.[34] For example, the behind-the-scenes 'green room' process in the World Trade Organization in which the European Union and the United States essentially broker a common position behind closed doors is an affront to the rest of the world – as is the notion that the head of the International Monetary Fund should always be a European and the head of the World Bank an American, irrespective of merit.

Financial decision-making should obviously include China, India, Brazil and representatives from Africa and the Middle East alongside the traditional group of seven industrialised countries and Russia. The International Monetary Fund should plainly be more than a debt collector for Western banks and enforcer of economic stringency. Similarly, the World Bank should have the financial resources to be a serious development institution. Yet the deficiencies have been allowed to continue for decades.

The charitable view is that these are design flaws that can be readily addressed with sufficient political will; a tougher appraisal is that they reflect no more than the power struggles and compromises that beset the creation of the institutions and have persisted ever since. There should be little surprise at the widespread perception that these institutions are no more than vehicles for Western power – indeed American power – with inherent institutional biases, because essentially the perception is correct. The broad political, economic and social agenda for such reform may be understood and even favoured by some within the International Monetary Fund and World Bank, but it conflicts with their long-standing institutional bias to favour efficiency over equity, to favour transactional market incentives rather than justification and accountability mechanisms and to suspect social spending rather than understand its value.

The reform agenda is not hard to outline. There should be wider membership of the key governing councils of every international institution, just as the UN Security Council should now include Japan, Germany, India and Brazil. International institutions should be able to finance themselves from the taxation of global 'bads', such as carbon-dioxide emissions. There should be higher standards of transparency and accountability. There should be a bias towards what, for want of a better term, I have called the Enlightenment agenda. Necessarily it will have a proper scepticism about legitimising doctrines of pre-emptive action against perceived threats, terrorist or otherwise; or at least insist that any such action should be regularly rejustified. There should be a broadening of the treaty and institutional network to regulate climate change, the arms race and the harbouring of terrorists, and to ensure better auditing and less tax evasion. There needs to be a drive for higher literacy, higher numeracy and better health standards.

If the need for such institutions is pressing in terms of global security and economic soundness, then no less urgent is the environmental need. During 2003 the concentration of carbon dioxide in the atmosphere hit the highest levels for 420,000 years.[35] Winter temperatures in some of the world's coldest places – western Canada, eastern Russia and Alaska – have risen by three to four degrees centigrade over the past fifty years.[36] Few scientists dispute the link between burning fossil fuels, increased carbon-dioxide emissions and the rise in temperatures. Yet the International Energy Agency projects that over the next twenty-five years coal use will rise by 51 per cent, oil by 57 per cent and natural gas by 89 per cent. Together those increases will bring a 62 per cent rise in carbon-dioxide emissions unless fuel efficiency improves remarkably.[37]

The impact on the global ecosystem is already evident and will escalate. The great ice sheets and glaciers melt; sea levels rise, ocean currents change their velocity and temperature and the weather and distribution of rainfall change. The Greenland ice sheet would not survive a three-degree-centigrade rise in world temperatures, now within the range of projections for 2100. If the Greenland ice sheet was lost, world sea levels would rise seven metres (twenty-three feet) with incalculable consequences.[38] China and India are already, with current weather patterns, chronically short of water; so is sub-Saharan Africa. In 2005 the Millennium Ecosystem Assessment, a four-year project involving 1300 researchers and scientists from ninety-five countries, announced that 60 per cent of the world's ecosystem services have been degraded and that species extinction is anything up to one thousand times the normal background rate. According to Jared Diamond, environmental despoliation has killed civilisations as disparate as the Khmer of Angkor Wat, the Norse Greenlanders and the Easter Islanders.[39] Ecosystems are part of what makes the earth habitable. The concern to preserve them is not the kooky preoccupation of the green brigade; it is the concern of every human being alive. Unless we take care, we will follow other species to extinction.

We urgently need a concerted international endeavour to redouble the efforts to lower carbon-dioxide emissions through taxation, regulation and greater efficiency. We also need to replace the Kyoto Treaty commitment to reduce carbon-dioxide emissions by 2012 to 95 per cent of 1990 levels with something much tougher and more encompassing. The European Union has signed and ratified the treaty; the United States, which produces a quarter of the world's carbon, has not because it wants less developed countries to share the pain, and Bush believes that lowering carbon-dioxide emissions might damage the American economy. The United States wants to free-ride off the rest of the world's commitment to rise to the environmental challenge and do nothing itself. It is the ultimate decadence. Meanwhile China's emissions of greenhouse gases are rising with explosive rapidity; it too is not a signatory of Kyoto.

To progress we need a belief in international action legitimised by a multilateral commitment to the rule of law and a self-confident rather than defensive, anxious West; precisely what we do not have. Within the European Union twenty years of high unemployment in Italy, Germany and France has undermined confidence in liberal capitalism and in the case for European integration around the commitment to enlarge four great freedoms of movement – of goods, people, money and services. There is a dangerous introspection, a desire to protect and a turning away from even the limited process of European governance that exists today. The French and Dutch 'No' votes in their referenda on the proposed so-called European Constitution (it was no such thing, but in fact another intergovernmental treaty) were but further evidence of the same negative malaise. It is all the more tragic in that the European Union is the most successful experiment with multilateral governance the world has ever seen, and its social model – as I have argued above – is not only attractive but eminently viable. In particular the Nordic countries, with their high and growing productivity, high employment, innovativeness and high social spending, show what Europe can become, and contradict the conventional criticism. Germany's recent economic success is a further sign that the European model can combine good social outcomes with economic dynamism. German confidence has returned: under Chancellor Merkel there is a renewed determination to kick-start the European project around environmental, energy and common foreign policy concerns.

In the Western effort to sell globalisation and manage China, the European Union has a crucial role: it offers a model of capitalism that is more attractive than the American and more sympathetic to Chinese concerns about equity and social solidarity. The European Union should be confident; it needs to reverse the doubt and fearfulness that has plagued it for most of the 2000s. Meanwhile in the United States the same mood that brought pre-emptive unilateralism and extra-legal detention without trial is informing the attitude towards multilateral institutions and international initiative. Global governance can go hang.

Britain seen through an Enlightenment prism

In a world in which Enlightenment values are never more important, Britain sounds a hesitant note. The country was lucky that circumstance, geography, Protestant passion and mercantile inventiveness allowed it to be the first European nation to develop the Enlightenment institutional infrastructure that would trigger industrial capitalism. But it was unlucky in that it did not go through the same intellectual, political and constitutional battles that characterised the embracing and entrenching of Enlightenment principles in other Western societies. As a result, the cultural and intellectual understanding of why it achieved what it did is singularly shallow. Today, for example, there is only a reluctant commitment to invest in developing everyone's individual capabilities in education and training, and a thin comprehension of why justification and accountability are so important in sustaining the integrity of both private and public organisations. Even the idea of a public realm does not go deep.

While the United States wrote the Enlightenment into its heart via the popular American Constitution, Britain never had the same opportunity. Its revolution against monarchy in the seventeenth century predated the Enlightenment, so that the constitutional settlement that followed – in any case organised from on high by an aristocratic elite – could not incorporate Enlightenment values because they were undeveloped. Instead Britain bolted Enlightenment concepts of the public realm, democratic accountability, freedom of the press, independent trade unions and even the rule of law on to its unwritten constitution with its still-feudal, monarchical core. As a result Britain's rulers, even if elected, retain the important discretionary executive and centralised powers of the crown. From Gladstone to Attlee, and now to Blair, well-intentioned reformism has always transmuted into forms of statism.

Thus Britain's particular character. Its glory is its parliament, the national debating chamber, and its great tradition that every man and woman is equal before the law, enshrined since Magna Carta. There is a commitment to liberty and an understanding that governments must argue their case, deliver it or give way to a government-in-waiting that is very powerful, and ultimately the guarantor of the country's democratic vitality. The weakness in its democratic system is that too many of the elements of a plural society and the values that underpin it are neither constitutional entitlements nor have sufficiently firm cultural roots to do their job well. Indeed the sheer power concentrated in the remnants of feudalism – crown-in-parliament – mean that the idea of the public interest is always stilted. Public purpose is not the consequence of free deliberation by citizens, but rather of their members of parliament who legislate over them. The focus is the state, not the public realm. This means that, while the government is accountable for its actions, it becomes the principal public actor – and the role of the intermediate network of public institutions, either in London or in the rest of the country, is downgraded and devalued.

The classic example is the weakness of local, city and regional government, which are creatures of Whitehall and Westminster. The Labour government's attempt to give executive power to towns and cities in the form of a mayor has not only been difficult to achieve constitutionally, with power held jealously at the centre, it has been little supported by citizens who see this culturally as adding 'more bureaucracy'. The success of the London mayor has been against the grain, and in any case his powers could be withdrawn by a subsequent national government exercising its feudally extensive power in the sovereign parliament. Power in cities, towns and regions cannot be constitutionally entrenched in the British system; rather, power can be delegated to them that can be taken away – not dissimilar to their status in China under the central control of the Communist Party.

There *are* examples of successful public institutions, such as the NHS and BBC, for which there is a strong cultural underpinning. Both free health care at the point of use and a national broadcaster that is constitutionally obliged to be fair have earned loyalty through their success, but it has been their practice rather than the principles on which they are founded that has saved them. The BBC is permanently under siege from commercial critics and the ideology that markets always do better; one falter and it could suffer death by neglect. The reason why successive governments have been unable consistently to invest in Britain's educational or transport infrastructure – Britain's road and rail network is nearly half the size per head of population as that in France or Germany – is that public investment is not characterised as a public action from which every citizen might benefit, but as the action of a state which is seen as acting against citizens as much as for them.

The institutions of pluralism are either taken for granted, with little cultural or intellectual support, or their role in keeping economy and society honest is traduced and misunderstood. Britain's Enlightenment tradition beats feebly, and sometimes not at all. For example, a free media is a cornerstone of a free society. Yet Britain's media has allowed itself to descend into editorialising, spinning, trivialising, misrepresenting and sensationalising, while simultaneously defending itself as responding to what its consumers want and resisting any attempt to hold it to account as an unwarranted state intrusion into its private affairs. And its complaint is partly true. In a society with a weak Enlightenment tradition too much criticism of the media is that it has become an intrusive, unjustifiable nuisance (an essential part of its role) rather than that it does not do its job of holding truth to power and empowering the citizenry. But then there is no public framework or tradition in which either the media properly understands its role or in which it can be legitimately criticised, or, crucially, that legitimately permits reform along the pluralist principles I suggested in Chapter 8 while respecting media independence. The media has become part of the problem of weak accountability and poor understanding of the public interest rather than the solution.

Similarly, neither business nor trade unions themselves see free trade unions in depoliticised terms; as crucial functional counterbalances to, and partners with, business in safeguarding worker interests in a pluralist economy and society, and which both enable and compel companies better to discharge their duty of care for their workforces. Business relapses into seeing unions as troublesome obstructions to productivity, weakening the management prerogative to manage and disrupting the smooth working of the economy. At the same time too many trade union leaders warrant the distrust by wanting to sell themselves as shock troops of socialism or, more moderately, as the workplace arm of the Labour Party. In this stand-off workers themselves come to be suspicious of the very institution that exists to protect and advance their interests; in the private sector only one in eight workers are trade union members, and in Britain's fast-growing service sector membership is even lower. Frozen into stasis over its purpose, trade union membership continues to atrophy.

This lack of embrace of Enlightenment values penetrates the heart of Britain's innovation, investment and education system, and is the chief explanation why Britain remains trapped – notwith-standing the consistently good years of economic growth since the pound's expulsion from the European Exchange Rate Mechanism in 1992 – in a halfway house between a fully fledged knowledge economy and a low-skill, low value-added, low-innovation economy. According to the *Business Week*/Interbrand survey of top global brands in 2006 – the most comprehensive survey of its kind – Britain has only five global brands in the top hundred; the UK's highest ranking brand is a bank, HSBC, at 28th, with the next an oil company, BP, at 76th. The European Union's Community Innovation Survey, the best source for monitoring trends in the European Union, puts the share of firms engaged in innovative activity at 43 per cent, 2 per cent below the EU-15 average. Germany, for example, reports 65 per cent. Productivity still trails the United States and the European Union average, and the country has an escalating trade deficit.

The weakness roots back to two key deformations: the education and training system and corporate indifference to investment and innovation. The education and training system does not do its Enlightenment job of ensuring everyone has a chance; despite the recent improvements in the number of students achieving GCSEs, just under half the cohort do not get the basic minimum of five GCSEs including C grades in mathematics and English, while a third of adults lack any educational qualification. Vocational training remains the system's undernourished Cinderella. In any case the objective of education and skills training is too frequently under-stood as the supply of business with the skilled workers it needs, rather than to invest democratically in enlarging individual capabilities for all. It is no surprise that the growing investment in university provision since the 1960s has benefited children of the better off; the proportion of children from richer families winning a university degree has more than doubled, while less than 10 per cent of children from poor families graduate.[40] Education in Britain, with the disproportionate access of the privately educated to the top universities, which in turn are the passport to the upper echelons of economy and society, remains focused on the solidification of class differences rather than on enfranchisement for all.

British business, like its American counterpart but without the compensation of a vast domestic market, is locked into a vicious circle of meeting the extravagant financial demands of footloose institutional shareholders or confronting takeover. Britain has not constructed a system of corporate ownership, governance or accountability that permits companies to develop their vocation as business builders. There is a long roll call of companies whose decline in fortunes has been because of – all or in part – an over-preoccupation with immediate profits or concern to avoid takeover; it could be ITV1, sacrificing programme budgets in order to prop the share price and witnessing its audiences dwindle, or BAA (British Airports Authority), vainly under-investing in airport facilities unsuccessfully to avoid the threat of takeover, and now owned by the Spanish company who itself borrowed £10 billion to buy it and whose own inadequacies have become a national scandal. The companies that do succeed in maintaining the pace of R & D are shielded from the financial markets' demands by government procurement; it is the NHS and the Ministry of Defence to which Britain owes its high-investment drug and defence industries. But in the main British firms struggle to meet the criteria for success in the knowledge economy set out by Zuboff and Maxmin earlier in this chapter; there is an insufficiently broad base of soft and hard skills from which to recruit, and the only way to meet the financial institutions' demands is to focus on the low-innovation end of the market.[41]

What has masked these weaknesses and permitted the growth of a large service sector is a decade-long consumer boom largely based on borrowing against the collateral of rising house prices. In the mid-1990s first-time buyers paid, on average, 2.9 times their income to buy their first house; by 2005 the ratio had risen to 4.5 – a measure of the real and ultimately unsustainable increase in house prices. Consumer debt, largely mortgages, stood at only 37 per cent of household income in 1975; by 2006 it had risen nearly fourfold to 150 per cent of household income – a cool £1.2 trillion. What can be predicted with certainty is that it cannot and will not again rise by four times over the next thirty years. Like China and the United States, the logic of large numbers will start to apply in Britain. Growth in living standards will require progressively ever more attention to the fundamentals, and redress of the Enlightenment deficiencies in the British system.

However Enlightenment convictions on which to build are insecure. The British socialist tradition has always been suspicious of pluralism, even as it has championed equality, and one-nation Toryism – the Enlightenment home inside British conservatism – has been buried beneath the free-market simplicities of Thatcherism. Nor are British citizens notably effective advocates of better education, better training and more equality of opportunity; they collude in the forces of market capitalism and business delivering an unequal market society because the Enlightenment drumbeat that calls for better is so weak.

Since its election in 1997 Britain's Labour government has uncertainly tried to build a more pluralist economy and society. Indeed, New Labour can be conceived as trying to capture the Enlightenment tradition for the left. It has had more success than either its critics or sometimes even its own supporters accept. By establishing independence for both the Bank of England and the Competition Commission, for example, it has created significant institutional bulwarks of pluralism. It has devolved power to Scotland, Wales and London. The investment in the health system has been substantial:

by 2008 spending in real terms will have doubled. There has been a sustained attempt at upgrading both the standards of vocational training and educational attainment for the mass of children. If inequality has not fallen very much, at least it has not risen.

But it has been patchy. Many of the strictures I directed at the United States in Chapter 11 apply in Britain, a society where the Enlightenment tradition is weaker. The trivialisation and lack of balance in the media, the inability to create progressive countervailing forces in the workplace and decline of trade unionism and the growing unfairness of the education system are all part of the British story as well. So is the growing fragility of the public realm. New Labour's weakness is that it has not even successfully explained to its own party, let alone the wider public, what it is doing and why – and how its ideas might address these issues. Blair may have tried to deliver the public interest through plural institutions, some of which are private, some private-public partnerships and some newly autonomous bodies – like foundation hospitals or schools – within the public sector, but he does not express it in those terms. The proper attempt to escape from the old typology that action is done either by the state or the market, and the advantages such an escape from the old categories opens up, are wilfully misunderstood and poorly explained. Critics on the left and right alike interpret this as privatisation and liberalisation.

What is happening is, in truth, more subtle – but Blair failed to explain himself. There is a tradition of pluralist progressive thinking in Britain from which he might have drawn – G. D. H. Cole, H. J. Laski and Richard Tawney – but he did not. Instead he has struggled to find a tradition or language that combines pluralism with public purpose to which the public, the media or his own party can relate, and in its absence has fallen back on using the state in a highly personalised way to achieve his ends, in the hope that practical success will validate his approach. But success would never be so clear-cut. Rather, he has been increasingly portrayed as an unprincipled manipulator of the media and state structures, careless of proper mechanisms of accountability. Unable and unwilling to talk the principled language of public purpose or Enlightenment pluralism, he has preferred to wrap himself up in the rhetoric of being non-ideological and practical.

The weakness has been especially obvious over the approach to terrorism and all questions involving civil liberty. Enlightenment instincts have simply been neglected and ignored. The same vacuum extends abroad. It was Blair's tragedy that his foreign policy betrayed his commitment to reclaiming Enlightenment principles for the left at home, and he was seduced by the trappings of the British state to weaken his embrace of pluralism. His political travails at the end of his premiership were tribute to the extent of his failure. But, in fairness, it was a philosophic insecurity that reflects the spirit of the times.

The last word

There is a dismaying lack of consensus over Enlightenment values – indeed whether to believe in the Enlightenment at all – throughout the West that lies beneath the surface of today's malaise. It propels the uncertainty and is the root cause of the political immobility. Rationalism and justification are under assault because they do not answer the question why. There is confusion over purpose and values. In China it reflects itself in its ideological crisis. If class war is over – from a party that now includes capitalists in its ranks – what are the values that justify one-party rule? Communism aimed to be more than a political creed; it sought, and for a period succeeded, to offer an answer to the universal question of how to live a life well. It does no longer. Simply, it is a moral and ideological empty vessel.

Political leaders everywhere need to feel they speak for a majority underpinned by a consensus over values. As the fundamentalisms of flag, tribe, nation and religion become ever more primitive and visceral as alternative answers, Western politicians become more nervous about continuing to argue for a politics based on rational law-making, multilateral institution building and collaboration. The attacks on stem cell research and Darwinian theories of natural selection in the United States are important not only because they are attacks on the willingness to accept proof as evidence of truth, the very core of the Enlightenment. They are important because they dramatise the gulf that has opened between the world of the secular and rational and the world of the believer. The bitter divisions within the United States between the crusading Christian fundamentalists and civil society are but one expression of this phenomenon; another is the rise of militant Islamic fundamentalism; another is the rise of nationalism within Europe and resistance to further European integration; another is the conservative faction in China wanting to stop the clock on the reform programme and return to old communist and nationalist verities. Reason is at loggerheads with faith and the ties of blood. In Britain the emergence of English nationalism alongside virulent euro-scepticism is part of the same story.

To urge the overcoming of these impulses is almost purposeless without recognising the deeper roots of what is happening today. The great German philosopher Jürgen Habermas, in his recent magisterial exploration of the future of human nature, insists that the emerging battle between faith, instinct and belief on the one hand and secularism, rationality and empiricism on the other is useless and self-destructive. The essence of human nature is to need both. It is impossible, he says, to try to box human nature into scientific rationalism, the logic of market transactions and justice based on no more than rational human principles. It is not that this universe is wrong or should be qualified in any way; it is that human nature also needs the richness of the morality and understanding of how knowledge is used that can be derived from religion. Equality, for example, can be a more powerful notion if it is understood that an equality before our maker is as profoundly based and more vividly understood than equality on any other basis. Similarly, morality can be better comprehended if we can find a language that differentiates between what is wrong and what is evil.[42]

Even the justification process, which I have argued is one of the pillars of the Enlightenment commitment to the rule of reason, is not just a rational process of claim and counter claim; it is animated, Habermas argues, by a sense of what ought or should take place. You do not necessarily have to be a believer or have faith to recognise the debt Western moral sensibilities owe religion (or Chinese morality owes to Confucianism).

Only when both parties to the debate within Western societies can respect each other's traditions and understand their contribution to the whole will we construct a basis for mutual respect – and then show the rest of the world the complexity of our own struggles to come to terms with the two impulses. To understand and present the West to others in these terms will be more persuasive, he argues, than simply praising the rule of the market while threatening overwhelming military force against those who dare challenge us. Our roots, as well as the times, demand that we do better than this.

Habermas' thesis is closely related to the core of this book. 'Hard' economics, politics and social realities need to be complemented, corrected and enriched by countervailing 'soft' forces. When the West creates and manages this interaction well it is the heart of our genius; too frequently we do not grasp its nature and today we are neglecting it at our peril. Suddenly the stakes of this failure have become higher. China, riven with contradictions and full of potential menace, is coming to terms with the bankruptcy of communism and the logical impossibility of continuing to grow as it has. It should borrow from, rather than be opposed to, the West. We have to enable this process rather than freeze it. Equally, the world is racked by crazy economic imbalances and imprudently regulated financial institutions. The doctrine that these should be left untouched because the primacy of the private and the market should always be respected has to be challenged; imbalances as severe as those today need be managed and high-risk financial institutions need to be regulated. The world's ecosystems are in peril; an international reaction is vital. Currently overshadowing everything is the fear that as Islamic terrorism cannot be beaten we should retreat into our national strongholds. Even there we will not be safe.

For the world is ever more interdependent. Both the benefits of cooperation and costs of non-cooperation have never been greater. There is an accident waiting to happen unless we find an accommodation over values – the precondition for cooperative action. The Writing is on the Wall.

ACKNOWLEDGEMENTS

I owe two people and one organisation above any others thanks for this book. The first person is Ed Victor, my agent, who suggested the concept after reading my first-ever column on China after my week-long lecture tour in Beijing and Shanghai in the autumn of 2003, and who persisted in arguing that I could take on this vast subject despite my misgivings. Nine months later he overcame my doubts and this book is the result. Ed has a deserved reputation for being one of the best in the business, and his conviction and gentle insistence have led me into territory that I have found endlessly interesting and rewarding. Whatever else, I know a great deal more about China – and the United States – than I did eighteen months ago!

The second person is Philippe Schneider, who joined me as a Mandarin-speaking researcher in December 2004 and who worked with me right to the last minute of the very last missed deadline. It was one of the best hires of my life. We became firm companions in an intellectual and political odyssey: as we joked, an 'Enlightenment' project in its own right. The depth and range of Philippe's reading, the quality of his background papers and the catholicism of his intellectual interests sometimes took my breath away, and were never less than excellent. He ensured, as a great researcher should and must, that I was fully aware of the literature on every subject I wrote about and the evidence is in the exhaustive list of references. He was indefatigable and a relentless chaser of facts and theories alike. He was also firmly committed to my ambition for the book, and his enthusiasm carried me along when sometimes it just seemed an ambition too far. This book and I owe him an enormous debt of gratitude.

And the organisation is the British Council. China regional director Michael O'Sullivan, Gary Hallsworth in Beijing, Jeff Streeter in Shanghai, Caroline Garden in Hong Kong and Christine Skinner in Guangzhou together arranged two programmes of visits and briefings that would have been impossible had I attempted them by myself. Nor should I forget Peng Yanni, the Beijing project manager who so carefully shepherded Philippe and me through our schedule. I compressed an enormous amount into my two journeys, and I was hugely impressed with the affection and regard with which the Council is held in China – and the depth and range of its contacts. And thanks to Michael for his suggestion to visit the Qing tombs – much further from Beijing than the Ming tombs, but more than worth the journey. Thanks also to my own researchers in Beijing, Liang Yan (Edera) and Li Jialin. Edera's vast range of potential interviewees was essential, and Li Jialin's background papers were detailed and well researched.

In no particular order I would like to thank Jeremy Sargent, Wang Ershan, Zhu Hui, Lui Siewying, Professor Lin Jiang, Li Yongning, Yang Zaigao, Yin Ningyu, Lu Tong, Neil Blakeman, Patrick Powers, Li Zhaoxi, Yang Dongning, Wang Jiangping, Hu Shuli, Professor Ding Ding, Stephen Green, Cong Yan, Professor Lin Shangli, Kong Quiyun, Professor Lu Feng, Fu Jun, Li Bozhong, Professor Hu Angang, David Concar, Robin Porter, Huang Ping, Sir Christopher Hum, Professor Shi Yinhong, Mao Yushi, Joseph Cheng, Dr Eden Woo, Stephen Bradley, Michael Elliott, Nic Dean and many others for the time they gave up to see me in China. The usual disclaimers about my being solely responsible for the opinions expressed here apply with even more force.

I also made a research trip to the United States in the January of 2006. I would like to thank Tony Saich, Dwight Perkins, Liz

Perry, Richard Cooper, Dani Rodrik, Richard Lester, Iain Johnston, Yasheng Huang, Kevin Lanzit, Commissioner Bill Reinsch and Larry Wortzel, Minxin Pei, Anatol Lieven, Rob Atkinson, Frank Jannuzi, Shahid Yusuf, Kaoru Nabeshima, Fred Bergsten, James Lilley, William Galston, Stephen Roach, Adam Segal and Walter Russell Mead for the time they freely gave up. In London, Geoff Mulgan, Peter Nolan, Howard Davies and Susan Lawrence all made helpful suggestions about people I should approach in China while David Held, Philip Dodd, Chris Patten and Jonathan Fenby have also contributed to the cause. Jonathan's detailed comments on the first three chapters, delivered days before the very last deadline, were especially helpful. In addition, Howard Davies offered insightful comments on an early draft. Thanks to them all, and once again the same disclaimer.

Then thanks to my editors at Little, Brown in London and Free Press (Simon & Schuster) in New York. Richard Beswick has been supportive and engaged throughout, resisting various suggestions for titles until I hit on this one, and feeding back comment on the chapters as I sent them. Similarly Fred Hills in New York, who was one of the great figures in American publishing; he gave me a good sense of how Americans will react to the thesis. After he retired in Easter 2006 his successor Emily Loose took up the challenge with dedication and commitment. In London Philippa Harrison read every chapter thoroughly and made typically shrewd, detailed and insightful remarks. Andrew Beven, proof-readers at Simon & Schuster and Little, Brown and finally my daughter Alice all contributed to the copy-editing process. My thanks to them all, and especially Alice, who came to my rescue in the final exhausting week.

I also benefited from a two-month sabbatical from the *Observer* and three months' semi-sabbatical from the Work Foundation; thanks to *Observer* editor Roger Alton and Work Foundation chairman Peter Ellwood respectively for their support. My colleagues at the Work Foundation have been encouraging when I flagged, and did not raise too many eyebrows as I became progressively more harassed towards the end. Sarah Holden operated beyond the call of duty in helping with the logistics of the America and China trips, and Steve Bevan's and Aine O'Keeffe's reaction – along with other Work Foundation colleagues at a mid-term seminar – kept my spirits up. And lastly, as every author knows, writing imposes a terrible strain on one's family. My two daughters followed the drama away from home, but Andrew (brainstorming for a title) and especially Jane had to experience it at first hand. She has now been through three of these exercises (*The State We're In* and *The World We're In* being Numbers One and Two). The love and support she offers – along with the occasional, but never accusatory, groan at another lost weekend or evening – is indispensable.

Will Hutton, 26 July 2006

NOTES

Chapter 1

1. Scott C. Bradford, Paul L. E. Grieco and Gary Clyde Hufbauer, 'The Payoff to America from Global Integration', in Bergsten (ed.), *The United States and the World Economy*, p. 105.
2. For the most bullish assessment, see 'Dreaming with the BRICs: The Path to 2050', Goldman Sachs Global Economics Paper 99, 2003. The deployment of China as rhetoric to subdue wage inflation is, at this stage, more important than its direct effect.
3. Angus Maddison in *The World Economy*, in table B-20, computes the rise in US GDP as a proportion of the world total from 8.9 per cent in 1870 to 19.1 per cent in 1913. China's GDP as a share of world output was 4.6 per cent in 1973, rising to 11.5 per cent in 1998. I compute a further rise to some 16 per cent in 2006.
4. See, for instance, *China 2020: Development Challenges in the New Century*, World Bank, 1997, Ravallion and Chen, 'China's (Uneven) Progress Against Poverty', the *OECD Economic Survey: China*, 2005 and various years of *Zhongguo tongji nianjian* [Statistical Yearbook of China], 2000–.
5. *OECD Economic Survey: China*, op. cit., p. 30.
6. *Quadrennial Defense Review Report*, Department of Defense, 6 February 2006, p. 29.
7. Adjusting for its low prices and wages in a measurement called Purchasing Power Parity (PPP), China is now unambiguously the world's second-biggest economy – worth $7.3 trillion compared with the US's $11.6 and Japan's $3.8 trillion.
8. This is how Jiang Zemin defined the 'three represents': 'viewing the course of struggle and the basic experience over the past eighty years and looking ahead to the arduous tasks and bright future in the new century, our Party should continue to stand in the forefront of the times and lead the people in marching toward victory. In a

word, the Party must always represent the requirements of the development of China's advanced productive forces, the orientation of the development of China's advanced culture, and the fundamental interests of the overwhelming majority of the people in China.' (from Jiang's speech at the Sixteenth CPC Congress).

9.   Zhao Suisheng, *A Nation-State by Construction*.

10. See Peak Oil Netherlands Foundation's *World Oil Production and Peaking Outlook* 2005, p. 7, Table 1.

11. Cited by Dr Gal Luft in his statement presented before the US–China Economic and Security Review Commission Hearing on China's Future Energy Development and Acquisition Strategies, 21 July 2005.

12. American consumers, estimate the investment bankers Morgan Stanley, have cumulatively saved $100 billion since the China boom began in 1978 by paying China prices rather than what they would have paid without the China effect.

13. Letter from President George W. Bush to Senators Hagel, Helms, Craig and Roberts, 13 March 2001.

14. *Business Week* Top 100 Brands 2005

15. Walt, *Taming American Power*, pp. 29–61.

16. Johnston, 'Chinese Middle Class Attitudes Towards International Affairs: Nascent Liberalization?'. (Though admittedly Johnston does not look directly at middle-class attitudes towards Taiwan.)

17. See Prestowitz, *Three Billion New Capitalists*, p. 76.

18. Oded Shenkar, *The Chinese Century: The Rising Chinese Economy and Its Impact on the Global Economy, the Balance of Power, and Your Job*, Wharton School Publishing, 2004.

19. John Maynard Keynes, 'National Self-Sufficiency', *Yale Review*, volume 22, number 4, 1933, pp. 755–769.

20. Harold James, *The End of Globalization*, p. 8.

21. Ibid., p. 11.

22. Table 3 Average tariffs on imported manufactured goods, Bordo, Eichengreen and Irwin, 'Is Globalization today really different from Globalization a hundred years ago?'.

23. Bordo et al., op. cit., Table 6.

24. Ibid.

25. Maddison, op. cit.

26. Taken from 'China and the World Economy: From T-Shirts to T-bonds', *The Economist*, 28 July 2005. For a more modest account, see Steven B. Kamin, Mario Marazzi and John W. Schindler, 'Is China "Exporting Deflation"?', Board of Governors of the Federal Reserve System International Finance Discussion Papers, number 791, 2004.

27. Roubini and Setser, 'The US as Net Debtor: The Sustainability of US External Imbalances'. Available at <pages.stern.nyu.edu/~nroubini/papers/Roubini-Setser-US-External-Imbalances.pdf>. From a slightly different perspective, see Dumas and Choyleva, *The Bill from the China Shop*.

28. Richard B. Freeman, 'Doubling the Global Labour Force', Centre for Economic Performance, 2004. In addition, estimates Freeman, there are 400 million new additions to the global workforce from India and 200 million from the ex-Soviet Union, constituting what will ultimately be a doubling of the world's effective labour force.

29. See note 9., above.

30. David Hale, 'China's Growing Appetites', *The National Interest*, 2004.

31. World Economic Forum on East Asia, Security and Sustainability, 15–18 June 2006. Available at <http://www.weforum.org/pdf/summit reports/eastasia2006/security.htm>.

32. Zweig, *Internationalizing China*

33. From communications from the localities to Party Central and State Council. Zhang Liang, *The Tiananmen Papers*, Nathan and Link (eds.), p. 398. The book gives an extraordinary account of the whole episode.

34. See Gilley, *China's Democratic Future*.

35. Nathan and Link, op. cit.

36. Wang Hui, *China's New Order: Society, Politics and Economy in Transition*, Theodore Huters (ed.), Harvard University Press, 2003.

37. Nathan and Link, op. cit.

38. Quoted in Nicholas Kristof and Sheryl WuDunn, *China Wakes*, Times Books, 1994, p. 82.

39. There is considerable dispute over the exact figures. For example, Nicholas Kristof and Sheryl WuDunn, Beijing correspondents of the *New York Times*, estimate that up to eight hundred unarmed people were killed and several thousand injured (Kristof and WuDunn, op. cit.) while Western news agencies at the time had a range of numbers. My figures are drawn from Nathan and Link, op. cit.

40. See table 4.1, Angang Hu, *Great Transformations in China*, OUP, 2006. The computations are on the basis of Purchasing Power Parity (PPP).

41. The Gini coefficient has risen to 0.465 in 2004, up from 0.403 in 1998, says the Chinese Bureau of National Statistics. Given it excludes corrupt income going to officials, the calculation is almost certainly too low.

42. *Financial Times* China Supplement, 8 November 2005. Xie Fuzhan, deputy director of the Development Research Council, is quoted:

'We need to create about twenty million new jobs a year.' Tony Saich (see below) quotes Lu Zhongyuan from the same centre as saying that China will need twenty-four million jobs a year.

43. Tony Saich, China: Socio Political issues 2005–2015, unpublished paper, Kennedy School of Government, Harvard University, 2005, p. 6.

44. Hu, op. cit., p. 259.

45. Tony Saich, 'China in 2005: Hu in Charge', *Asian Survey*, volume 46, number 1, 2006, p.42.

46. 'Power not socialism in today's Chinese ideology', *Financial Times*, 25 July 2006.

47. Xinhua News Agency, 'China Becoming a Growth Engine for the World', Hu Jintao's speech to the 2005 Fortune Global Forum, <http://www.china.org.cn/english/2005/May/128956.htm>. Accessed 13 August 2005. See also Ira Kalish, 'The World's Factory: China Enters the 21st Century', A Deloitte Research Consumer Business Study, 2003.

48. Hu, op. cit.

Chapter 2

1. See Spence, *The Search for Modern China*.

2. Max Weber, *The Religion of China*, Free Press, 1968, and *The Protestant Ethic and Other Writings*.

3. Douglass C. North, 'The Paradox of the West', in Richard W. David (ed.), *The Origins of Modern Freedom*, Stanford University Press, 1995, pp. 7–34.

4. Finlay, 'China, the World and World History in Joseph Needham's *Science and Civilisation*'.

5. See Perdue, *China Marches West*.

6. Angus Maddison, *The World Economy: Historical Statistics*, OECD, 2004.

7. Deng, *The Premodern Chinese Economy*, pp. 46–7.

8. Ringmar, *The Mechanics of Modernity in Europe and East Asia*, p. 159.

9. Tawney, *Land and Labour in China*.

10. Deng, op. cit.

11. Mark Elvin, *The Pattern of the Chinese Past*, Stanford University Press, 1973.

12. Between the Song and Qing dynasties, on average government tax revenue represented 7.1 to 9.3 per cent of Chinese agricultural GDP or 5 to 7 per cent of its total GDP. Deng, op. cit., p. 164.

13. See Li Bozhong, *Agricultural Development in Jiangnan*.

14. Deng, op. cit., p. 170.

15. Gu Yanwu, a seventeenth-century Confucian scholar, personified this tradition.
16. 'China and Europe, 1500-2000', American Council on Education, 2004, available at <http://afe.easia.columbia.edu/chinawh/web/s10/ideas.pdf>
17. Deng, op. cit.
18. Ibid.
19. In the late Ming dynasty some two thousand officials were dismissed as a result of one inspection by the Censorate. Ringmar, op. cit., p. 150.
20. Deng, op. cit., p. 110.
21. Fairbank, *The United States and China*.
22. Habermas, *The Structural Transformation of the Public Sphere*. See also Bayly, *The Birth of the Modern World 1780–1914*.
23. See Joel Mokyr, 'The Enduring Riddle of the European Miracle; The Enlightenment and the Industrial Revolution', paper presented to the University of California Conference on Economic Convergence and Divergence in Historical Perspective, Irvine 2002.
24. Ibid.
25. Jared Diamond, *Guns, Germs and Steel: A Short History of Everybody for the Last 13,000 Years*, Vintage, 1998.
26. Tilly, *Coercion, Capital and European States*. See also Jones, *The European Miracle*.
27. Acemoglu, Johnson and Robinson, 'The Rise of Europe: Atlantic Trade, Institutional Change, and Economic Growth'. The balance of power between competing groups lies at the heart of their account of democratisation. Acemoglu and Robinson, *Economic Origins of Dictatorship and Democracy*. See also Johnston, *Syndromes of Corruption*, pp. 216–19.
28. Having examined a variety of competing explanations, this is the conclusion Peter Perdue reaches. In his eyes, conflict-driven innovation essentially stopped when the Qing finally put down the last nomadic empire in 1760. See Peter C. Perdue, 'Constructing Chinese Property Rights: East and West', in Huri Islamoglu (ed.), *Constituting Modernity: Private Property in the East and West*, I. B. Tauris, 2004.
29. Braudel, *Civilization and Capitalism*.
30. Keynes, *A Treatise on Money*.
31. Ringmar, op. cit.
32. This point is made forcibly by Mokyr, op. cit.
33. Mokyr, 'The Great Synergy: the European Enlightenment as a factor in Modern Economic growth'.

34. Angus Maddison, *Growth and Interaction in the World Economy: The Roots of Modernity*, A.E.I. Press, 2005.

35. There is something of a ritual in brief histories of China to quote, at this point, Emperor Qian Long's famous retort to Lord Macartney's trade mission to China in 1793: China has 'not the slightest need for your country's manufactures'. I thought I would spare readers the ritual, at least in the main body of the text – but Qian Long's statement remains a telling insight into the Chinese mentality at the time.

36. See Zhang Doqing, *Zhongguo Jingjishi Cidan*, [Encyclopedia of Chinese Economic History], quoted in Kent Deng, 'Statebuilding – the original push for institutional changes in modern China, 1840–1950', Working paper 0104, The Global Economic History Network, London School of Economics, 2004.

Chapter 3

1. Schoppa, *Revolution and Its Past*.

2. Ibid.

3. Spence and Schoppa, op. cit.

4. Blecher, *China Against the Tides*, p. 21.

5. Fenby, *Generalissimo*.

6. Spence, op. cit.

7. Spence, op. cit.

8. See Womack (ed.), *Contemporary Chinese Politics in Historical Perspective*. In particular, see his contribution 'In Search of Democracy: Public Authority and Popular Power in China'.

9. Quoted in Spence, op. cit., p. 495.

10. John K. Fairbank, Edwin O. Reischauer and Albert Craig, *China: Tradition & Transformation*, Allen & Unwin, 1989, p. 670.

11. Quoted in Blecher, op. cit., p. 23.

12. Bramall, *Sources of Chinese Economic Growth 1978–96*, pp. 154–5.

13. Selden, *The Political Economy of Chinese Development*. This self-reinforcing dynamic is a running theme throughout Roderick MacFarquhar's magisterial three-volume *Origins of the Cultural Revolution*.

14. Blecher, op. cit., pp. 52–72.

15. Uncertainty surrounds the number that died as a result of the Great Leap Forward. Numbers range from 16.5 million to a more debatable 40 million. The *Cambridge History of China* opts for a narrower range between 16 and 27 million. Chang and Halliday put the figure higher, at 37 million, while computer modelling by the US Bureau of the Census puts it around 30 million: <http://countrystudies.us/china/33.htm>. The 30 million estimate is widely, though not universally, accepted.

16. See Min C. Tsang, 'Education and National Development in China', *China Review*, 2000, p. 6.
17. See Lin, Fang Cai and Zhou Li, *The China Miracle*, Chinese University Press, 2003.
18. Bramall, op. cit., p. 137.
19. Bramall, op. cit., p. 158. In analysing the Indian experience, Nobel Prize winner Amartya Sen also praises this aspect of China's development. See, for instance, Dreze and Sen, *India*, especially pp. 85–6.
20. Qian Yingyi, 'The Process of China's Market Transition (1978–98): The Evolutionary, Historical, and Comparative Perspectives'.
21. Yusuf, Nabeshima and Perkins, *Under New Ownership*, p. 50.
22. From Chang and Halliday, *Mao: The Unknown Story*.
23. Zhao Suisheng, op. cit., p. 241
24. Professor Maurice Meisner, 'The Significance of the Chinese Revolution in World History', Asia Research Centre, London School of Economics and Political Science, Working Paper 1. See also his *Marxism, Maoism, and Utopianism*.
25. 'Politics as Vocation', in H. H. Gerth and C. Wright Mills (trans. and ed.), *From Max Weber: Essays in Sociology*, OUP, 1946, pp. 77–128.
26. 16 May 2006 marked the fortieth anniversary of the start of the Cultural Revolution. The event remains shrouded in officially mandated silence, characteristic of the CCP's unwillingness to grapple with its historical ambiguities. See, for instance, 'China Ignoring the Past', *The Economist*, 18 May 2006.
27. Moore, *Social Origins of Dictatorship and Democracy*.
28. Karl Polanyi, *The Great Transformation*.
29. 14th Annual Friedrich Hayek lecture, delivered by Andrew Neil, 28 November 2005.

Chapter 4

1. Cited by Qian Yingyi, 'The Process of China's Market Transition (1978–98): The Evolutionary, Historical, and Comparative Perspectives'.
2. Discussed by Peter Nolan in *China at the Crossroads*, pp. 7–9.
3. Barry Naughton, 'Deng Xiaoping: the Economist', in Lin (ed.), *China*, p. 388.
4. Baum, *Burying Mao*.
5. See Baum, op. cit.
6. Naughton, *Growing Out of the Plan*. See also William Byrd, *The Market Mechanism and Economic Reforms in China*, M. E. Sharpe, 1991.
7. Yusuf, Nabeshima and Perkins, op. cit., Table 1.2.

8. Modigliani and Cao, 'The Chinese Saving Puzzle and the Life-Cycle Hypothesis'.

9. Jeffrey D. Sachs and Wing Thye Woo, *China's Transition Experience, Reexamined*, World Bank, 1996. See also their 'The Real Reasons for China's Growth', *China Journal*, 1999.

10. Qian Yingyi, op. cit.

11. Naughton, op. cit.

12. See World Bank, *Under New Ownership*, op. cit.

13. *OECD Economic Survey: China*, op. cit., Table 1.3, p. 29.

14. Qian Yingyi, 'The Institutional Foundations of China's Market Transition', paper prepared for World Bank Development Conference, 1999.

15. Qian Yingyi, op. cit., p. 8.

16. *The Economist* China Survey 23 March 2006.

17. Professor Li Bozhong showed me thousands of property titles that had been used in Anhui province to reclaim land that dated from the seventeenth century.

18. Bramall, op. cit., pp. 250–1.

19. Naughton, op. cit., p. 390.

20. Qian Yingyi, op. cit., p. 11.

21. Chong-en Bai, David D. Li and Yijiang Wang, 'Thriving on a Tilted Playing Field', in Hope, Yang and Mu Yang Li (eds.), *How Far Across the River*.

22. Oi, *Rural China Takes Off*. See also Whiting, *Power and Wealth in Rural China*.

23. Steinfeld, *Forging Reform in China*, pp. 237–48.

24. This characterisation arguably surfaces in some of the arguments of Jean Oi, whose work is otherwise very illuminating.

25. Studwell, *The China Dream*, p. 36.

26. Tsai, *Back Alley Banking*, Chapter 4.

27. Liu Yaling, 'Reform from Below: The Private Economy and Local Politics in the Rural Industrialization of Wenzhou'.

28. See Yang, *Remaking the Chinese Leviathan*.

29. See Huang Yasheng, 'Institutional Development and Private Sector Development', in *China*, Wilson Centre's Asia Report Series number 129, 2005.

30. Lee Branstetter and Nicholas Lardy, 'China's Embrace of Globalisation', in *China*, Wilson Centre's Asia Report Series number 129, 2005.

31. Studwell, op. cit., p. 15.

32. Studwell, op. cit., p. 75.

33. Tseng and Zebregs, 'Foreign Direct Investment in China: Some Lessons for Other Countries'.

34. 'Keeping Tabs on China's Growth', *Business Week*,<http://www.businessweek.com/globalbiz/content/may2006/gb20060524_346105.htm?chan=globalbiz_asia_today%27s+top+story>.
35. OECD, op. cit., Figure 1.1.
36. Export shares of FIEs of total exports in three countries, Taiwan, China and Indonesia, from Huang Yasheng, *Selling China*, Table 8.1.
37. Ira Kalish, *The World's Factory: China Enters the 21st Century*, Deloitte Research, 2004.
38. 'The debate of China's becoming a world factory', The Academy of China's Economic Reform and Development, speech by Wu Jinlian, Renmin University, 2004.
39. Nolan, op. cit., p. 20.
40. Huang Yasheng, *Selling China*.

Chapter 5

1. Some of these themes are echoed by Zheng Yongnian, *Globalization and State Transformation in China*.
2. Ravallion and Chen, 'China's (Uneven) Progress Against Poverty'.
3. Joshua Ramo, former foreign editor of *Time* magazine, coined this phrase in 'The Beijing Consensus' for the Foreign Policy Centre, 2004.
4. 'Promote the Building of a Clean Government', in Jiang Zemin, *On the 'Three Represents'*, Foreign Language Press, 2002, pp. 119–47.
5. Nicholas Lardy, cited by Dali L. Yang, 'Economic Transformation and State Rebuilding in China', in Naughton and Yang (eds.), *Holding China Together*.
6. Yang, *Remaking the Chinese Leviathan*, p. 67.
7. Blecher, op. cit., p. 106.
8. Naughton and Yang, op. cit., p. 8.
9. Blecher, op. cit., p. 106.
10. Yang, op. cit., p. 71.
11. Zhiyue Bo, 'The Institutionalisation of Elite Management', in Naughton and Yang, op. cit., p. 86.
12. From Yang, op. cit.
13. Sun Yan, 'Corruption, Growth, and Reform: The Chinese Enigma', *Current History*, volume 104, number 683, 2005, pp. 257–63. For a fuller account see her *Corruption and Market in Contemporary China*.
14. See Huntingdon, *Political Order in Changing Societies*.
15. Lu, *Cadres and Corruption*.
16. *Observer*, 26 June 2005. See also Rose-Ackerman, *Corruption and Government*.
17. Kynge, *China Shakes the World*, pp. 153–4.
18. Ibid., pp. 158–159.

19. Wedeman, 'Anticorruption Campaigns and the Intensification of Corruption in China'.

20. Lubman, *Bird in a Cage*. Sceptical of the CCP's 'instrumental' approach to law is William Alford's 'Double-edged swords cut both ways: law and legitimacy in the People's Republic of China'. For a more upbeat assessment, but one that is still sensitive to the contradictions, see Peerenboom, *China's Long March Toward Rule of Law*.

21. Shandong Xinhuanet, 13 December 2003, cited in 'Enforcement of Civil Judgements: Harder than Reaching the Sky', *China Law and Governance Review*, issue 2, 2004. Available at <http://www.chinareview.info/pages/legal.htm>.

22. Statement to the Senate Foreign Relations Committee by Minxin Pei, director, China Program, Carnegie Endowment for International Peace, 7 June 2005.

23. 'Enforcement of Civil Judgments', op. cit.

24. Minxin Pei, statement to the Senate Foreign Relations Committee, op. cit.

25. Ye Zhang, 'China's Emerging Civil Society', working paper at the Center for Northeast Asian Policy Studies, The Brookings Institution, 2003.

26. Guo Zhenglin and Bernstein, 'The Impact of Elections on the Village Structure of Power: the relations between the village committees and the Party branches'. See also Alpermann, 'The post-election administration of Chinese villages'.

27. 'Back on the Leash', *The Economist*, 18 August 2005.

28. John G. Palfrey, Jr., executive director, Berkman Center for Internet and Society, Harvard Law School, evidence to the US–China Economic and Security Review Commission, 14 April 2005. A complete study of Internet filtering in China, as of 2005, may be found at <http://www.opennetinitiative.net/china/>.

29. Karl Taro Greenfeld, 'The Virus Hunters', *Foreign Policy*, 2006.

30. Ibid., p. 8.

31. Isabel Hilton, 'Beijing's Media Chill', *openDemocracy*, 15 February 2006. Available at <http://www.opendemocracy.net/democracychina/chill_3272.jsp>

32. Pei, *China's Trapped Transition*, p. 154.

33. Ibid., pp. 92–5.

34. Dickson, *Red Capitalists in China*.

35. Ru Xin, Lu Xueyi and Li Peilin (eds.), *2005 Zhongguo shehui xingshi fenxi yu yuce* [Analysis and forecast on China's social development, 2005].

36. Dr Richard Baum's evidence to the US–China Economic and Security Review Commission, 'China's State Control Mechanism and Methods', 14 April 2005.
37. Murray Scott Tanner's evidence to the US–China Economic and Security Review Commission, 'China's State Control Mechanism and Methods', 14 April 2005.
38. Gilboy and Heginbotham, 'The Latin Americanization of China'.
39. Cited by Tony Saich, 'Satisfaction with Government Performance: Public Opinion in Rural and Urban China', unpublished paper, 2005, p. 8.
40. Described by Elizabeth Perry in her *Challenging the Mandate of Heaven*.
41. Minxin Pei takes the raw numbers from the World Bank's Governance Matters III and turns them into rankings. Pei, op. cit., pp. 5–6.
42. Quoted by Pei, op. cit., p. 4.
43. Baum evidence to the US–China Economic and Security Review Commission, op. cit.
44. Baum evidence to the US–China Economic and Security Review Commission, op. cit.

Chapter 6

1. Wolf, *Why Globalization Works*, p. 144.
2. *OECD Economic Survey: China*, 2005, p. 96.
3. World Bank, *Under New Ownership*, op. cit., p. 16.
4. 'The Struggle of the Champions', *The Economist*, 6 January 2005.
5. From a foreign perspective, see 'Over the Wall', *The Economist*, 3 November 2005.
6. Walter and Howie, *To Get Rich is Glorious*, pp. 36–43.
7. According to the 2006 ISS Global Institutional Investor study, which interviewed 322 multinationals worth a combined $27,000 billion, the market value of all listed companies in China dropped by 50 per cent between 2001 and 2005. 'China told to refine corporate governance', *Financial Times*, 16 April 2006.
8. World Bank, *Under New Ownership*, op. cit., p. 90
9. Guy S. Liu and Pei Sun, 'China's Public Firms: How much privatisation?', in Green and Liu (eds.) *Exit the Dragon?* However, other chapters within the same volume, notably Stephen Green's 'The Privatization Two-Step at China's Listed Firm' (pp. 125–44), assert that these structures are inherently transitory and the movement is towards increased privatisation – but concede that increased regulation may be required to inhibit a tendency towards asset stripping.
10. Porter, Schwab and Lopez-Claros, *The Global Competitiveness Report 2005–2006*.

11. See Huang, *Selling China*.
12. Heytens and Karacadag, quoted in World Bank, *Under New Ownership*, op. cit., p. 14.
13. OECD, op. cit., p. 96.
14. OECD, op. cit., p. 52.
15. Minxin Pei, 'The Dark Side of China's Rise', *Foreign Policy*, web edition, 2006, p. 2.
16. 'The Myth of China Inc.', *The Economist*, 1 September 2005
17. Edward Steinfeld, Forging Reform in China: The Fate of State-Owned Industry, CUP, 1998.
18. OECD, op. cit., pp. 85–8. Recent studies have confirmed this finding. See David Dollar and Shang-Jin We, 'Das (Wasted) Kapital: Firm Ownership and Investment Efficiency in China', IMF Working Paper WP/07/9.
19. Davin A. Mackenzie, 'A healthy financial sector requires enterprises that deserve financing', to Conference on Financial Sector Reform in China, 2001. See also Wank, *Commodifying Communism*.
20. *Asia Times*, 10 August 2005 and 'The Myth of China Inc.', *The Economist*, 1 September 2005.
21. *The Economist*, op. cit.
22. *The Economist*, op. cit.
23. George Gilboy, 'The Myth Behind China's Miracle', *Foreign Affairs*, web edition, 2004, p. 4. Available at <http://www.foreignaffairs.org/20010701faessay83405/george-j-gilboy/the-myth-behind-china-s-miracle.html>.
24. Edward Steinfeld, 'China's Shallow Integration: Networked Production and the New Challenges for Late Industrialisation', for the Commission on US–China Economic and Security Review, 2003.
25. Ibid.
26. Poncet, 'Measuring Chinese Domestic and International Integration'.
27. Ibid., p.17.
28. Y. Rao, B. Lu. and C. Tsou, ' Transition from Rule by Man to Rule by Merit – Comments on National Planning of Science and Technology', *Nature*, volume 432, number 7015, 2004.
29. Segal and Wilson, 'Trends in China's Transition toward a Knowledge Economy'.
30. Elizabeth Economy, 'China's Environmental Challenge', *Current History*, volume 104, 2005. See also her more extensive monograph *The River Runs Black*.
31. Economy, op. cit., p. 279.
32. Nathan Nankivell, 'China's Pollution and its Threat to Domestic and Regional Stability', *Jamestown Review*, China Brief, volume 5, issue 22, 2005. Available at <http://jamestown.org/publications_ details.

php?volume_id=408&issue_id=3505&article_id=2370389>. However, contrast this with Elizabeth Economy, who puts the figure at just over 300,000.

33. Nathan Nankivell, 'The National Security Implications of China's Emerging Water Crisis', *Jamestown Review*, China Brief, volume 5, issue 17, 2005. Available at <http://jamestown.org/publications_ details.php?volume_id=408&issue_id=3422&article_id=2370095>

34. Economy, op. cit., p. 279.

35. World Bank, op. cit., pp. 6–8.

36. For a general overview of the challenges and responses, see Huang, Saich and Steinfeld (eds.), *Financial Sector Reform in China*.

37. Weijian Shan, 'The World Banks' China Delusion', *Far Eastern Economic Review*, September 2006, and 'China's Low-Profit Growth Model', *Far Eastern Economic Review*, November 2006.

38. The classic account is Lardy, *China's Unfinished Economic Revolution*.

39. Studwell, op. cit., points to the findings of Stu Fulton, a financial systems specialist working with PWC. After three years in the field, his conclusion was that 50 per cent of total portfolios were NPLs, a figure that rose to as high as 70–80 per cent in some branches.

40. 'A Great Big Banks Gamble', *The Economist*, 27 October 2005.

41. Ibid.

42. Podpiera, 'Progress in China's Banking Sector Reform: Has Bank Behavior Changed?'.

43. Reported in the *Financial Times*, 3 May 2006.

44. *Financial Times*, 31 May 2006

45. World Bank, *Under New Ownership*, op. cit.

46. Hu Angang, op. cit., Table 3.1.

47. Qu Hongbin and Sophia Ma Xiaoping, 'China Economic Insight (Vol. 25) – Balancing Act', HSBC Global Research, 2006.

48. Qu Hongbin and Sophia Ma Xiaoping, op. cit., p. 3

49. The anecdote is given by Qu Hongbing and Sophia Ma Xiaoping. They also describe how the local government of Jian, in Guangxi province, has built a breathtakingly modern eight-lane highway in the city centre, even though it is home to only two hundred thousand people and fewer than ten thousand cars.

50. Olivier Blanchard and Francesco Giavazzi, 'Rebalancing Growth in China', MIT Working Paper 05-32, 2005, say that the renminbi is 30 per cent undervalued, and quote unpublished work from Ricardo Haussman and Dani Rodrik supporting this judgement. Morris Goldstein of the Institute for International Economics in Washington also computes that the renminbi is 30 per cent under-valued in a paper for the Cato Institute, 2005.

51. Blanchard and Giavazzi, op. cit.

52. Michael Pettis, 'China's Last Option: Let the Yuan Soar', *Far Eastern Economic Review*, June 2007.

53. Edward Lim, Michael Spence and Ricardo Hausmann, 'China and Global Economy: Medium Term Issues and Options', Center for International Development Harvard University Working Paper 126, 2006.

54. Pei, op. cit., p. 173.

55. Ibid.

56. Ibid.

57. Ibid., p. 174.

58. Tony Saich, 'Development and Choice in Asia's Giants', in Bruce Gilley and Edward Friedman (eds.), *Comparing China and India*, Palgrave MacMillan, 2005, p. 231.

59. Pei, op. cit., p. 171.

60. Ibid., p. 170.

61. Cheng Li, 'Hu's Policy Shift and the Tuanpai's Coming-of-Age', *China Leadership Monitor*, number 15, pp. 4–5. The paper can be accessed at <www.chinaleadershipmonitor.org>

62. This point is forcefully made by Thomas Palley, 'External Contradictions of the Chinese Development Model: Export-led Growth and the Dangers of Global Economic Contraction', *Journal of Contemporary China*, volume 15 (46), 2006.

63. David Metcalf and Jianwei Li, 'Chinese Unions – Nugatory or Transforming; an Alice Analysis', CEP Discussion Paper 708, 2005.

Chapter 7

1. Dani Rodrik, 'Goodbye Washington Consensus, Hello Washington Confusion?', 2006. Available at <http://ksghome.harvard.edu/~drodrik/Lessons%20of%20the%201990s%20review%20_JEL_.pdf>

2. Diamond, op. cit. For instance, Diamond attributes delays in food production and their knock-on effects for economic, political and military organisation to the absence of domesticated animals. Eurasia's native cows, sheep, goats, horses and pigs, which were relatively docile, cheap to feed and capable of being bred in captivity, were important to its story of development. The same was not true of Africa, i.e. the African buffalo, zebra, bush pig, rhino and hippopotamus were violent and difficult to keep in captivity.

3. Bloom and Sachs, 'Geography, Demography, and Economic Growth in Africa'.

4. See Wing Thye Woo, 'The Washington Consensus: Misunderstanding the Poor by the Brightest', paper presented at the FONDAD-organised Conference, 'Stability, Growth and the Search

for a New Development Agenda: Reconsidering the Washington Consensus', 2004.

5. John Williamson, 'What Should the World Bank Think about the Washington Consensus?', cited by Wing Thye Woo, op. cit., p. 17.

6. See *The Global Competitiveness Report 2004–5*, World Economic Forum, Palgrave Macmillan, 2005.

7. Dani Rodrik, 'Institutions for High Quality Growth: What they are and how to acquire them', paper prepared for the International Monetary Fund Conference on Second Generation Reform, 1999.

8. See Amartya Sen, *Development as Freedom*, OUP, 1999.

9. Stern, Dethier and Rogers, *Growth and Empowerment*. See also Ellerman, *Helping People Help Themselves*.

10. Joseph Stiglitz compares Latin America's average 2.7 per cent growth rate over the 1990s with 5.4 per cent over the 1960s – a tribute to a different policy approach and mix.

11. Scott, *Seeing Like a State*.

12. See 'The Geopolitics of Sexual Frustration', *Foreign Policy*, 2006.

13. Ibid.

14. These comments are drawn from the discussion by Yanzhong Huang and Dali L. Yang, 'Population Control and State Coercion in China', in Naughton and Yang, op. cit., and Amartya Sen's *Development as Freedom*, op. cit.

15. For a typology of the different unintended consequences that can accompany intervention, see Sam D. Sieber, *Fatal Remedies: The Ironies of Social Intervention*, Plenum Books, 2001.

16. Sen, op. cit.

17. Sen, op. cit., pp. 221–3.

18. Tyler, *Why People Obey the Law*.

19. Halperin, Siegle and Weinstein, *The Democracy Advantage*.

20. In particular, see chapters 1 and 2, 'Exposing a 50-Year-Old Myth' and 'Setting the Record Straight'.

21. Halperin, Siegle and Weinstein, op. cit., p. 13.

22. In particular, see chapter 4, 'Democracy and Security'.

23. Sunstein, *Why Societies Need Dissent*.

24. Surowiecki, *The Wisdom of Crowds*.

25. For a useful synthesis of case studies, see Kay, *The Truth About Markets*.

26. Florida and Gates, 'Technology and Tolerance'.

27. The BBC introduced the waterholing technique in the early 2000s under director-general Greg Dyke. An account of how it works and its success is provided in 'Creativity' by The Work Foundation, 2005.

28. Lester and Piore, *Innovation*.

29. See Barry Lynn, 'Up to the Old-Fashioned Power of the New Oligopolies', *Financial Times*, 14 February 2006. For a more historically informed discussion, see Lynn's *End of the Line*.

30. Jürgen Krönig, 'Hotting it Up', in John Lloyd and Jean Seaton (eds.), *What Can be Done? Making the Media and Politics Better*, *Political Quarterly* special issue book, Blackwell, 2006, pp. 14–22.

31. Zaller, 'Market Competition and News Quality'. See also Castells, *The Power of Identity*.

32. Dunsire, 'Tipping the Balance: Autopoiesis and Governance'. See also Scott, 'Analysing Regulatory Space: Fragmented Resources and Institutional Design', and Hirschman, 'Pillars of Order: Social Conflicts as Pillars of Democratic Market Society'.

Chapter 8

1. Arjun Appadurai, 'The Capacity to Aspire: Culture and the Terms of Recognition', in Vijayendra Rao and Michael Walton (eds.), *Culture and Public Action*, Stanford University Press, 2004.

2. Schiller, *The New Financial Risk in the 21st Century Order*, p. 8. Quoted by Roger C. Altman, Peter R. Orszag, Jason E. Bordoff and Robert E. Rubin, 'An Economic Strategy to Advance, Opportunity, Prosperity and Growth', The Brookings Institute Hamilton Project, 2006.

3. See John Armour and Douglas Cumming, 'The Legal Road to Replicating Silicon Valley', Centre for Business Research, Cambridge University Working Paper 281, <http://www.cbr.cam.ac.uk/pdf/WP281.pdf>

4. In discussing the historical relevance of the East Asian experience for the Middle East, Marcus Noland and Howard Pack make a similar argument. Partly because of this, he is sceptical of popular arguments that stress an activist industrial policy and the strategy of picking winners. Noland and Pack, 'The East Asian Industrial Policy Experience: Implications for the Middle East'.

5. de Soto, *The Mystery of Capital*.

6. This figure is strongly contested by many. Christopher Woodruff in *Journal of Economic Literature*, volume 49, 2001, argues that the unrealised price of peasant property is $3.6 trillion, which would be further reduced by translating collateral into loans. Even so, the figure remains large.

7. de Soto, op. cit.

8. See, for instance, David Dyzenhaus, 'Form and Substance in the Rule of Law', in C. Forsyth (ed.), *Judicial Review and The Constitution*, Hart Publishing, 2000, and his 'Law as Justification:

Etienne Mureinik's Conception of Legal Culture' in *South African Journal on Human Rights* 11, 1998.

9. For an overview of Smith's moral philosophical vision, see Evensky, *Adam Smith's Moral Philosophy*.

10. Wilkinson, *The Impact of Inequality*. See Richard Sennett, *Respect in a World of Inequality*, Norton, 2003.

11. Alan Greenspan, 'Capitalizing Reputation,' at the Financial Markets Conference of the Federal Reserve Bank of Atlanta, Sea Island, 2004, cited by Bogle, *The Battle for the Soul of Capitalism*.

12. See the collection of essays in Gintis, Bowles, Boyd and Fehr (eds.), *Moral Sentiments and Material Interests*.

13. Gintis et al. draw a distinction between what they call 'weak reciprocity', cooperation premised on the expectation that individuals will obtain future benefits (as associated with the work of evolutionary biologist Robert Trivers) and 'strong reciprocity', 'the disposition to cooperate with others and to punish those who violate norms of cooperation, at personal cost, even when it is implausible to expect that these costs will be repaid either by others or at a later date'.

14. Gintis et al., op. cit., p. 12.

15. Axelrod, *The Evolution of Cooperation*.

16. For a discussion of how humans differ from other animals, see, for instance, Stevens and Hauser, 'Why be nice? Psychological constraints on the evolution of cooperation'.

17. In so doing, they build on the kind of work developed by Antonio Damasio. A. R. Damasio, *Descartes' Error: Emotion, Reason and the Human Brain*, Putnam, 1994.

18. Steven Pinker, *The Blank Slate: The Modern Denial of Human Nature*, Viking Penguin, 2002, p. 271.

19. Leda Cosmides and John Tooby, 'Better Than Rational: Evolutionary Psychology and the Invisible Hand', *American Economic Review*, volume 84, number 2, 1994, p. 329. See also Barkow, Cosmides and Tooby, *The Adapted Mind*.

20. Dan M. Kahan, 'The Logic of Reciprocity: Trust, Collective Action and Law', *Michigan Law Review*, volume 102: 71, 2003.

21. Richard Wilkinson, 'Social Corrosion, Inequality and Health', in Giddens and Diamond (eds.), *The New Egalitarianism*, p. 191.

22. Easterly, Ritzen and Woolcock, 'Social Cohesion, Institutions and Growth'. Available at <www.nyu.edu/fas/institute/dri/DRIWP17.pdf>. See also their 'On "good" politicians and "bad" policies – social cohesion, institutions, and growth', World Bank Policy Research Working Paper 2448, 2000.

23. Knack and Keefer, 'Does social capital have an economic payoff? A

cross-country investigation'. See also Hilton L. Root, *Capital and Collusion: The Political Logical of Global Economic Development*, Princeton University Press, 2006.

24. Alexis de Tocqueville, *Democracy in America*, Hackett, 2000, cited by Wilkinson, op. cit., p. 1.

25. Collins and Porras, *Built to Last*, pp. 72–3.

26. In *Built to Last*, op. cit., the authors describe how profits are not the 'why' of Boeing – the 'why' of Boeing is about 'aviation pioneering, adventure, challenge and contribution', p. 81.

27. Unilever Annual Report 2004.

28. Porras and Collins, op. cit., p. 58.

29. 'Cracking the Performance Code', The Work Foundation, 2005.

30. On the Asian Financial Crisis, see Godement, *The Downsizing of Asia*. For an excellent overview of the Asian Values debate, see Peerenboom, 'Beyond Universalism and Relativism: The Evolving Debates about "Values in Asia"'. Available from SSRN. See also Lucien W. Pye, 'The Asian Values Ballyhoo: Patten's Common Sense on Hong Kong and Beyond', *Foreign Affairs*, 1998, which places the debate in its rather contingent political context.

31. Emblematic of this tendency is Bell and Chaibong (eds.), *Confucianism for the Modern World*.

32. Kim Dae Jung, 'Is Culture Destiny? The Myth of Asia's Anti-Democratic Values', *Foreign Affairs*, 1994.

33. See, for instance, Katz, *The System that Soured*, and McCormack, *The Emptiness of Japanese Affluence*.

34. Jeff Kingston, *Japan's Quiet Revolution: Social Change and Civil Society in 21st Century*, Routledge, 2004, p. 54.

35. Ibid., pp. 70–94.

36. '*Economist* Survey: Japan, The Sun Also Rises', *The Economist*, 6 October 2005.

37. Amartya Sen, *The Argumentative Indian*.

38. Ibid., p. 23.

39. In a survey of twenty-five emerging market economies conducted in 2000 by Credit Lyonnais Securities Asia, India ranked sixth in corporate governance, China nineteenth.

40. Cited by Huang Yasheng and Tarun Khanna, 'Can India Overtake China?' *Foreign Policy* 137, 2003, pp. 74–81. See also Basu, 'India and the Knowledge Economy: The "Stealth Miracle" is Sustainable', and, more generally, Edward Friedman and Bruce Gilley, *Asia's Giants: Comparing China and India*, Palgrave Macmillan, 2005, which provides a sprightly, judicious reassessment of India's institutional advantages.

41. This point is powerfully made by Meghnad Desai, 'India and China: An Essay in Comparative Political Economy'.

42. UNDP, *Human Development Report*. Statistics available at <http://hdr.undp.org/statistics/data/>

43. For evidence, see K. Hoff and P. Pandey, 'Belief systems and durable inequalities – An experimental investigation of Indian caste', World Bank Policy Research Working Paper 3351, 2004.

44. Joshua C. Ramo, *The Beijing Consensus, notes on the new physics of Chinese power*, Foreign Policy Centre, 2004.

Chapter 9

1. Quoted in Goldstein, *Rising to the Challenge*. See also Christopher R. Hughes, *Chinese Nationalism in the Global Era*.

2. Quoted in Wu Xinbo, 'China: Security Practice of Modernizing and Ascending Power', in Alagappa (ed.), *Asian Security Practice*.

3. For an account of Li Hongzhang's modernisation efforts see Jonathan Spence, *The Search for Modern China*, op. cit.

4. Quoted in Zhao Suisheng, *A Nation State by Construction*.

5. The full text of Li Zhaoxing's 7 March 2004 press conference is available at <http://english.people.com.cn/200403/07/eng20040307_136794.shtml>.

6. Zheng Bijian, 'China's Peaceful Rise to Great Power Status', *Foreign Affairs* 2005.

7. Mearsheimer, *The Tragedy of Great Power Politics*.

8. Goldstein, op. cit.

9. Thomas J. Christensen, 'Looking Beyond the Nuclear Bluster: Recent Progress and Remaining Problems in PRC Security Policy', *China Leadership Monitor*, number 15. Available at <http://www.chinaleadershipmonitor.org/20053/tc.html>

10. Louisa Lombard, 'China's Africa Card', *Foreign Policy* 2006. Available at <http://www.foreignpolicy.com/story/cms.php?story_id=3419>.

11. Confirmed in author's conversation with Jonathan Fenby, then editor of the *South China Post*, and with Chris Patten, governor of Hong Kong. See also Jonathan Dimbleby, *The Last Governor: Chris Patten and the Handover of Hong Kong*, Time Warner Books, 1998.

12. Adrian Karatnycky (ed.), *Freedom in the World: The Annual Survey of Political Rights and Civil Liberties, 2001–2002*, Freedom House, 2002.

13. Interview with author, 2 February 2006.

14. Stephen Green.

15. Report to Congress of the US–China Economic and Security Review Commission 2005, p. 19.

16. Ibid., pp. 44–5.

17. *The Economist*, 18 February 2006.

18. <http://usinfo.state.gov/eap/Archive/2006/Apr/04-929128.html>

19. Edward M. Graham and David M. Marchick, *US National Security and Foreign Direct Investment*, Institute of International Economics, 2006, p. 102.

20. Ibid., note 19.

21. 'Pricey Oil's Path to Your Pocket', *Business Week*, 27 April 2005, <http://www.businessweek.com/bwdaily/dnflash/apr2005/nf200504 27_2905.htm>, accessed 10 October 2005.

22. Statement by Dr Gal Luft, presented before USC Hearing on China's Future Energy Development and Acquisition Strategies, 21 July 2005.

23. Cited by the *New York Times*, 'The Breaking Point', 21 August 2005.

24. 'The Future of Oil', Institute for the Analysis of Global Security, <www.iags.org/futureofoil.html>, accessed 8 March 2006.

25. 'The List: The Top Five Global Chokepoints', *Foreign Policy*, 2006.

26. Ibid.

27. Michael L. Ross, 'Does Oil Hinder Democracy?', *World Politics* 53, 2001, pp. 325–61.

28. Jeffrey D. Sachs and Andrew M. Warner, 'Natural Resource Abundance and Economic Growth', NBER Working Paper W5398. Also see Paul Collier and Anke Hoeffler, 'On Economic Causes of Civil War' *Oxford Economic Papers* 50, 1998, pp. 563–73.

29. See Paul Collier and Anke Heoffler, *Greed and Grievances in Civil War*, World Bank, 2001.

30. Christopher Dickey, 'The Oil Shield', *Foreign Policy*, 2006, pp. 37–40.

31. See Michael T. Klare, 'The Twilight Era of Petroleum', *Tomdispatch*, 2005.

32. Dr David Zweig, director Centre of China's Transnational Relations, Hong Kong University of Science and Technology, 'The Foreign Policy of a Resource Hungry State'.

33. Li Zhibiao, researcher at CASS, is quoted in the *Financial Times* (23 February 2006): 'China wants to have diversified channels in case of disruptions. It's the same as the US policies (on oil).'

34. Quoted in Zweig and Bi, 'China's Global Hunt for Energy'.

35. Ibid. See also *Jamestown Review*, China Brief, volume 5, issue 21, 2005.

36. Zweig and Bi, op. cit.

37. Statement by Vincent Wei-cheng Wang, 'Democratic Consolidation or Electioneering Nationalism? The 2004 Taiwan Presidential Election and Its Implications', presented before the USCC hearing on China's Military Modernization and Cross-strait Balance, 15 September 2005; see also 'Turning Taiwanese', *The Economist*, 13 January 2005.

38. Sheng, 'Cross Strait Relations and Public Opinion on Taiwan'.
39. Carpenter, op. cit., p. 90.
40. Eric McVadon, Evidence to the US–China Economic and Security Review, 15 September 2005.
41. The 2005 Department of Defence Annual Report to Congress on 'The Military Power of the People's Republic of China'.
42. Ibid.
43. See Kent E. Calder, 'China and Japan's Simmering Rivalry', *Foreign Affairs*, 2006.
44. Cited by Carpenter, *America's Coming War with China*, p. 153.
45. Robert Zoellick speech to National Committee on US–China Relations, 21 September 2005.
46. See Heginbotham and Twomey, 'America's Bismarkian Asia Policy'.
47. Roh had only a forty-five-minute audience with Bush; Koizumi was given the five-star treatment at the Bush ranch.
48. Jeff Kingston, op. cit., p. 227.
49. The textbooks in question remain highly controversial. According to an article in *Asahi Shinbun* (September 2005) they have been adopted in only 0.04 per cent of Japan's junior high schools since their introduction in 2001, a figure which falls considerably short of the 10 per cent penetration target that the Japanese Society for History Textbook Reform had set itself. Thanks to Yoko Enomura for helping track down much of the Japanese material.
50. The ten members of ASEAN are: Brunei, Myanmar, Cambodia, Indonesia, Thailand, Vietnam, Singapore, Malaysia, Philippines and Laos.
51. Hu Angang, op. cit., p. 50.
52. Zhao Suisheng, *A Nation State by Construction*. See also: Howard French, 'China's Textbooks Twist and Distort History', *New York Times*, 6 December 2004; statement by Professor Edward Friedman, 'Chinese Nationalism and American Policy', presented before the USCC hearing on State Control Mechanisms and Methods, 14 April 2005.
53. Gries, 'Chinese Nationalism: Challenging the State'.
54. Edward Friedman, 'Preventing War between China and Japan', in Friedman and McCormick (eds.), *What if China Doesn't Democratise?*
55. Heginbotham and Twomey, op. cit., p. 250.

Chapter 10

1. See Bairoch, *Economics and World History*, p. 40, Table 3.3.
2. Greenfield, *The Spirit of Capitalism*.
3. Ibid., p. 417.
4. LaFeber, *The New Empire*.

5. Ferguson, *Colossus*. See also Zakaria, *From Wealth to Power*.
6. Maier, *Among Empires*, p. 78.
7. Alfred T. Mahan, *The Influence of Sea Power upon History, 1660–1783*, Dover Books, 1987.
8. Lake, *Power, Protection, and Free Trade*. For a discussion of the relationship between free trade and security interests, see Gowa, *Allies, Adversaries, and International Trade*.
9. Eckes and Zeiler, *Globalization and the American Century*. See also Forsberg, *America and the Japanese Miracle*.
10. X, 'The Sources of Soviet Conduct', *Foreign Affairs*, 1947.
11. Cited by Frieden, *Global Capitalism*, p. 267.
12. In Johnson, *Blowback*.
13. Eckes and Zeiler, op. cit., p. 139.
14. Drake and Nicolaidis, 'Ideas, Interests and Institutionalization: Trade in Services and the Uruguay Round'.
15. Reynolds, *One World Divisible*, p. 517.
16. Braithwaite and Drahos, *Information Feudalism*.
17. Between 1980 and 2001 the US brought 856 suits, compared to 784 for the European Union. Maurizio Zanardi, 'Antidumping: A Problem in International Trade', 2005, available at <http://darkwing.uoregon.edu/%7Ebruceb/adpage.html>, US Antidumping Database and Links. For information on dumping since the inception of the WTO: <http://www.wto.org/english/tratop_e/ adp_e/ adp_e.htm>
18. Blonigen, 'Evolving Practices of US Antidumping Activity'.
19. Barfield, *High-Tech Protectionism*.
20. Bhagwati and Irwin, 'The Return of the Reciprocitarians: US Trade Policy Today'.
21. 'America's Place In The World 2005: Opinion Leaders turn cautious, public looks homeward', Pew Research Center for the People and the Press and the Council on Foreign relations. Available at <http://people-press.org/reports/pdf/263.pdf>
22. 'Bush Approval Falls to 33%, Congress Earns Rare Praise', Pew Research Center for the People and the Press, 15 March 2006. Available at <http://people-press.org/reports/display.php3?ReportID=271>
23. Ibid.
24. Glaeser and Shleifer, 'The Rise of the Regulatory State'.
25. Friedman, *The Moral Consequences of Economic Growth*, p. 107.
26. see Kloppenberg, *The Virtues of Liberalism*.
27. Goldin and Katz, 'The "Virtues" of the Past: Education in the First Hundred Years of the New Republic'. See also Claudia Goldin, 'The Human-Capital Century And American Leadership: Virtues Of The Past', *Journal of Economic History*, volume 61, 2001, pp. 263–92.

28. 'Closing the Growth Gap', *The Economist*, 27 October 2005.

29. Goldin, op. cit., pp. 275–6.

30. Gentzkow, Glaeser and Goldin, 'The Rise of the Fourth Estate: How Newspapers Became Informative and Why it Matters'.

31. In Glaeser and Shleifer, op. cit.

32. Chandler, *The Visible Hand*.

33. In Glaeser and Shleifer, op. cit.

34. Berle and Means, *The Modern Corporation and Private Property*.

35. Schwarz, *The New Dealers*. Gary Brechin, 'Keeping the Faith', *San Francisco Chronicle*, 27 December 2005, <http://www.sfgate.com/cgi-bin/article.cgi?file=/chronicle/archive/2005/12/27/EDG2IGCOES1. DTL>, accessed 20 February 2006.

36. Many innovations owe their creation to government support. For a comprehensive overview, see <http://www.nsf.gov/od/lpa/nsf50/ nsfoutreach/htm/home.htm>

37. I adapted this idea from a paper by Stephen Jenkins and Frank Cowell, 'Dwarves and Giants in the 1980s', Department of Swansea Discussion Paper 93-03. The calculations (which are a rule of thumb) are based on the *New York Times* study on class, together with IRS tax return numbers.

38. Uchitelle, *The Disposable American*.

39. Muriel Siebert, 'To Encourage Recovery, Encourage Investors', *New York Times*, 6 August 2002, cited by Kochan, *Restoring the American Dream*.

40. 'How Many People Lack Health Insurance and for How Long', Congressional Budget Office Report, 2003, cited in Kochan, op. cit.

41. The 2005 Employment Policy Institute reports that the middle-earning group of households, defined as those with half to twice the median, shrank to 60.7 per cent in 2002 from 68.0 per cent in 1979.

42. Piketty and Saez, 'The Evolution of Top Incomes: a historical and international perspective'.

43. Stephen Roach, 'Globalization's New Underclass', Global Economic Forum, <http://www.morganstanley.com/GEFdata/ digests/20060303-fri.html>, accessed 4 February 2006.

44. 'Minding the Gap', *Wall Street Journal*, 6 March 2006. <http://online.wsj.com/public/article/SB114182443308492484.html >, accessed 14 March 2006.

45. Gøsta Esping-Andersen, 'Inequality of Incomes and Opportunities', in Giddens and Diamond (eds.), op. cit.

46. Ton Hertz computation from the University of Michigan survey cited by David Wessel in 'Moving Up: Challenges to the American Dream', *Wall Street Journal*, 13 May 2005.

47. The World Value Survey (1983–1997) in Alesina and Glaeser, *Fighting Poverty in the US and Europe.*

48. Interviewed in *Mother Jones*, 7 February 2005.

49. *American Prospect*, 27 March 2006.

50. See Bradford, Grieco and Hufbauer, op. cit.

51. 11,120 jobs are embedded in every net $1 billion of trade deficit with China, estimate the EPI (see Palley, below); the 2005 $202 billion trade deficit thus creates 2.24 million cumulative lost job opportunities.

52. See I. Thomas Palley, *Trade, Employment and Outsourcing; some observations on US-China relations in Offshoring and the Internationalisation of Employment*, ILO, 2006, pp. 82-84.

53. See <http://www.emcc.eurofound.eu.int/erm/>

54. Uchitelle, op. cit.

55. Bradford, Grieco and Hufbauer, op. cit.

56. The data in this paragraph is taken from Levy and Murnane, *The New Division of Labor.*

57. Dew-Becker and Gordon, 'Where did the Productivity Growth Go? Inflation Dynamics and the Distribution of Income'.

58. Paul Krugman, 'Graduates versus Oligarchs', *New York Times*, 27 February 2006.

Chapter 11

1. McCarty, Poole and Rosenthal, *Polarized America*, p. 47.

2. 'Will White Evangelicals Desert the GOP?', Pew Research Center commentary on public opinion, 2 May 2006. Available at <http://pewresearch.org/obdeck/?ObDeckID=22>

3. Galston and Kamarck, 'The Politics of Polarization'.

4. Mark Noll, 'The Old Religion in a New World', cited by Phillips, *American Theocracy*, p. 105.

5. Micklethwait and Wooldridge, *The Right Nation*, p. 325.

6. Cited by Thomas Gallagher, 'Politics and the Economy', in Keene (ed.), *Flying on One Engine.*

7. Bogle, op. cit., p. 74.

8. Ibid., p. 94.

9. Ibid., p. 96.

10. Baily, Bartelsman and Haltiwanger, 'Downsizing and Productivity Growth: Myth or Reality?'.

11. See *Mergerstat* and *Business Week*, 'Mergers: Why Most Big Deals Don't Pay Off', 14 October 2002, <http://www.businessweek.com/magazine/content/02_41/b3803001.htm>, accessed 2 March 2006.

12. *Business Week*, op. cit.

13. Matthias M. Bekier, Anna J. Bogardus and Tim Oldham, 'Is the

belief that mergers drive revenue growth an illusion?', *McKinsey Quarterly*, number 4, 2001.

14. 'Unlocking Shareholder Value: The Key to Success', KPMG, 2001.

15. Nina Munk, *Fools Rush in: Steve Case, Jerry Levin and the Unmaking of AOL Time Warner*, Harper Collins, 2004. See also Alec Klein, *Stealing Time: Steve Case, Jerry Levin and the Collapse of AOL Time Warner*, Simon & Schuster, 2004

16. Matthew T. Bodie, 'AOL Time Warner and the False God of Shareholder Primacy', Hofstra University Legal Studies Research Paper 05-21. Available at SSRN: <http://ssrn.com/abstract= 776228>

17. Quoted in Gretchen Morgenson, 'What are mergers good for?', *New York Times*, 5 June 2005.

18. Lucien A. Bebchuk and Jesse M. Fried, 'Pay without Performance', Discussion Paper 528, Harvard John M. Ohlins Discusion Series, 2005. See also their book *Pay without Performance*.

19. Will Hutton, *The World We're In*, Little, Brown, 2002.

20. Bogle, op. cit.

21. Roe, 'The Inevitable Instability of American Corporate Governance'.

22. Roe, op. cit.

23. Baumol, Blinder and Wolff, *Downsizing in America: Reality*.

24. Freeman and Rogers, *What Do Workers Want?*. See also Lipset, Meltz, Gomez and Katchanovski, *The Paradox of American Unionism*.

25. Ehrenreich, *Bait and Switch*.

26. Hutton, op. cit. See also OECD, 'Education at a Glance', available at <http://www.oecd.org/dataoecd/41/13/35341210.pdf>

27. See generally, Bowen, Kurzweil and Tobin, *Equity and Excellence in American Higher Education*.

28. Robert L. Woodbury, 'Social Contracts Erode at Colleges', <http://www.utexas.edu/conferences/africa/ads/1392.html>, accessed 2 April 2006.

29. Two million new jobs were created in 2005, representing a gain of 1.5 per cent: less than half of the average growth rate of 3.5 per cent for the same stage of previous business cycles that lasted as long. See Lee Price, 'Why people are so dissatisfied with today's economy', Employment Policy Institute Issue Brief 219, 2006

30. Farber, 'What do we know about Job Loss in the United States? Evidence from the Displaced Workers Survey, 1984–2004'.

31. New America Foundation, 'Decline of Broadcasters' Public Interest Obligations', Policy Backgrounder, 2004.

32. For a discussion of the Internet's role in this transformation, see Sunstein, *republic.com*.

33. Hacker and Pierson, *Off Center*, p. 176.
34. Michael Massing, 'The Press; The Enemy Within', *New York Review of Books*, volume 52, number 20, 2005. See also his 'The End of News', *New York Review of Books*, volume 52, number 19, 2005.
35. Bartels, 'Homer Gets a Tax Cut: Inequality and Public Policy in the American Mind'. See also Jacob S. Hacker and Paul Pierson, 'Abandoning the Middle: The Bush Tax Cuts and the Limits of Democratic Control, *Perspectives on Politics*, volume 3, number 1 2005, pp. 32–53.
36. Benabou, 'Unequal Societies: Income Distribution and the Social Contract'.
37. Freeman, 'What, Me Vote?'.
38. 'American Democracy in an Age of Rising Inequality', Task Force on Inequality and American Democracy, American Political Science Association, 2004, p. 7. Available at <http://apsanet.org/imgtest/taskforcereport.pdf>
39. Ibid.
40. cited in Hacker and Pierson, op. cit, pp. 122–3.
41. Ibid., pp. 124–5
42. Burden, 'Candidate positioning in U.S. congressional elections'.
43. Hacker and Pierson, op. cit., pp. 39–43
44. Ibid.
45. William G. Gale, and Peter R. Orszag, 'Bush Administration Tax Policy: Summary and Outlook', *Tax Notes*, 2004, pp. 1279–84.
46. Suskind, *The Price of Loyalty*.
47. Friedman, op. cit.
48. Introduction, 'The National Security Strategy of the United States of America', September 2002. Available at <http://www.whitehouse.gov/nsc/nss.html>
49. Nicholas Lemann, 'How it Came to War. When did Bush decide that he had to fight Saddam?', *New Yorker*, 31 March 2003.
50. Ignatieff, op. cit.
51. Hans Blix, *Disarming Iraq: The Search for Weapons of Mass Destruction*, Bloomsbury, 2004.
52. Paul R. Pillar, 'Intelligence Policy and the War in Iraq', *Foreign Affairs*, 2006.
53. Ibid.
54. Quoted in the *Observer*, 14 May 2006, p. 8.
55. They include retired Army Maj-Gen. Charles Swannack, former Central Command Chief Marine Gen. Anthony Zinni, Army Maj-Gen. Paul Eaton, Marine Lt-Gen. Gregory Newbold and Army Maj-Gen. John Batiste.

56. George Packer, *The Assassin's Gate: America in Iraq*, Farrar, Straus and Giroux, 2005, cited by Francis Fukuyama, 'After Neoconservatism', *New York Times*, 19 February 2006.

57. 'Iraq Body Count: War Dead Figures', *BBC News*, 15 May 2006. Available at <http://news.bbc.co.uk/1/hi/world/middle_east/4525412. stm>

58. 'Project Syndicate: The True Costs of the Iraq War', February 2006. <http://www.project-syndicate.org/commentary/stiglitz67>. Joseph Stiglitz and Linda Bilmes, a budget expert at Harvard, estimate that the Iraq war's overall costs are likely to settle in a range of one to two trillion dollars, vastly higher than official estimates.

59. 'Conflict contributes to rising insecurity over energy supply', *The Times*, 7 March 2006. Available at <http://www.timesonline.co.uk/article/0,,5-2072761,00.html>

60. 'Iraqi voters defy the bombers', *Guardian*, 31 January 2005.

61. Report by Alvaro Gil-Robles, Commissioner for Human Rights, On his Visit to the United Kingdom 4–12 November 2004. Available at <http://www.unhcr.org/cgi-bin/texis/vtx/home/opendoc.pdf?tbl= RSDCOI&id=4402c3c94>

62. Ackerman, *Before The Next Attack*.

63. Ibid.

Conclusion

1. Quoted by Guy de Jonquieres in 'The Critical Skills Gap', *Financial Times*, 12 June 2006. Available at <http://www.ft.com/cms/s/733ea3c8-fa38-11da-b7ff-0000779e2340.html>

2. Berger, *How We Compete*, p. 120.

3. David Birnbaum, *Birnbaum's Guide to Winning the Great Garment War*, Third Horizon Press, 2000. Cited by Berger, op. cit., p. 124.

4. Berger, op. cit., p. 125.

5. Ibid., p. 260.

6. Atkinson, *The Past and Future of America's Economy*, p. 124.

7. Berger, op. cit., p. 169.

8. Ibid., p. 68.

9. Ibid., p. 111.

10. Peter Lindert, 'Growing public: is the welfare state mortal or exportable?', lecture delivered at the World Bank, 17 April 2005.

11. See Jeffrey D. Sachs, 'Lessons from the North', Project Syndicate, 2006. On the benefits of child-centred redistribution, see Gøsta Esping-Anderson, op. cit.

12. Zuboff and Maxmin, *The Support Economy*.

13. Ronald Inglehart, *Modernisation and Postmodernisation: Cultural, Economic and Political Change in 43 Societies*, Princeton University Press, 1997. Cited by Zuboff and Maxmin, op. cit., p. 96.

14. For a discussion of definitions of the knowledge economy, see the *Ideopolis Report*, The Work Foundation, 2006.

15. 'Competitive advantage from better interactions', *McKinsey Quarterly*, number 2, 2006.

16. David A. King, 'The Scientific Impact of Nations', *Nature* 430, 2004, pp. 311–16.

17. See The Work Foundation Knowledge Economy Paper 1, 2006, at <www.theworkfoundation.com>.

18. Garrett, 'The Three Worlds of Globalisation: Market Integration, Economic Growth and the Distribution of Income in High, Middle and Low-Income Countries'.

19. See Stephen Roach, 'Scale and the China Challenge', Morgan Stanley Global Economic Forum, 19 June 2006. Available at <http://www.morganstanley.com/GEFdata/digests/20060619-mon.html>

20. See the *International Herald Tribune*: <http://www.iht.com/articles/2006/06/12/bloomberg/sxchitrade.php>

21. See the recent promotion of Qiu He to Deputy Governor of Jiangsu province. He has excelled at old-fashioned mobilisation to the detriment of more lasting institution-building, reported by Joseph Fewsmith in *China Leadership Monitor*, number 17, 2006.

22. Cheng Li, 'Hu's Policy Shift and the Tuanpai's Coming-of-Age', *China Leadership Monitor*, number 15, 2005.

23. Roderick MacFarquhar, 'Rotting from the Inside Out', FP Roundtable: Tale of Two Chinas, *Foreign Policy*, 2006, pp. 71–2. The shock-as-precursor-to-reform thesis forms the centrepiece of Bruce Gilley's crystal ball-gazing in *China's Democratic Future*, op. cit.

24. Offer, *The Challenge of Affluence*.

25. Dumas and Choyleva, *The Bill from the China Shop*.

26. Howard Davies, in his 2005 lecture on financial reform at the London School of Economics, cites Andrew Sheng, chairman of the Hong Kong Securities and Futures Commission, who claims that the return on US fdi (mostly equity) is 12–15 per cent per annum compared to the long-term return on US Treasuries of 4 per cent per annum.

27. Eichengreen, 'Global Imbalances: The New Economy, the Dark Matter, the Savvy Investor and the Standard Analysis'.

28. Boughton, Silent Revolution, p. 208.

29. Robert Brenner, *The Boom and the Bubble: The US in the World Economy*, Verso Books, 2003, p. 64.

30. Stephen Jen, 'The Plaza Accord, Japan, and Lessons for China', Morgan Stanley Global Economic Forum, 4 July 2005. Available at <http://www.morganstanley.com/GEFdata/digests/20050704-mon.html>

31. Barshefsky, 'With or Without Doha'.

32. Ibid.

33. Jochen Sanio, 'Should Hedge Funds Be Regulated?', delivered at the Goldman Sachs Ten Top Financial Risks to the World Economy Conference, 30 September 2005.

34. Joseph E. Stiglitz, 'The Overselling of Globalisation', in Weinstein (ed.), *Globalization: What's New?* See generally, Held, *Global Covenant*.

35. See James Gustave Speth, afterword prepared for the paperback edition of *Red Sky at Morning: America and the Crisis of the Global Environment*, Yale University Press, 2005, p. 3.

36. Speth, op. cit., p. 4.

37. Cited by Speth, op. cit., p. 9.

38. Speth, op. cit., p. 5

39. Jared Diamond, *Collapse: How Societies Choose to Fail or Survive*, Penguin, 2005.

40. Jo Blanden, Paul Gregg and Stephen Machin, 'Social Mobility in Britain: Low and Falling', *CentrePiece*, 2005.

41. Geoff Mason, 'In Search of High Value Added Production: How Important Are Skills?', Department for Education and Skills research report 663, 2005.

42. 'Faith and Knowledge', in Habermas, *The Future of Human Nature*.

BIBLIOGRAPHY

Acemoglu, Daron, 'Technical Change, Inequality and the Labor Market', *Journal of Economic Literature*, volume 40 (2002), pp. 7–72

Acemoglu, Daron, Simon Johnson and James Robinson, 'The Rise of Europe: Atlantic Trade, Institutional Change, and Economic Growth', *The American Economic Review*, volume 95, number 3 (2005), pp. 546–79

Acemoglu, Daron and James A. Robinson, *Economic Origins of Dictatorship and Democracy* (Cambridge: CUP, 2006)

Ackerman, Bruce, *Before The Next Attack: Preserving Civil Liberties in an Age of Terrorism* (New Haven: Yale University Press, 2006)

Aghion, Philippe and Steven N. Durlauf (eds.), *Handbook of Economic Growth*, volumes 1A and 1B (London: Elsevier North-Holland, 2005)

Alagappa, Muthiah (ed.), *Asian Security Practice: Material and Ideational Differences* (Stanford: Stanford University Press, 1998)

Albert, Michel, *Capitalism against Capitalism* (London: Whurr Publishers, 1993)

Alesina, Alberto and Edward L. Glaser, *Fighting Poverty in the US and Europe: A World of Difference* (Oxford: OUP, 2004)

Alford, William, 'Double-edged swords cut both ways: law and legitimacy in the People's Republic of China', *Daedalus* (1993)

Alpermann, Björn, 'The post-election administration of Chinese villages', *China Journal*, volume 46 (2001), pp. 45–68

Amsden, Alice, *The Rise of 'The Rest': Challenges to the West from Late-Industrialising Economies* (Oxford: OUP, 2001)

Ansolabehere, Stephen, Roy Behr and Shanto Iyengar, *The Media Game: American Politics in the Television Age* (New York: Macmillan, 1993)

Aoki, Masahiko, Hyung-Ki Kim and Masahiro Okuno-Fujiwara (eds.), *The Role of Government in East Asian Economic Development: Comparative Institutional Analysis* (Oxford: Clarendon Press, 1997)

Arendt, Hannah, *The Human Condition* (New York: Doubleday Anchor, 1958)

Arrighi, Giovanni, *The Long Twentieth Century* (London: Verso Books, 1994)

Arrighi, Giovanni, Takeshi Hamashita and Mark Selden (eds.), *The Resurgence of East Asia: 500, 150 and 50 Year Perspectives* (London: Routledge, 2003)

Asian Development Bank, *Country Economic Review: People's Republic of China*, CEP-PRC 2000-09, 2000

Atkinson, Robert D., *The Past and Present of America's Economy* (Cheltenham: Edward Elgar, 2004)

Autor, David H., Lawrence F. Katz and Melissa S. Kearney, 'Trends in US Wage Inequality: Re-Assessing the Revisionists', unpublished, 2005

Axelrod, Robert, *The Evolution of Cooperation*, (London: Penguin, 2004)

Baily, Martin N., Eric J. Bartelsman and John Haltiwanger, 'Downsizing and Productivity Growth: Myth or Reality?' Small Business Economics 8(4) (1996), pp. 259–78, reprinted in David G. Mayes (ed.), *Sources of Productivity Growth* (Cambridge: CUP, 1996)

Bairoch, Paul, *Economics and World History – Myths and Paradoxes* (Brighton: Wheatsheaf, 1993)

Barber, Benjamin R., *Jihad vs McWorld: Terrorism's Challenge to Democracy* (New York: Ballantine Books, 2001)

Bardhan, Pranab, *Scarcity, Conflicts and Cooperation: Essays in the Political and Institutional Economics of Development* (Cambridge, MA: MIT Press, 2005)

Barfield, Claude, *High-Tech Protectionism: The Irrationality of Antidumping Laws* (Washington DC: American Economic Institute, 2003)

Barkow, Jerome H., Leda Cosmides and John Tooby, *The Adapted Mind: Evolutionary Psychology and the Generation of Culture* (Oxford: OUP, 1992)

Barry, Brian, *Why Social Justice Matters* (Cambridge: Polity, 2005)

Barshefsky, Charlene, 'With or Without Doha', *Foreign Affairs*, WTO special edition (2005)

Bartels, Larry, 'Homer Gets a Tax Cut: Inequality and Public Policy in the American Mind', *Perspectives on Politics*, volume 3, number 1 (2005), pp. 15–31

Basu, Prasenjit K., 'India and the Knowledge Economy: The "Stealth Miracle" is Sustainable', in Prasenjit K. Basu, Brahma Chellaney, Parag Khanna and Sunil Khilani, *India as a New Global Leader* (London: Foreign Policy Centre, 2005)

Bates, Robert H., Avner Greif, Margaret Levi, Jean-Laurent Rosenthal and Barry R. Weingast, *Analytic Narratives* (Princeton: Princeton University Press, 1998)

Bauer, Joanne R. and Daniel A. Bell, *The East Asian Challenge for Human Rights* (Cambridge: CUP, 1999)

Baum, Richard, *Burying Mao: Chinese Politics in the Age of Deng* (Princeton: Princeton University Press, 1994)

Baumol, William J., *The Free Market Innovation Machine: Analyzing the Growth Miracle of Capitalism* (Princeton: Princeton University Press, 2004)

Baumol, William J., Alan S. Blinder and Edward N. Wolff, *Downsizing in America: Reality, Causes and Consequences* (Russell Sage Foundation, 2003)

Bayly, C. A., *The Birth of the Modern World 1780–1914* (Oxford: Blackwell Publishing, 2004)

Bebchuk, Lucien A, and Jesse M. Fried, *Pay without Performance: The Unfulfilled Promise of Executive Compensation* (Cambridge, MA: Harvard University Press, 2004)

Beck, Ulrich, *The Brave New World of Work* (Cambridge: Polity, 2001)

Beck, Ulrich, Anthony Giddens and Scott Lash (eds.), *Reflexive Modernization: Politics, Tradition and Aesthetics in the Modern Social Order* (Stanford: Stanford University Press, 1994)

Beisner, Robert L., *From the Old Diplomacy to the New* (Arlington Heights: Harlan Davidson, second edition 1986)

Bell, Daniel A. and Hahm Chaibong (eds.), *Confucianism for the Modern World* (Cambridge: CUP, 2003)

Benabou, Roland, 'Unequal Societies: Income Distribution and the Social Contract', *American Economic Review*, volume 90 (2000), pp. 96–129

Ben-Ner, Avner and Louis Putterman, *Economics, Values and Organization* (Cambridge: CUP, 1999)

Berger, Suzanne, *How We Compete: What Companies Around the World are Doing to Make It in Today's Global Economy* (New York: Doubleday, 2005)

Bergsten, Fred (ed.), *The United States and the World Economy* (Washington DC: Institute for International Economics, 2005)

Berle, Adolf A. and Gardiner C. Means, *The Modern Corporation and Private Property* (New York: Harcourt, Brace & World, [1932] 1968)

Bernstein, Peter L., *Against the Gods: The Remarkable Story of Risk* (New York: John Wiley, 1996)

Bhagwati, Jagdish (ed.), *Going Alone* (Cambridge, MA: MIT Press, 2002)

Bhagwati, Jagdish, 'From Seattle to Hong Kong', *Foreign Affairs*, WTO special edition (2005)

Bhagwati, Jagdish and Douglas Irwin, 'The Return of the Reciprocitarians: US Trade Policy Today', *The World Economy* 10 (1987), pp. 109–30, reprinted in Kevin O'Rourke (ed.), *The International Trading System: Globalization and History* (Camberley: Edward Elgar, 2005)

Blanchard, Olivier, Jean Pisani-Ferry and Charles Wyplosz, *L'Europe Declassée* (Paris: Flammarion, 2005)

Blanchard, Olivier, Francesco Givazzi and Filipa Sa, 'The US Current Account and the Dollar', *Brookings Papers on Economic Activity* 1 (2006), pp. 1–49

Blecher, Marc, *China against the Tides: Restructuring through Revolution, Radicalism and Reform* (London: Continuum International Publishing, 2003)

Blinder, Alan, 'Offshoring; the next Industrial Revolution', *Foreign Affairs*, volume 85, number 2 (2006)

Blonigen, Bruce A., 'Evolving Practices of US Antidumping activity', NBER Working Paper 9625, 2003

Bloom, David and Jeffrey D. Sachs, 'Geography, Demography, and Economic Growth in Africa', *Brookings Papers on Economic Activity* 2 (1998), pp. 207–73

Bobbitt, P., *The Shield of Achilles – War, Peace and the Course of History* (London: Allen Lane, 2002)

Bogle, John C., *The Battle for the Soul of Capitalism* (New Haven: Yale University Press, 2005)

Boltanski, Luc and Eve Chiapello, *The New Spirit of Capitalism* (London: Verso Books, 2005)

Bordo, Michael D., Barry Eichengreen and Douglas A. Irwin, 'Is Globalization Today Really Different than Globalization a Hundred Years Ago?' NBER Working Paper 7195, 1999

Boughton, James M., *Silent Revolution: The International Monetary Fund 1979–1989* (Washington DC: International Monetary Fund, 2001)

Bowen, William G., Martin A. Kurzweil and Eugene M. Tobin, *Equity and Excellence in American Higher Education* (Charlottesville: University of Virginia Press, 2005)

Braithwaite, John and Peter Drahos, *Information Feudalism: Who Owns the Knowledge Economy* (New York: W. W. Norton, 2003)

Bramall, Chris, *Sources of Chinese Economic Growth 1978–96* (Oxford: OUP, 2000)

Braudel, Fernand, *Civilization and Capitalism, 15th–18th Century: The Wheels of Commerce*, volume 2 (Berkeley: University of California Press, 1992)

Bronfenbrenner, Kate and Stephanie Luce, 'The Changing Nature of Corporate Global Restructuring: The Impact of Production Shifts on Jobs in the US, China and Around the Globe', submitted to the US–China Economic and Security Review Commission, 2004

Burden, Barry, 'Candidate positioning in US congressional elections', *British Journal of Political Science* 34 (2) (2004), pp. 211–27

Buss, David M., *Evolutionary Psychology: The New Science of the Mind* (Boston: Allyn and Bacon, 1999)

Buzen, Barry and Rosemary Foot, *Does China Matter? A Reassessment* (Oxford: Routledge, 2004)

Card, David and John E. DiNardo, 'Skill-Biased Technological Change and Rising Wage Inequality: Some Problems and Puzzles', *Journal of Labor Economics* 20 (2002), pp. 733–83

Carpenter, Ted Galen, *America's Coming War with China* (Basingstoke: Palgrave Macmillan, 2006)

Castells, Manuel, *The Rise of the Network Society: The Information Age: Economy, Culture and Society*, volume 1 (Oxford: Blackwell Publishing, second edition 2000)

Castells, Manuel, *The Power of Identity: The Information Age: Economy, Culture and Society*, volume 2 (Oxford: Blackwell Publishing, second edition 2004)

Castells, Manuel, *End of Millennium: The Information Age: Economy, Society and Culture*, volume 3 (Oxford: Blackwell Publishing, second edition 2000)

Chan, Sylvia, *Liberalism, Democracy and Development* (Cambridge: CUP, 2002)

Chandler, Alfred, *The Visible Hand* (Cambridge, MA: Harvard University Press, 1977)

Chandler, Alfred D. Jr. and James W. Cortada (eds.), *A Nation Transformed by Information* (Oxford: OUP, 2000)

Chang, Ha-Joon, *Kicking Away the Ladder: Development Strategy in Historical Perspective* (London: Anthem Press, 2002)

Chang, Jung and Jon Halliday, *Mao: The Unknown Story* (London: Random House, 2005)

Chang, Maria Hsia, 'The Thought of Deng Xiaoping', *Communist and Post-Communist Studies*, volume 29, number 4 (1996), pp. 371–94

Chen, An, 'The New Inequality', *Journal of Democracy*, volume 14, number 1 (2003)

Chen, Jie, 'Assessing Political Support in China', *Journal of Contemporary China* 6 (16) (1997), pp. 551–67

Christensen, Clayton M., *The Innovator's Dilemma* (Boston: Harvard Business School Press, 1997)

Cline, William R., 'Doha and Development', *Foreign Affairs*, WTO special edition (2005)

Cohen, Daniel, *Modern Times: The New Nature of Capitalism in the Information Age* (Cambridge, MA: MIT Press, 2003)

Cohen, Daniel, *Globalization and Its Enemies* (Cambridge, MA: MIT Press, 2006)

Cohen, Edward S., *The Politics of Globalization in the United States* (Washington DC: Georgetown University Press, 2001)

Collier, Paul, *Economic Causes of Civil Conflict and their Implications for Policy* (Washington DC: World Bank, 2000)

Collins, Jim and Jerry I. Porras, *Built to Last: Successful Habits of Visionary Companies* (New York: HarperBusiness, 1994)

Deng, Kent, *The Premodern Chinese Economy: Structural Equilibrium and Capitalist Sterility* (London: Routledge, 2003)

Desai, Meghnad, 'India and China: An Essay in Comparative Political Economy', International Monetary Fund Conference on India and China, New Delhi, 2003

de Soto, Hernando, *The Mystery of Capital: Why Capitalism Triumphs in the West and Fails Elsewhere Else* (London: Black Swan, 2001)

Destler, I. M., *American Trade Politics* (Washington DC: Institute for International Economics, fourth edition 2005)

Dew-Becker, Ian and Robert Gordon, 'Where did the Productivity Growth Go? Inflation Dynamics and the Distribution of Income', paper presented at the 81st meeting of the Brookings Panel on Economic Activity, 2005

Dickson, Bruce, *Red Capitalists in China: The Party, Private Entrepreneurs, and Prospects for Political Change* (Cambridge: CUP, 2003)

Diamond, Larry, 'Thinking About Hybrid Regimes', *Journal of Democracy* 13(2) (2002), pp. 21–35

Dixit, Avinash K., *Lawlessness and Economics: Alternative Modes of Governance* (Princeton: Princeton University Press, 2004)

Drake, William J. and Kalypso Nicolaidis, 'Ideas, Interests and Institutionalization: Trade in Services and the Uruguay Round', *International Organization*, volume 46, number 1 (1992), pp. 37–100

Dreze, Jean and Amartya Sen, *India: Economic Development and Social Opportunity* (New York: OUP, 1995)

Drifte, Reinhard, *Japan's Foreign Policy for the 21st Century* (Basingstoke: Palgrave Macmillan, 1998)

Dumas, Charles and Diana Choyleva, *The Bill from the China Shop: How Asia's Savings Glut Threatens the World Economy* (London: Profile Books, 2006)

Dunn, John, *Setting People Free: The Story of Democracy* (London: Atlantic Books, 2005)

Dunsire, Andrew, 'Tipping the Balance: Autopoiesis and Governance', *Administration and Society*, volume 28, number 3 (1996), pp. 299–334

Dutton, William, Brian Kahin, Ramon O'Callaghan and Andrew W. Wyckoff, *Transforming Enterprise: The Economic and Social Implications of Information Technology* (Cambridge, MA: MIT Press, 2005)

Easterly, William, *The Elusive Quest for Growth: Economists' Adventures and Misadventures in the Tropics* (Cambridge, MA: MIT Press, 2001)

Easterly, William, *The White Man's Burden: Why the West's Efforts to Aid the Rest have done Much Ill and so Little Good* (New York: Penguin, 2006)

Easterly, William, Jo Ritzen and Michael Woolcock, 'Social Cohesion, Institutions and Growth', unpublished paper, 2005

Eckes Jr., Alfred E. and Thomas W. Zeiler, *Globalization and the American Century* (Cambridge: CUP, 2003)

Economy, Elizabeth, *The River Runs Black: The Environmental Challenge to China's Future* (Ithaca: Cornell University Press, 2004)

Ehrenreich, Barbara, *Bait and Switch: The (Futile) Pursuit of the American Dream* (New York: Metropolitan Books, 2005)

Eichengreen, Barry, 'Global Imbalances: The New Economy, the Dark Matter, the Savvy Investor, and the Standard Analysis', *Journal of Policy Modelling*, forthcoming, 2006

Ellerman, David, *Helping People Help Themselves: From the World Bank to an Alternative Philosophy of Development Assistance* (Ann Arbor: University of Michigan Press, 2006)

Evensky, Jerry, *Adam Smith's Moral Philosophy: A Historical Perspective and Contemporary Perspective on Markets, Law, Ethics and Culture* (Cambridge: CUP, 2005)

Fairbank, John, *The United States and China* (American Foreign Political Library; Cambridge MA: Harvard University Press, 1989)

Fairbank, John King, *China: A New History* (Cambridge, MA: Harvard University Press, 1992)

Farber, Henry, 'What do we know about Job Loss in the United States? Evidence from the Displaced Workers Survey, 1984–2004', Princeton Working Paper 498, 2005

Fenby, Jonathan, *Generalissimo: Chiang Kai-shek and the China He Lost* (New York: Simon & Schuster, 2003)

Feng, Yi, (Cambridge, MA: MIT Press, 2005)

Democracy, Governance, and Economic Performance: Theory and Evidence

Ferguson, Niall, *The Cash Nexus: Money and Politics in Modern History, 1700–2000* (London: Penguin, 2002)

Ferguson, Niall, *Colossus: The Rise and Fall of the American Empire* (London: Penguin, 2004)

Fernie, Sue and David Metcalf (eds.), *Trade Unions: Resurgence or Demise?* (London: Routledge, 2005)

Finlay, Robert, 'China, the World and World History in Joseph Needham's *Science and Civilisation*', *Journal of World History*, volume 11, number 2 (2000), pp. 265–303

Florida, Richard, *The Rise of the Creative Class* (New York: Basic Books, 2002)

Florida, Richard and Gary Gates, 'Technology and Tolerance', The Brookings Institution Survey Series, 2001

Fogel, Robert William, *The Fourth Great Awakening and the Future of Egalitarianism* (Chicago: Chicago University Press, 2000)

Fortin, Nicole M. and Thomas Lemieux, 'Institutional Changes and Rising Wage Inequality: Is there a Linkage?', *Journal of Economic Perspectives*, volume 11, number 2 (1997), pp. 75–95

Forsberg, Aaron, *America and the Japanese Miracle: The Cold War Context of Japan's Postwar Economic Revival 1950–1960* (Chapel Hill: University of North Carolina Press, 2000)

Frank, Robert H. and Philip Cook, *The Winner-Take-All Society* (New York: Free Press, 1995)

Frankel, Jeffrey, 'Globalization and the Economy', in J. Nye and J. Donahue (eds.), *Governance in a Globalizing World* (Washington DC: Brookings Institution, 2002)

Freeman, Richard B., 'What, Me Vote?', NBER Working Paper W9896, 2003

Freeman, Richard B. and Joel Rogers, *What Do Workers Want?* (Ithaca: Cornell University ILR Press, 1999)

Frieden, Jeffrey A., *Global Capitalism: Its Fall and Rise in the Twentieth Century* (London: W. W. Norton, 2006)

Friedman, Benjamin M., *The Moral Consequences of Economic Growth* (New York: Knopf, 2005)

Friedman, Edward and Barrett L. McCormick (eds.), *What If China Doesn't Democratize: Implications for War and Peace* (Armonk: M. E. Sharpe, 2000)

Friedman, Thomas L., *The World Is Flat: The Globalized World in the Twenty-first Century* (London: Penguin, 2005)

Fukuyama, Francis, *After the Neocons: America at the Crossroads* (London: Profile Books, 2006)

Galbraith, J. K., *American Capitalism: The Concept of Countervailing Power* (London: Hamish Hamilton, 1952)

Gale, William, 'Effects of Recent Tax Cuts on Marginal Tax Rates', Tax Policy Center: Urban Institute and Brookings Institution, 2005

Galston, William A., *Public Matters: Politics, Policy and Religion in the 21st Century* (Lanham: Rowman & Littlefield, 2005)

Galston, William A. and Elaine C. Kamarck, 'The Politics of Polarization', The Third Way Middle Class Project, 2005

Garrett, Geoffrey, 'The Three Worlds of Globalization: Market Integration, Economic Growth and the Distribution of Income in High, Middle and Low-Income Countries', UCLA Working Paper, 2004

Gates, Hill, *China's Motor: A Thousand Years of Petty Capitalism* (Ithaca: Cornell University Press, 1996)

Gentzkow, Matthew, Edward Glaeser and Claudia Goldin, 'The Rise of the Fourth Estate: How Newspapers Became Informative and Why it Matters', NBER Working Paper 10791, 2004

Giddens, Anthony and Patrick Diamond (eds.), *The New Egalitarianism* (Cambridge: Polity, 2005)

Gilboy, George, 'The Myth Behind China's Miracle', *Foreign Affairs* (2004)

Gilboy, George J. and Eric Heginbotham, 'The Latin Americanization of China', *Current History* (2004), pp. 256–61

Gilley, Bruce, *China's Democratic Future: How It Will Happen and Where it Will Lead* (New York: Columbia University Press, 2004)

Gilpin, Robert, *Global Political Economy: Understanding the International Order* (Princeton: Princeton University Press, 2001)

Gilpin, Robert, *The Challenge of Global Capitalism* (Princeton: Princeton University Press, 2001)

Gintis, Herbert, Samuel Bowles, Robert Boyd and Ernst Fehr, *Moral Sentiments and Material Interests: The Foundation of Cooperation in Economic Life* (Cambridge, MA: MIT Press, 2005)

Gittings, John, *The Changing Face of China: From Mao to Market* (Oxford: OUP, 2005)

Glaeser, Edward and Andrei Shleifer, 'The Rise of the Regulatory State', *Journal of Economic Literature*, volume 41, number 2 (2003), pp. 401–25

Godement, François, *The Downsizing of Asia* (Oxford: Routledge, 1998)

Goldin, Claudia and Lawernce F. Katz, 'Decreasing (and then Increasing) Inequality in America: A Tale of Two Half-Centuries', in F. Welch (ed.), *The Causes and Consequences of Increasing Income Inequality* (Chicago: University of Chicago Press, 2001)

Goldin, Claudia and Lawrence F. Katz, 'The "Virtues" of the Past: Education in the First Hundred Years of the New Republic', NBER Working Paper 9958, 2003

Goldstein, Avery, *Rising to the Challenge: China's Grand Strategy and International Security* (Stanford: Stanford University Press, 2005)

Goodman, David S. and Gerald Segal, *China Deconstructs: Politics, Trade and Regionalism* (London: Routledge, 1995)

Goody, Jack, *East in the West* (Cambridge: CUP, 1996)

Goos, Maarten and Alan Manning, 'Lousy and Lovely Jobs: The Rising Polarization of Work in Britain', unpublished paper, Centre for Economic Performance London School of Economics, 2003

Gowa, Joanne, *Allies, Adversaries and International Trade* (Princeton: Princeton University Press, 1994)

Gray, John, *The Moral Foundations of Market Institutions* (London: IEA Health and Welfare Unit, 1992)

Gray, John, *False Dawn: The Delusions of Global Capitalism* (New York: New Press, 1999)

Green, Stephen and Guy S. Liu (eds.), *Exit the Dragon? Privatization and State Control in China* (Oxford: Blackwell Publishing, 2005)

Greenfield, Liah, *The Spirit of Capitalism* (Cambridge, MA: Harvard University Press, 2003)

Greider, William, *One World, Ready or Not: The Manic Logic of Global Capitalism* (New York: Touchstone, 1998)

Greider, William, *The Soul of Capitalism: Opening Paths to a Moral Economy* (New York: Simon & Schuster, 2003)

Gries, Peter Hay, 'Chinese Nationalism: Challenging the State?' *Current History*, volume 104, number 683 (2005), pp. 251–6

Guo Yong and Angang Hu, 'The administrative monopoly in China's economic transition', *Communist and Post-Communist Studies* 37 (2004), pp. 265–80

Guo Zhenglin and Thomas Bernstein, 'The Impact of Elections on the Village Structure of Power: the relations between the village committees and the Party branches', *Journal of Contemporary China* 13(39) (2004), pp. 257–75

Habermas, Jürgen, *The Structural Transformation of the Public Sphere* (Cambridge: Polity, 1999)

Habermas, Jürgen, *The Future of Human Nature* (Cambridge: Polity, 2003)

Hacker, Jacob S. and Paul Pierson, *Off Center: The Republican Revolution and the Erosion of American Democracy* (New Haven: Yale University Press, 2005)

Halperin, Morton H., Joseph T. Siegle and Michael M. Weinstein, *The Democracy Advantage: How Democracies Promote Prosperity and Peace* (New York: Routledge 2005)

Hanser, Amy, 'Made in the PRC: China's Consumer Revolution', *Current History*, volume 104, number 683 (2005), pp. 272–7

Hart, Oliver, *Firms, Contracts and Financial Structure* (Oxford: Clarendon Press, 1995)

Hartwell, R. M., *The Industrial Revolution and Economic Growth* (London: Methuen, 1971)

He Qinglian, *Zhongguo de Xianjing* [China's Pitfall] (Hong Kong: Mingjing Chubanshe, 1998)

Heginbotham, Eric and Christopher P. Twomey, 'America's Bismarckian Asia Policy', *Current History*, volume 104, number 683 (2005), pp. 243–50

Held, David, *Global Covenant: The Social Democratic Alternative to the Washington Consensus* (Cambridge: Polity, 2004)

Held, David and Anthony McGrew (eds.), *The Global Transformations Reader* (Cambridge: Polity, second edition 2003)

Hirschman, Albert, 'Pillars of Order: Social Conflicts as Pillars of Democratic Market Society', *Political Theory*, volume 22, number 22 (1994)

Hirschman, Albert, *The Passion and the Interests: Political Arguments for Capitalism Before Its Triumph* (Princeton: Princeton University Press, 1997)

Hiscox, Michael J., *International Trade and Political Conflict: Commerce, Coalitions and Mobility* (Princeton: Princeton University Press, 2002)

Hope, Nicholas C., Dennis Tao Yang and Mu Yang Li, *How Far Across the River?* (Stanford: Stanford University Press, 2003)

Hu, Angang, *Guoqing yu Fazhan* [The National Condition and Development] (Beijing: Qinghua Daxue Chubanshe, 2005)

Hu, Angang, *Yuanzhu yu Fazhan* [Support and Development] (Beijing: Qinghua Daxue Chubanshe, 2005)

Huang, Yasheng, *Selling China: Foreign Investment During the Reform Era* (Cambridge: CUP, 2002)

Huang, Yasheng, Tony Saich and Edward Steinfeld (eds.), *Financial Sector Reform in China* (Cambridge, MA: Harvard University Press, 2005)

Hughes, Christopher R., *Chinese Nationalism in the Global Era* (Oxford: Routledge, 2006)

Hughes, Neil C., 'A Trade War with China?', *Foreign Affairs* (2005)

Huntingdon, Samuel, *Political Order in Changing Societies* (New Haven: Yale University Press, 1968)

Hussain, Athar, 'Repairing China's Social Safety Net', *Current History*, volume 104, number 683 (2005), pp. 268–71

Ignatieff, Michael, *The Lesser Evil: Political Ethics in an Age of Terror* (Princeton: Princeton University Press, 2004)

Inglehart, Ronald and Christian Weizel, *Modernization, Cultural Change, and Democracy: The Human Development Sequence* (Cambridge: CUP, 2005)

International Institute for Strategic Studies, *Military Balance 2005–2006* (Oxford: Routledge, 2005)

International Monetary Fund, *World Economic Outlook: Globalization and External Balances* (Washington DC: International Monetary Fund, 2005)

International Monetary Fund, *World Economic Outlook: Building Institutions* (Washington DC: International Monetary Fund, 2005)

Irwin, Douglas A., *Free Trade Under Fire* (Princeton: Princeton University Press, 2002)

Irwin, Douglas A., 'Tariffs and Growth in Late Nineteenth Century America', *The World Economy* 24 (1) (2001), pp. 15–30

Isaacs, Harold, *Scratches on Our Mind: American Views of China and India* (New York: M. E. Sharpe, 1958)

James, Harold, *The End of Globalization: Lessons from the Great Depression* (Cambridge, MA: Harvard University Press, 2001)

James, Harold, *The Roman Predicament: How the Rules of International Order Create the Politics of Empire* (Princeton: Princeton University Press, 2006)

Johnson, Chalmers A., *MITI and the Japanese Miracle* (Stanford: Stanford University Press, 1982)

Johnson, Chalmers A., *Blowback: The Costs and Consequences of American Empire* (New York: Time Warner Books, 2002)

Johnston, Alistair Iain, *Cultural Realism: Strategic Culture and Grand Strategy in Chinese History* (Princeton: Princeton University Press, 1998)

Johnston, Alistair Iain, 'Chinese Middle Class Attitudes Towards International Affairs: Nascent Liberalization?', *China Quarterly*, 179/1 (2004)

Johnston, Alistair Iain and Robert Ross (eds.), *Engaging China: The Management of an Emerging Power* (London: Routledge, 1999)

Johnston, Michael, *Syndromes of Corruption: Wealth, Power and Democracy* (Cambridge: CUP, 2005)

Jones, Eric L., *The European Miracle: Environments, Economies and Geopolitics in the History of Europe and Asia* (Cambridge: CUP, 2003)

Jones, Eric L., *Cultures Merging: A Historical and Economic Critique of Culture* (Princeton: Princeton University Press, 2006)

Kagan, Robert and William Kristol, *Present Dangers: Crisis and Opportunity in American Foreign and Defense Policy* (San Francisco: Encounter Books, 2000)

Kahan, Dan M., 'The Logic of Reciprocity: Trust, Collective Action and Law', *Michigan Law Review*, vol 102: 71 (2003)

Katz, Richard, *The System that Soured: The Rise and the Fall of the Japanese Miracle* (Armonk: M. E. Sharpe, 1998)

Kaufmann, Daniel, Aart Kraay and Massimo Mastuzzi, 'Governance Matters IV: Governance Indicators for 1996–2004', The World Bank, Working Paper 3630, 2005

Kay, John, *The Truth About Markets: Their Genius, Their Limits, Their Follies* (London: Allen Lane, 2003)

Keene, Thomas R. (ed.), *Flying on One Engine: Fourteen Views of the World Economy* (New York: Bloomberg Press, 2005)

Keynes, John Maynard, *A Treatise on Money: Volume 2* (London, Palgrave MacMillan, 1971)

King, Desmond, *The Liberty of Strangers: Making the American Nation* (Oxford: OUP, 2005)

Kissinger, Henry, *Does America Need a Foreign Policy: Toward a Diplomacy for the 21st Century* (New York: Touchstone, 2002)

Klare, Michael, *Blood and Oil: How America's Thirst for Petrol is Killing Us* (London: Penguin, 2005)

Kletzer, Lori, *Imports, Exports and Jobs: What Does Trade Mean for Employment and Job Loss?* (Michigan: Upjohn Institute for Employment Research, 2002)

Kloppenberg, James, *The Virtues of Liberalism* (New York: OUP, 1998)

Knack, S. and P. Keefer, 'Does social capital have an economic payoff? A cross-country investigation', *Quarterly Journal of Economics* 112(4) (1997), pp. 1251–88

Kochan, Thomas A., *Restoring the American Dream: A Working Families' Agenda for America* (Cambridge, MA: MIT Press, 2005)

Kornai, Janos and Susan Rose-Ackerman, *Building a Trustworthy State in Post-Socialist Transition* (Basingstoke: Palgrave Macmillan, 2004)

Kynge, James, *China Shakes the World: The Rise of a Hungry Nation* (London: Weidenfeld & Nicolson, 2006)

LaFeber, Walter, *The New Empire: An Interpretation of American Expansion, 1860–1898* (Ithaca: Cornell University Press, 1963)

LaFeber, Walter, *The Cambridge History of American Foreign Relations: Volume 2, The American Search for Opportunity, 1865–1913* (Cambridge: CUP, 1995)

Lake, David, *Power, Protection, and Free Trade: International Sources of US Commercial Strategy, 1887–1939* (Ithaca: Cornell University Press, 1988)

Lampton, David, *Same Beds, Different Dreams: Managing US -China Relations 1989–2000* (Berkeley: University of California Press, 2002)

Landau, Ralph, Timothy Taylor and Gavin Wright (eds.), *The Mosaic of Economic Growth* (Stanford: Stanford University Press, 1996)

Landes, David, *The Wealth and Poverty of Nations* (New York: W. W. Norton, 1998)

Lardy, Nicholas, *China's Unfinished Economic Revolution* (Washington DC: The Brookings Institution, 1998)

Lardy, Nicholas, *Integrating China into the Global Economy* (Washington DC: The Brookings Institution, 2001)

Lee, David S., 'Wage Inequality in the US during the 1980s: Rising Dispersion or Falling Minimum Wage?', *Quarterly Journal of Economics* 114 (1999), pp. 977–1023

Leifer, Michael (ed.), *Asian Nationalism* (Oxford: Routledge 2000)

Lemieux, Thomas, 'Decomposing Changes in Wage Distributions: A Unified Approach', *Canadian Journal of Economics* 35(4) (2002), pp. 646–88

Lester, Richard K. and Michael J. Piore, *Innovation: The Missing Dimension* (Cambridge, MA: Harvard University Press, 2004)

Levy, Frank and Richard J. Murnane, *The New Division of Labor: How*

Computers are Creating the Next Job Market (Princeton: Princeton University Press, 2004)

Lewis, William W., *The Power of Productivity: Wealth, Poverty and the Threat to Global Stability* (Chicago: University of Chicago Press, 2004)

Li Bozhong, *Agricultural Development in Jiangnan, 1620–1850* (Basingstoke: Palgrave Macmillan, 1998)

Lieberthal, Kenneth, *Governing China: From Revolution through Reform* (London: W. W. Norton, 1995)

Lieven, Anatol, *America: Right or Wrong* (London: Harper Collins, 2004)

Lin, Chun (ed.), *China, Volume 2, The transformation of Chinese Socialism* (Aldershot: Ashgate-Dartmouth, 2000)

Lin, Yimin, *Between Politics and Markets: Firms, Competition, and Institutional Change in Post-Mao China* (Cambridge: CUP, 2002)

Lin, Justin Yifu, Fang Cai and Zhou Li, *The China Miracle*, (Hong Kong: Chinese University Press, 2003)

Lind, Michael, *Vietnam: The Necessary War – A Reinterpretation of America's Most Disastrous Military Conflict* (New York: Simon & Schuster, 2002)

Lind, Michael, *Made in Texas: George W. Bush and the Southern Takeover of American Politics* (New York: Basic Books, 2004)

Lindert, Peter H., 'Voice and Growth: Was Churchill Right?', *Journal of Economic History* 63 (2003), pp. 315–50

Lindert, Peter H., *Growing Public: Social Spending and Economic Growth since the Eighteenth Century. Volume 1 – The Story* (Cambridge: CUP, 2004)

Lipset, Seymour Martin, Noah M. Meltz, Rafael Gomez and Ivan Katchanovski, *The Paradox of American Unionism: Why Americans Like Unions More Than Canadians Do, but Join Much Less* (Ithaca: Cornell University ILR Press, 2004)

Liu Yaling, 'Reform from Below: The Private Economy and Local Politics in the Rural Industrialization of Wenzhou', *China Quarterly* 130 (1992)

Lorsch, Jay W., Leslie Berlowitz and Andy Zelleke, *Restoring Trust in American Business* (Cambridge, MA: MIT Press, 2005)

Lovett, A. William, Alfred E. Eckes Jr. and Richard L. Brinkman, *US Trade Policy: History, Theory and the WTO* (Armonk: M. E. Sharpe, 2004)

Lu, Xiaobo, *Cadres and Corruption: The Organizational Involution of the Chinese Communist Party* (Stanford: Stanford University Press, 2001)

Lubman, Stanley B., *Bird in a Cage: Legal Reform in China After Mao* (Stanford: Stanford University Press, 2000)

Lynn, Barry, *End of the Line: The Rise and Coming Fall of the Global Corporation* (New York: Doubleday, 2005)

McCarty, Keith T. Poole and Howard Rosenthal, *Polarized America: The Dance of Ideology and Unequal Riches* (Cambridge, MA: MIT Press, 2006)

McCormack, Gavan, *The Emptiness of Japanese Affluence* (Armonk: M. E. Sharpe, second edition 2001)

McCormick, Barrett and Jonathan Unger (eds.), *China after Socialism: In the Footsteps of Eastern Europe or East Asia?* (Armonk: M. E. Sharpe, 1995)

MacFarquhar, Roderick, *Origins of the Cultural Revolution*, 3 volumes (Oxford: OUP, 1974, 1983, 1999)

McNeil, John Robert and William H. McNeil, *The Human Web: A Bird's Eye of World History* (New York: W. W. Norton, 2004)

Machin, Stephen and Anna Vignobles, *What's the Good of Education? The Economics of Education* (Princeton: Princeton University Press, 2005)

Maddison, Angus, *The World Economy: A Millennial Perspective* (Paris: Development Centre of the OECD, 2001)

Maddison, Angus, *Growth and Interaction in the World Economy: The Roots of Modernity* (Washington DC: AEI Press, 2005)

Mahbubani, Kishore, *Can Asians Think?* (Singapore and Kuala Lumpur: Times Books International, 1998)

Maier, Charles S., *Among Empires: American Ascendancy and Its Predecessors* (Cambridge, MA: Harvard University Press, 2006)

Mankiw, Gregory N. and Phillip L. Swagel, 'Antidumping: The Third Rail of Trade Policy', *Foreign Affairs*, WTO special edition (2005)

Mansfield, Edward D., *Power, Trade & War* (Princeton: Princeton University Press, 1994)

Maravall, Jose M. and Adam Przeworski, *Democracy and the Rule of Law* (Cambridge: CUP, 2003)

Marglin, Stephen A. and Juliet B. Schor, *The Golden Age of Capitalism: Reinterpreting the Post-war Experience* (Oxford: Clarendon Press, 1990)

Maslow, A., *Motivation and Personality* (New York: Harper Row, 1987)

Massing, Michael, 'The End of News', *New York Review of Books*, volume 52, number 19 (2005)

Massing, Michael, 'The Press; The Enemy Within', *New York Review of Books*, volume 52, number 20 (2005)

Marquand, David, *Decline of the Public* (London: Polity, 2004)

Mayer, Frederick W., *Interpreting NAFTA: The Science and Art of Political Analysis* (New York: Columbia University Press, 1998)

Mead, Walter Russell, *Special Providence: American Foreign Policy and How It Changed the World* (New York: Knopf, 2001)

Mead, Walter Russell, *Power, Terror, Peace, and War: America's Grand Strategy in a World at Risk* (New York: Vintage, 2005)

Mearsheimer, John, *The Tragedy of Great Power Politics* (New York: W. W. Norton, 2001)

Meisner, Maurice, *Marxism, Maoism, and Utopianism: Eight Essays* (Madison: University of Wisconsin Press, 1982)

Meisner, Maurice, *Mao's China and After: A History of the People's Republic* (New York: Free Press, third edition 1999)

Meisner, Maurice, 'China's communist revolution: a half-century perspective', *Current History* (1999), pp. 243–8

Menand, Louis, *The Metaphysical Club* (London: Flamingo, 2002)

Micklethwait, John and Adrian Wooldridge, *The Right Nation: Why America is Different* (London: Penguin, 2005)

Modigliani, F. and Shi Larry Cao, 'The Chinese Saving Puzzle and the Life-Cycle Hypothesis', *Journal of Economic Literature*, volume 42 (2004), pp. 145–70

Mokyr, Joel, *The Lever of Riches: Technological Creativity and Economic Progress* (Oxford: OUP, 1990)

Mokyr, Joel, 'The Great Synergy: the European Enlightenment as a factor in Modern Economic growth', keynote address, European Association for Political and Evolutionary Economics, Maastricht 2003

Mokyr, Joel, *The Gifts of Athena: The Historical Origins of the Knowledge Economy* (Princeton: Princeton University Press, 2004)

Moore, Barrington, *Social Origins of Dictatorship and Democracy: Lord and Peasant in the Making of the Modern World* (Boston: Beacon Press, 1993)

Moore, Mike, *A World Without Walls: Freedom, Development, Free Trade and Global Governance* (Cambridge: CUP, 2003)

Morgan Stanley, *Global Restructuring: Lessons, Myths and Challenges*, International Investment Research, 1998

Morgan Stanley, *India and China: A Special Economic Analysis*, Equity Research, Asia/Pacific, 2004

Mueller, John, *Retreat from Doomsday: The Obsolescence of Major War* (New York: Basic Books, 1989)

Mulgan, Geoff, *Good and Bad Power: The Ideals and Betrayals of Government* (London: Penguin, 2006)

Narayan, Deepa (ed.), *Measuring Empowerment: Cross-Disciplinary Perspectives* (Washington DC: The World Bank, 2005)

Nathan, Andrew J., 'Authoritarian Resilience', *Journal of Democracy*, volume 14, number 1 (2003)

Nathan, Andrew J. and Perry Link, *The Tiananmen Papers: The Chinese Leadership's Decision to Use Force against their Own People – In their Own Words* (New York: Public Affairs, 2001)

Nathan, Andrew J. and Bruce Gilley, *China's New Rulers: The Secret Files* (London: Granta Books, 2002)

Naughton, Barry J., *Growing Out of the Plan: Chinese Economic Reform, 1978–1993* (Cambridge: CUP, 1995)

Naughton, Barry J. and Dali Yang, *Holding China Together Diversity and National Integration in the Post-Deng Era* (Cambridge: CUP, 2004)

Nee, Victor and Richard Swedberg (eds.), *The Economic Sociology of Capitalism* (Princeton: Princeton University Press, 2005)

Nelson, Richard, *Technology, Institutions and Economic Growth* (Cambridge, MA: Harvard University Press, 2006)

Nivola, Pietro S., 'Thinking About Political Polarization', The Brookings Institution Policy Brief 139, 2005

Nolan, Peter, *China and the Global Business Revolution* (Basingstoke: Palgrave Macmillan, 2001)

Nolan, Peter, *China and the Global Economy* (Basingstoke: Palgrave Macmillan, 2001)

Nolan, Peter, *China at the Crossroads* (Cambridge: Palgrave Macmillan, 2004)

Noland, Marcus, 'Religion, Culture and Economic Performance' Working Paper 03-8, Institute for International Economics Washington DC, 2003

Noland, Marcus and Howard Pack, 'The East Asian Industrial Policy Experience: Implications for the Middle East' Working Paper 05-14, Institute for International Economics, Washington DC, 2005

North, Douglass C., *Understanding the Process of Economic Change* (Princeton: Princeton University Press, 2005)

Nye, Joseph, S., *Soft Power: The Means to Success in World Politics* (New York: Public Affairs, 2005)

Nye, Joseph S., Philip D. Zelikow and David C. King, *Why People Don't Trust Government* (Cambridge, MA: Harvard University Press, 1997)

O'Brien, Kevin J., *Reform Without Liberalization: China's NPC and the Politics of Institutional Change* (Cambridge: CUP, 1990)

Obstfeld, Maurice and Kenneth Rogoff, 'The Unsustainable US Current Account Position Revisited', NBER Working Paper 1086, 2004

OECD, *Dynamising National Innovation Systems* (Paris: OECD, 2002)

OECD, *Economic Surveys – China*, volume 2005/13 (Paris: OECD, 2005)

Offer, Avner, *The Challenge of Affluence: Self-Control and Well-Being in the United States and Britain Since 1950* (Oxford: OUP, 2006)

Ohmae, Kenichi (ed.), *The Evolving Global Economy: Making Sense of the New World Order* (Boston: Harvard Business School Press, 1995)

Oi, Jean, *Rural China Takes Off: Institutional Foundations of Economic Reform* (Berkeley: University of California Press, 1999)

Oi, Jean C. and Andrew G. Walder (eds.), *Property Rights and Economic Reform in China* (Stanford: Stanford University Press, 1999)

Olson, Mancur, *The Rise and Decline of Nations* (New Haven: Yale University Press, 1982)

Panagariya, Arvind, 'Liberalizing Agriculture', *Foreign Affairs*, WTO special edition (2005)

Patten, Chris, *East and West* (London: Pan Books, 1999)

Patterson, James T., *Restless Giant: From Watergate to Bush v. Gore* (Oxford: OUP, 2005.)

Peak Oil Netherlands Foundation's World Oil Production and Peaking Outlook, Netherlands 2005

Peerenboom, Randall, *China's Long March Toward Rule of Law* (Cambridge: CUP, 2002)

Peerenboom, Randall, 'Beyond Universalism and Relativism: The Evolving Debates about "Values in Asia"', University of California Los Angeles School of Law, Research Paper 02-23, 2002

Pei, Minxin, *China's Trapped Transition: The Limits of Developmental Autocracy* (Cambridge: Harvard University Press, 2006)

Perdue, Peter C., 'Constructing Chinese Property Rights: East and West', in Huri Islamoglu (ed.), *Constituting Modernity: Private Property in the East and West* (London: I. B. Tauris, 2004)

Perdue, Peter C., *China Marches West: The Qing Conquest of Eurasia* (Cambridge, MA: Belknap Press, 2005)

Perlstein, Rick, *Before the Storm: Barry Goldwater and the Unmaking of the American Consensus* (New York: Hill & Wang, 2001)

Perry, Elizabeth, *Challenging the Mandate of Heaven: Social Protest and State Power in China* (Armonk: M. E. Sharpe, 2002)

Perry, Elizabeth and Mark Selden (eds.), *Chinese Society: Change, Conflict and Resistance* (London: Routledge, 2000)

Phillips, Kevin, *American Theocracy* (New York: Viking, 2006)

Piketty, Thomas and Emmanuel Saez, 'The Evolution of Top Incomes: A Historical and International Perspective', NBER Working Paper 11955, 2006

Podpiera, Richard, 'Progress in China's Banking Sector Reform: Has Bank Behavior Changed?', International Monetary Fund Working Paper WP/06/71

Polanyi, Karl, *The Great Transformation* (New York: Octagon Books, 1944 and 1980)

Pomeranz, Kenneth, *The Great Divergence: China, Europe and the Making of the Modern Economy* (Princeton: Princeton University Press, 2000)

Poncet, Sandra, 'Measuring Chinese Domestic and International Integration', *China Economic Review* 14 (1) (2003), pp. 1–21

Porter, Michael E., Klaus Schwab and Augusto Lopez-Claros, *The Global Competitiveness Report 2005-2006 Policies Underpinning Rising Prosperity* (Basingstoke: Palgrave Macmillan, 2005)

Prestowitz, Clyde, *Rogue Nation: American Unilateralism and the Failure of Good Intentions* (New York: Basic Books, 2003)

Prestowitz, Clyde, *Three Billion New Capitalists: The Great Shift of Wealth and Power to the East* (New York: Basic Books, 2005)

Putnam, R. D., *Bowling Alone* (New York: Touchstone Books, 2000)

Qian Yingyi, 'The Process of China's Market Transition (1978–98): The Evolutionary, Historical, and Comparative Perspectives', paper prepared for the Journal of Institutional and Theoretical Economics symposium on 'Big-Bang, Transformation of Economic Systems as a Challenge to New Institutional Economics', Wallerfangen/Saar 1999

Ravallion, Martin and Shahoua Chen, 'China's (Uneven) Progress Against Poverty', World Bank Policy Research Working Paper 3408, 2004

Rawski, T. G., 'Will Investment Behavior Constrain China's Growth?', *China Perspectives* 38 (2001), pp. 28–35

Resnick, Mitchel, *Turtles, Termites, and Traffic Jams: Explorations in Massively Parallel Microworlds* (Cambridge, MA: MIT Press, 1997)

Reynolds, David, *One World Divisible: A Global History since 1945* (London: W. W. Norton, 2001)

Ridley, Matt, *The Origins of Virtue* (London: Penguin, 1997)

Ringmar, Erik, *The Mechanics of Modernity in Europe and East Asia* (London: Routledge, 2005)

Robinson, Joan, *Aspects of Development and Underdevelopment* (Cambridge: CUP, 1979)

Rodrik, Dani, 'Where Did All the Growth Go? External Shocks, Social Conflict and Growth Collapses', *Journal of Economic Growth* (1999)

Rodrik, Dani (ed.), *In Search of Prosperity: Analytic Narratives on Economic Growth* (Princeton: Princeton University Press, 2001)

Rodrik, Dani, 'Feasible Globalizations', NBER Discussion Paper 9129, 2002

Roe, Mark J., 'The Inevitable Instability of American Corporate Governance', Harvard John M. Olin Center for Law, Economics and Business Discussion Paper 493, 2004

Rose-Ackerman, Susan, *Corruption and Government: Causes, Consequences, and Reform* (Cambridge: CUP, 1999)

Rosecrance, Richard, *The Rise of the Trading State: Commerce and Conquest in the Modern World* (New York: Basic Books, 1986)

Rothschild, Emma, *Economic Sentiments: Adam Smith, Condorcet and the Enlightenment* (Cambridge, MA: Harvard University Press, 2001)

Roubini, Nouriel and Brad Setser, 'The US as a Net Debtor: The Sustainability of the US External Imbalances', unpublished manuscript, Stern School of Business, New York University, 2004

Bibliography

Rowe, W. T., *Hankow: Commerce and Society in a Chinese City, 1796–1889* (Stanford: Stanford University Press)

Ru Xin, Lu Xueyi, and Li Peilin (eds.), *2005 Zhongguo shehui xingshi fenxi yu yuce* [Analysis and forecast on China's social development, 2005] (Beijing: Social Sciences Academic Press, 2004)

Sabel Charles and Joshua Cohen, 'Directly Deliberative Polyarchy', *European Law Review* 3 (4) (1998), pp. 313–42

Sachs, Jeffrey D. and Andrew M. Warner, 'Natural Resource Abundance and Economic Growth', NBER Working Paper W5398, 1995

Sachs, Jeffrey D. and Wing Thye Woo, 'Structural Factors in the Economic Reforms of China, Eastern Europe and the Former Soviet Union', *Economic Policy* (1994), pp. 102–45

Saich, Tony, *Governance and Politics of China* (Basingstoke: Palgrave Macmillan, second edition 2004)

Sapir, André, Philippe Aghion, Giuseppe Bertola et al., *An Agenda for a Growing Europe; The Sapir Report* (Oxford: OUP, 2004)

Schedler, Andreas, Larry Diamond and Marc F. Plattner, *The Self-Restraining State: Power and Accountability in New Democracies* (Boulder: Lynne Rienner, 1999)

Schiller, Robert, *The New Financial Risk in the 21st Century Order* (Princeton: Princeton University Press, 2003)

Schoppa, R. K., *Revolution and Its Past: Identities and Change in Modern Chinese History* (Upper Saddle River: Prentice Hall, 2002)

Schuck, Peter H., *The Limits of Law; Essays on Democratic Governance* (Boulder: Westview Press, 2000)

Schwarz, Jordan, *The New Dealers: Power Politics in the Age of Roosevelt* (New York: Knopf 1993)

Scott, Colin, 'Analysing Regulatory Space: Fragmented Resources and Institutional Design', *Public Law* (2001), pp. 283–305

Scott, James C., *Seeing Like a State: How Certain Schemes to Improve the Human Condition Have Failed* (New Haven: Yale University Press, 1998)

Segal, Adam, *Digital Dragon: High-Technology Enterprises in China* (Ithaca: Cornell University Press, 2002)

Segal, Adam and Ernest J. Wilson, III, 'Trends in China's Transition toward a Knowledge Economy', *Asian Survey*, volume 45, number 6 (2005), pp. 886–906

Selden, Mark, *The Political Economy of Chinese Development* (Socialism and Social Movements Series; Armonk: M. E. Sharpe, 1992)

Sen, Amartya, *Development as Freedom* (New York: Knopf, 1999)

Sen, Amartya, *The Argumentative Indian: Writings on Indian History, Culture, and Identity* (London: Penguin, 2005)

Sennett, Richard, *The Culture of the New Capitalism* (New Haven: Yale University Press, 2005)

Setser, Brad, 'The Chinese Conundrum: External Financial Strength, Domestic Financial Weakness', paper produced for CESifo Conference: Understanding the Chinese Economy, 2005

Shambaugh, David (ed.), *The Modern Chinese State* (Cambridge: CUP, 2000)

Shang-Jin Wei and Arvind Subramanian, 'The WTO Promotes Trade Strongly, but Unevenly', NBER Working Paper 10024, 2003

Sheng, Andrew, Xiao Geng and Yuan Wang, 'Property Rights and Original Sin in China: Transactions Costs, Wealth Creation and Property Rights Infrastructure', paper given at Stanford Center for International Development Conference, 2004

Sheng, Emile C. J., 'Cross Strait Relations and Public Opinion on Taiwan', *Issues & Studies* 38, number 1 (2002), pp. 17–46

Shevchenko, Alexei, 'Bringing the party back in: the CCP and the trajectory of market transition in China', *Communist and Post-Communist Studies* 37 (2004), pp. 161–85

Shiller, Robert, *The New Financial Order: Risk in the 21st Century* (Princeton: Princeton University Press, 2003)

Shleifer, Andrei and Lawrence Summers, 'Breach of Trust in Hostile Takeovers', in A. Auerbach (ed.), *Corporate Takeovers: Causes and Consequences* (Chicago: University of Chicago Press, 1988)

Shleifer, Andrei and Robert. W. Vishny, *The Grabbing Hand: Government Pathologies and Their Cures* (Cambridge: Harvard University Press, 1999)

Silverstein, Michael J. and John Butman, *Treasure Hunt: Inside the Mind of the New Consumer* (New York: Portfolio Books, 2006)

Skocpol, Theda, *The Missing Middle: Working Families and the Future of American Social Policy* (New York: W. W. Norton, 2000)

Skocpol, Theda, *Diminished Democracy: From Membership to Management in American Civil Life* (Norman: University of Oklahoma Press, 2003)

Spence, Jonathan, *The Search for Modern China* (London: Norton, second edition 1999)

Speth, James Gustave, *Red Sky at Morning: America and the Crisis of the Global Environment* (New Haven: Yale University Press, 2005)

State Statistical Bureau, *Zhongguo tongji nianji* [China Statistical Yearbook] (Beijing: China Statistics Press, 2003)

Steedman, Hilary, 'Skills for All', *Centrepiece* (2005/06), pp. 24–7

Steil, Benn, David G. Victor and Richard R. Nelson, *Technological Innovation and Economic Performance* (Princeton: Princeton University Press, 2002)

Steinfeld, Edward, *Forging Reform in China: The Fate of State-Owned Industry* (Cambridge: CUP, 1998)

Stephenson, Hugh (ed.), *Challenges for Europe* (Basingstoke: Palgrave Macmillan, 2004)

Stern, Nicholas, Jean-Jacques Dethier and F. Halsey Rogers, *Growth and Empowerment: Making Development Happen* (Cambridge, MA: MIT Press, 2005)

Stevens, Jeffrey R. and Marc D. Hauser, 'Why be nice? Psychological constraints on the evolution of cooperation', *Trends in Cognitive Sciences*, volume 8, number 2 (2004), pp. 60–5

Stewart, Thomas A., *The Wealth of Knowledge: Intellectual Capital and the 21st Century Organization* (New York: Doubleday, 1997)

Stiglitz, Joseph, 'The New Development Economics', in G. M. Meier and J. E. Rauch, *Leading Issues in Economic Development* (New York: OUP, 2000), pp.352–5

Stiglitz, Joseph, *Globalization and its Discontents* (London: Allen Lane, 2002)

Studwell, Joe, *The China Dream: The Elusive Quest for the Greatest Untapped Market on Earth* (London: Profile Books, 2005)

Sunstein, Cass, *Why Societies Need Dissent* (Oliver Wendell Holmes Lectures; Cambridge, MA: Harvard University Press, 2003)

Sunstein, Cass, *republic.com* (Oxford: Princeton University Press, 2002)

Surowiecki, James, *The Wisdom of Crowds: Why the Many Are Smarter Than the Few and How Collective Wisdom Shapes Business, Economies, Societies and Nations* (New York: Doubleday, 2004)

Suskind, Ron, *The Price of Loyalty: George W. Bush, the White House and the Education of Paul O'Neill* (New York: Simon & Schuster, 2004)

Suskind, Ron, *The One Percent Doctrine: Deep Inside America's Pursuit of Its Enemies Since 9/11* (New York: Simon & Schuster, 2006)

Sutton, John, *Technology and Market Structure* (Cambridge, MA: MIT Press, 2001)

Tabb, William K., *Economic Governance in the Age of Globalization* (New York: Columbia University Press, 2004)

Tamanaha, Brian Z., *On The Rule of Law: History, Politics, Theory* (Cambridge: CUP, 2004)

Tanner, Murray, *The Politics of Lawmaking in Post-Mao China: Institutions, Processes and Democratic Prospects* (Oxford: OUP, 1999)

Tawney, Richard, *Land and Labour in China* (London: George Allen & Unwin, 1937)

Taylor, Charles, *Modern Social Imaginaries* (Durham, NC: Duke University Press, 2004)

Thompson, Edward P., *Whigs and Hunters* (London: Penguin, 1977)

Tilly, Charles, *Coercion, Capital and European States, AD 990–1990* (Cambridge: Basil Blackwell, 1990)

Tsai, Kellee S., *Back Alley Banking: Private Entrepreneurs in China* (Ithaca: Cornell University Press, 2002)

Tseng, Wanda and Harm Zebregs, 'Foreign Direct Investment in China: Some Lessons for Other Countries', International Monetary Fund Policy Discussion Paper, PDP/02/03

Tucker, Nancy B. (ed.), *Dangerous Strait: The US–Taiwan–China Crisis* (New York: Columbia University Press, 2005)

Turner, Adair, *Just Capital – The Liberal Economy* (Basingstoke: Macmillan, 2001)

Tyler, Tom, *Why People Obey the Law* (New Haven: Yale University Press, 1990)

Uchitelle, Louis, *The Disposable American: Layoffs and their Consequences* (New York: Knopf, 2006)

United Nations Development Program, *Human Development Report* (Oxford: OUP, assorted years)

Venables, Anthony J. and Stephen Redding, 'Economic Geography and International Inequality', *Journal of International Economics* 62, number 1 (2004), pp. 53–82

Verba, Sidney, Steven Kelman, Gary Orren et al., *Elites and the Idea of Equality: A Comparison of Japan, Sweden and the United States* (Cambridge, MA: Harvard University Press, 1987)

Waldron, Jeremy, *The Dignity of Legislation* (Cambridge: CUP, 1999)

Walt, Stephen M., *Taming American Power: The Global Response to US Primacy* (New York: W. W. Norton, 2005)

Walter, Carl E. and Fraser J. T. Howie, *To Get Rich is Glorious: China's Stock Markets in the 80s and 90s* (Basingstoke: Palgrave Macmillan 2001)

Wank, David L., *Commodifying Communism: Business, Trust, and Politics in a Chinese City* (Cambridge: CUP, 1999)

Warsh, David, *Knowledge and the Wealth of Nations: A Story of Economic Discovery* (New York: W. W. Norton, 2006)

Weber, Max, 'Politics as Vocation', in H. H. Gerth and C. Wright Mills (trans. and eds.), *From Max Weber: Essays in Sociology* (New York: Oxford University Press, 1946), pp. 77–128

Weber, Max, *The Protestant Ethic and Other Writings* (London: Penguin, 2005)

Wedeman, Andrew, 'Anticorruption Campaigns and the Intensification of Corruption in China', *Journal of Contemporary China* 14(42) (2005), pp. 93–116

Weinstein, Michael M., *Globalization: What's New?* (New York: Columbia University Press, 2005)

Whiting, Susan, *Power and Wealth in Rural China: The Political Economy of Institutional Change* (Cambridge: CUP, 2000)

Wilkinson, Richard, *The Impact of Inequality: How to Make Sick Societies Healthier* (London: The New Press, 2005)

Williamson, Oliver E., *The Economic Institutions of Capitalism* (New York: The Free Press, 1985)

Wilson, Edward O., *Consilience: The Unity of Knowledge* (London: Abacus Books, 1998)

Wolf, Charles Jr., K. C. Yeh, Benjamin Zycher et al., *Fault Lines in China's Economic Terrain* (Santa Monica: Rand, 2003)

Wolf, Martin, *Why Globalization Works* (London: Yale University Press, 2004)

Womack, Brantly (ed.), *Contemporary Chinese Politics in Historical Perspective* (Cambridge: CUP, 1991)

Wong, R. Bin, *China Transformed: Historical Change and the Limits of the European Experience* (Ithaca: Cornell University Press, 1997)

Woo, Wing Thye, 'The Washington Consensus: Misunderstanding the Poor by the Brightest', paper presented at the FONDAD-organised conference, 'Stability, Growth and the Search for a New Development Agenda: Reconsidering the Washington Consensus', 2004

Wood, Adrian, *North-South Trade, Employment and Inequality: Changing Fortunes in the Skill-Driven World* (Oxford: Clarendon Press, 1994)

Wood, Gordon S., *The Radicalism of the American Revolution* (New York: Vintage, 1993)

World Bank, *The State in a Changing World* (Oxford: OUP, 1997)

World Bank, *The Right to Tell: The Role of Media in Economic Development* (Washington DC: World Bank, 2002)

Wrigley, E. A., *Continuity, Chance and Change* (Cambridge: CUP, 2001)

Wrong, Brian, *The Problem of Order: What Unites and Divides Society* (Cambridge, MA: Harvard University Press, 1995)

Xiao, Geng, 'What is Special about China's reforms?', World Bank Research Paper Series number 23, 1991

Xiao, Gongqin, 'The Rise of the Technocrats', *Journal of Democracy*, volume 14, number 1 (2003)

Yahuda, Michael B., *The International Politics of the Asia-Pacific Since 1945* (Oxford: Routledge, 2004)

Yan Sun, *Corruption and Market in Contemporary China* (Ithaca: Cornell University Press, 2004)

Yang, Dali, *Remaking the Chinese Leviathan: Market Transition and the Politics of Governance in China* (Stanford: Stanford University Press, 2004)

Yergin, D. and J. Stanislaw, *The Commanding Heights: The Battle between Government and Marketplace that is Remaking the World* (New York: Touchstone Books, 2000)

Yusuf, Shahid, Kaoru Nabeshima and Dwight Perkins, *Under New Ownership* (Washington DC: The World Bank 2006)

Zakaria, Fareed, *From Wealth to Power: The Unusual Origins of America's World Role* (Princeton: Princeton University Press, 1998)

Zaller, John, 'Market Competition and News Quality', paper prepared for presentation at the annual meetings of the American Political Science Association, Atlanta 1999

Zhao Suisheng, *A Nation State by Construction; Dynamics of modern Chinese Nationalism* (Stanford: Stanford University Press, 2004)

Zheng Yongnian, *Globalization and State Transformation in China* (Cambridge: CUP, 2004)

Zuboff, Shoshana and James Maxmin, *The Support Economy: Why Corporations Are Failing Individuals and the Next Episode of Capitalism* (New York: Viking Penguin, 2002)

Zweig, David, *Internationalizing China: Domestic Interests and Global Linkages* (Ithaca: Cornell University Press, 2002)

Zweig, David and Bi Jianhai, 'China's Global Hunt for Energy', *Foreign Affairs* (2005)

INDEX

Index